THE MIDDLE EAST MILITARY BALANCE

1992-1993

Shlomo Gazit - Zeev Eytan - Amos Gilboa

Edited by Shlomo Gazit

First published 1993 by Westview Press

Published 2019 by Routledge
52 Vanderbilt Avenue, New York, NY 10017
2 Park Square, Milton Park, Abingdon, Oxon OX14 4RN

Routledge is an imprint of the Taylor & Francis Group, an informa business

Library of Congress Catalog Card Number:
86-50920

Library of Congress Cataloging-in-Publication Data

ISBN 13: 978-0-367-29397-0 (hbk)
ISBN 13: 978-0-367-30943-5 (pbk)

Printed in the United Kingdom
by Henry Ling Limited

JCSS Publications

JCSS Publications present the findings and assessments of the Center's research staff. Each paper represents the work of a single investigator or a team. Such teams may also include research fellows who are not members of the Center's staff. Views expressed in the Center's publications are those of the authors and do not necessarily reflect the views of the Center, its trustees, officers, or other staff members or the organizations and individuals that support its research. Thus the publication of a work by JCSS signifies that it is deemed worthy of public consideration but does not imply endorsement of conclusions or recommendations.

Contents

Page

Preface
Part I **Strategic Developments** 1
Chapter 1 The Middle East: Main Strategic
Trends 3
Shlomo Gazit
Chapter 2 The Regional Arena: Key Issues 26
Ephraim Kam
Chapter 3 The Arab-Israel Peace Process 45
Joseph Alpher
Chapter 4 US-Israel Strategic Cooperation 68
Dore Gold
Chapter 5 The US and Gulf Security 79
Dore Gold
Chapter 6 Arresting Weapons Proliferation 93
Shai Feldman
Chapter 7 The Palestinian Struggle 120
David Tal

Part II **Main Middle East Armies** 127
Chapter 8 Introduction 129
Amos Gilboa
Chapter 9 The Egyptian Armed Forces 136
Amos Gilboa
Chapter 10 The Iranian Armed Forces 144
Amos Gilboa
Chapter 11 The Iraqi Armed Forces 150
Amos Gilboa
Chapter 12 The Israel Defense Forces 158
Amos Gilboa
Chapter 13 The Jordanian Armed Forces 171
Amos Gilboa
Chapter 14 The Saudi Armed Forces 175
Amos Gilboa
Chapter 15 The Syrian Armed Forces 181
Amos Gilboa

Page

Tables and Figures

Table I   Incidents of Riots and Disorder,
              by Region   122
Table II   Terrorist Activity Since Beginning
              of Intifada   122
Table III   Terrorist Activity in 1991-1992,
              by Region   123
Table IV   Fatalities by Terrorist Attacks in
              the Territories   123
Table V   Punitive Sealing and Demolition of
              Homes   124
Table VI   Deportations by Region   124
Table VII   Border Infiltration Attempts:
              January 1991-December 1992   125

Figure I   76

Part III   **Regional Military Forces**   191
              Introductory Note   193
              1. Algeria   195
              2. Bahrain   207
              3. Egypt   214
              4. Iran   233
              5. Iraq   250
              6. Israel   266
              7. Jordan   283
              8. Kuwait   292
              9. Lebanon   301
              10. Libya   311
              11. Morocco   324
              12. Oman   335
              13. Palestinian Military and   344
                  Paramilitary Forces
              14. Qatar   353
              15. Saudi Arabia   360
              16. Sudan   376
              17. Syria   385
              18. Tunisia   397
              19. United Arab Emirates (UAE)   406
              20. Yemen   418

		Page
Part IV	**Comparative Tables and Figures**	427
	Glossary of Weapons Systems	
	List of Abbreviations	
	Chronology: Key Strategic Events 1992-93	
	Maps	

Comparative Tables and Figures, by Zeev Eytan

Table 1	Major Armies of the Middle East	428
Table 2	Major Air Forces of the Middle East (including Air Defense Forces)	432
Table 3	Major Navies of the Middle East	436
Table 4	The Israel-Syria Military Balance	438
Table 5	Eastern Front-Israel Military Balance	440
Table 6	Arab-Israel Military Balance (Israel vs. Arab Coalition, including Egypt and Iraq)	442
Table 7	Arab-Israel Military Balance 1984-1992	444
Table 8	The Iran-Iraq Military Balance	446
Table 9	The USA in the Middle East: Financial Aid (Military), Arms Sales, Advisors, Trainees and Facilities	448
Table 10	The USSR/Russia in the Middle East: Arms Sales, Advisors, Trainees and Facilities	450
Table 11	France in the Middle East: Arms Sales, Advisors and Trainees	451
Table 12	Britain in the Middle East: Arms Sales, Advisors, Trainees, and Cooperation in Arms Production	452
Table 13	Surface-to-Surface Missiles and Rockets in Service in Middle Eastern Armies	453

		Page
Figure 1	Tanks in Major Middle East Armies	430
Figure 2	Surface-to-Surface Missiles & Rockets in Service in Middle East Armies	431
Figure 3	Combat Aircraft in the Middle East	434
Figure 4	Missile Craft in Major Middle East Navies	435

Glossary of Weapons Systems, by Zeev Eytan 455
Army 456
Air Force 469
Navy 487
Chronology 501
List of Abbreviations 512

Maps 515

1. The Middle East
2. Southern Lebanon
3. Israel: Northern Front
4. Israel and the Arab East
5. The Persian Gulf
6. The Iran-Iraq Border
7. Israel-Egypt
8. Eastern Mediterranean
9. Northern Red Sea
10. North Africa and the Sahara

Preface

The *Middle East Military Balance 1992-1993* covers the year 1992 as well as the first months of 1993. As the previous edition of the *Balance* (1990-1991) covered events through 1991, we have now closed the time-gap that resulted from the 1991 Gulf War.

The year 1992 witnessed the separate but parallel development of three strategic trends. The outcome of each, indeed the critical question of which of these courses first reaches fruition, will probably be of vital importance in the future.

The first trend is the political peace process, which opened dramatically in Madrid in October 1991, and was designed to achieve an agreed settlement of the Arab-Israel conflict. During the period under review, the bilateral and multilateral committees continued to reconvene despite the many obstacles they faced, and the relatively meager progress they registered. Joseph Alpher reviews the process of negotiations and brings us to the temporary break in the talks, at the beginning of 1993.

A second key process has little in common with the Arab-Israel conflict. This is the strengthening of the Islamic activist movement in the region. Radical Islam appears to thrive primarily on political, social and economic frustration and distress in most of the Middle Eastern countries. It enjoys Iranian encouragement and assistance–money, weapons, training and organization. Dr. Ephraim Kam analyzes these and additional strategic developments in Iran and the Arab countries of the Middle East.

The third course is the arms race in the Middle East-- conventional and nonconventional. Here events appear to justify a review of military developments among the main regional powers, including an update on the Israel Defense Forces. We are indebted to Brigadier General (res) Amos Gilboa, who is not a member of our staff, for undertaking this task. In a separate chapter, Dr. Shai Feldman analyzes the Middle East arms control process. And David Tal provides a data update (to the end of 1992) on the Palestinian armed struggle against Israel. His figures do not include the escalation in Palestinian operations of early

1993, or the consequences of Israeli countermeasures. These will be dealt with in next year's *Balance*.

Turning to a different sphere of interest, 1992 witnessed changes of government in Israel and in the United States, but not, to the disappointment of many, in Baghdad. Dr. Dore Gold analyzes the dynamics of US policy toward both the Gulf and Israel.

In parts III and IV of this year's *Balance*, Dr. Zeev Eytan presents, as usual, a detailed data update regarding the countries and armed forces in the area.

Incidentally, this year the entire book is, for the first time, the product of JCSS's own desktop printing operation. We hope this will enhance our efficiency in preparing the *Balance* on an annual basis.

Finally, the authors are indebted to all members of the senior research staff of the Jaffee Center for their critical review of drafts of the various chapters. Special thanks are due to Major General (res) Aharon Yariv, Head of Center, for his overall involvement and guidance, and to Joseph Alpher, Director of Center, for his diligent efforts in bringing this book to the public.

S.G.
June 1993

PART I

STRATEGIC DEVELOPMENTS

1. The Middle East: Main Strategic Trends

Shlomo Gazit

This introductory chapter reviews the main strategic trends of the period between October 1991 and late 1992-early 1993. For the sake of clarity of presentation, there will be some overlapping with events already covered in last year's *Military Balance* (1990-1991), either because of the continuity of some of the developments or because, in some cases, new data has been disclosed that was unknown a year ago.

The chapters that follow will discuss in detail some of the trends presented here. Here again, in the interests of comprehensiveness, there may be some minor repetition.

Most of the strategic developments in 1992 had their origin in the past. They could be expected to impact beyond the year in review, and to characterize trends in coming years. One exception to this rule was Israel's change of government, following the general elections that were held in June 1992. The importance of this change is in its expression of new and different Israeli national and strategic priorities, that might be expected to redound upon regional developments.

In reviewing the main strategic trends, we shall discuss six topics:

*   The Persian Gulf, 1-2 years after Desert Storm;
*   The impact of global developments on the Middle East;
*   Facing the era of nonconventional weaponry;
*   Arab unity and Islamic activism;
*   Evolution of the Palestinian position; and
*   The political change in Israel.

The Persian Gulf, 1-2 Years After Desert Storm

The situation in the Gulf area remained fluid in 1992. In many ways, decisive developments had not yet ripened for the key actors.

The first such actor was the US, together with the other members of the coalition that supported Washington during the crisis and the war that followed. In March 1991, immediately after the defeat of Iraq's military forces, many observers ignored the international and regional conditions and naively thought that the US could continue the war so as to ensure the complete and immediate demise of Saddam Hussein. Those critics, seeing President Bush and the US at the peak of their military power and political prestige, concluded incorrectly that the time was ripe for the remolding of the Middle East, and for solving the latent conflicts in the region.

But Washington refrained from doing so. There were many reasons--regional as well as American domestic--to justify this position. Yet they could not dispel the intense feelings of disappointment and frustration among the critics. Contrary to the hopes and expectations voiced at the conclusion of hostilities, there was no new regional order; Saddam Hussein and his regime were still in power; and Iraq's armed forces (despite their heavy losses) were rehabilitated and reorganized, and effectively supported the regime.

By early 1993, some two years after the war, there were no large allied forces in the area that could support firm political demands and take effective positions against Baghdad, threatening Saddam with the use of overwhelming military force were he not to comply. Furthermore, while there had been clear justification to demand the liberation of Kuwait, there was no such cause that appeared to justify a new world coalition against Iraq. Neither the physical elimination of Saddam Hussein nor the need to prevent Iraq from joining the nuclear 'club,' were weighty enough factors to realign coalition forces for a major new military move.

Meanwhile, in Iraq Saddam Hussein had survived, in spite of the embargo and various other sanctions. He had successfully subdued regional uprisings as well as the attempts against his person or regime. The credit went mostly to his strengthened personal guard.

Despite international admonitions, he continued to brutally subdue the Kurds in northern Iraq. A clear and decisive allied intervention, operating from military bases in Turkey, soon forced Baghdad to accept the establishment of a Kurdish safe haven in the north, in which Iraqi forces were not allowed to operate, as well as to acquiesce in an agreement which established a Kurdish self-governing unit there. A Kurdish government was formed in July 1992 with a prime minister and a legislative council. Unfortunately, this did not put an end to the suffering of the Kurds.

Washington had supported the Kurdish uprising against Saddam Hussein, but it did not take long to discover that Turkey, an ally and a member of the NATO Alliance, was opposed to a Kurdish autonomy so extensive as to strengthen the Kurdish separatist movement in Turkey. Additional neighboring states were also wary. Thus the foreign ministers of Turkey, Iran and Syria met in November 1991 and condemned the establishment of a de facto sovereign Kurdish state. They warned the Kurds that they would not allow such an entity to bring about the disintegration of Iraq. Iranian Foreign Minister Ali Akbar Velayati characterized the situation in northern Iraq as one that might "affect the national security of the three countries."

From the Turkish standpoint, matters became even more complicated. The Kurdistan Workers' Party (PKK), a Turkish Kurdish separatist movement, had been fighting since 1984 for an independent state in southeastern Turkey. In 1991-92 the PKK found sanctuary in Iraqi Kurdistan, and were striking at Turkish targets from across the border. These activities forced Turkey to initiate a major military operation against the rebels. More than 20,000 Turkish troops, armed with tanks and helicopters, were operating inside northern Iraq in November 1992, and four more Turkish Army divisions were on standby.

Iraq's own Kurds did not support the Marxist, separatist PKK, but they were trapped between the two opposing parties and were afraid that they might be facing a prolonged Turkish military presence and occupation of their autonomous area. Thus in October 1992 the Kurdish regional parliament bowed to Turkish demands and decided to expel the PKK from Iraqi Kurdistan. The Turks in turn vowed that their troops would be out of Iraq before the winter snows.

At the same time, Baghdad continued its attempt to suppress the Shi'ites in southern Iraq. There were good reasons for the Iraqis to consider the Shi'ite rebellion as the more dangerous one. The predominance of Shi'ites in the south made them a natural ally of Iran, while the common border made it easier for Tehran to help the rebels.

In August of 1991 the US, British and French had issued a new ultimatum, warning Iraq not to use its combat aircraft south of the 32nd parallel. It was hoped that this would protect the uprising in the south from severe Iraqi retribution. Further, Iraqi compliance would damage the prestige of Saddam's regime, while

5

an Iraqi military response could serve as a good pretext to punish Iraq with military force. Saddam Hussein told the Iraqi people that he completely rejected the ultimatum, yet refrained from sending his aircraft south of the 32nd parallel. However, this limited show of force by the allies only appeared to demonstrate the limits of their options for initiating a new military move.

Meanwhile, UN inspectors were responsible for uncovering and destroying the Iraqi infrastructure of nonconventional weapons. Their effectiveness proved to be quite limited. In spite of laborious investigations, and the destruction of some Iraqi installations, the inspectors recognized that Iraq continued to hide R&D efforts, production lines and residual stocks. Further, Saddam adopted a policy of challenging and even ridiculing the foreign inspectors, who, under the circumstances, often had to stand helplessly by. Saddam knew that were he to succeed in concealing his activities, it would be an enormous achievement for Iraq; while if he were to fail in hiding his arms efforts, neither he nor Iraq would risk punishment more severe than current restraints.

The list of alleged Iraqi violations was impressive:

* It was reported as early as July 1991 that American intelligence satellites discovered Iraqis burying equipment vitally needed for the uranium enrichment process.
* It was revealed in November 1991 that the international inspectors had discovered highly enriched--or weapons grade--uranium inside Iraq. According to their judgement, this could mean either that Iraq had developed in the past, and perhaps retained, an undiscovered capability to enrich uranium to high levels, or that Iraq had acquired some quantity of highly enriched uranium from another source.
* UN inspectors accused Iraq in November 1991 of failing to account for some 300 Scud missiles.
* A heli-borne surprise raid, made by UN weapons experts in December 1991, uncovered chemical bomb production equipment that the Iraqis had tried to hide inside a sugar factory.
* A Bush administration official revealed in April 1992 that Saddam was holding easily hidden biological agents in secret locations, retaining this "ace in the hole" in order to rearm quickly when it became possible or necessary.

*   After a three-week showdown in Baghdad, Rolf Ekeus, head of the UN Special Commission in Iraq, reported in July 1992 that the Iraqi government had agreed to allow UN weapons inspectors to search the Agriculture Ministry. Ekeus added, however, that he was concerned that all documents on ballistic missiles and chemical and biological weapons may have been removed or destroyed during the three weeks of waiting.

*   In September 1992 David Kay, a former head of the UN inspectors who led three controversial and at times risky missions to Iraq, claimed that Iraq's promises that its nuclear weapons program had been halted could not be believed in the face of Baghdad's consistent behavior of lying, deception and attempting to frustrate the work of the inspection teams.

Not only was Iraq hiding as much of its nonconventional infrastructure as possible, but all its scientists and engineers who were responsible for nonconventional development and production remained in Iraq. If called upon to renew their work, they could presumably render Iraq a nuclear power within a few years.

To sum up, Iraq's military forces were seriously crippled, and its political standing constrained. Yet Iraq continued to pose a serious military threat to all its immediate neighbors as well as to Israel.

The Impact of Global Developments on the Middle East

Most countries in the Middle East were greatly influenced by the dramatic international changes of the early 1990s. Four major developments stand out.

First, of course, came the disintegration of the Soviet Union and its disappearance as a leading superpower and leader of the Communist Bloc. The USSR was replaced by 15 independent republics. All were on the verge of economic collapse, and their stability and cohesiveness from an ethnic political standpoint were also highly dubious. Under the circumstances, it was not surprising that the national priorities of Russia, as well as the other republics, were directed toward domestic affairs. They had little short-term pretension of getting involved in global strategy, nor could they maintain their political, military and, in some exceptional cases, even economic support for countries that were until recently their clients and proteges--in the Middle East as in other areas.

The implications of these new developments for regional client states were, inevitably, a strong sense of abandonment. In the short term, troubling and urgent problems of East and Central Europe almost completely pushed aside the Third World and its problems. In many ways, the Arab countries in the Middle East were no exception. They discovered that they were no longer as important as they had believed themselves to be in the past. Nor, following the collapse of the Soviet empire and the military defeat of Iraq, was the western world as sensitive to their doings, or as appreciative of their favors, as it once was. The threat of an oil embargo, for example, could not dictate major strategic decisions in the 1990s as it had in the 1970s and in the 1980s.

The development that accompanied the Soviet collapse--the emergence of the US, by default, as the only remaining superpower--was even more remarkable. Global strategy, such as it was, was now directed from one single center, Washington, even if the US did at times prefer, because of its international position, to work through the UN in order to lend legitimization to its policies. It is doubtful, were it not handled this way, that the international military coalition charged with Operation Desert Storm against Iraq could have been formed.

Thus sanctions were imposed by the UNSC against Libya, upon the demand of the western troika--the US, the UK and France--because Tripoli refused to hand over six Libyan terrorists accused of two acts of mass terrorism in 1988 and 1989 (blowing up American and French passenger aircraft). Such sanctions would not have been possible within the framework of the former world order, which was constantly guided by East-West conflict considerations. While few if any Arab countries harbored feelings of empathy or esteem for Libyan leader Qaddafi, they were all bothered by these developments, as they clearly reflected western disregard for Arab positions.

This compelled Arab leaders to reach out for American attention, and quite naturally this became a two-way process. Thus, on the one hand, Arab and other Muslim countries searched for new relationships that would replace their lost liaison with Moscow, while, on the other hand, the US did not miss the opportunity to open and develop relations with Arab countries that had hitherto been inaccessible, when the world was divided between the two superpowers. This also had an immediate and positive impact on the US image as a possible 'honest broker,' charged with the role of advancing the regional peace process.

A third international development, of a very different nature, involved the huge stocks of weapons systems and other military hardware that remained 'on the shelf' in the newly independent republics as well as in other countries of the former Soviet Bloc. A large number of military experts, scientists and engineers in these countries found themselves unemployed and without a reasonable income, and were liable to hire out to Third World countries where they might assist in the development of a local military industrial infrastructure.

The gravity of their failing economies and their vital need for foreign currency forced the newly-independent republics to sell almost anything and at very attractive prices. In some cases the only consideration that did prevent sales was fear of US sanctions or punishment. From the point of view of potential consumer states, these deals also had disadvantages. Arms transactions now lost their political character, and became purely commercial transactions from the suppliers' standpoint. This had several negative implications:

* The purchasing country now had to pay full price for military hardware. There were no long-term credits, nor were there realistic chances that debts would be erased in the future (as was the case so often in the past).

* From a technical point of view, it was quite possible that in a few years time this new exporters' market would have nothing new to offer; one could hardly expect the former Eastern Bloc countries to maintain a sophisticated weapons industry only for Middle East and other Third World customers. Thus the immediate advantage of these cheap bargains might be neutralized in the not too distant future.

* Consequently, in the event of war in the Middle East, there was no longer a guarantee that supplier countries would support the consumer countries with air- or sealifts of weapons, ammunition and spares to replace those lost in battle. The realization that at the end of a war an Arab country might find itself exposed, vulnerable, and unable

immediately to rebuild its military forces, could in future deter Arab leaders considering military action.

* Finally, one could not ignore new international realities: the Cold War was over, there was no East-West arms race and no fear that a local or regional military confrontation could escalate and force the powers into a major war that they were trying so hard to avoid. This could impact upon future American policy and decisionmaking regarding a regional conflict. In considering a possible direct military intervention, the US would be aware of the different new international circumstances. There would be little danger that a considered American intervention would bring the USSR to support the other side, and no fear that such an American act would escalate into an uncontrollable East-West war. On the other hand, the absence of superpower rivalry might reduce the incentive for American intervention.

The fourth major development involved Iran. There were some who thought and hoped that the disappearance of Ayatollah Khomeini from the Iranian political scene would mark the beginning of Iranian moderation, and the adoption by Tehran of pragmatic policies aiming at closer involvement within the international system. By 1993 these hopes were not reflected in Iranian behavior. On the other hand, Tehran did act forthrightly to exploit Iraq's post-war political and military weakness, in two directions: For one, Tehran continued to consider Iraq, quite justifiably, as its most dangerous potential enemy. The Iran-Iraq War, which had lasted for some eight years, was never resolved politically, and Iran felt a need to ready itself for a new military confrontation in the not too distant future. Thus Tehran exploited Iraqi weakness and isolation during the Gulf Crisis to extract reconfirmation by Baghdad of the 1975 Algiers Agreement (signed by Saddam Hussein and the late Shah), which formalized Iranian rights in the Shatt al-Arab and was a key reason for Iraq's invasion in 1980. Iran also confiscated more than one hundred Iraqi combat aircraft which sought shelter during the 1991 Desert Storm fighting. And in another direction, Iran capitalized on the internal disarray in Iraq to encourage and support the Shi'ite uprising in the south.

A precondition for all these initiatives was the urgent need to acquire and absorb masses of weapons systems, both conventional as well as nonconventional. During its eight years of war with Iraq, Iran had lost or spent a major part of its arms, and had no access to foreign markets where it could find replacements. Now this was no longer the case: the weapons export markets of Eastern Europe, together with tempting Chinese and North Korean propositions, changed things completely. Thus Iran adopted a military five-year plan to turn itself, by the middle or end of the decade, into a military power that would boast a 'decisive strategic capability.' Tehran dedicated 18 percent of its annual budget toward this end, in addition to $2 billion in hard currency set aside for military acquisitions from foreign suppliers.

The biggest international concern, however, was with Iran's attempts to acquire nonconventional weapons as well as ballistic missile delivery systems, some with a range of 1,000 km or more. Reliable information indicated that Iran sought to achieve a nuclear capability by the end of the decade.

The other direction was Iran's ongoing sponsorship, with fervor and dynamics still as strong as they were 12 years ago, of subversive and terrorist activity. One peripheral but indicative example was Tehran's decision to double the prize it placed on the head of author Salman Rushdie. We have already mentioned Iranian support for the Shi'ite rebellion in southern Iraq. Additional examples include cooperation with the fundamentalist regime in Khartoum in sponsoring regional subversion, Tehran's support for Hizballah in Lebanon, and its sponsorship of a number of Palestinian organizations that opposed the Arab-Israel peace process.

Another, different crisis developed in the summer of 1992 between Iran and the United Arab Emirates in the Gulf. Iran occupied three small islands--Abu Musa, Big Tunb and Little Tunb--at the southern end of the Persian Gulf, dominating the passage through the Straits of Hormuz. The island of Abu Musa is not only important for its strategic location, but also comprises a large oil field. The UAE tried to mobilize inter-Arab support, but no Arab party was ready to undertake military operations against Iran, and the latter emerged triumphant from this crisis.

Facing the Era of Nonconventional Weapons

The search for nonconventional arms is not new in the Middle East. Egypt was the first country to initiate, in the 1960s, a program to develop and produce ballistic missiles, with the assistance of foreign scientists and engineers. About the same time, during the war in Yemen, Egyptian forces, supporting the revolutionary government that had overthrown the king in 1962, used chemical weapons against Yemenite troops.

According to unconfirmed reports from non-Israeli sources, Israel has successfully developed nuclear weapons, and has developed Jericho ballistic missiles with ranges in excess of 1000 km. By 1992 five Arab/ Muslim countries--Iraq, Syria, Egypt, Iran and Libya--were actively developing and producing chemical weapons or maintained a proven production capability. The same five were probably also involved in the development of biological weapons, which is easier to conceal.

But the most dramatic development concerning the possible introduction of nonconventional weapons into the Middle East was, no doubt, the disclosure of the full scope and variety of Iraq's efforts. The Saddam Hussein regime's megalomania and insatiable expansionist ambition brought Baghdad to invest heavily in a major effort to develop and produce nuclear weapons. The destruction of Iraq's Osiraq nuclear reactor near Baghdad by the Israel Air Force in June 1981, did not put an end to these ambitions; on the contrary, it probably only impelled Iraq to continue even more decisively, and to work simultaneously in several directions and in a far more secretive way. One may assume that were it not for the Gulf War, Iraq would already have joined the exclusive 'nuclear club.' But a nuclear program was not the only direction in which Iraq worked. The UN inspectors succeeded in uncovering a disturbing picture of Iraq's intentions and activities to acquire and produce medium-range ballistic missiles, and to acquire or produce chemical and biological weapons.

Other Middle East countries actively involved in the nuclear field by 1992 were Algeria and Iran. We have already noted the assessments that Iran was making a concentrated nuclear effort, with the goal of developing nuclear weapons by the year 2000.

This returns us to the possibility that a former Soviet republic would agree to sell nuclear warheads or fissionable material from its existing arsenal. It is frightening to consider, from this point of view, the process of banalization that nuclear weaponry underwent in the early 1990s. It was only 'yesterday' that humanity looked upon nuclear weapons as a nightmare threatening the very destruction of life on earth. Now, all of a sudden, we became aware of tens of thousands of nuclear devices, spread across a number of former Soviet republics. Not only was control problematic; according to some rumors there were serious doubts as to the reliability of records concerning categories and locations of weapons, not to speak of quantities: one version referred to the existence of 27,000 nuclear devices, another to 30,000, and a third spoke of 34,000.

Little wonder, then, under these circumstances, that rumors proliferated to the effect that Iran had received, or was about to receive, several nuclear devices purchased from Kazakhstan, or that it was planning to mount its nuclear devices on Silkworm ballistic missiles received from China. While Iran almost certainly was striving toward such goals, for the time being these rumors appeared to have no serious foundation.

Lastly, as there was little sense in producing weapons of mass destruction unless one also had the means of delivery, a significant Arab effort was directed toward developing bombs and ballistic missiles. From the standpoint of the Arab-Israel conflict, ballistic missiles offered a great advantage to the Arabs, as they could balance and evade the near-absolute superiority of the Israeli Air Force, and permit accurate hits against Israeli civilian targets, with no danger of interception (as was witnessed during the Gulf War). Pre-war Iraq had also tried to produce a supergun, with a possible range of hundreds of kilometers, that may have been intended to fire artillery shells with nonconventional warheads.

Arab Unity and Islamic Activism

The dramatic developments of the Gulf crisis and war had, at least for the time being, killed any hopes of realizing the goal of Arab unity that had been held out to the Middle East for half a century. The regional behavior of Saddam Hussein and the Iraqi Ba'ath Party in 1990 did briefly generate, among some Arab circles, new expectations of enhanced Arab political and military power that would permit close political, military and economic cooperation in an area spreading from the Persian Gulf to the Atlantic Ocean, and based on the belief that Arabs were one nation sharing a joint mission. Subsequently, the military defeat of Baghdad in the Gulf War delivered a deadly blow to this dream. The blow was a double one: not only was the idea of Arab political unity weakened, but the course of the Gulf Crisis affected the other aspect of unity--the possibility of a joint Arab stand vis-a-vis the outside world. Iraq's aggression against other Arab countries created an inter-Arab split that forced some Arab states to join hands with foreign powers while seeking protection against Iraq.

On another level, the crisis and war may have promoted the strengthening of the territorial Arab nation-state--one where an indigenous population shares a collective consciousness. It was a US diplomat that claimed "I don't think that Washington sees an Arab landscape out there anymore. We see Egyptians, we see Saudis, we see Libyans and Algerians. While there is still some appreciation of the concept of Arab solidarity, it no longer plays a role in our calculation."

Furthermore, despite temporary difficulties in oil supply during the crisis and war, there was neither serious world panic nor a dramatic 'oil rush,' as in the 1970s and 1980s. This was all the more remarkable since the crisis and war took place in the geographic center of the world's largest oil reserves. These developments--or lack thereof--reflected a dramatic decline in the strength and capability of the Arab oil-producing countries to exert political pressure.

Turning from Arab unity to Islamic activism, the new and aggressive threat presented by the latter development received its greatest impetus in 1979, with the spectacular success of the Khomeini revolution in Iran. The Iranian revolution aroused new hope among many deprived and frustrated people in the Middle East region, while generating grave feelings of concern in almost all the status quo regimes in the area. Political leaders in the region did of course pay lip-service in public to the supremacy of Islam and Islamic law; their true feelings, however, were better expressed by the steps taken in most countries to suppress the Islamic threat.

Prior to the Gulf Crisis, Iraq served as the main barrier to Iranian aggression and expansion in the Middle East. An indirect result of the weakening of Iraq, together with parallel developments in the independent Central Asian republics, was the renewed threat of Islamic activism throughout the region. One school of thought claimed that this new threat to regional stability would dissolve and disappear on its own, just as in the past. But another school took the threat seriously and considered it to be a most dangerous new phenomenon.

These fears were at least partially realized after a group of officers, headed by General Omar Bashir, took power in Khartoum in 1989. The military rulers were heavily influenced by the National Islamic Front in Sudan to adopt Islamic religious law for the state and to effect close relations with Iran. The extremist Sudanese government allowed the Iranians to establish training bases in Sudan, as well as operational centers that promoted clandestine and terrorist activities deep inside the territory of Sudan's northern neighbor, Egypt. Initial attacks targeted Egyptian Coptic Christians. July 1992 witnessed the beginning of a series of terrorist attacks mainly targeting western tourists visiting sites along the Upper Nile.

The most important Egyptian organization initiating these attacks was Gamaa al-Islamiya. Its aim was to depose President Husni Mubarak's moderate pro-western regime and to replace it with one based on Islamic law. In justifying the attacks, one of the group's spokesmen claimed that "the tourists were coming from the West and the West wanted to destroy Islam. One should not consider these tourists and visitors as innocent travellers that have no involvement in this confrontation."

Earlier, the Algerian government had allowed the open participation of Islamic activists in a democratic political process. The Islamic Salvation Front (ISF) won 49 percent of the vote in the first round of elections held in December 1991, and seemed certain to sweep the vote in a second round. These disturbing results led the Algerian government to cancel the second round of elections, to impose a general state of national emergency, to outlaw the ISF and its activities and to arrest most of its leaders.

General elections were also held in Kuwait, in October 1992 (with the participation of only five percent of residents and 14 percent of the citizenry). These were the first elections since Kuwait's liberation; the outcome showed a considerable increase in the number of opposition members elected, including those representing the Islamic activist movement. Because of Kuwait's very special economic advantages, and in view of its highly constrained "democracy," it was premature to expect a strong impact of these elections on government and society, and it was still farfetched to expect Kuwait to adopt Islamic law too.

The general elections to the parliament in Jordan, which were held shortly after the Gulf War, were another case where Islamic activist representatives were elected. The Hashemite regime responded by gradually and cautiously acting against the Islamic movement to remove it from positions of political power and constrain its influence. Jordan's success in dealing with the Islamists would also depend on specific local circumstances. The year 1992 witnessed an enhancement of Jordanian relations with its former Arab supporters and allies in the area as well as with the US; Jordan was thus gradually emerging from its isolation. Another intriguing issue was the deteriorating health of King Hussein. In August 1992 the King underwent surgery to remove a malignant growth, following which his exact medical status was not clear. The King appeared to be openly preparing his people for his departure from the throne. This raised the issue of whether a successor regime could handle the Islamic opposition as skillfully.

Another new and troubling development was the appearance on the international scene in the early 1990s of six independent Islamic republics in the Caucasus and Central Asia-- former Soviet republics with a total population of some 60 million. With the exception of the former communist system that had incorporated them all, and the Islamic religion, there was more to separate these entities than to unite them: there were major differences in their economic and educational-technological development, and there were major differences in the character of their internal problems. And yet one could not ignore the shared potential threat--the overall conditions of distress that characterized all the newly-independent republics of the former USSR could prove to be a perfect hothouse for the breeding of extremist Muslim movements. These movements would surely seek to manipulate urgent current problems for their own consolidation. In this regard the Islamic movements enjoyed an important organizational advantage, as effective networks of mosques and religious preachers quickly spread all over the country with Saudi, Iranian and other support.

By early 1993 it was impossible to predict the outcome of these developments. The population of these republics was mostly Sunni. They did not have a tradition of strict religious observance, and the communist way of life no doubt had left its mark. They had no tradition of extremism, and appeared to prefer gradual reforms while preserving a secular way of life that tolerated alcohol and encouraged women to fully share the responsibilities of wage earning. Such external expressions of personal behavior are vitally important in the process of enforcing religious law in a Muslim society.

The outcome of these conflicting attitudes would also be decided by the competition between two neighbors, Shi'ite Iran with its bent for exporting revolution, and Turkey, which represented modernization and close relations with Europe and the West (as expressed during the Gulf War), and which preserved strict separation between state and religion. Turkey's main problem, however, was the scarcity of its resources when it came to financing and assisting the new republics. Saudi Arabia, too, would probably play an important role. As a conservative but pro-western religious state, Saudi Arabia could buttress the opposition to Iran and reinforce the support Turkey received from the West.

The ethnic composition of these republics would also probably impact upon this confrontation. Five were ethnically close to Turkey, while only one (Tajikistan) was related to Iran. One Iranian tactic vis-a-vis these states was economic. Tehran played a primary role in an initiative launched in 1992, to expand the Economic Cooperation Organization (ECO)--founded originally in the 1960s by Iran, Turkey and Pakistan--to include the newly independent Muslim republics of the former Soviet Union.

Coincidentally with an enlarged ECO summit hosted by Tehran in February 1992, Iranian President Rafsanjani announced the formation of 'a cooperation organization of Caspian Sea littoral states,' with headquarters in Tehran. This initiative came as a surprise to Turkey, and stole the limelight accorded to Ankara's own initiative, some two weeks previously, to set up a Black Sea Cooperation Zone.

In another move depicted as a challenge, or balance, to Turkey's influence among the Turkic peoples of Azerbaijan and Central Asia, Tehran hosted a meeting between Iranian and Tajik leaders and heads of Afghani Islamic parties, in affirmation of their shared Persian linguistic bond.

Turkey, for its part, stepped up its campaign for influence in the Muslim republics by operating a satellite TV station designed to broadcast seven hours of news and programs to Turkic speakers between the Adriatic Sea and the Chinese border.

Yet both Iran and Turkey were also interested in managing their economic as well as cultural and Islamic relationships, and looked for ways to contain regional rivalries. By promoting an expanded ECO, Iran was proceeding in conjunction with, rather than in direct opposition to, Turkey. The presence of a sizeable Azeri population in Iran, and the Turkic link between Azeris and the majority of Turkey's population rendered both Tehran and Ankara sensitive to the possible domestic repercussions for themselves of a war in Transcaucasia.

Central Asia was a classic instance of a power vacuum demanding the attention of contenders for predominance. The potential rewards of extending power were compounded by fear of the consequences of regional turmoil and the ascendance of rival powers. For the time being, the external powers appeared to understand that in Central Asia the ground was not yet fertile for proselytizing Iranian-style Islamic militancy (or, for that matter, Saudi Arabia's Islamic conservatism).

Evolution of the Palestinian Position

The bilateral Arab-Israel peace talks, together with the multilateral talks, had their start in the fall of 1991. They were, no doubt, the most important development in years in Israel-Arab relations and in enhancing a political solution to the Palestinian problem. This could not have taken place were it not for some important changes in the Palestinian position. They were a direct ramification of the Gulf War, as well as an indirect reaction to general conditions at the time.

In the past, the Palestinians had refused to enter any negotiations with Israel that would be restricted to an open-ended interim agreement (i.e., one that did not define, from the very beginning of the process, the political end-goal to which both parties would commit themselves). Contrary to this past position, the Palestinians agreed (in the summer of 1991) to enter bilateral talks by accepting the procedural conditions which were imposed by Israel: the Palestinians would be members of a joint

Jordanian-Palestinian delegation; no residents of East Jerusalem or of the Palestinian diaspora could be official members of the delegation; and the agenda would be restricted to the establishment of the ISGA (the Interim Self-Governing Administration).

Two main factors caused the Palestinians to change their mind: on the one hand, a strong feeling that their policy had failed to serve their interests, and on the other, the hope that the new 'window of opportunity' opened after the Gulf War, carried some reward for them.

The Palestinian sense of disappointment and failure resulted from a number of background developments. First among these was a cumulative fatigue after four difficult and painful years of the Intifada. After some initial achievements, especially on the political and public relations levels, the Intifada had largely disappeared from the international media and the world's TV screens, to be replaced by new and more dramatic international developments. The Palestinian struggle was once again forgotten.

Then too, Israel had learned to live with the Intifada, from both a political and a military standpoint. Intifada-generated external pressures on Israel had decreased substantially, and while pressures from within Israeli society did continue, these had become little more than a containable nuisance. As for the military-security standpoint, the Intifada had changed its character-- there were fewer popular demonstrations, roadblocks with burning tires and stone-throwing, and more terrorist acts organized by the various Palestinian organizations or carried out by individuals armed with a knife, an axe, a firebomb or any other improvised weapon. Another dimension of Palestinian terrorist activity was the killing of hundreds of Palestinians suspected of being 'collaborators' with the Israeli administration. This made the work of the Israeli General Security Service in the Territories increasingly difficult. The essential Israeli military response was to use regular troops for 'police' duties in the territories; these were younger soldiers of higher physical fitness, who knew the local neighborhoods and the Palestinian modus operandi because of their longer stay in the area. The IDF also formed special undercover units that proved to be very effective in achieving tactical surprise by soldiers disguised as local civilians.

The main Palestinian concern was Israel's political response, which was manifested in the massive establishment of new Israeli settlements (especially in the West Bank). This served as blatant proof in Palestinian eyes that Israel not only had no intention to withdraw from the Territories, but was planning to consolidate its presence there. Unless there was a quick political settlement, the new reality in the Territories might no longer be reversible through negotiations and political agreement.

Yet another aspect of the Intifada was the severe economic crisis in the Territories, which eroded whatever reserve resources Palestinians had. One of the Palestinians' main sources of income, if not the main one, was work in Israel. The immediate result of the Intifada's policy of 'separation' was tens of thousands of newly unemployed Palestinians (especially in the Gaza Strip). But because of frequent general strike days, and restrictions imposed by Israel to minimize security risks, there was even a serious cut in the income of those who continued to work in Israel (working fewer days every month and fewer hours per day). Furthermore, it did not take long before the local economy could no longer manage as an independent entity, and Palestinians were gradually forced to return to buy all they needed in Israel.

Nor could one ignore the shift of power and influence within Palestinian society. The strengthening of the Hamas and Islamic Jihad movements came mostly as a reaction to the failure of Fatah's (the PLO mainstream) strategy to produce political results. Hence the dual images of, on the one hand, pressure on the mainstream to continue negotiations in order to reach an agreement before it was too late and the various 'refusal' factions took over; and on the other hand, collaboration by those same refusal factions with Hamas to incite the local population and promote terrorist activity--all with the hope of foiling any chance of an agreement.

Over a long period of time Israel had avoided taking steps to suppress Hamas' activities. Only after a series of attacks by extremist Islamic factions did Israel alter its policy radically-- arresting some 1200 Hamas and Islamic Jihad activists. It followed this by deporting 414 of them to Lebanon in mid-December 1992. The Beirut government's stubborn refusal to allow the deportees to enter its territory generated a serious political controversy. One of the immediate consequences was a PLO refusal to renew peace talks with Israel.

Last came the implications of the Gulf War. The Palestinians in general and the PLO in particular were among the very few Arab parties that had openly supported Saddam Hussein and his aggressive policies. This brought about a serious disenchantment between the Palestinians and their traditional Arab supporters. Hundreds of thousands of Palestinians that had been living and working in the rich Gulf states were expelled, and could no longer remit their earnings to their families. The Saudis and the Emirates also stopped their institutional financial support to the Palestinians. And serious reservations about the PLO and the Palestinians in general were now voiced throughout the Arab world, the world-at-large (with special emphasis on the US), and even among the Israeli Left and peace movements.

Thus an additional outcome of the Gulf conflict involved Palestinian finances. PLO financial resources dried up almost entirely, and the organization was sharply constrained in its support for institutions and adherents in the West Bank and Gaza. In contrast, Hamas now received Saudi as well as Iranian funding with which to develop its popular base in the Territories. Hamas diligently applied this largess to developing welfare institutions and acquiring weapons.

Yet there was also a sharp sense among Palestinians that an opportunity had presented itself, that should not be missed. Here again, a number of factors were at play:

* The deep American involvement in the process, and the application by the US of heavy pressures, largely through the medium of special shuttle trips to the Middle East during 1991 by Secretary of State James Baker.
* The promises Washington gave to the various Arab parties, including the Palestinians, as to the negotiations process and its ultimate goals.
* Israeli concessions regarding the identity of the 'advisors' to the Palestinian delegation (these included residents of East Jerusalem and others openly identified as official delegates of the PLO).
* And the Syrian decision to join the process. This boosted Palestinian hopes that the Syrian position during the negotiations would support the Palestinian demands. On the other hand, it implied that were the Palestinians to abstain from joining the talks, a bilateral Syrian-Israeli agreement might leave the Palestinians in perfect isolation (a situation which Israel sought to bring about, according to the Palestinian belief).

All these factors brought the Palestinians to join the process.

Yet, after some twelve months of talks, and despite the fact that the newly-elected government in Israel (July 1992) included in its platform a clear policy statement offering territories for peace, the bilateral Israeli-Palestinian negotiations were still at a standstill. The Palestinian delegation, from the very first day of the meetings, sought to invalidate the agreed terms of the initial invitation to the Madrid Conference and to the talks. Again and again, and through constant appeals to the media, the Palestinians asked to be recognized as an independent delegation representing a state-in-the-making. They wished to negotiate a PISGA ("Palestinian Interim Self-Governing Authority") that would have initial attributes of political sovereignty, and would be assured in advance of complete independence at the end of five years of an interim agreement.

The members of the Palestinian delegation were aware of the inoperability of these demands, and of the grave psychological damage that would be visited upon the Palestinian public once it came face-to-face with bitter realities as compared to the high expectations that the leadership had raised. Indeed, one of the main problems of the Palestinian delegation was its lack of natural and authoritative leadership. The 15-person delegation was constantly pressured by the PLO leadership in Tunis, embarrassed by infighting, and subjected to Chairman Arafat's extreme and unacceptable demands.

Under these circumstances, the Palestinians once again had good reason to be concerned lest Israel reach a bilateral agreement with Jordan or with Syria, and thereby eliminate the possibility of effective Arab pressure being applied to Israel to accommodate Palestinian demands.

The Political Change in Israel

The Israeli general elections for the 13th Knesset were held on June 23, 1992. The Likud government, which had been in power for 15 years, was replaced by a new Labor-led government headed by Yitzhak Rabin.

This outcome was not necessarily an expression of change in Israeli public opinion regarding peace process and security issues. During the campaigning that preceded election day, these topics were often of peripheral interest, and it was doubtful whether they carried a major impact on the vote. Rather, the outcome appeared to have been more heavily influenced by non-security factors. For one, Labor succeeded in generating a sense of personal competition for the position of prime minister between Mr. Rabin and Mr. Shamir--a contest won by Rabin. Then too, the Likud was hindered by sharp public criticism of the outgoing government's failing economic and social policies. Further, first-time new immigrant voters from the former USSR gave Labor 3-4 new seats in the Knesset. These voters were almost completely absorbed with their immediate personal problems of unemployment and absorption. And there was, very possibly, a strong popular feeling that the Likud policy of massive Jewish settlement in Judea and Samaria as the top national priority, was responsible for the lack of any progress in the social and economic areas.

The new government formed by Rabin was based on a coalition of three parties--Labor (with 44 seats), Meretz (with 12 seats) and Shas (with 6 seats). This was a rather narrow and fragile coalition, supported by 62 out of 120 MKs (barely 52 percent of the Knesset). Rabin could also count on the support of five MKs from predominantly Arab parties on major votes on foreign affairs. Yet no Israeli government would dare attempt to pass a resolution dealing with painful political and security decisions without a Jewish majority in parliament.

Nevertheless, the first steps of the new government indicated a clear intention to move ahead on the peace process. In keeping with its policy regarding a change in the order of national priorities, the new government initiated a direct challenge to right-wing parties and their supporters, by ordering a complete freeze of plans to establish new settlements and to initiate new construction in most of the Judea and Samaria (West Bank) areas. In many cases it was even decided to stop work on houses that were already in the process of construction.

The Israeli delegations to the bilateral and multilateral peace talks also received new and very different instructions. These emphasized more openness and flexibility, and a clear intention to reach agreements based on the principle of territorial compromise, both in the West Bank and Gaza as well as in the Golan Heights. Finally, the new government initiated a number of confidence-building measures. These included the cancellation of an expulsion order against a number of Palestinians who held central positions in the popular uprising, and the release of hundreds of prisoners and detainees. Other gestures were the replacement of Yossi Ben-Aharon, the head of Israel's delegation to the bilateral talks with Syria (identified completely with Likud positions) with Professor Itamar Rabinovich, and the decision to join the multilateral committee on refugees (a committee which had been boycotted by the Likud government).

The political change in Israel naturally raised new hopes for the success of negotiations. During the talks that ensued, several procedural understandings were agreed by the parties; gaps on substance however, remained, and it was still too early to say if and how they could be bridged.

Another result of the political change in Jerusalem was the renewed intimacy of relations between Israel and the US. One of Rabin's first steps as prime minister (after a visit to Cairo where he met with President Mubarak) was to meet with President Bush (as well as with his main challenger, Governor Clinton). This visit opened a new page in bilateral relations, after considerable deterioration during the last year of the Likud government. The US responded immediately with a gesture, approving $10 billion in loan-guarantees for the absorption of new immigrants. This was followed by the delivery of combat helicopters and additional weapons systems.

All these steps carried an important message to the Arabs: if they had harbored any hope of seeing Israel isolated and shorn of US political and military support, these hopes had to be abandoned for the time being.

***

We opened this survey with the statement that most strategic developments in 1992 had their roots in processes that started at least several years earlier. The year concluded with a development that did not belong to the Middle East region, but would undoubtedly have a significant influence on events there: the election of Bill Clinton as president of the US for the coming four years. By early 1993 it was premature, of course, to analyze Clinton's policy on Middle Eastern problems. He had repeatedly spoken of the need to change American national priorities in favor of a prompt solution to serious economic and social domestic problems. Thus one could expect a series of measures emphasizing the need to curb the budgetary deficit, reduce the defense budget, renew economic growth, bring down unemployment rates, fight the spread of drugs and AIDS, improve public health programs and curb the spread of crime. With these priorities one could also expect a cut in American foreign aid programs, and perhaps serious new constraints on the American capability to intervene strategically in different parts of the world, as well as some reluctance to become involved in international conflicts that might demand an American military, economic or even political engagement.

During his first weeks in office, Clinton made clear his intention to maintain his predecessor's policies regarding Iraq and Saddam Hussein, to carry on with the aid operation in Somalia, and to deepen US involvement in the internal convulsions in former Yugoslavia. As for the Arab-Israel conflict, Secretary of State Warren Christopher's first trip abroad was designed to renew bilateral peace negotiations. It reflected a Clinton decision, again, to pursue his predecessor's successful policy and, indeed, even to extend the scope of American involvement.

2. The Regional Arena: Key Issues
Ephraim Kam

From 1990 through 1992 important changes took place within the Arab system. These stemmed from three main sources: (a) The Gulf crisis, which changed the balance of power in the Arab world, particularly in the Gulf area, and affected the Arab-Israel peace process as well as the role of the powers in the Middle East. (b) The collapse of the Soviet Union, which affected not only the powers' involvement in the region, but also the behavior of the Arab actors affiliated to them. And (c) internal issues within most of the Arab states, which created a shift in the inner balance of power in some of them. Prominent among the internal issues were economic distress, which enlarged the circle of dissatisfaction with regime policies; growing demands on the part of various groups for a share in power and for democratization; a greater tendency to return to Islamic sources as a solution to socio-economic and personal distress; and health problems of key leaders. The outcome was a growing potential risk of instability for several Arab regimes--though most were still relatively stable--or at least significant constraints upon their freedom of action.

These factors brought about a series of changes in the Arab arena. First, a new inter-Arab balance of power emerged: the pragmatist bloc was strengthened, led by the tripartite axis of Egypt, Saudi Arabia and Syria; the radical group was further weakened, and its most militant member, Iraq, was isolated. By early 1993 this new realignment seemed to be stable, despite differences of opinion that emerged among its leading members.

Second, the defeat of Iraq considerably weakened its capability to threaten its neighbors. It also significantly reduced its potential contribution to the threat toward Israel. And yet the Gulf area remained the main source of instability in the Middle East. The Gulf crisis did not generate any sort of outcome that could restore the balance of power among its three main components, after it had been basically undermined since the early 1980s.

Thus *Iraq* was still led by a radical regime that strove to change the conditions imposed on it. Saddam Hussein's regime was weak, and faced many problems. Yet the combination of its vision of Iraq as a regional military power, its motivation and survivability, its military and economic potential, and the capacity it had acquired to produce nonconventional weapons--all these presented Iraq as a problematic and potentially threatening local power in the long run. Whenever international sanctions and supervision were removed, Iraq would be able to reconstruct a major part of its previous military capability.

Iran sought rapidly to exploit Iraq's weakness. It allocated extensive resources for a military buildup, including the development of nonconventional capabilities. The combination of its extreme radical approach, drive to export the Islamic revolution, growing military capability, economic and manpower potential, and the vacuum left by Iraq--all bolstered Iran as a growing threat toward its neighbors as well as toward other moderate Arab regimes. At the same time, it also projected a growing threat toward Israel, due to its developing long-range strategic arm (nonconventional capabilities, surface-to-surface missiles, modern air force), its involvement in Lebanon and in terrorism, its attempts to influence the Islamic movement in the Territories, and its efforts to obstruct the Arab-Israel peace process.

The Gulf crisis emphasized the inherent military weakness of *Saudi Arabia and the Gulf emirates*. The solution they sought to that weakness was to institutionalize their reliance on the United States in order to deter future enemies, and to protect their independence when deterrence failed. Saudi Arabia added to this reliance a far-reaching force-building program, which in turn would contribute to the acceleration of the arms race in the Middle East. While this solution was apparently the best available for the Gulf states, it had its own inherent weaknesses. The exposure, since the Gulf Crisis, of the limits of American power to affect local developments--even when the United States was the sole world superpower--presumably indicated to the Gulf leaders that their security was not guaranteed even under an American umbrella.

Third, from 1989 on, Islamic fundamentalism acquired a significant momentum in the Arab world. Its success was based on its appeal to the masses and its ability to suggest simple answers to socio-economic distress, its organizational effectiveness, its capability to exploit democratization processes initiated by some Arab regimes, and on Iranian encouragement and funding. In a few years time it registered an impressive string of victories: Sudan was under Islamic rule; the Algerian government had to use force in order to contain the stunning electoral success of the Islamic movement; the Islamic groups in Jordan posed the most significant political challenge to the regime; the Islamic groups in Kuwait played a major role in the victory of the opposition candidates in parliamentary elections; radical Islamic groups in Egypt continue to challenge the regime and attack government targets; the Islamic movement posed the strongest opposition to the Tunisian regime, which was forced to dismantle it; Hizballah was strengthened in Lebanon, and, for the first time, sent several of its members to the newly-elected parliament; and the Islamic groups in the Territories posed a growing challenge both to Israel and the PLO. In a way, Islamic fundamentalism replaced traditional Arab radicalism, which diminished as a political power. Potentially, however, Islamic radicalism--though still an opposition force within most Arab states--was more dangerous than Arab radicalism, both for moderate Arab regimes and for Israel.

And fourth, the more convenient environment for the Arab-Israel peace process following the Gulf Crisis, the changing approach of Syria toward the process, the expectations of the Palestinians in the Territories to advance negotiations as an outcome of the Intifada--all these created a consensus among most Arab parties to exploit the potential opportunities of the peace process to bring about a political settlement of the Arab-Israel conflict, on the basis of territories-for-peace.

The Inter-Arab Balance of Power

The Gulf crisis undermined the former set of balances and changed alignments within the Arab arena. Iraq was weakened and isolated, and lost much of its central position in the Arab system. Syria affiliated itself to the so-called Arab pragmatist bloc, and its approach toward the peace process showed indications of significant change. Jordan distanced itself from Iraq, and began to move back to its traditional place within the pragmatist bloc. Looked at from the standpoint of the Arab radical bloc, the crisis further strengthened the position of the pragmatist camp: Iraq, the most militant member of the Arab radicals, was defeated; Syria, another outstanding representative of the radicals, preferred to join the anti-Iraq coalition, as well as the peace process; Libya, the third pillar of Arab radicalism, came under heavy American pressure, due to its involvement in terrorism. Thus, the traditional radical group, already weakened during the 1980s, barely existed after the crisis; and the new momentum that characterized the peace process after 1991 seemed to justify the political approach taken by the pragmatist camp.

Since the Gulf Crisis, a coalition headed by Egypt, Saudi Arabia and Syria took over the lead in the Arab world. Though its original aim was to contain the Iraqi threat, its sphere of common interests was much wider: to build a new order in the Middle East, mainly by stabilizing the situation in the Gulf and advancing a political solution to the Arab-Israel conflict on the basis of terms acceptable to the Arabs. In particular, its members agreed on the need to exploit the American commitment to advance the peace process, and to coordinate their negotiating strategies, though they might differ regarding specific issues pertaining to the process. They also agreed on the need to prevent future attempts by radical forces to change the regional balance of power. On the other hand, as the Iraqi threat diminished, the leading members of the coalition significantly differed regarding the required system of security arrangements in the Gulf. This controversy was accompanied by the failure of Egypt and Syria to institutionalize economic aid from Saudi Arabia and the Gulf emirates on a long-range basis for the future.

To a large extent, *Egypt* emerged from the Gulf crisis as the central Arab power. Saudi Arabia and Syria preferred to cooperate with Egypt rather than challenge it. Iraq was weakened so much that it could not threaten Egypt's strategic position and leadership, at least for the coming years. Egypt was perceived as a regional strategic asset for the United States and the West, and as the most important stabilizing force in the Middle East and the main Arab channel of influence. It developed a close relationship with most Arab states, and played an important role behind the scenes in the Arab-Israel peace process, taking full advantage of its open communications with all participants.

Yet despite its improved position, Egypt was unhappy with developments in the Arab arena. Beyond its disappointment with the policy of the Gulf states, which will be discussed later, Egypt was frustrated by the situation in its own neighborhood--in Sudan, Algeria and Libya. Of great concern to Cairo was the "revolution" in Sudan of the Islamic junta of General Bashir that had seized power in 1989, particularly insofar as the regime in Khartoum developed close relations with Iran, which financed large shipments of arms from China to Sudan. Egypt had always been deeply concerned with the internal situation in Sudan, regarding it as its strategic backyard. In its view, Iranian influence in Sudan turned it into a center of fundamentalist subversion, and a source of encouragement for the Egyptian Islamic movement. Hence Egypt insisted that the Sudanese regime distance itself from the Islamic movement and cut links with foreign radical Islamic groups. To a lesser extent, Egypt was unhappy with the strengthening of the Islamic movement in Algeria, and the implications this might have on other North African states.

Libya was often a cause of concern for Egypt, due to its radical orientation and involvement in terrorism. After the Gulf War it had to cope with the possibility of an American military move against Libya. In April 1992 the Security Council, led by the western powers, imposed aerial, arms and diplomatic sanctions against Libya until its government abided by the Council's demands: to surrender two Libyans suspected of the 1988 bombing of Pan Am 103 over Lockerbie in Scotland; to permit questioning of four other suspects believed to be involved in the 1989 explosion of a French airliner over Niger; and to cease all forms of terrorist action and all assistance to terrorist groups. As the sanctions failed to force Qadhafi to comply, American military action appeared at times to be imminent. Against this background, Egypt helped Libya to defuse the tension by trying to convince the western powers to avoid force, and rely on compromise. Egypt believed that an American strike against Libya would alienate most of the Arabs and might amplify the latent resentment stirred up by the military operation against Iraq. In any case, the likelihood of American military action against Libya appeared to decline toward the end of 1992.

Saudi Arabia focused most of its attention on the Gulf arena, rather than on inter-Arab affairs or the peace process. The Gulf crisis had exposed its vulnerability to external threats on the part of Iraq--despite its defeat--or Iran. The Saudi reply to these threats was a combination of four components: further weakening of Iraq by encouraging American pressure on Saddam Hussein's regime and supporting limitations on its military capabilities; developing Saudi military power on the basis of far-reaching force-building programs; securing an American commitment to help

Saudi Arabia deter its enemies and contain possible attack if deterrence failed; and promising small steps toward internal reform in order to reduce internal pressures on the regime.

Syria further established its position within the pragmatist camp. On the basis of its active participation in the peace process and direct negotiations with Israel, as well as its improving relations with the United States, Damascus projected a more moderate, responsible image. Its enhanced position in the Arab world and in the international arena compensated Syria, at least partly, for the loss of Soviet strategic backing. Its alliance with Iran, though constant, took a lower profile than in former years. In any case, Iran's attempts to obstruct the peace process apparently did not affect the Syrian attitude toward the process.

Thus by the end of 1992 the Arab system was characterized by a lower degree of inter-Arab divisions and conflicts. Yet new frameworks for political and economic cooperation among Arab governments did not develop, as some had expected, and the role of Iraq in Arab affairs remained problematic.

Instability in the Gulf

In 1992 the Gulf arena was still the most important source of instability in the Middle East. Two radical forces, Iraq and Iran, threatened to change the balance of power in the Gulf and beyond. The remaining local forces, especially Saudi Arabia and the Gulf emirates, were too weak to contain these threats without external military backing.

Iraq's strategic power was significantly damaged. A considerable portion of its military capability was destroyed, it faced severe internal difficulties, aggravated by international sanctions, and it was politically isolated, lacking the ability to play a major role in Arab politics. Yet Saddam Hussein remained in power, and managed to reconstruct part of his military power. More importantly, even after his defeat Saddam appeared not to have given up his vision of building Iraq as a regional power. He projected a determination to preserve, to the extent possible, Iraq's military capabilities, especially its nonconventional strategic programs. These were perceived by him as the basis for leading Iraq back to regional hegemony.

The international supervision and sanctions compelled Saddam to adopt a cautious policy, and project a willingness to cooperate with the international inspectors. He clearly wanted to avoid a military confrontation with the United States, but at the same time he probably felt that political constraints and reduced military power in the Gulf limited the American freedom of action. Hence he maneuvered between his desire to conceal his nonconventional programs and hide his weapons arsenals on the one hand, and his fear of American military action on the other. His policy was to manifest stubbornness in the face of international pressure, but to back down at the last minute and agree to limited cooperation with United Nations inspectors when the risk of military retaliation seemed too high. He presumably sought to survive until international sanctions were lifted, to probe American determination without provoking military punishment, and to preserve military capabilities as a basis for reconstructing his power.

By 1993, it was still too early to judge to what extent this policy succeeded from Iraq's viewpoint. If Saddam had hoped to ease the sanctions, he was apparently disappointed. The limitations on Iraqi flights over southern Iraq imposed in August 1992, and the American attacks on Iraqi military targets in January 1993 presumably manifested to Saddam the limits of his maneuverability: the American administration, aiming at his collapse, was still able to rally its allies--despite some reservations on the part of Egypt--to apply new pressures. Moreover, as of January 1993 Iraq's border with Kuwait was relocated northward by Security Council mandate, bisecting Iraqi's only port, Umm Qasr, and granting Kuwait control over part of the large Iraqi oil field at Rumeila. The move thus created another potential area of dispute in the future. With the departure of the Bush administration, Saddam had some hopes that the Clinton administration would be more flexible and lighten the pressures, and he signaled his willingness to open a new chapter with the United States. In any case, his policy of maneuvering between conflicting pressures always involved risks of miscalculation on both sides. And yet the key question was whether Iraq would be able to maintain its threatening military potential in the future, despite the sanctions.

With the Iraqi threat removed *Iran* now formed another source of potential instability. Tehran harbored its own aspirations for regional hegemony, and moved quickly to fill the vacuum created by Iraq's weakness. It had long been conducting a radical policy, with an emphasis on exporting the Islamic revolution. That policy's newest manifestations were growing support for fundamentalist and radical organizations, developing contacts with the Islamic regime of Sudan, Iran's role in Lebanon, enhanced by the strengthening of Hizballah, and its attempts to obstruct the Arab-Israel peace talks. Moreover, Iranian moves to fully annex three disputed small strategic islands in the Gulf, and the purchase of two or three submarines from Russia, were perceived by the Gulf states and Egypt as a new initiative by Tehran to control the entrance to the Gulf. And on the periphery, Iran competed with Turkish connections and Saudi money to acquire influence within the Central Asian Muslim republics of the former USSR.

But the most worrisome aspect of Iran's activity was its military buildup, despite its deep economic troubles. The core of this buildup were programs for developing a long-range strategic arm based on a modern air force, surface-to-surface missiles, and above all--nonconventional military capabilities. At the same time, Iran had an interest in projecting a positive image of pragmatism, in order to recruit the European credits and investments that were crucial for its crippled economy, to improve its international position, and probably to blur the threatening impact of its military buildup. Hence Tehran displayed an openness toward the West, as indicated by the release of western hostages in Lebanon, and improved its relations with Arab regimes. This did not necessarily reflect a genuine ideological change in Iran's radical approach, but rather the more pragmatic and flexible policy image that generally characterized the Rafsanjani regime.

The lessons of the Iraqi invasion of Kuwait, together with the potential threat still projected by both Iraq and Iran, compelled the members of the anti-Iraq coalition to consider a new system of post-war security arrangements to protect the Gulf states. It soon became apparent, however, that the Arab members of the coalition were unable to agree on this issue. The controversy involved two sets of problems. First, what was the main source of threat? Was it Iraq, as Saudi Arabia and Kuwait claimed? Or was it Iran, as Egypt suggested? And should future security arrangements involve Iran, as the Iranians demanded? But the more controversial problem had to do with the composition of a defense force for the Gulf. Would it be a local force, based on troops from the Gulf states? Or would it be an Arab force, including expeditionary forces from other Arab states, mainly Egypt and Syria? And should it be backed by American troops, as the best deterrence against potential threats?

Already in March 1991, Egypt, Syria and the six Gulf states (the "six plus two") declared in Damascus that they would establish an Arab Force to defend the Gulf; it was understood that the Gulf states would provide bases and funding for the force, while Egypt and Syria--the bulk of the troops. Within weeks, however, controversy emerged: Kuwait preferred to be protected by an American-British brigade to be stationed there, without any Arab component. In May 1991 Egypt and Syria reacted by withdrawing their expeditionary forces from Kuwait. Under pressure from the other Gulf states, Kuwait ultimately agreed to incorporate 5,000 Egyptian and 1,000 Syrian soldiers in the force. Oman had a different plan: it envisaged a force of 100,000 troops drawn exclusively from the Gulf states, with some Iranian involvement; at the same time, each Gulf state could have separate bilateral military agreements with Egypt, Syria or the United States. Neither of these concepts, nor their variations, were accepted, and no agreement was reached regarding the nature, size, structure or command of the force.

The disagreement reflected differing perceptions within the coalition. Egypt and Syria insisted on building an all-Arab defense force, in which they would play a major role. This in turn would bring them generous financial aid. Egypt also suggested that such a force was necessary to contain the growing Iranian threat. Most of the Gulf states, on the other hand, preferred a strong American commitment to their security, though without a visible American military presence on their soil. They also argued that an Arab force could not be relied upon, given the nature of Arab politics. The Gulf states' aversion to a security alliance with Egypt and Syria was partly affected by Iran's objection to the idea, based on the claim that only littoral states should participate in the protection of the Gulf.

As it became clear that no collective security measures could be expected from the Arab coalition, the main Gulf states began to develop their own solutions. Saudi Arabia planned to expand its armed forces considerably, and to create a 200,000-strong army on the basis of a massive arms acquisition program. With an improved military capability the Saudis expected to deter a future enemy, or to slow its attack until American reinforcements arrived. Kuwait had a different concept. In September 1991 it concluded a defense pact with the United States. The ten-year agreement was aimed at achieving close cooperation between the two parties, improving the military capabilities of Kuwait's armed forces, and deterring any aggression or threat to Kuwait's security. The idea was to enable the rapid deployment of significant American forces in Kuwait when needed, by prepositioning military equipment there, rather than basing troops permanently in the Gulf. In February 1992 Kuwait and the United Kingdom signed a separate memorandum on security cooperation, and Kuwait intended to conclude a similar agreement with France. In October 1991 Bahrain too signed a defense agreement with the United States.

Needless to say, the agreements angered both Egypt and Iran. Cairo was displeased because it was now denied any role in the defense of the Gulf, and because of the failure of the anti-Iraq coalition to develop a framework for close political and economic cooperation. Egypt was also irritated by the Gulf states' failure to meet its expectations of obtaining generous long-range economic aid in gratitude for its contribution to Iraq's defeat. And Egypt was concerned about the tendency of some Gulf states to seek an understanding regarding Gulf security with Iran, which was regarded by Egypt as a major threat to the region.

Iran, for its part, opposed the presence and involvement of American forces in the Gulf, and insisted on its own participation in security arrangements there. Controversy over Gulf security was reflected also in the differing Arab approaches toward the banning of Iraqi flights over southern Iraq after August 1992, and regarding American air attacks on Iraq in January 1993. Saudi Arabia and Kuwait supported the American moves, as they continued to regard Saddam's Iraq as the main threat to their security. Egypt and Syria, on the other hand, were more hesitant. They were concerned about the possibility that increasing the pressure on Iraq would lead to its disintegration, and hence to further growth of the Iranian threat.

In conclusion, two years after the Gulf crisis the Arab system was still unable to suggest its own solution to the instability in the Gulf. The concept of an Arab force to guarantee Gulf security was rejected. The sense of individual vulnerability generated by the crisis pushed the Gulf states to think more seriously about a Gulf confederation. Yet by early 1993 no significant steps had been taken in that direction. As in the 1990-1991 crisis, the Gulf states seemed likely once again to rely on American protection in future crises.

Regime Stability

From 1970 to 1993, no central Arab regime had collapsed. Even the Gulf Crisis did not change this picture of relative stability. Yet some Arab regimes faced severe internal pressures that might affect their stability in the future. These problems stemmed from four main sources: (a) Economic distress, which formed a major risk for many Arab regimes, especially in Egypt, Jordan, Iraq, Algeria and Sudan. (b) Fundamentalist Islamic movements, which exploited socio-economic pressures to gain power and influence, especially in Egypt, Jordan, Algeria and Sudan. (c) The outcome of the Gulf War, which affected mainly the stability of the Iraqi regime, but also, to a lesser extent, that of the Gulf states. (d) The personal survivability of some Arab leaders, who were threatened by health problems or possible assassination attempts. Here the outstanding cases in point were King Hussein of Jordan and President Asad of Syria.

The main question mark in this regard referred to the future of Saddam Hussein's regime in *Iraq*, in the wake of the severe internal distresses and external pressures caused by the war. On the surface, the regime seemed to have consolidated its position. The army, the Ba'ath Party and the security services were still loyal to the regime. The damaged infrastructure was partly repaired. The food supply improved, and even prices were stabilized, though at a high level. Many Iraqis blamed Saddam for their hardships, but at the same time their hatred was also directed against the United States. Moreover, many Iraqis did not support Saddam's removal under American pressure lest his regime's collapse trigger a civil war and bring about the disintegration of Iraq.

On the other hand, Saddam's regime faced heavy pressures, which threatened its stability and viability. For one, the Iraqi economy was in a severe crisis. Beyond the significant damage to its infrastructure during the war, Iraq suffered seriously from international economic sanctions: there was a real shortage of raw materials and spare parts, and a partial shortage of foodstuffs and medicines; industry was partly paralyzed; inflation and unemployment rates were very high, medical services limited and, due to sanctions, the reconstruction of the economy was inadequate, and growth impossible. Secondly, since the war the Iraqi regime faced considerable internal unrest. The Kurds, despite the defeat of their post-war uprising, controlled part of northern Iraq and confronted the army from time to time. Turkey's repeated violations of Iraqi sovereignty, by its massive attacks on Turkish Kurdish rebel concentrations inside Iraqi territory, emphasized Saddam's weakness. In the south, especially along the border with Iran and in the marsh areas, Shi'ite groups, partly supported by Iran, conducted guerrilla operations against government targets. Overall, a variety of Iraqi opposition movements became more active against Saddam's regime than ever before, encouraged by the American administration and some Arab governments.

Saddam employed a variety of measures to counter these threats. He rewarded the army and security services generously, cultivated the Ba'ath Party as a counterweight to the army, often reshuffled senior officials who were perceived as a potential threat to him, and allocated military units and resources to defend the regime's sensitive targets, especially in Baghdad. In all, Saddam drew strength from the opposition's weakness as a real alternative to his regime. And yet by the beginning of 1993 Saddam's regime was itself weak, and its survivability was questionable in view of the heavy pressures being exerted upon it.

The Gulf Crisis affected the internal affairs of other Gulf states as well, especially *Saudi Arabia* and *Kuwait*. Some of these governments sensed that following their exposure to severe external threat, they now had to defuse domestic pressures for democratization and respond to the internal ferment that accompanied the crisis. In order to strengthen their stability in wartime, Saudi Arabia and Kuwait had promised during the crisis to introduce political reforms.

Thus in March 1992 Saudi Arabia suggested that it establish an advisory consultative council with power to propose, but not pass, legislation. Earlier, it had repatriated some 800,000 Yemenite migrant workers in order to reduce the number of foreigners in the Kingdom. The Kuwaiti regime, which had been traumatized by the Iraqi invasion, took three major steps in order to restabilize its authority: it reduced the number of non-Kuwaiti Arabs in the emirate, and in particular expelled or "encouraged to leave" nearly 300,000 Palestinians; it provided generous financial grants to each Kuwaiti family; and, in response to opposition and popular calls, it held parliamentary elections in October 1992, in which opposition candidates won about 70 percent of the seats. The stunning victory of the opposition candidates, about half of whom belonged to the Islamic movement, probably did not immediately endanger the ruling family. But it must have signaled the regime that it could not long ignore public support for the opposition and its demands without risking internal unrest. This consideration probably convinced the regime to appoint six opposition members, including three of Islamic persuasion, as cabinet ministers.

It was not clear, however, to what extent these political reforms would be significant. The ruling family in Saudi Arabia, for example, had repeatedly promised reforms since the 1960s, yet significant moves were consistently delayed. The newly pledged consultative council--hardly a far-reaching step--was no exception: by early 1993 it had still not been established. Obviously the Gulf regimes liked to move cautiously in balancing the demands of rival internal forces, like conservatives and liberals. Yet the more important consideration was their fear that opening up the political process would increase rather than contain pressures on the regime.

Iran had not been directly involved in the Gulf crisis, but its strategic position was affected. Indeed it benefited considerably from the war, especially due to the weakening of Iraq. Yet Iran faced severe economic problems: high inflation, widespread unemployment, shortages of basic products, and a deteriorating infrastructure. The economic crisis caused, for the first time under Rafsanjani's regime, recurrent outbreaks of unrest, albeit of limited proportions, within the population; it also fueled criticism by Rafsanjani's opponents against his policies. The regime, for its part, sought to implement a five-year economic plan and to project an image of efficiency and openness, in order to attract foreign investment. By the beginning of 1993, Rafsanjani still enjoyed solid political strength. Iran's economic problems, however, created a potential long-term threat to the regime's stability.

The other outstanding development pertaining to the stability of Arab regimes was the growing power of Islamic fundamentalist movements--especially in Algeria, Egypt, Jordan,

Kuwait, Lebanon, and Sudan. We have already discussed Sudan and Kuwait. Alongside them, the greatest success of the Islamic fundamentalist movement was in *Algeria*. The main religious party there, the Islamic Salvation Front (FIS), was founded in 1989 and rapidly gained considerable power by exploiting a nascent democratization process, growing discontent and frustration, and the weakness of both the regime and the other opposition parties. The shock came in 1991. Despite the regime's efforts to curb FIS, it scored overwhelming success in the first round of general elections in September 1991: it won 188 seats in the parliament, and needed only 28 additional seats in a second round runoff scheduled for January 1992, to gain an outright majority. FIS's decisive victory forced the regime, supported by the army, to react. By early 1992 it had canceled the second round of the elections, imposed a state of emergency, banned FIS, and made an attempted to dismantle it by arresting its leaders and thousands of its supporters. The outcome was a wave of violence across the country and a long series of armed clashes between the security forces and Islamic activists, which soon cost the life of the newly appointed head of state, Mohammed Boudiaf.

The regime's efforts to eliminate the Islamic movement were accepted with relief by most Arab governments, as the prospect of an Islamic regime in Algeria had aroused fears of a fundamentalist tide sweeping the Arab world, especially in North Africa. This would encourage similar groups in other Arab states, the more so since in the Algerian case--as in Sudan, and unlike in Iran--it was a Sunni Islamic threat. Most concerned were the neighboring regimes in Tunisia and Morocco, where fundamentalist parties had been banned, and even in Libya, which also had experienced troubles with Islamic activists. Egypt, which had been fighting fundamentalism since the 1970s, explicitly supported the crackdown against the Algerian Islamic movement.

From mid-1992 the Algerian regime conducted "total war" against the Islamic groups, and escalated its emergency steps with the objective of eradicating them. Although many of their leaders and activists were indeed arrested or killed, the Islamic groups were nevertheless far from being eliminated. Moreover, the regime's efforts to overcome the economic crisis--the key to undermining the Islamic movement--did not bear fruit. Thus by the beginning of 1993, the regime was facing a declining economy, internal insecurity and disturbances, and growing public dissatisfaction.

For many years, *Egypt*'s stability depended to a large extent on its success in preventing significant unrest stemming from socio-economic distress, and on its ability to contain the threat posed by the opposition, especially the fundamentalist Islamic movement. During 1991-1992 Egypt began to reap the economic rewards of the Gulf Crisis. The financial aid received from Saudi Arabia facilitated a limited improvement in the economic situation. It was characterized by an enhanced supply of goods and stable low prices for basic products, rather than by a significant increase in investment and development.

And yet, from May 1992 on, there was also a significant rise in radical Islamic activity in Egypt, mainly in Upper Egypt and Cairo. Assaults on government officials, security forces and Copts increased sharply. The main target, however, was tourist groups, with the overt goal of obstructing tourism to Egypt, the country's primary source of foreign currency, thereby destabilizing the economy and the regime. Government efforts to suppress the Islamic groups were partially successful. While it seemed unlikely that this violence would actually destabilize the regime, it did nevertheless have considerable nuisance value, and the regime found it difficult to suppress these groups altogether.

In *Jordan*, the end of the Gulf Crisis enabled the regime to overcome some of its internal and external difficulties. By distancing itself from Iraq, and by actively participating in the peace process, the regime managed to repair most of the damage caused to relations with the United States and Europe. It also succeeded in improving its relations with Egypt, Syria and, to a lesser extent, Saudi Arabia. This led to the renewal of American economic assistance to Jordan. The defeat of Iraq also cooled nationalistic fervor in Jordan, and to some extent eroded popular support for Islamic fundamentalism. This made it easier for the regime to act, however gradually and cautiously, against the Islamic movement, and to begin removing its representatives from positions of political power. Moreover, the end of the Gulf Crisis and the beginning of the Arab-Israel peace process considerably reduced Iraqi and Syrian constraints formerly imposed on Jordan's freedom of action; it also somewhat moderated tensions between Jordanians and Palestinians within the Kingdom, stirred up by the Intifada.

But the most important problem that the Jordanian regime

encountered in the post-Gulf War period was the health of King Hussein. In August 1992 the King underwent surgery to remove a malignant growth; he was required to undergo chemotherapy treatments in the United States for some time afterwards. By the beginning of 1993 his exact condition remained unclear. In any event, in his public remarks the King began to prepare his people for his possible departure from the throne.

The regime faced a number of additional problems. The Jordanian economy was still in severe crisis, with high rates of unemployment and poverty, and this in turn encouraged the rise of Islamic movements. Islamic groups still posed a powerful challenge to the regime, due to their organizational infrastructure and status as the single largest faction in parliament. While the Islamic groups did not endanger the stability of the regime, they did somewhat restrict its freedom of action, especially as they opposed peace talks with Israel, and demanded conservative social policies.

In this context, the regime hesitated to continue the democratization process. Three years of experimentation with democratization had increased the weight of the opposition, mainly the Islamic movement, in Jordanian politics in general and in parliament in particular. Moreover, the events in Algeria served as a warning to the regime of the need to exercise caution in broadening political freedoms. Still, the regime continued expanding democratization in Jordan: in July 1992 the government passed a law permitting the establishment of political parties, prohibited in Jordan since 1957. The government also intended to hold multi-party elections for parliament in November 1993, for the first time since 1954, and many parties began to organize accordingly. Though the regime was surprised by the success of the opposition in the 1989 elections, it nevertheless obviously believed it could control the democratization process. It remained to be seen whether the coming elections would not once again play into the hands of the opposition.

All told, then, by the beginning of 1993 the Hashemite regime seemed to be relatively stable. Its capacity to cope with both its internal and external problems had improved, compared with its difficult position during the Gulf crisis. There were, however, growing concerns in Jordan regarding long-term stability. This, due to two developments that emerged in 1992: the possibility that autonomy for the Palestinians in the Territories would affect the internal situation in Jordan, and King Hussein's health problems.

Health problems could play a key role regarding the stability of the regime in *Syria* as well. By and large President Asad's health did not affect his political functioning, and his regime was stable, facing no significant opposition or new threats. Arab economic assistance given to Syria following the Gulf War helped it cope with the economic difficulties it had faced since the mid-1980s. Even the Syrian policy of stabilizing the Lebanese system seemed to be relatively successful, despite many difficulties. However the regime was still anxious to ensure that its negotiations with Israel and its growing openness toward the West generated no internal criticism or pressures.

Finally, a comment is in order regarding the *PLO*. By mid-1991 the organization was at a low ebb. Its support for Iraq during the Gulf Crisis isolated the PLO in the international and Arab arenas. It lost the financial support of the Gulf states, where hundreds of thousands of Palestinians were forced to leave. The collapse of the Soviet Union deprived the PLO of important political and military support. The Intifada faced growing difficulties, and the rise of a local leadership in the Territories potentially threatened the domination of the diaspora PLO leadership. Thus as the peace talks progressed, that leadership repeatedly had to decide to what extent the Territories' delegation would be allowed to move in a process that fell far short of meeting its conditions.

During 1992, however, the PLO gradually repaired some of the damage. It used its indispensable role as the sole representative of the Palestinians to improve its relations with most of the Arab leaders--including Syria's Asad, with whom Arafat met in October 1991 in Damascus, after a decade of mutual animosity-- and with the Europeans. It also played a key role in the peace process. The PLO was still the dominant force among the Palestinian organizations and groups, and Arafat's Fatah was dominant within the PLO.

And yet, by the beginning of 1993, despite this improvement, the PLO still faced considerable problems and threats. Its relations with the Gulf states remained strained, which meant a continuing shortfall of funding for the Palestinians in the Territories and for the Intifada. A direct dialogue with the American administration had not been renewed, and the PLO remained suspicious of American intentions regarding the peace process. The behind-the-curtain role that the PLO leadership was forced to play contributed to the strengthening and independence of the local leadership in the Territories, while the PLO was also concerned about the possibility of a Syrian move toward a settlement of the Syrian-Israeli conflict that ignored the Palestinian issue.

Conclusion

In the spring of 1991, the prevailing feeling in the Arab world was that the end of the Gulf Crisis would bring about a new order in the Middle East. The defeat of Iraq, coupled with America's extraordinary involvement in containing the aggression, were expected to create new opportunities for solving central regional conflicts.

Two years later, it could hardly be said that a new order had come to the Middle East. Indeed, while there was less division within the Arab world, Arab governments still found it difficult to agree to common strategies. Egypt had become the central Arab power, but it coordinated Arab efforts, rather than leading the Arab world. The peace process had developed a significant momentum, but the obstacles in its way were even more significant. The Arab pragmatist approach had been strengthened, but emerging Islamic radicalism was replacing traditional Arab radicalism.

A new order in the Middle East was also intended to reduce regional instability. By and large, this aim had not been achieved. The Iraqi threat was considerably diminished, yet Iraq retained its potential to reconstruct a major part of its arsenal in the future. More importantly, the growing threats posed by Iran and Islamic fundamentalism--which nurtured one another--had acquired crucial importance during the years 1990-1993. They threatened the internal stability of most moderate Arab regimes, and Israeli and western interests as well. They were, evidently, the face of future instability in the region.

It was still too early to judge how deep-rooted these developments would be. More time was needed to determine whether they would bring about any genuine turnover in the Middle East and within the Arab world. Eventually, the answer would depend primarily on developments in six crucial sectors: the fate of Iraq and its future regional role; the chances of the Arab-Israel peace process; the economic situation in the main Arab states; the future of Islamic fundamentalism; the increasing Iranian threat; and the stability of key Arab regimes.

3. THE ARAB-ISRAEL PEACE PROCESS

Joseph Alpher

The year that followed the Madrid Conference of October 1991 witnessed the unfolding of a multi-track peace process between Israel and its Arab neighbors. The principal effort--a series of bilateral meetings between Israel and Syria, Jordan, Lebanon and the Palestinians--may be divided into two distinct phases.

The first commenced with the Madrid Conference of October 1991 and ended with the Israeli elections and the ensuing change of government in Jerusalem. That change facilitated progress, particularly on the Syrian-Israeli track, where negotiations now appeared to offer the prospect of a new strategic departure, and in Jordanian-Israeli talks, where the one-year anniversary of Madrid produced an agreed agenda that defined the parameters of a future peace agreement. Progress was less evident on the Israeli-Palestinian track, where a considerable perceptual gap continued to separate the two sides, although by late 1992 small informal working groups were moving ahead. A secondary but, in the long term, equally significant effort--five multilateral forums for discussing regional issues--developed more slowly, its progress essentially linked to the bilateral track.

The US presidential election in November 1992 was potentially an important development for the process, insofar as the defeat of President Bush bespoke the departure of James Baker, who had successfully conceived, implemented and guided an extremely complex international structure for Middle East negotiations. Those negotiations, however historic their impact, nevertheless might still falter unless Washington maintained a high-profile role in shepherding them. Thus it was not surprising that the second phase of the process ground to a halt with Bush's defeat; the Arabs, and particularly the Syrians, wished to take the measure of the Clinton administration before proceeding. The crisis that developed over Israel's subsequent expulsion of over 400 Palestinian Islamic militants, exacerbated and prolonged the freeze.

45

Madrid and the First Five Rounds of Negotiations

Prior to the convening of the historic peace conference in Madrid on October 30, the United States outlined its position and summarized the undertakings it made during the long prenegotiation process, in "letters of assurances" to the various actors. These constituted an exercise in diplomacy--at times, in constructive ambiguity--that defined, in writing, the parameters within which Washington intended to channel the process:

Thus the Palestinians were told (all emphases added) that "the United States is determined to achieve a comprehensive settlement of the Arab-Israeli conflict," whereas Israel, in reply to its demand that the goal of the process be peace agreements, was granted that "the United States wants to establish peace in the Middle East." While Israel was informed that "the US will not support the creation of an independent Palestinian state," the Palestinians were told that the US "will accept any outcome agreed by the parties.... confederation is not excluded" (confederation presupposes the prior existence of two independent states, thus implying the possible creation of an independent state of Palestine). And while the Palestinians were offered "an end to the Israeli occupation.... Palestinians should gain control over political, economic and other decisions that affect their lives," the administration acknowledged that the Israeli government of Yitzhak Shamir held "its own interpretation of Security Council Resolution 242"--an allusion to Shamir's contention that Israel need not give up any more territories. (Indeed, even the Labor Party that succeeded the Likud in power in the summer of 1992, ultimately was bound to argue for far-reaching territorial adjustments in the West Bank that were presumably unacceptable to Washington.)

Several of the assurances did not display this sort of symmetry. Jordan and the Palestinians were given an undertaking that Jerusalem, though not represented in their joint delegation, may be discussed in the talks; that the US does not recognize Israel's annexation of East Jerusalem; and that Jerusalem Arabs should be allowed to participate in autonomy elections. Moreover the Palestinians were guaranteed an opportunity to put their case separately, despite being part of a joint delegation with Jordan. In contrast, Jerusalem was not mentioned in American assurances to Israel, presumably because the two sides could not agree as to how the issue should be approached. And the Palestinians' insistence on their right to a separate delegation was to delay the opening of negotiations for weeks, precisely because it had not been cleared in advance with Israel.

For its part Israel was further assured of US intentions to end the Arab economic boycott of Israel and to repeal the 1975 UNGA Zionism-is-Racism resolution (which the UN general Assembly did, in December 1991, despite lack of Arab support). The US also accepted that Israel was "entitled to secure and defensible borders;" reconfirmed President Ford's 1975 commitment to then Prime Minister Rabin regarding "the importance of the Golan Heights to Israel's security" and offered to "give its own guarantees to any border agreed upon between Israel and Syria" (a formulation that does not preclude even complete Israeli withdrawal); and reaffirmed its commitment "to Israel's security and to the maintenance of Israel's qualitative edge." Syria (which, alone, did not publish its assurances) was presumably led by Washington to understand that it would support an extensive, if not complete territories-for-peace exchange on the Golan, as well as Israeli withdrawal from southern Lebanon.

All the parties to the conference were assured by the United States that a Palestinian autonomy agreement was sought within one year of the start of negotiations; that it would last five years; and that in the third year, negotiations would be renewed regarding the final status of the Territories.

The Madrid Conference itself featured a series of addresses, and replies, or rebuttals, by the heads of delegations, followed by the initiation of direct bilateral talks between Israel and its Arab neighbors. The speeches, for the most part, were remarkable for their dedication to a rational peace process; President Bush made prominent mention of normalization and open borders as components of the peace he envisaged. Syrian Foreign Minister Farouq al-Shar'a was the lone exception, setting a tone that Damascus then maintained by an abortive last minute attempt to sabotage the bilateral talks. Certainly little happened at Madrid to substantiate American hopes that this face-to-face confrontation would effect an immediate dramatic breakthrough in the regional actors' attitudes toward one another. Still, the Madrid Conference succeeded in launching the extremely complex structure of negotiations that Secretary Baker had formulated.

Negotiations

Following these bumpy beginnings in Madrid, talks continued throughout the winter and spring in a series of five bilateral meetings held in Washington. Little progress was made, as the substantive gaps between Israel and each Arab partner were laid out, and the United States--pressed in particular by Israel to give the parties a chance to sort out their differences on their own, and mindful of Israeli internal political considerations, i.e., pressure from the extreme Right to dismantle Shamir's coalition--dismissed Arab pressures to intervene actively.

The case of Israel and Syria in particular appeared to illustrate the common wisdom that, for the most part, the Arabs and Israelis were going through the motions in order to please the Americans: Syria insisted that Israel commit itself to returning all of the Golan, and withdrawing completely on all other fronts as well, before substantive talks could begin; Israel demanded a prior detailed Syrian commitment to a genuine peace agreement as the goal of negotiations, before agreeing to hear Syria's territorial claims. Israeli-Lebanese talks were equally unproductive. Beirut clearly could not proceed without a green light from Damascus; nor, in fact, could it claim to control the southern third of the country sufficiently to offer Israel security in return for withdrawal.

Israel-Syria-Lebanon represented one 'triangle' of talks in Washington. A second--Israel, Jordan and the Palestinians--progressed along different lines during the first five meetings. Here the initial center of controversy was the procedural issue of the nature of the Jordanian-Palestinian negotiating "partnership." The Israeli government emerged from the 1991 Gulf War and the cumulative effects of the Intifada with a new and more positive assessment of the Hashemites, both as a strategic buffer between Israel and Iraq, and as a partner in a Palestinian agreement that would present virtually no territorial demands upon Israel. Hence it insisted that the principle of a joint Palestinian-Jordanian delegation be maintained to a maximum extent even when autonomy issues were discussed. The Palestinians, never happy with the procedural concessions and the partnership with Jordan that they had been obliged, in their weakness, to accept, wished to detach themselves to the greatest extent possible; and Jordan, weak economically and politically and fearful of antagonizing its many residual enemies on the inter-Arab scene, remained neutral. As a result, in December and January the three delegation heads met in a State Department corridor--unable to agree on a format for the delegations to meet in conference rooms.

Once this obstacle was finessed (with a symbolic Jordanian presence in the Palestinian-Israeli negotiations on an interim settlement), Jordanian-Israeli talks took on a friendly and businesslike atmosphere, and sought to concentrate on specifics. Amman itself had few minor territorial and other disagreements with Israel. But it insisted on prior progress in the Israeli-Palestinian talks before formally resolving them. Indeed, the latter talks were the most eventful. When Israel and the Palestinians did sit down together, they each presented their concepts of the interim period arrangements. The substantive gap that emerged clearly represented each side's strategic concept, as well as its internal political considerations. Thus Israel offered a minimalistic version of autonomy, focusing on aspects of self-government that did not involve any Palestinian control over the land or security, and that left the Israeli government as the source of authority. This constituted a retreat from some provisions of the Camp David Autonomy Framework that Prime Minister Shamir had earlier reluctantly embraced. The framework, for example, postulated the withdrawal of Israeli armed forces to "designated locations" in the Territories and the delineation of limited responsibility for security to an enhanced local police force, buttressed by Jordan. Shamir's new position bespoke Israel's claim that the spread and extent of its settlements in the West Bank now made it impossible to consider giving security responsibility to the Palestinians, as specified at Camp David. It was also a retreat from the readiness that Israel had displayed in the autonomy talks that ended a decade earlier, to discuss an alternative source of authority. It obviously reflected Shamir's own ideological predilections, but also his fear of alienating right wing voters yet further; even the initial minimalistic Israeli autonomy offer was embodied in a draft document that bore no official Israeli letterhead, and was called "Ideas for peaceful coexistence in the territories during the interim period."

The Palestinians, for their part, presented a "model of the Palestinian Interim Self-Government Authority (PISGA)" that described a sovereign state in everything but name, and rendered largely meaningless the concept of an open-ended, interim, confidence-building period that they had been forced to endorse in order to enter the process and avoid regional political isolation. Their leadership also appeared to fear the reaction of constituents who doubted the entire process. Moreover the Palestinian delegation displayed a tendency to escalate disputes by publicizing them, as competition was intense among diverse circles of negotiators and advisors: West Bankers and Gazans in the actual negotiating team, East Jerusalem intellectuals in a primary advisory capacity, pro-PLO exile academics from Europe and the US in a secondary advisory capacity, and a high-level PLO official, usually Nabil Shaat, consulting with Tunis from a nearby hotel room.

Withal, the moment the very notion of autonomy (with its implication of even minimal functional territorial compromise) surfaced on the agenda, two of the Likud's extreme right-wing coalition partners, Tehiya and Moledet, left the Israeli government. This precipitated a political crisis that culminated in an agreement between Likud (now leading a minority government) and Labor to advance the date for new Knesset elections from November to June 1992. It also ensured that little progress would take place in Israeli-Arab peace negotiations prior to the summer of 1992.

Multilateral Talks

In late January 1992 Moscow hosted the opening of the multilateral conference. This framework was designed to address the main problems confronting the Middle East on a regional scale. Following the grand opening, the conference split into five working groups that focused on issues of regional security and arms control, water, refugees, economy and environment, and that were scheduled to meet every few months in diverse world capitals.

Like Madrid, the Moscow conference was little more than a procedural beginning. Yet it was notable for the presence--for the first time at the same table with Israel--of all the Gulf states and some of those from North Africa. From the Israeli standpoint, it also served as the ultimate incentive for Moscow, Beijing and even New Delhi to establish full diplomatic relations (in order to qualify to host or attend the conference).

From a substantive standpoint, however, the absence from at least some of the meetings of three key delegations signaled the implicit limitations of the multilateral process. Syria refused to attend any of the sessions because, it argued, no bilateral progress had yet been made with Israel. Certainly Syrian attendance would be critical for the ultimate success of the arms control and water "baskets" of the Moscow process. The Palestinians were not allowed to be seated in Moscow because they insisted on bringing "outsider" diaspora representatives, in violation of the guidelines they had accepted prior to Madrid. Once a compromise was worked out between the Palestinians and the Americans, Israel responded by boycotting the refugee and economy working groups, lest it be seated alongside diaspora Palestinians.

To sum up this first phase of the peace process, it was ostensibly largely a procedural triumph. In reality, it represented a far-reaching political breakthrough. Essentially, the United States had succeeded in putting into place an impressive, multidimensional process reminiscent, in its complexity, of the 1919 Versailles Peace Conference. Israelis were speaking directly on political issues for the first time with Syrians and Palestinians. By and large, the key actors had persevered at the conference table. Certain apparently unavoidable rituals of mutual accusation (who started the '67 war, the meaning of 242) were acted out. The parties began to get to know one another. The international community was signed on. Of particular importance were those who would ultimately be called upon to bankroll Middle East peace settlements: Japan, the EEC and the Gulf states.

But progress in the two main bilateral sets of negotiations, Israel-Syria and Israel-Palestinians, was minimal. The Shamir government refused to introduce a territorial dimension, and insisted that the Palestinians suffice for now with measures that improved their quality of life, but little more; Syria refused to offer a peace settlement or even define the nature of peace; and the Palestinians, having agreed (largely out of post-Gulf War weakness) to discuss an open-ended interim arrangement, now demanded that the yardstick for approval of interim measures be their compatibility with a Palestinian state as the final status.

The talks in general were characterized by a total lack of confidence in both directions. The Syria-Israel negotiations, in particular, featured a tendency by both sides to define negotiating goals in the most ultimate terms possible, rather than seeking to identify feasible intermediate goals. Meaningful Israeli offers to institute reciprocal CBMs and informal behind-the-scenes discussions were rejected by the Arabs, while the US refused to even contemplate active intervention in the process until such measures were tried, and had failed. Meanwhile, the Shamir government's policy of massive settlement was day-by-day eroding any conceivable territorial basis for peace with the Palestinians.

This brings us, chronologically and topically, to a brief discussion of the only change of leadership among the actors at the peace talks during the first year--one that significantly affected the tenor of negotiations.

The Israeli Elections

We have noted that the June 23, 1992 Knesset elections in Israel were precipitated by the peace process. That process, and attendant issues, were thus very much at the center of the election debate. And the election results--a clear Labor plurality and mandate to form a government, but perpetuation of the broad divide in Israeli politics between territorial hawks and doves--mirrored the Israeli political dilemma regarding the process, yet generated a dramatic new departure toward a settlement.

The results--a Center-Left majority (with key ultra-orthodox assistance) of 62 out of 120 Knesset seats, with Labor gaining 44 mandates and Likud only 32--were seen in the Likud (and in the Tehiya Party, which lost its Knesset representation entirely) as a failure for the Right. Prime Minister Yitzhak Shamir announced he would resign from the Likud Party leadership and the Knesset as soon as a successor had been chosen. Defense Minister Moshe Arens announced his immediate departure from politics. In the soul-searching that accompanied this process, numerous reasons were offered for the voters' loss of confidence in the Likud after 15 years in which it dominated Israeli politics: widespread corruption, highlighted by the State Controller's reports, constant bickering and infighting among the leadership echelon, acquiescence to political demands by the ultra-orthodox, economic setbacks, a sharp decline in Russian Jewish immigration, and the crisis in relations with the United States. Even a rise in Arab violence against Israelis in the months preceding elections--stabbings inside Israel, Hizballah attacks in southern

Lebanon, a terrorist attack in Eilat--failed to produce the "classic" effect of moving voters toward the Right. On the contrary, the reaction in Bat Yam, scene of a particularly brutal stabbing of a young girl in late May, was heightened electoral support for the Left.

Many of these tendencies were direct spinoffs of Likud insistence on giving budgetary and ideological priority to settling Judea, Samaria and Gaza--whatever the strategic and economic cost to Israel. Both Shamir and Arens granted after the election that voters--particularly youth and Russian immigrants--had rejected the Likud's ideological priority of the Greater Land of Israel. Arens, in a major post-election surprise, declared that this was not his priority either, and suggested that at a minimum, the Gaza Strip was dispensable. "The Likud," he added, "was seen by the public as going nowhere. Statements by Shamir reinforced this image.... For years we have ignored the Palestinians.... In Judea and Samaria we have to reach a settlement with them. We can't ignore their problem." Shamir remained adamant, suggesting that a revitalized Likud would eventually win back the Israeli voter, and declaring that he would have "conducted autonomy negotiations for ten years, and meanwhile we would have reached half a million Israelis in Judea and Samaria" (days later, apparently recognizing the damage done by this statement to his credibility as a peace negotiator, he declared he had been misunderstood).

Correspondingly, a central aspect of Rabin's electoral strategy focused on linking the peace issues--the stalemated talks, the Likud's territorial intransigence and the issue of Israel's settlements in the West Bank--with Israel's economic stalemate, the collapse of Russian immigration, and the deterioration in relations with the United States. Whatever else may have motivated the Israeli electorate in terms of issue salience, Rabin emerged from the elections with a sense that he had been given a clear mandate to enforce a new order of priorities in Israeli policymaking--one that downgraded the effort to construct settlements in the West Bank and Gaza in favor of urgent domestic social and economic needs, and a territories-for-peace policy in negotiations with the Arabs. In a dramatic inaugural address to the Knesset on July 13, Rabin offered Israelis the option of changing both their priorities and their world view:

We are no longer an isolated nation and it is no longer true that the entire world is against us. We must rid ourselves of the feeling of isolation that has afflicted us for almost 50 years. We must join the campaign of peace, reconciliation and international cooperation that is currently engulfing the entire globe, lest we miss the train and be left alone at the station.

In his official reply to Rabin's speech, outgoing prime minister Shamir clearly stated the opposition's rejection of Rabin's new order of priorities:

The Israeli governing system has taken a step down. There is alienation from any Zionist and Jewish content. ...we did not hear the words Land of Israel [the term used to encompass Judea, Samaria and Gaza] even once in MK Rabin's speech.... the Jewish state cannot exist without a unique ideological content. We will not exist for long if we become just another country that is mostly devoted to the welfare of its residents.... what was presented before us today contains no vision and the tendency to neglect the future for the sake of immediate achievements.... It aspires to peace now, for achievements now, at the expense of basic national goals.

Rarely had Israel's most substantive national controversy been laid out so clearly by its leaders as in the days following Labor's election victory.

The Peace Process Resumes

In the aftermath of Israel's elections, its new government took on the role of catalyst, or protagonist, in the resumed talks--though at times in ways not entirely consistent with Rabin's earlier plans. Prior to his election triumph, Yitzhak Rabin had signaled clearly the ways in which he intended to alter Israel's approach to the Arab-Israel peace process. He would base it on the territories-for-peace principle, accelerate autonomy talks, and search for ways to facilitate the process through confidence-building measures and, where possible, a more liberal attitude toward the Palestinians' day-to-day problems. Rabin's position also reflected a view he had often voiced in criticism of the negotiating structure that James Baker had put into place during 1991. Only by negotiating sequentially with its Arab neighbors, Rabin believed, could Israel make progress toward peace; parallel and multilateral meetings were bound to escalate Arab demands and complicate negotiations. Consequently he hinted that he would place priority on what appeared to him--and, he believed, to Israelis in general--to be the most urgent issue, an interim autonomy settlement with the Palestinians, and would move the Syrian track to the back burner.

Even before Israel returned to the negotiating table in Washington in late August 1992 for a month of intensive talks, Rabin was obliged to revise his strategy. In talks held in July with Baker and with Egypt's President Mubarak, he was apprised of the emphasis they placed on the Syrian track in order to maintain both the inter-Arab acceptability of the process, and the American commitment to the Syrians to produce a forthcoming Israeli approach to the territorial issue. This was backed up by an increasingly overt Israeli intelligence assessment that indicated that Damascus' reappraisal of its strategic situation was indeed far-reaching: the changes in the global, inter-Arab and economic scene that had brought the Syrians into face-to-face negotiations with Israel in the first place, also appeared to dictate a readiness on Asad's part to end the conflict with Israel.

Hence the renewal of negotiations featured a two-pronged Israeli effort to produce new progress, with the key innovation in the Syrian sphere.

Syria-Israel

Professor Itamar Rabinovich, who replaced Yossi Ben Aharon as chief Israeli negotiator, opened the renewed talks in late August 1992 with a new departure: a declaration that Israel agreed to apply UNSC Resolution 242, with its territories-for-peace element, to its negotiations with Syria. Israel was prepared to discuss the territorial element on the Golan, alongside discussion of peace and security arrangements. Rabinovich also improved the atmosphere of talks, for example by avoiding rancorous cataloguing of Syria's plentiful transgressions against human rights.

This new approach immediately altered the tenor of the negotiations. Syrian delegation leader Ambassador Muaffaq al-Alaf abandoned his tight-lipped approach, and replied in kind: Syria was, he said, prepared to offer Israel peace in return for territories; it recognized that both sides had legitimate security interests to be taken into account; it could envisage a "delinked" Syrian-Israeli peace, achieved prior to a final settlement of the Palestinian issue; peace could be "delivered" by the Syrians in parallel with Israel's withdrawal; and that withdrawal could, once the principle was agreed, be implemented in stages. The Syrians presented many of these positions in writing--the first written document they had ever offered Israel.

These developments were almost without precedent in 43 years of Syrian-Israeli conflict. They led to a carefully orchestrated series of conciliatory statements for home consumption by both Syrian and Israeli leaders. Asad spoke publicly of a "peace of the brave." Rabin told Israeli audiences that Israel should prepare to offer Syria part of the Golan, and even to remove some settlements there. This provoked controversy within Israel over the Golan settlements issue, that reminded many Israelis of the debate over the fate of the Sinai Peninsula that accompanied the Begin-Sadat peace initiative in 1977-78.

By late 1992 a number of key points of contention continued to separate the two sides:

* Israel agreed in principle to discuss the territorial dimension, but only after the Syrians clarified their interpretation of the concept of peace. Jerusalem also signaled its intention that withdrawal be partial, not complete, and that it involve mainly Israel's military deployment rather than settlements. Rabin's repeated statements regarding partial withdrawal--e.g., "withdrawal on the Golan, not from the Golan"--were clearly unacceptable to Damascus, which wanted Israel to commit itself to a complete withdrawal.

* Meanwhile Syria's references to peace remained vague; spokespersons talked of a peace agreement, not a treaty, and rejected the notion of "normalization" in the short term; nor had Syria yet offered any explicit recognition of Israel and its right to exist.

* Syria insisted that any demilitarization arrangements be territorially symmetrical, despite the vast asymmetry between the land mass and configuration of the two countries.
* Syria continued to reject Israeli suggestions that the two sides institute confidence-building measures on a modest scale; it also rebuffed any notion of interim agreements; it continued to insist that the two sides first reach a comprehensive agreement in principle on the final outline of a settlement.
* Syria continued to hold the Israel-Lebanon talks hostage to progress in its own negotiations with Israel--and to condone Iranian-sponsored terrorism from Lebanon against Israel--despite the relative ease with which progress could have been made in that sphere, and the obvious Syrian interest in effecting an Israeli withdrawal from southern Lebanon.
* Israel rejected Syria's traditional demand for some sort of linkage between a bilateral settlement and progress (including withdrawal) on the Palestinian front as well as the Lebanese. On the other hand, Syria helped engineer a pact among all the Arab negotiating parties, and Egypt, in mid-October 1992, that each could proceed at its own pace toward reaching agreement with Israel (although none would sign a separate peace).
* Syria continued to boycott the multilateral talks on arms control and other issues, insisting that, first, progress be registered at the bilateral level.
* Perhaps most significantly, Asad indicated that he would settle for no less than the total withdrawal achieved 15 years earlier by Sadat on the Egyptian front. Yet the Syrian leader seemed unable, or uninterested for the present, in effecting the kind of atmosphere of reconciliation that had characterized the Israel-Egypt talks of 1977-79, and that had helped persuade Israelis ultimately that it was in their interest to give up all of the Sinai.

The Syrian position was also undoubtedly affected by the impending US presidential elections. Syria had engineered major changes in its global orientation--joining both the anti-Iraq coalition and the peace process--in close coordination with Bush and Baker. Asad attributed to them not only credibility, but a relatively congenial position, one that offered the prospect of eventual total Israeli withdrawal on the Golan. Clinton, on the other hand, seemed likely to deemphasize the substantive aspects of the process, reemphasize inconvenient human rights issues, and be more responsive to pressures by the organized American Jewish community.

Hence the looming prospect of a Bush defeat appeared to trigger a change of approach. A brief Syrian attempt, in mid-September, to effect a "crisis" in the talks and spur American intervention, seemed to reflect Syrian ignorance of the improved state of American-Israeli coordination (following Israel's elections) as well as Bush's obvious election-time reluctance to bring about any new tensions with Israel. Clinton's victory appeared to prompt Syrian decisions to allow an escalation of Hizballah activity against Israel in November, and to suspend the emigration of Syrian Jews. Damascus was apparently serving notice on Washington that the new administration should take Syria seriously, and should reaffirm Baker's commitments, if it hoped to renew progress in the peace process.

Nevertheless, the talks registered progress. The negotiators persevered even when tensions flared on the Lebanese-Israeli border in November. Most of the aforementioned differences were declared negotiable by the parties. By November-December 1992, more than one year after Madrid, an agreed "statement of principles" that laid out the parameters of substantive talks, appeared achievable. Statements by the Syrian leadership appeared to reaffirm Damascus' commitment to the process, and hinted at a Syrian readiness to entertain the possibility of an interim agreement, and to 'go it alone' if the Palestinians held up progress.

Israel-Palestinians

The Israeli-Palestinian talks on an interim autonomy settlement in the West Bank and Gaza also registered new progress in Washington. But it was more modest, and was often obfuscated by the conceptual gap that continued to overshadow the talks.

Unilateral Israeli CBMs in the security sphere (Rabin retained the defense ministry in his new government) that preceded the talks--release of detainees, cancellation of deportation orders, relaxation of travel restrictions, dismantling of barricaded streets and houses--were met by indifference or derision from the Palestinians, and were not reciprocated (e.g., by ceasing violent aspects of the intifada). Nor did Rabin's principal new departure--a partial settlement freeze--elicit great enthusiasm. The Palestinians pointed out that some 10,000 building starts would continue, and that Rabin had packaged the freeze more for American consumption (to obtain the long-delayed loan guarantees) than for the Palestinians.

Indeed, in general Rabin's initial confidence-building moves, while unilateral and therefore an innovation, were guarded in nature. Thus much of the building that would continue in the Territories was in so-called "security regions" (the Jordan Valley, Maaleh Adumim, Gush Etzion) destined by Rabin to remain part of Israel under any solution. This tended to placate many of the settlers, while the US government insisted on deducting huge loan sums against the ongoing construction.

Nor did Israel replace its chief negotiator, Dr. Elyakim Rubinstein, whom the Palestinians consider to be a hawk, or offer any dramatic new breakthrough with regard to autonomy. Rather, Rubinstein emphasized that Israel now sought to maintain a continuous dialogue, in a more flexible mode than previously, aimed at producing rapid progress: an outline agreement on the authority of an administrative council by February 1993, and elections to that council in April or May. This, against the strategic backdrop of Rabin's overall readiness eventually to invoke territorial compromise on all fronts, and his emphasis on the need for Israel to disengage from direct rule over the Palestinians.

Thus, upon resumption of negotiations in late August 1992, Rubinstein produced a detailed document describing the functions to be attributed to the council, including a Palestinian police force, tax collecting, education, health, etc.--even a standards institute. The document indicated that Israel saw itself as the source of authority for autonomy, although some issues, such as disposition of water and land resources, might be referred to a joint Israeli-Palestinian authority, and others to a joint Israeli-Palestinian-Jordanian liaison unit. By dint of omission, security issues were still to be left in Israel's hands during the five-year autonomy period.

The Palestinians acknowledged some progress in these Israeli positions. But they still insisted that the parties first reach agreement on the broad outlines of PISGA, and that these find expression in institutions of far more extensive authority. In particular, the Palestinians demanded that the autonomy agreement itself be the source of authority, and that, rather than the small administrative council that Israel proposed, they elect a 180-member legislative council.

Moreover, the Palestinians continued to reject Israel's suggestion, embodied in its new proposals, that the parties begin by discussing noncontroversial issues, such as transfer of authority over health facilities, on a non-conditional basis, in order to build confidence. They saw this Israeli approach as designed to entrap them in inconsequential details, while avoiding the necessity to discuss the broad principles and framework of autonomy. In the words of delegation leader Dr. Haider Abd al-Shafi, the Palestinians would not agree to "make it easier for Israel to rule" by taking over administrative functions alone. Indeed, the Palestinians countered by demanding that Israel register its commitment to eventual territorial withdrawal in accordance with 242, despite the interim nature of the settlement being discussed. Palestinian spokespersons also insisted that Israel agree to discuss the status of Jerusalem, as well as transfer of some initial security authority to them, and a partial withdrawal of Israeli forces.

One hopeful sign by October 1992 was an indication of implicit Palestinian readiness to coordinate directly with Israel on security issues. Another was a readiness to meet in informal three-person working groups. These discussed the definition of the interim period, and the status of state lands. The two sides finally agreed in October to move to a discussion of a detailed negotiating agenda, after Israel reportedly undertook to drop the adjective "administrative" from its definition of the Palestinian autonomous council, and to acknowledge Palestinian self-rule over Arab-populated lands (rather than the Arab population alone). But the Palestinians now complained that by offering them autonomy only over Palestinian-populated lands in the Territories, Israel was implicitly granting a parallel "autonomy" to its settlements in the Territories, thereby laying the groundwork for large scale annexations.

Thus the basic Palestinian insistence on defining in advance the far limits of autonomy in all spheres, continued to run headlong into a gradualistic Israeli approach. As one senior Israeli official summarized the situation in October 1992, "the Palestinians continue to judge every proposal in terms of how much closer this brings them to a state; we propose that the standard be, to what extent does the proposal improve upon their current situation."

It would be difficult to bridge this key substantive gap unless both Israel and the PLO showed greater flexibility. But progress was also being hampered by basic faults in both sides' procedural approach. Indeed, as we have seen, procedure itself frequently takes on substantive importance for both. For one, as Rabin noted in early September, "the Palestinians want to discuss the symptoms of the conflict [e.g., human rights abuses], rather than the actual problem [i.e., ending the conflict that produced the abuses]." In other words, Palestinian priorities were so politicized that it was impossible to discuss practicalities.

This reflected the Palestinians' ongoing difficulties with leadership and command-structure. Their delegation was hampered in its decisionmaking on all sides. Back home, in the West Bank and Gaza, Islamic extremists whipped up opposition to Palestinian concessions. In Tunis, part of the PLO leadership seemed bent on obstructing any progress that appeared to award the peace negotiators with a leadership status that might challenge its own mantle--while other members of the leadership circle were more accommodating toward the needs and status of the actual negotiators.

This highlighted the inherent weakness of any Palestinian peace delegation not led overtly by the PLO. The Madrid procedural formula that excluded the PLO had, in a way, locked the process in a vicious circle. True, Rabin did agree, in a new departure, not to obstruct consultations by the "insider" leadership with the Tunis "outsiders," in the hope that this might facilitate Palestinian deliberations. He also agreed, under pressure from Foreign Minister Peres, that non-PLO "outsiders" participate in the multilaterals. But his steadfast refusal well into 1993, apparently motivated at least in part by a reluctance to alienate parts of the Israeli body politic, to negotiate directly even with Faisal Husseini (a resident of East Jerusalem), not to mention the official PLO, appeared to exacerbate the Palestinians' negotiating and decisionmaking problems, to the detriment of the entire process.

Israel could hardly claim to be "putting the Palestinians to the test," unless and until it allowed them to field their strongest team--one that it had, in any event, already implicitly recognized. This contention received support from virtually half of Rabin's Cabinet in the aftermath of the December 1992 mass expulsion of Palestinian Islamic militants. In effect, large parts of the Israeli Left now argued that the use of a strong "stick" against extremists, which they had reluctantly supported, required that a tastier "carrot" also be proffered.

Yet it was not clear that even an overt PLO negotiating team could overcome the Palestinians' many internal rifts and contradictions. The gains made in the West Bank and Gaza by Islamic fundamentalist movements that opposed the peace process, appeared to signal that the long-term effects of the 1991 Gulf War were particularly salient among the Palestinians: the PLO was discredited on the inter-Arab scene, and its coffers were empty due to Saudi and Kuwaiti ire. Meanwhile, Hamas and the Islamic Jihad were riding the wave of Islamic fundamentalism generated by Iraq's humiliation at the hands of the West. And Iran, freed from the Iraqi threat, was becoming increasingly active in supporting the anti-peace camp.

Israel-Jordan

The most dramatic advance in the process prior to the American elections was registered in the Jordanian-Israeli sphere. We have noted that the bilateral issues separating the two countries as they entered the process were minor, and centered on peripheral border and water disputes. But Amman also signaled early on in the talks in Washington that it would not, indeed could not, move ahead of the inter-Arab consensus: Israel would have to register progress with the Palestinians, perhaps with Syria too, before King Hussein could sign a peace treaty with Israel.

What remained ambiguous was the degree of flexibility these parameters granted Jordanian and Israeli negotiators. This was clarified at the close of the seventh round of negotiations, in late October 1992, when Jordan itself leaked the contents of an "agenda" for negotiations that had been agreed, and that awaited King Hussein's approval. Though it left much for future negotiation (indeed the Jordanians, under inter-Arab pressure, soon demanded to renegotiate parts of it), the agenda appeared to comprise all the parameters of an eventual peace. Thus it placed Jordan at the vanguard of the peace process, yet without committing it to a formal step that might draw excessive inter-Arab (especially Syrian) ire. At the same time it created an incentive for Syria to finalize its own agenda with Israel.

The Israeli-Jordanian document appeared also to reflect internal political incentives upon both Rabin and Hussein, to produce a recognizable sign of progress in the otherwise sluggish talks. Perhaps both leaders also sought to provide President Bush with a final election boost.

The contents of the agreed agenda were remarkable on several accounts. All the mandatory elements--economic and human contacts, water and refugee issues--were there. But Jordan could also claim to fellow Arabs that it had extracted Israel's first formal commitment to divest itself, "as a matter of priority and as soon as possible," of weapons of mass destruction. For its part Israel could argue that the above arms control goal was to be achieved only "in the context of a comprehensive...peace," i.e., at the end of the entire process. This formula indeed presaged a new Israeli departure on nuclear arms control issues in the region. Israel had also succeeded in reducing the two countries' border disputes to the issue of "demarcation of the international boundary" established under the British mandate--rather than one of returning conquered territory. And it obtained from Jordan a commitment to a peace treaty--not merely an "agreement," as Syria had hitherto insisted. In return, Israel granted that the objective of talks was indeed "comprehensive peace"--the inter-Arab catch-phrase that Syria has championed.

Israel-Lebanon

Throughout both phases of the process that began in Madrid, the Israeli-Lebanese sphere was undoubtedly the least productive. The Lebanese, clearly subject to Syrian hegemony, appeared to have no genuine negotiating strategy other than demanding that Israel fix a timetable for carrying out UNSC Resolution 425, which mandated its withdrawal from the South. Israel responded with a two-pronged strategy. First, it suggested discussing a peace treaty. When Lebanon, not unexpectedly, refused even to peruse a suggested draft, Israel countered by offering to discuss CBMs on a level unrelated to the disagreement in principle: increasing Lebanese government activity in the Southern Security Zone, a joint military liaison team, etc. But this tactic too ran headlong into the Lebanese precondition that Israel first accept the "political contour" of 425.

Israel in fact endorsed the need ultimately to withdraw from Southern Lebanon, but only as part of a peace package. It also insisted that Syrian forces withdraw from the large sections of Lebanese territory they occupied. While this last demand would ultimately probably prove to be a flexible negotiating stance, it did reflect the basic assessment in Jerusalem of the key to a Lebanese settlement: an Israeli accommodation with Syria. Thus for the time being Israel could only hope to ensure that, when a breakthrough with Syria did occur, the Israeli-Lebanese talks would be ripe for progress.

Conclusion

A brief summary is in order regarding the principal actors' primary considerations in the process, as they emerged after more than a year of negotiations. The Palestinians' objective was statebuilding; they sought to minimize the timeframe and maximize the content of the interim phase. Syria wished to recover all of the Golan, maximalize political fallout on the inter-Arab scene, and exploit the entire exercise in order to facilitate a major reorientation in its relationship with the United States--while keeping to a minimum the degree of intimacy involved in its peace with Israel. Jordan sought an agreement that would enable it to manage its own Palestinian threat and to reestablish itself in Arab and American good graces both financially and strategically, while avoiding friction with its hegemonic neighbor, Syria. Lebanon hoped eventually to rid itself of both Syrian and Israeli occupation. Yet it knew this was impossible unless and until Damascus and Jerusalem made their own deal.

As for Israel, it sought to exploit the window of opportunity produced by the fall of the USSR and the Second Gulf War, to generate, with American help, a regional rapprochement, and to reduce the profile of the Palestinian threat to daily stability. This, it hoped, would also allow it to defuse or preempt the more distant and amorphous threats of a nuclear Middle East and of militant Islam, while maintaining its key alliance with the US.

Finally the primary facilitator, the United States, wished to exploit the historic opportunity provided by its exclusive superpower role, to stabilize and institutionalize its regional influence, guarantee its economic interests, and reduce the nuclear threat posed by radical Third World states. And Egypt, a secondary but nonetheless important facilitator too, exploited the process to shed the last remnants of its post-Camp David isolation, enhance its inter-Arab profile, and spearhead regional cooperation with Washington.

Meanwhile the multilateral talks ground on, gradually laying the infrastructure for eventual broader cooperation and, here and there--e.g., in the realm of Israeli-Jordanian cooperation on water issues, and better understanding of ecological issues--registering measurable progress.

In the short and medium terms, the process was liable to be most affected by a number of domestic issues among the key actors, as well as regional trends. It was not clear by early 1993 to what extent the removal of James Baker and his team might delay, or reformulate, the elaborate mechanism he had wrought. There was, after all, no official "architecture" to this process; by and large, Baker had been coordinating it intuitively, and with admirable success. Could Warren Christopher be as successful? Would President Clinton provide the same forceful White House backing that Bush had offered Baker? The initial activity of the new administration appeared to suggest that President Clinton would play a far less active role on foreign policy matters than did Bush: this did not bode well for the Middle East peace process.

Inside Israel, Rabin faced ample potential political problems. He had defined his timeframe to correspond with a regional post-Gulf War "window of opportunity" in which Israel could negotiate from a position of relative strength. That window was likely, within a few years, to be closed by the emergence of Iran and/or Iraq as nuclear powers and by the threat of increasingly militant Islamic movements in the region. This roughly corresponded with Rabin's maximum term of office, four years. Yet more immediate dangers--the rise of a Palestinian "refusal" front, a possible new American approach to the peace process--could even shorten that timeframe considerably. Rabin's original game plan had been to produce a quick autonomy agreement, for which he felt he had a clear mandate from Israel's voters, and then, presumably, reassess his options. Now, the prospect of compromise agreements with Jordan, the Palestinians and Syria--coupled with the shaky nature of his coalition--threatened to arouse enough domestic dissent to precipitate early elections. Certainly it was not clear how Rabin intended to neutralize the opposition to any interim agreement on the part of the 110,000 Israelis settled in the Territories by previous Israeli governments.

Turning to the Arab players, by late 1992 there emerged the possibility that, despite (or perhaps because of) the Israeli-Jordanian agreement, dramatic progress between Syria and Israel, possibly coupled with stalemate or a waiting game on other fronts, might give Damascus a veto power over the entire process. Whether this would hinder or enhance flexibility and progress was not clear. Certainly Palestinian fears of a separate Israeli-Syrian deal that essentially ignored their dilemma, explained some of the erratic behavior of the Palestinian delegation. Moreover, in one of those paradoxes that frequently characterize events in the Middle East, Syria's "strategic ally," Iran, together with a number of extremist Palestinian and Lebanese Shi'ite organizations under the Syrian or Iranian wing, were whipping up opposition to the process in Lebanon, Jordan and the Territories. Israel appeared to be resigned to talking with Syria even as the latter winked at terrorism against it--this being seen as Damascus' tried-and-true modus operandi.

But this delicate balancing act could easily get out of hand, to the detriment of the peace process. Indeed, it came to a head with Israel's mass deportation of some 414 Hamas and Islamic Jihad activists on December 18, 1992. Here Prime Minister Rabin's goals were to traumatize the Muslim militant movements, save the peace process from their aggressive intentions, and save his own government, in view of public reaction to a series of brutal killings of Israeli security personnel.

In these he may have succeeded. The immediate result, however, was strong anger on the part of all Arabs, and particularly Palestinians, at what appeared to them to be a dangerous precedent of mass "transfer." The deportation provoked an unexpected display of toughness by the new Lebanese prime minister, Rafiq al-Hariri. And it generated an Arab refusal to return to the peace process even after the delay generated by the inauguration of a new American president. It also created an unexpected challenge to US-Israel relations at a time when the nurturing of a positive Rabin-Clinton relationship was judged by both to be a key factor in proceeding with the process. Thus early contacts between the new administration and the Israeli and Arab governments were devoted largely to working out acceptance of a series of compromises, whereby Rabin softened various aspects of the deportation in order to enable the Arab-Israel peace talks to reconvene.

There were regional and global dangers to the process as well: militant Islam, a rampant Middle East arms race, the potential spillover effect of new tensions in the Gulf, and instability in nearby areas of the former Soviet Union and Yugoslavia, to name but a few. Yet for the time being, it was two strong and complementary emotions--shared by Israel, most of the Arabs, and the US alike--that would continue to spur the process: cumulative fatigue with Arab-Israel wars, and growing fear of what the next war might be like.

4. US-Israel Strategic Cooperation
Dore Gold

Prior to the June 23 Israeli elections, President Bush, National Security Advisor Brent Scowcroft and Secretary of State James Baker were reluctant to speak explicitly about the strategic relationship between the US and Israel. Administration remarks about strategic cooperation were chiefly left to Secretary of Defense Richard Cheney and lower level officials in the departments of Defense and State.

Thus in October 1991 Cheney declared before the Jewish Institute of National Security Affairs in Washington that "strategic cooperation with Israel remains a cornerstone of US defense policy." Questioned in April 1992 after a spate of press analyses discounting the strategic value of Israel to the US, Baker spoke more reservedly about military ties, emphasizing the centrality of "shared values" in the relationship. Moreover, he admitted that global developments had affected strategic cooperation: "Our relationship with Israel was based on a couple of things. It was based on the strategic cooperation. Yes. It was based on shared values. Strategic cooperation is still important, as far as the US is concerned. We don't say that that's no longer important. We recognize the change."

But during Prime Minister Yitzhak Rabin's August 1992 summit meeting with President Bush at Kennebunkport, Maine, the administration's tone on this subject changed. In answer to a reporter's question Bush said: "Israel is not only important as a friend, but they have demonstrated strategic reliability...it is in our security interests to retain the kind of relationship we have militarily and every other way with Israel."

The future of the strategic relationship under the Clinton administration would be largely dependent on the latter's national security strategy in the years ahead. Clearly, Secretary of Defense Les Aspin planned far deeper cuts in the US force structure than his predecessor, Cheney. Aspin was also interested in reducing the "forward presence" of the US armed services worldwide, placing greater emphasis on American rapid deployment capabilities.

Thus with forward-deployed ships, the future US Navy would reduce the number of ship visits to Haifa. Yet by the same token, a facility in the Eastern Mediterranean might be of increasing importance for maintaining a reduced Sixth Fleet. Similarly, the number of overseas exercises could dwindle, but prepositioning could increase in importance for the new Aspin Pentagon.

In the following pages we shall look in some detail at developments in the US-Israeli strategic relationship, as governments changed in both countries.

The Bush-Shamir Period: Managing Strategic Ties and Political Disagreement

The outstanding feature of the US-Israeli strategic relationship from the end of the Gulf War until the Israeli elections was the dilemma of how both parties could continue their military ties despite their deep political differences over the peace process and Israel's settlement policy.

Washington preferred to separate the two components of the relationship, and strove to achieve a delicate balance. It did not allow any demonstration of the continuing military ties to be interpreted as an approval of Israeli policies, but at the same time it avoided giving the impression that political differences could diminish the strategic relationship.

Such a balance was almost impossible to achieve. In the lead-up to the Madrid Peace Conference, Washington was extremely sensitive to any Israeli action that might reduce the prospects for convening this opening event of the Arab-Israel peace process. Thus when the Israel Air Force conducted a reconnaissance mission over western Iraq in early October 1991, the US issued a strongly worded protest. This came only two weeks after President Bush's September 12 outburst attacking pro-Israel forces in Congress for seeking approval of Israel's request for $10 billion in loan guarantees, after he had sought a 120-day delay. Previously, Israel had unsuccessfully sought improved cooperation with the US in the event of renewed allied air strikes against Iraq.

In the political climate created by continuing US-Israeli tensions, repeated leaks over the sensitive area of technology transfer appeared during mid-March 1992. The worst, in the *Washington Times*, contended that Israel had transferred Patriot parts and technology to the PRC. Subsequent leaks included a report from the State Department Inspector General alleging the unauthorized transfer of US technology by Israel to third parties through its domestically-produced cluster bombs, Mapatz anti-tank missiles, and Python III air-to-air missiles. After an American team completed an inspection of Israeli Patriot missiles, including a check on the actual serial numbers on Patriot parts, Israel was cleared by the Department of Defense regarding the Patriot transfers.

These scandals appeared in the press largely at the initiative of elements in the US national security bureaucracy that were never sympathetic to Israel. Nonetheless, the reports left an impression among some circles on the Israeli side that Bush and Baker were actually orchestrating a campaign to damage Israel's reputation in the eyes of the American public, and that they were seeking to dismantle the strategic relationship that their predecessors, Reagan and Shultz, had erected in the 1980s. Others in Israel viewed these incidents as the inevitable fallout from the deterioration in bilateral relations due to disagreements over Israel's settlements policy in the West Bank and Gaza.

Further reinforcing these impressions in Jerusalem were the appearance in March 1992 of a spate of articles in both the *New York Times* and the *Washington Post* that sought to explain the deterioration in the US-Israel relationship in terms of a decline in Israel's strategic importance after the end of the Cold War. These news analyses derived their political importance from the fact that they were written by chief diplomatic reporters at the State Department, who were believed generally to initiate such articles only after deep background meetings with the secretary of state. Even without such prompting by American officialdom--the stories were written in the wake of the technology transfer scandal reports--these analyses were perceived to mark a changing view on Israel that was emerging in the American capital.

Within Israel itself, the depth of concern about the future of the strategic relationship crossed party lines. One of the harshest critics of the administration's behavior regarding the Patriot scandal in particular, was the commander of the Israel Air Force during the Gulf War, Maj. General (res.) Avihu Ben Nun. While no longer in active service, his critique reflected views in the defense establishment that were alarmed by the emerging trends in US-Israel relations.

These reactions led the US Embassy in Tel Aviv to make strategic cooperation a central point in its public pronouncements during the spring of 1992. At nearly every public appearance Ambassador William Harrop focused on the continuity that existed in the strategic ties between the two countries, despite political differences between the Bush administration and the Shamir government.

Bush and Rabin Seek New Understandings

Yitzhak Rabin's election as prime minister presented an opportunity for renewing the US-Israel strategic relationship. First, the political strains that inevitably affected overall bilateral ties no longer loomed in the background. The restored political understanding between the two countries led to the administration's quick approval of Israel's request for a $10 million loan guarantee package that had served as a central point of friction between the administration and the previous Israeli government since the end of the Gulf War.

Secondly, the Rabin visit to the presidential residence at Kennebunkport in August 1992 occurred three months before what already appeared as an extremely difficult reelection for President Bush. As the American elections neared, domestic considerations inevitably strongly entered the conduct of US policy toward Israel, and influenced Washington's willingness to improve Israel's access to advanced American weaponry.

Third, Bush's desire to complete a major arms sales package with Saudi Arabia involving 72 F-15XP aircraft, deepened the administration's readiness to reach an understanding with Israel over a compensatory package. The president officially notified Congress of his intent to make the sale on September 15, giving Congress 30 days to pass a resolution of disapproval.

Neither the US nor Israel explicitly spoke about their strategic discussions in this period in terms of compensation for the Saudi F-15s. The Bush administration had argued in the past that arms sales to Saudi Arabia did not undermine Israel's security. For its part, the Israeli Cabinet expressed its formal disapproval of the sale. But with both Bush and Clinton supportive of the sale. Prime Minister Rabin admitted that he "did not like [fighting] losing battles."

Thus in early October the US and Israel issued a joint communique over the results of their intensified military discussions, which they said were initiated for the purpose of "the preservation and maintenance of Israel's qualitative military edge." The communique outlined a number of measures upon which both countries had agreed. First was the supply of 25 Apache and 10 Blackhawk helicopters, as part of the transfer to Israel of defense items (up to $700 million) drawn down from US military stocks. While these helicopters were no answer to the planned expansion of Saudi airpower, they allowed the Israel Air Force to shift funds to its F-16 procurement budget, thereby helping preserve the regional balance in combat fighters.

Secondly, the prepositioning of advanced military equipment (up to $200 million) in Israel was ordered, in accordance with earlier approved legislation. Third came agreement on closer ties between the two countries' armed forces and cooperation on technology upgrades. And finally, the communique welcomed Israeli participation in the Global Protection System (GPS).

The US military establishment had claimed that the accelerated closure of American bases overseas had created a backlog for the armed services over the disposition of excess equipment. The new US-Israeli package designated for the drawdown program some advanced American weapons systems that Israel badly needed. Moreover, while Apache helicopters were no answer to the enhancement of Saudi air capabilities, their acquisition through the drawdown program would at least allow the Israel Air Force to divert greater funding to the expansion of its fleet of latest generation F-16s.

While the new US-Israeli strategic understandings appeared to represent a breakthrough in their military relations, in reality the package the administration was offering contained many elements that had been committed previously. Thus the $700 million drawdown had already been passed by Congress during the 1990 Desert Storm buildup, but had been only partly utilized.

Like the drawdown proposal, the idea of prepositioning US equipment in Israel was not new. A $100 million stockpile already existed. Appropriations for the additional $200 million in prepositioning had already been approved at congressional initiative during the Gulf buildup.

The agreement on closer cooperation between the two countries' armed forces was not well-defined, and required further negotiations. But these would be conducted well after Israel had lost its bargaining leverage in the aftermath of the American elections and the F-15 sale to Saudi Arabia. Thus, as US officials admitted in late September, there were still difficulties to be overcome in US-Israeli strategic cooperation.

The area of technology cooperation remained inadequately defined as well. True, in letters from Secretary of Defense Richard Cheney and Acting Secretary of State Lawrence Eagleburger prior to the American elections, Israel was promised that its status as a recipient of American technology would be brought up to the level of a NATO ally. But Israel needed specific technologies, rather than a general definition that placed it in the category of Belgium, Greece, or Turkey; in many cases, Israel required access to technologies that were not made available even to these countries. Here too, the execution of any technology transfer agreements was postponed until after the American elections.

The invitation to Israel to join the Global Protection System involved a program in which, ostensibly, Israeli participation should have been automatic; hence it did not appear to entail a genuine upgrading of the strategic relationship. The GPS idea had evolved in the course of 1992 as a new framework for international cooperation in missile defense for the SDI program. During May 1992 Secretary of State James Baker received several complaints asking why Israel had not already been invited like other SDI allies. On June 4 he wrote to Rep. Jon Kyl (Rep.-Ariz.), "it is our hope that Israel will participate fully in this initiative as it moves forward." Thus the American intention to include Israel in GPS already existed considerably before the Bush-Rabin summit. The announcement was clearly delayed for the appropriate political occasion.

Unlike previous international SDI efforts, GPS was centered around Russian-American collaboration. Moscow sought American technology to enhance its early-warning capability against the proliferation threat. Washington was chiefly interested in Russian political backing for the SDI program and for modification of the 1972 Soviet-American Anti-Ballistic Missile (ABM) Treaty, that had inhibited SDI testing in the past.

Nor did membership in the GPS program give SDI participants new rights or privileges. Russian-American working groups established at the June 1992 Bush-Yeltsin summit dealt with technology cooperation, the study of missile proliferation, the modification of current arms control agreements and, most importantly, the definition of the concept of GPS itself. In short, GPS was still in the concept-definition phase. Because the program was associated with the most politically-controversial part of the SDI program in the American domestic debate, the chances that GPS would continue under a Clinton presidency were slim.

Not only did Israel's "qualitative edge" package, received at the time of the F-15XP sale, contain many uncertainties, but US assurances regarding the F-15XP itself were not wholly adequate. Acting Secretary of State Lawrence Eagleburger's letter to Israel in this regard was not made public. The administration underlined the importance of the letter when it claimed that commitments regarding the military buildup to a third country (Saudi Arabia) were contained, for the first time, in an Israeli-American understanding. Previously, during the F-15A/B sale to Saudi Arabia in 1978, the administration had made commitments regarding limitations on the aircraft to Congress, and not to Israel. Still, Israeli negotiators close to the US-Israeli discussions expressed concern that the letter was not explicit enough about the commitment not to base the aircraft at Tabuk--apparently relying instead on a general formulation that the aircraft would not be deployed "offensively." This commitment was important to Israel because Saudi Arabia had violated its past understandings with the US over Tabuk during September 1992.

Nor was there any indication of assurances to Israel that prevented the F-15XP from being upgraded to a full F-15E in the future. The Reagan administration, for example, upgraded the first Saudi F-15A/B package sold during the Carter administration, with conformal fuel tanks and bomb racks. Such a move remained a distinct possibility for the Clinton administration with the F-15XP, especially if mainly software modifications were involved.

In sum, the Rabin-Bush summit definitely generated a new political climate between the US and Israel. But on the strategic level, the administration package designed to sustain Israel's qualitative edge contained many older commitments that simply had not been fulfilled. Other parts of the new understanding involved negotiations that would only be completed after the

American elections. In the case of GPS, Israel was given access to a program to which it was almost certain to have been invited in any case.

Current and Future Strategic Cooperation

Current programs in the US-Israeli strategic relationship remained substantial in 1992. Appropriations for funding US-Israeli programs increased in 1992 by about 20 percent and reached $250 million. Joint training programs continued with aircraft from the US Air Force in Europe. The US Marine Corps, as well, used Israeli training facilities. The Israel and US navies also engaged in joint training.

The US Sixth Fleet increasingly found Haifa to be a preferred port in the Mediterranean. Already, the number of US Navy ship visits to Israel in 1992 reached 50 (see Figure 1), recovering from a temporary drop to 42 during 1991 because of the Gulf War, when no US ships came to Israel for nearly three months. Expansion plans were underway in 1992 that would boost its importance in the future. A $15 million first phase of a program to deepen Haifa Port was begun. This would allow the US Navy to dock some of its largest ships, like its Aegis-class cruisers, for servicing, and would permit the servicing of up to eight US Navy vessels simultaneously.

A second phase of Haifa's expansion was in the planning stage. If implemented, it would allow Israel to accommodate US aircraft carriers in port. Admiral (ret.) Carl Trost, former chief of naval operations, told the American journal *Security Affairs* that Haifa had not been well-located for the US Navy during the Cold War, but with the shift of attention to projection power in the Middle East, the Sixth Fleet's need for facilities in the Eastern Mediterranean had increased. The deepening of Haifa Port for aircraft carriers might allow the US Navy, in the future, to home-port a carrier in Haifa. This option was at least being investigated in early 1993. According to Vice Admiral (ret.) William Rowden, who commanded the Sixth Fleet from 1981-83, "if you want to reduce the number of carriers, you can do so by home-porting in Haifa." Certainly for the Aspin Pentagon, that sought to cut the US Navy, the home-porting option seemed worthy of a thorough examination.

US Navy Ship Visits to Israel
1982-1992*

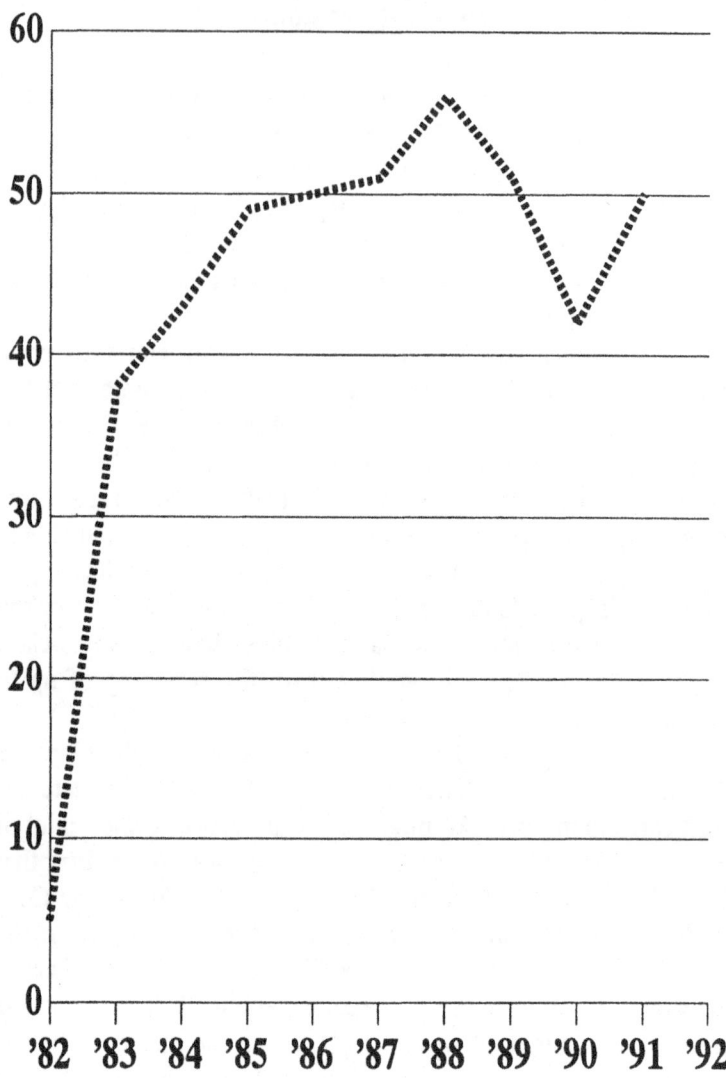

*Source: US Embassy, Tel Aviv

Yet alongside these positive signs in the US-Israel strategic relationship, some longer-term difficulties nonetheless loomed on the horizon. Speaking before the Senate Caucus on US-Israel Security Cooperation on October 1, Carl W. Ford, Principal Deputy Assistant Secretary of Defense for International Security Affairs, outlined some of the limitations to the relationship. Most of these, in Ford's judgment, were on the Israeli side. On the purely technical level the US had only partial access to Israeli training areas because of the needs of the IDF: "when our commanders from EUCOM come down and say, 'Boy we would sure like to bring our Apaches down and use that helicopter training range that you have,' we find that we must work on...Saturdays and holidays, because the facilities are taken up year round by the IDF."

> But a strategic limitation existed in the relationship as well: Another limitation, of course, is the longstanding view on the part of Israel, one in which I think most of us share their viewpoint on...that not one ounce of American blood should be spilled in the defense of Israel...this limitation is an important one at least in terms of the very narrow focus of the Defense Department. There is only so much we can do in terms of interacting with Israel without having the mission or contingency mission of coming to their support.

Ford then explained that it was difficult to deepen US-Israeli strategic cooperation without reconsidering Israel's self-reliance in its own actual defense:

> In terms of going much beyond where we are now there have to be some changes on both their part and our part to get us an opportunity to make our operations and interactions with Israel the same as they are with Great Britain and Germany or other countries that are prepared to have at least the notion of a contingency that at some point things might be so bad they would want to call on the US.

The Ford testimony was significant. It represented one of the first times a high-level US official proposed in public altering the basic ground rules of the US-Israel relationship by giving the American armed forces a direct role in Israel's defense. This new conception, by Ford's own admission, grew out of the experience of the Gulf War in which US Army units manned Patriot batteries in the defense of Israel against Iraqi missile attacks.

Further, this line of thinking must be understood in the context of the discussion over the purpose of any increased American prepositioning in Israel. Israel's interests in prepositioning were clear-cut: in the event of war, American equipment on the ground would shorten resupply times and eliminate the need for any massive airlift to Israel as in 1973. But from the US perspective, prepositioning could be useful in two main scenarios: equipping American forces in the Persian Gulf (thus far USCENTCOM had preferred to leave Israel out of Gulf contingencies), or equipping US forces coming to Israel's defense. This latter scenario could express itself in several contexts in the years ahead. A softening of Israel's traditional opposition to a greater American role in its security might be sought in the context of the arrangements for an Israeli-Syrian peace treaty: for example, in the event of a proposal for an American ground force deployment on the Golan Heights.

Equivalent proposals might be raised in the context of arms control discussions as well. Moreover, should American fiscal constraints force cutbacks in Israel's $1.8 billion security assistance package, Israel might be confronted with proposals for compensation in the form of greater American protection in selective roles relevant to Israel's defense.

5. The US and Gulf Security
Dore Gold

The Gulf War became an almost paradigmatic conflict for US military planners as they looked at the nature of future security challenges in the post-Cold War period. Most importantly, it represented a fundamental shift for the Department of Defense in the definition of the principal threats to the United States. Previously, during the period of Soviet-American rivalry, those threats were viewed as global. Now they were formally defined as regional in character.

Thus, General Colin L. Powell, Chairman of the Joint Chiefs of Staff, reported the "National Military Strategy of the United States" in January 1992 as follows:

> Because of the changes in the strategic environment, the threats we expect to face are regional rather than global. We will, of course, deter and defend against strategic nuclear attacks as we have for the past forty years. We will also retain the potential to defeat a global threat, should one emerge. However our plans and resources are primarily focused on deterring and fighting regional rather than global wars.

The Department of Defense codified the new approach in its annual five-year projection of defense challenges called "Defense Guidance." Leaked to the American press in two versions, the document identified the need for the US to cope in the future with regional "hegemons." Both American arms control policy and regional strategy focused on a primary US interest in preserving regional balances of power. Arms control was intended to deny destabilizing weaponry to ambitious states that were already adequately armed, while arms sales were seen as an alternative instrument to protect regional balances.

Where neither of these instruments could protect regional stability, the Bush administration sought to deploy a forward American military presence to balance hegemonial powers. US strategy in the Middle East was essentially derived from this view of American interests and instruments of policy.

But there was a wide gap between what might have been the preferred mix of measures to assure Middle Eastern stability, and what in the end American policymakers were left to employ by default. The notion of developing an inter-Arab security system in which Egyptian forces would collaborate with the GCC states--in accordance with the March 1991 Damascus Accords--still did not progress. Saudi Arabia itself resisted American plans to preposition heavy equipment for the US Army on its soil. And the US Central Command (USCENTCOM) had still not completed negotiations with any Gulf state on the establishment of a forward headquarters.

This resulted in an American Gulf security policy in 1992 that shifted from initiatives to build up new security arrangements, to reliance on extensive arms transfers to the Arabian Peninsula. Globally, US arms sales--which stood at about $12 billion during 1988 and $11 billion in 1989--increased to about $14 billion in 1990, $24 billion in 1991, and $24 billion in the first nine months of 1992 alone. US arms deliveries, as opposed to new sales, also increased from $9.6 billion in 1990 to $13.5 billion in 1991; in contrast, arms deliveries of the next top four arms exporters declined during the same period. From August 1990, the time of the Iraqi invasion of Kuwait, to late 1992, arms orders for the Middle East reached $32.3 billion.

US Perceptions of the Growing Iranian Threat

While outstanding differences remained between the US and Iraq in the aftermath of Desert Storm, one of the new features of the postwar period was a growing awareness of the renewed threat of Iran to US interests. Tehran was a driving force behind the spread of militant Islam, and through deepening ties with regional partners like Sudan, it worked to undermine the regimes of Egypt and several states in North Africa. In parallel Iran began an intensive military buildup, despite its domestic economic difficulties, that promised to change significantly the balance of power in the Persian Gulf.

A financially strapped Russia was the main source of Iran's new arms. Tehran's rearmament program included MiG-29s, MiG-31s, SU-24s, SA-5s, Kilo-class submarines, and a number of mini-submarines. Iran was reportedly interested in the 6000 km range TU-22M3 Backfire bomber; the Russians were working on an export version of the aircraft. In the Gulf itself, the Iranians began to assert exclusive sovereignty over the island of Abu Musa near the Straits of Hormuz. Since 1972, after its seizure by the Shah, it had been under the joint control of Iran and the United Arab Emirates.

US officials were not all in complete agreement about the immediacy of Tehran's threat to the Gulf. With all of its new activism, Iran would still require several years to absorb its new military purchases with adequate training for crews and the establishment of appropriate logistical support. For example, Rear Admiral Ted Shaefer, the Director of US Naval Intelligence, noted that the Iranians did not very successfully operate the midget-submarines that they had acquired from North Korea; they still needed to improve their ability to detect targets and coordinate with patrol aircraft.

Iran would also need time to reach significant breakthroughs in its nonconventional and missile programs. The Nodong (or Scud-D) missile from North Korea that would give Iran the ability to strike targets 1000 kilometers away--including Israel--was still under development. During late November 1992, CIA director Robert Gates said that Iran was not a problem today, "but three, four, five years from now it could be a serious problem."

Those taking a less alarmed view of Tehran in Washington pointed to the fact that post-Khomeini Iran was still spending less money than in the days of the military buildup under the Shah. Moreover, Iraqi expenditures in 1989-90, after the end of the Iran-Iraq War, far outstripped what Iran was now spending. Considering the low baseline of the Iranian order-of-battle of main platforms (combat aircraft, tanks, missiles) back in 1988, Tehran had a long way to go before it could become a threatening regional power.

American policy reflected this ambiguity in defining Iran as a clear-cut threat. Thus, most of Iran's hard currency was coming through oil sales made on the open market to US companies. Also, the US did little to halt the massive Russian arms sales to Iran, though it did express some concern over the specific sale of Kilo-class submarines.

Certainly had Iran's militant profile in former Soviet Central Asia been of considerable concern, then Washington would not have had great difficulty persuading Moscow to hold off on its conventional arms sales. Thus vis-a-vis Iran, the lack of a more robust US security structure in the Persian Gulf was not yet a major problem in 1992, but could pose serious difficulties in the not too distant future.

The Iraqi Threat and The Southern No-Fly Zone in Iraq

In the short term, the failure to establish full security arrangements may not have caused a great sense of urgency in the case of Iraq either, because of the limited extent of its capabilities after the Gulf War. The Defense Intelligence Agency (DIA) released its own data on the Iraqi armed forces in August 1992, after the second anniversary of the Iraqi invasion of Kuwait: Iraqi ground forces stood at 40 percent of their pre-war strength in manpower; the army had organized 28 divisions with 2,500 tanks, down from 54 divisions and 5,500 tanks. General Norman Schwarzkopf's replacement as CENTCOM commander-in-chief (CINCCENT), General Joseph Hoar, noted that the extent of Iraq's "demonstrated offensive capability" was limited to the conduct of "multi-division operations in a counter-insurgency environment." Iraq, he believed, had no real aviation capability.

But Iraq had by no means disappeared as an American concern. After the March 1991 ceasefire negotiated between the US and Iraqi military commanders at Safwan, a number of outstanding military issues continued to demand special American military involvement against Iraq. First, UN sanctions against Iraq had not been dropped. This required a continuing American naval presence to inspect shipping bound for Iraq in the Gulf, and even ships heading for the Jordanian port of Aqaba in the Red Sea.

Secondly, Iraq was gradually breaking out of ceasefire limitations over the use of its airpower. The US had already given Baghdad permission to use military helicopters--though not fixed-wing aircraft--for the transport of Iraqi officers at the Safwan military-to-military talks at the end of the Gulf War; the Iraqi armed forces during 1991 had exploited this American concession to use helicopters in tasks involving civil unrest, especially against the Kurdish population in the north and the Shi'ites in the south.

After March 1991, in order to protect the Kurds from Iraqi reprisals no Iraqi aircraft--helicopters or fixed wing--were permitted to fly north of the 36th parallel inside of Iraq itself. Even after the last of some 20,000 coalition forces withdrew from northern Iraq the following July, the US reserved the right to conduct reconnaissance flights over the Kurdish security zone, while continuing to prohibit Iraqi overflights.

This postwar regime limiting Iraqi air activity broke down a year after the ceasefire in the Gulf War. In April 1992, after eight Iranian Phantom F-4s struck bases of the Mujahideen i-Khalq deep in the interior of Iraq, Baghdad commenced regular use of the fixed-wing aircraft of the Iraqi Air Force outside of Iraqi Kurdistan. Aside from defending the airspace of central Iraq, the Iraqi Air Force intensified operations against the Shi'ite population in the south. In dealing with these activities, US humanitarian concerns for the Kurdish and Shi'ite populations of the north and south were generally counterbalanced by Washington's strategic interest in preserving the territorial integrity of the Iraqi state.

Third, UN Security Council Resolution 687, that established the ceasefire, created a UN Special Commission (UNSCOM) that was to oversee an inspection and disarmament regime. Iraq, on repeated occasions, chose to defy UNSCOM demands. In the brinkmanship that generally followed these Iraqi challenges, the threat of the use of American and coalition military force yielded only partial successes.

In September 1991 a UN-Iraqi standoff over documents on the Iraqi nuclear program ended with Baghdad backing down, but only after they had removed all documents from the site. The UN Security Council had already passed Resolutions 707 and 715 that found Baghdad to be in violation of previous UN resolutions regarding programs to produce its weapons of mass destruction. On February 19, 1992 the Security Council warned Iraq of "serious consequences" if it did not meet its arms control obligations. The cumulative impact of these Iraqi acts of defiance altered American considerations about the necessity of military action.

By August the enhanced Iraqi air operations against the Iraqi Shi'ites set the stage for the last military showdowns between Saddam Hussein and the Bush administration. The US was not going to address Iraq by executing punishing air strikes, but rather by placing limitations on Iraqi air activity that could be politically embarrassing for the regime of Saddam Hussein. US National Security Advisor Brent Scowcroft explained on August 19, "There is increasing evidence that he is pursuing genocidal policies in the south. What we're saying is that we're going to monitor and watch what he's doing there. And in order to do that with reconnaissance, he has to stop flying."

In the meantime, countervailing concerns about preventing any development that could affect Iraq's integrity had changed; democratic elections had already been held in the north for a Kurdish parliament, while Saudi Arabia began an open dialogue with the Iranian-supported Shi'ite opposition. The implied threat to Iraq's territorial integrity was thought to be a possible means to drive the Iraqi officer corps to seek Saddam Hussein's overthrow in order to avert the country's dismemberment; this latter consideration may have been part of the Bush administration's calculation in seeking to escalate the confrontation with Baghdad.

From the military point of view, total US forces in the Gulf region in mid-August 1992 stood at 24,000. By comparison, only 10,000 US personnel were located in and around the Gulf in August 1990, when Saddam Hussein ordered the invasion of Kuwait. Approximately 70 land-based American aircraft were deployed in Saudi Arabia, including eight F-117A stealth fighters.

Another 70 naval aircraft were deployed at sea on the USS Independence, which operated with its ten-ship battle group in the northern Persian Gulf. Rear Admiral Raynor A.K Taylor, constituent commander of CENTCOM's naval forces (CENTNAV) had a total of 22 ships at his disposal, including five cruisers and destroyers armed with sea-launched cruise missiles. At least 4,000 soldiers from the US Army and Marine Corps were involved in military exercises in Kuwait at about this time, as well.

In order to prepare for possible air operations against Iraq, General Michael A. Nelson, the air component commander of CENTCOM (CENTAIR), was sent to Riyadh with approximately 30 aides to set up a forward headquarters. Finally on August 27 President Bush ordered Operation "Southern Watch"--the creation of a no-fly zone in southern Iraq, south of the 32nd parallel, in which the Iraqi military was prohibited from operating both fixed-wing aircraft and helicopters. But US Navy pilots were informed that the no-fly zone did not affect Iraq's deployment of surface-to-air missile batteries, such as those that remained around Basra City.

Britain and France jointly supported the creation of the zone. Aircraft of all three countries began to fly in the zone's airspace to monitor Iraqi compliance. However, few combat aircraft were actually needed to monitor the zone, since US and Saudi AWACS provided radar coverage over the southern third of Iraq from Saudi airspace. For its part, Iraq did not initially challenge the three coalition members, except to concentrate its aircraft at an airfield close to the 32nd parallel.

By the close of 1992 the no-fly zone had done little to change the postwar military situation in Iraq. Indeed, Iraqi aircraft now regularly flew between the 36th and 32nd parallels in central Iraq despite the prohibitions contained in the local ceasefire agreements that restricted the Iraqis to the use of military helicopters alone. The flights of Iraqi combat aircraft in the central region were not challenged by the coalition partners. Moreover, since the coalition aircraft that monitored the zone were not given the mission to engage in any air-to-ground combat, they could do little about the ten Iraqi divisions still operating on the ground against the Shi'ites in the south.

Indeed, since the Iraqi Air Force was no longer grounded, and its pilots could again accumulate flight hours, it did not take a great deal of time for the Iraqis to begin challenging US aircraft in the southern no-fly zone. The shift of the aircraft carrier USS Kitty Hawk from the Persian Gulf to the waters off Somalia in December may also have given the Iraqi leadership the sense that the US had other security concerns. On December 27, after two such challenges, a US F-16 shot down an Iraqi MiG-25 over the southern zone. Iraqi air activity continued to be provocative in the days that followed; on January 2, 1993 for example, an Iraqi MiG-25 tried to intercept a U-2 surveillance aircraft flown by the United Nations. Moreover, within ten days Baghdad began shifting SA-2 and SA-3 air defense batteries into the southern no-fly zone, near Tallil Air Base and Nasiriya; a battery of SA-2 missiles was also deployed in the northern no-fly zone, 40 kilometers north of Mosul. After an Iraqi incursion into Camp Khor, a former Iraqi naval base at Umm Qasr that became Kuwaiti territory as a result of UN border modifications, the Security Council warned Baghdad on January 11 of "serious consequences."

The US, Britain, and France launched a raid with 80 strike aircraft (and 30 support aircraft) against the southern no-fly zone on January 13. Most of the aircraft flew from Saudi airbases, while some 35 planes came from the USS Kitty Hawk, after it was ordered back to the Persian Gulf at the end of December 1992.

Two command posts, at Tallil Air Base and al-Amara, were destroyed while two radar sites, at Najaf and Samawa, were partly damaged. Of the four mobile SAM batteries targeted, only one was destroyed; the Department of Defense attributed the poor results to the effects of dense cloud cover on the laser-guided munitions of the F-117 Stealth Fighter. Further raids were carried out on January 17 and 18. During the former, 45 Tomahawk cruise missiles were launched at an industrial complex near Baghdad; in the latter raid, 18 strike aircraft (supported by 51 planes) hit anti-aircraft sites in both the northern and southern zones.

The January US raids on Iraq did compel Baghdad to accept the terms of the UN weapons inspection teams--terms that previously it had sought to modify by insisting that UN inspectors arrive on Iraqi aircraft. On January 19, Iraq announced a ceasefire in its struggle against the no-fly zones, but within days Baghdad was again directing anti-aircraft radars at US aircraft in the north as well as in the south.

Thus Iraqi behavior had not been decisively modified. The no-fly zones had not weakened the power of Saddam Hussein, either. Finally, regional support for the US attacks on Iraq was declining, with Saudi Arabia and Turkey remaining the main coalition partners, but with increasing expressions of doubt about supporting any further attacks.

Emerging Postwar Security Arrangements

Original US postwar plans for the defense of Saudi Arabia were based on the prepositioning of large stores of American equipment, sufficient to equip a corps-level force reaching three divisions. These plans would have created the infrastructure for the eventual deployment of a force the same size as the army the Bush administration planned for post-Cold War Europe.

But for most of 1991 and 1992, *Saudi Arabia* was not willing to accept even a scaled-down version of this original plan-- one that would have involved heavy equipment for manning up to six brigades of American troops. General Joseph Hoar admitted the problem to the House Armed Services Committee on March 16, 1992: "The one thing that we have been unable to do, which is a disappointment to me, has been the prepositioning of sufficient heavy assets, armor assets, in the region."

The US also sought to preposition support equipment for five to six fighter wings consisting of approximately 400 aircraft as well as naval support. Hoar was more optimistic in this regard: "I would characterize the air force prepositioning as very achievable in the short haul, and we are very positive about the navy prepositioning, which is relatively minor, but it's a fleet hospital and some logistics equipment that we could use, and shore-based activities to support ships in the region." Saudi Arabia was reluctant to sign a special memorandum with the US government and instead based its postwar defense relationship on the 1977 Military Training Mission Treaty between the two countries.

In the meantime, Washington signed new defense memoranda with *Kuwait, Qatar,* and *Bahrain.* According to US Army Chief of Staff Gordon Sullivan, the Defense Department succeeded in prepositioning equipment in Kuwait for a token force of six army platoons with additional materiel afloat. Other reports mentioned that a battalion's worth of equipment had been stored. Kuwait sought to buttress the new accord during 1992, with parallel agreements with Britain and France.

In early August 1992, 1,900 troops from the 112th Marine Expeditionary Unit began two weeks of desert war games in Kuwait. Later, during mid-August 1992, the US held joint military exercises with the Kuwaiti Armed Forces, code-named Operation Intrinsic Action, that involved 2,400 American troops from the 1st Cavalry Division and the 5th Special Forces Group.

Elsewhere in the Gulf, Washington renewed its 1980 facilities access agreement with *Oman.* Outside the Gulf, while *Egypt* remained one of the cornerstones of American military strategy in the Middle East, Cairo, like Riyadh, refused to accept the prepositioning of heavy US Army equipment. Cairo also was not supportive of American attempts to bring military pressure to bear on Baghdad in order to implement the UNSCOM inspections of Iraqi nonconventional weapons programs. Like Syria, Egypt did not support the coalition's air strikes on Iraq during January 1993.

In November 1991, General Joseph Hoar spoke with the *Jordan*ian chief of staff, Field Marshal Abu Taleb, about resuming joint exercises. By March 1992, Hoar could say: "We have reason to look forward to a new, more constructive future with Jordan."

During the 1980s, the US had conducted special operations exercises with the Jordanians, such as Shadow Hawk in June 1984. The first post-Gulf War US-Jordan joint military exercise was finally held in September 1992. By December, the Department of State was including Jordan along with six other countries that were expected to provide either troops or supplies for Operation Restore Hope in Somalia.

Military relations with *Pakistan* remained clouded due to differences with regard to nuclear proliferation issues. But in the new atmosphere of the post-Cold War era, the US military was now seeking to establish an expanded military relationship with neighboring *India* that included joint exercises and reciprocal visits between both countries' military colleges. It was too early to see where the US-Indian relationship was heading, for the two countries had outstanding differences in the proliferation field. Nonetheless, it is useful to recall that India had historically been the cornerstone of Britain's Gulf policy for much of the period prior to World War II, providing manpower and materiel.

Finally *Turkey*, while formally a NATO country with a European orientation, had nonetheless been critical for the projection of US power against Iraq. But in 1992 it was by no means evident that Turkish bases would still be available for regional contingencies. During September the Turks indicated that they were not ready to open their airfields to assist in establishing the no-fly zone in southern Iraq. And while they continued to provide base support for the no-fly zone in northern Iraq, the Turks were reconsidering their policy in this regard, too.

After the third coalition strike against Iraq in January 1993, Turkish Foreign Minister Hikmet Cetin noted: "It is difficult to justify the operation in Iraq while there is a bloodbath in Bosnia and Herzegovina." In short, US postwar security arrangements toward the end of 1992 appeared still underdeveloped and, in many cases, much more fragile than they were in March 1991 at the end of the Gulf War.

Arms Transfers

The largest American arms sale to the Middle East in recent years involved a $9 billion arms package that included 72 F-15XP aircraft to Saudi Arabia. It was announced by President

Bush on September 11, 1992. Forty-eight of the aircraft were to be configured for air-to-ground missions, while 24 would serve in air-to-air roles. This latest arms sale package for Saudi Arabia also included 900 AGM-65D/G Maverick missiles, 600 CBU-87 cluster bombs, 700 GBU-10/12 bombs, and 600 air-to-air missiles (AIM-9S and AIM-7M).

The F-15XP itself was a specially designed export derivative of the F-15E. Its ground attack version contained low-altitude navigation and targeting pods with lesser capabilities than the LANTIRN (Low Altitude Navigation/ Targeting Infrared for Night) systems installed in the F-15E. For example, the Sharpshooter targeting pod sold to the Saudis cannot track multiple targets like the full LANTIRN on the F-15E; instead, to hit each target a Saudi F-15XP would have to make a separate pass.

Moreover the resolution of the F-15E's APG-70 radar was modified from 2.6 meters at 37 kilometers to 18.9 meters at 27.7 kilometers. By late 1992 it had not yet been decided whether the F-15XP would be powered by the high thrust General Electric F110-129 engine, or the low-thrust Pratt and Whitney F100-229 engine that was mounted on the current Saudi F-15 fleet.

The F-15XP sale was by no means the last major American aircraft sale to Saudi Arabia. The Royal Saudi Air Force still had to replace its aging fleet of F-5 fighters from the 1970s. Back in February 1990, General Schwarzkopf mentioned to the Senate Armed Services Committee the need to replace Saudi Arabia's fleet of F-5 aircraft: "if their aging F-5s are not replaced by our aircraft, the US share (of the Saudi aerospace market) will be less than 20 percent." In 1990 the Saudis, in fact, had 98 F-5s, including 15 F-5A/Bs configured for air-to-air combat and 83 F-5E/Fs configured as multi-role aircraft. Thus in addition to the 72 F-15XPs, it could be expected that Saudi Arabia would seek between 83 and 98 ground attack aircraft--either the F-16 or the F-18.

The US sale of F-15XPs to Saudi Arabia was not politically controversial. With the US economy still in recession and thousands of jobs at McDonnell Douglas in Missouri at stake, President Bush's challenger from the Democratic Party, Governor Clinton, also gave qualified support for the sale. Moreover, Israel offered only pro-forma opposition to the F-15XP package. Thus Congress did not block the sale. Nevertheless, several incidents in 1992 could have presented Saudi Arabia with a considerably more difficult time stopping a resolution of disapproval under different political circumstances.

First, during April the Bush administration confirmed that Saudi Arabia had conducted unauthorized transfers of US-made military equipment to Iraq, Syria and Bangladesh: an undisclosed number of 2,000 pound bombs were given to Iraq in 1986 along with British-made Lightning fighter-bombers, while in the cases of Bangladesh and Syria, a 1991 transfer of military transport vehicles was involved. Saudi Arabia claimed that the transfers were inadvertent. Nonetheless they involved a violation of the US Arms Export Control Act.

Secondly, in September 1992 Saudi Arabia deployed some of its already operational F-15s, purchased in the first F-15A/Bs arms package in 1978, at Tabuk Airbase near southern Israel, in violation of US-Saudi understandings made during the Carter administration. Previously, Saudi Arabia had only deployed these aircraft at Daharan, Khamis Mushayt, and Taif Airbases. While occurring in the context of the establishment of the no-fly zone in southern Iraq, the Tabuk incident could have had an impact on the F-15XP package since, according to the testimony of US officials, the 1978 Tabuk limitations were to apply to the 1992 F-15XPs as well.

Together, the 72 F-15XPs, in addition to the 60 F-15A/Bs from 1978 and 36 F-15C/Ds from 1990, would give the Royal Saudi Air Force 168 F-15s in the latter part of the 1990s. Moreover, the Saudis could well seek another 98 F-16 or F-18 aircraft in 1993 or 1994. With 48 Tornado aircraft, after the completion of the Yamama II agreement with British Aerospace (and 72 Tornados already operational), in total Saudi Arabia would have over 380 front-line aircraft later in the decade, making Riyadh a major air power in the region. CENTCOM was generally supportive of this expansion program since it improved the interoperability of the American and Saudi military establishments, in an era in which the American military was anticipating large cutbacks in the defense budget.

Aircraft were not the only weapons that the US was selling. Kuwait agreed during October 1992 to buy 236 M-1 A2 advanced battle tanks instead of the British Challenger tank. The M-1 A2 and Challenger were expected to compete in late 1992 for a 390-tank arms package in the United Arab Emirates as well. Previously, Saudi Arabia had purchased 465 M-1 A2 tanks (315 in

1989 and 150 in 1990) as well as 150 M-60 A3 tanks. These purchases would permit the creation of at least two armored divisions and help Saudi Arabia realize its goal of creating a significantly larger ground force order-of-battle, instead of relying on American prepositioning and rapid deployment alone.

From a purely strategic viewpoint, the expansion of Saudi Arabia's ground forces was precisely what the Kingdom required for its defense, especially since the Saudi leadership was unwilling to accept the prepositioning of heavy American equipment that would allow the US to play an early role on the ground in the event of another regional crisis like the Iraqi invasion of Kuwait.

During the first stages of the Desert Shield buildup in 1990, rapidly deployed US ground forces with inadequate equipment were used only to defend Saudi ports and airfields, while the small Saudi Army was deployed along the Kuwaiti border and was expected to absorb an Iraqi invasion of Saudi Arabia had Saddam Hussein decided to continue his ground offensive. At that time, the concept of operations proposed that US airpower and light mobility forces utilize the depth of Saudi Arabia in order to destroy extended lines of Iraqi armor, once Baghdad broke through the lightly defended Saudi forward lines. This early Desert Shield division of responsibility between the US and Saudi Arabia could be expected to be resumed in the future as long as the US had no way of achieving a rapid buildup of its ground forces.

In consequent recognition of the need to expand Saudi Arabia's ground capability, US and Saudi officials reached the conclusion that the kingdom should aspire to enlarge its armed forces from 90,000 to 200,000 men, in order to reach an equivalent of the initial Desert Shield force (of October 1990) that seemed to deter Saddam from invading the kingdom. It was especially important in this regard to expand the Saudi Army and National Guard, rather than the Air Force. After all, American air power could still be relied upon to reach the kingdom in real time in the event of a regional contingency.

But strategic logic was not the only factor behind the pattern of US arms sales in the region. Cutbacks in procurement on the part of the armed services forced the American defense industry to look to exports as a means of protecting entire production lines and keeping them from closing down; that appeared to be the case, for example, with the F-15E and its export derivative, the F-15XP.

Thus the drive for exports threatened to accelerate the Middle East arms race, as US firms were tempted to export increasingly more sensitive technologies in order to survive. Already in November 1992, the Defense and Commerce Departments were considering an export proposal from Litton Itek Optical Systems to sell a reconnaissance satellite to the United Arab Emirates. That the administration did not reject the proposal out of hand indicated the readiness of US officials to consider weapons exports that would never have even been imagined several years earlier.

6. Arresting Weapons Proliferation
Shai Feldman

In late January 1992, representatives of a number of Arab states and Israel convened at the House of Unions in Moscow to launch the Multilateral Negotiations on the Middle East. It was within this framework that the multilateral Working Group on Arms Control and Regional Security held its first meeting. Subsequently, the group held its second meeting in Washington in May 1992, and its third meeting in Moscow, in mid-September. Thus, for the first time in the history of the Middle East, a regional arms control process was officially launched. It was complemented by considerable international diplomatic activity, aimed at arresting the proliferation of conventional and mass destruction weapons and technologies in the Middle East.

The International and Regional Context

The New Global Environment
Global and regional factors seem to have converged in the aftermath of the Gulf War to create new opportunities for arms control in the Middle East. At the global level, the end of the Cold War has eliminated the superpowers' competition in the region. This was formerly a major source of the arms race, and thus a major obstacle to arms control in the Middle East. Containing the expansion of one another's influence in the region was the primary objective of both. In turn, this seemed to require the strengthening of allies, largely by providing them with more and better weapons. The desire to gain influence among allies was also seen as requiring that they be supplied with arms, so that they become dependent on their suppliers for maintenance and spare parts. Given the superpowers' tendency to view the Middle East as a testing ground for their weapons--and to regard the combat performance of their allies as a test of their own relative standing-- they could hardly cooperate in controlling the flow of arms to the region.

These superpower-level obstacles to the application of arms control in the Middle East became largely irrelevant following the end of the Cold War and the breakup of the Soviet Union. Indeed, the end of the Cold War also created general international support for limiting further proliferation, particularly in the realm of mass destruction weapons. In this regard, the cumulative effect of the agreements reached in recent years--primarily between Washington and Moscow--might also affect positively the attitude toward arms control in the Middle East. These agreements include the Intermediate-range Nuclear Forces (INF) Treaty, which resulted in reducing the stockpiles of theater nuclear weapons in Europe; the Conventional Forces in Europe (CFE) agreement, reducing the size of the conventional forces deployed by NATO and the Warsaw Pact in Europe; and both Strategic Arms Reduction Talks (START-I and START-II) agreements, in the framework of which the United States and the Soviet Union committed themselves to reduce their strategic nuclear forces by some two thirds.

These agreements created a historical precedent: for the first time in the post-World War II era, the two superpowers agreed to reduce the size of their armed forces, rather than merely to place limitations on their capacity to enlarge them. Indeed, the cumulative effect of these agreements was the creation of an atmosphere of a 'disarmament race' which could affect other regions of the world, including the Middle East. In addition, these agreements made the US and Russia more immune to the criticism voiced in the Third World, to the effect that while preaching non-proliferation in different regions, the superpowers refused to dismantle their own huge arsenals.

In the post-Gulf War period, these developments were reinforced by a number of important non-proliferation proposals advanced by western leaders, some specifically directed at the Middle East. The most salient among these were advanced by Canada's Prime Minister Brian Mulroney, and by Britain's Prime Minister John Major. The first called for a total suspension of arms transfers to the Middle East, while the latter was aimed at making all arms transfers transparent by establishing an international arms transfer register, in which deliveries of major weapon systems would be noted.

Following these proposals, US President George Bush issued on May 29, 1991 a comprehensive arms control initiative for the Middle East. His nonproliferation proposal encompassed the full array of weapons: conventional, missiles, nuclear, chemical and biological weapons. Shortly thereafter, President Francois Mitterand announced his own initiative, in the context of which he committed France to sign the 1968 Nuclear Nonproliferation Treaty (NPT).

As a direct result of the Bush initiative, top level officials of the five permanent members of the UN Security Council (the P-5) convened in Paris on July 9, 1991 and on October 17, 1991, and in Washington in May 28, 1992, in order to define guidelines for limiting conventional arms transfers to the Middle East. Meanwhile, the leaders of the seven major industrial states (the G-7) held a summit in London in mid-July 1991, and agreed to recommend to the UN General Assembly that an international arms transfer register be established. By November 1991 the Assembly adopted the G-7 proposal with minor changes.

Meanwhile, South Africa completed the procedure for signing the NPT, and after intensive persuasion by US Secretary of State James Baker, China announced in November 1991 that it intended to follow suit. It also told the July 1991 P-5 meeting that it would abide by the stipulations of the Missile Technology Control Regime (MTCR) limiting the export of surface-to-surface missiles and the technologies needed to develop and produce such missiles.

The decisions of France, South Africa, and China to sign the 1968 Nuclear Nonproliferation Treaty, were very important given their past contribution to the proliferation of nuclear technologies. In the past, France contributed to the establishment of key nuclear programs in Iraq and Pakistan; and, to a somewhat lesser degree, the outcome of China's conduct was similar. At a minimum, their signature created an atmosphere less conducive to further nuclear weapons proliferation.

In turn, the cumulative effect of these developments probably affected North Korea's decision to accept South Korea's proposal to transform their region into a nuclear weapons free zone, to provide a more complete account of its nuclear program, and to allow International Atomic Energy Agency (IAEA) experts to visit its installations. These steps complemented an earlier development in Latin America, strengthening the Tlateloco Nuclear Weapons Free Zone (NWFZ): in December 1991, Brazil and Argentina decided to become effective members of the NWFZ and to implement mutual intrusive verification measures, so that compliance with its provisions could be assured. Thus, developments in the Korean Peninsula and in Latin America may also have contributed to the creation of an atmosphere more conducive to arms control in the Middle East.

Finally, by mid-July 1992, President Bush contributed another push for regional arms control by announcing a new "Nonproliferation Initiative." Substantively the initiative did not break now ground; rather, it largely comprised a repackaging of previous US initiatives and a generalization of the ideas elaborated in the president's May 1991 Middle East arms control initiative to other regions.

Developments in the Region

Simultaneously, a number of developments within the Middle East encouraged some of the region's states to place arms control higher on their national agendas. First, the cumulative impression left by the destruction caused by the Iran-Iraq War and the Gulf War may have crystallized the need to prevent further weapons proliferation. Indeed, the Iran-Iraq War provided a number of precedents in this respect, such as the first massive use of ballistic missiles and--for the first time since World War I--the battlefield use of chemical munitions.

During the Gulf War, Israel--a state perceived by its neighbors as possessing nuclear weapons--and the United States, a superpower controlling the world's largest nuclear arsenal, experienced the first use of surface-to-surface missiles and the threat to use chemical weapons against them. As it turned out, the region was spared the catastrophe which retaliation to the use of chemical weapons might have brought about.

Yet some in the region may have concluded that urgent action was needed to diminish the danger that the region would not be so lucky next time around. Thus the Jordanians, concerned about the possibility that they might become prime victims of the fallout created by an exchange of nonconventional munitions between the Arab states and Israel, understandably seemed eager to encourage arms control in the region.

Indeed, post-Gulf War revelations regarding the dimensions of Iraq's nonconventional capabilities seemed to have shaken Egypt as well. As Egypt was the only Arab state at peace with Israel, President Mubarak and his government probably regarded the possible specter of an Israeli-Iraqi exchange of nonconventional munitions as a political and strategic nightmare. Moreover, the magnitude of Iraq's nuclear program and the prospects that, had Saddam only refrained from invading Kuwait, the program might have provided Iraq with a deliverable nuclear capability within a few years--must have created enormous anguish in Cairo: against the backdrop of millennia-long rivalry, Mesopotamia would have upstaged the Nile Delta in an important attribute of national power. In turn, such concern may partly explain Egypt's focus on the need to pursue nuclear nonproliferation in the region.

Other outcomes of the Gulf War may also have contributed to advancing an arms control process in the Middle East. With the defeat of Iraq's military might, the forces of the most destabilizing power in the region diminished considerably. Correspondingly, Iraq's capacity to torpedo any regional arms control process was reduced. In addition, the post-Gulf War inspection of Iraq's missile and nonconventional weapons development activity--though conducted in the context of Saddam's surrender rather than in the framework of a regional arms control process--did provide the region's states with some experience in implementing intrusive verification measures.

Also, the post-Gulf War revelations regarding the extent of assistance which Iraq's missile and nonconventional weapons development programs received from the advanced industrial states, may have created greater readiness among the latter governments to accept supplier restraints. The political embarrassment created by these revelations may have resulted in greater willingness among some of these principal suppliers to limit the scale and pace of weapons proliferation in the Middle East.

Yet the most important of the regional factors encouraging an arms control process was the launching of the Arab-Israel bilateral negotiations in Madrid in October 1991, and the launching of the Middle East multilateral talks in Moscow in January 1992. First, after decades characterized by the absence of direct communication and negotiations among the region's states, Egypt and Israel had engaged each other in direct negotiations in late 1977, leading to peace and the establishment of diplomatic relations between the two countries. Now, with the advent of the Madrid and Moscow processes, a large number of Arab states-- most notably, Syria and Jordan--began to follow in Egypt's footsteps by engaging Israel in direct negotiations and communication. Thus a key prerequisite for an arms control process--namely that the parties be engaged in some form of negotiations and relations--was met.

The dramatic inauguration of this new phase in the Arab-

Israel peace process reflected the decision of key Arab governments--with Syria playing a pivotal role--to shift their emphasis from force to diplomacy. While this did not imply that the pursuit of military strength had been abandoned, it did mean that that pursuit was subordinated to the requirements of diplomacy.

In addition, the delicate nature and critical importance of the diplomatic process required that it be protected from destabilizing weapons proliferation. Thus a viable arms control process became critically important for peacemaking. Moreover, since resolution of its political disputes with its Arab neighbors was likely to require that Israel withdraw from most of the territories it occupied since 1967, and since Israel would not withdraw unless proper security arrangements were implemented, the conflict's resolution would inevitably require the application of effective confidence-building measures, too. Thus the launching of the new phase in Arab-Israeli negotiations created for the first time a possibility as well as an imperative to discuss the application of arms control and confidence-building in the Middle East.

The Arms Control Agenda for the Middle East: Conventional Weapons

The agenda for limiting the proliferation of weapons in the Middle East in the aftermath of the Gulf War, was propelled forward by the initiative launched by US President Bush on May 29, 1991. The importance of the initiative lay in its comprehensive nature, as well as in Washington's unique role in the region. Consequently, the initiative led other states and international organizations to take a number of steps designed to slow the pace of weapons proliferation in the Middle East.

The agenda for controlling conventional weapons proliferation in the Middle East included initiatives at a number of different levels: direct efforts to arrest conventional arms transfers to the region; attempts to achieve greater transparency with respect to such transfers; efforts to create a consulting mechanism among arms suppliers; initiatives to create a data bank on Middle East arsenals; and finally, suggestions for controlling the defense expenditures of the region's states.

Limiting Arms Transfers to the Middle East

We have noted that, following the Gulf War, Canada's Prime Minister Brian Mulroney suggested a moratorium on all transfers of conventional weapons to the Middle East. Similar initiatives were taken in the US Congress, notably by Rep. Dante Fascell, chairman of the House Committee on International Relations, within the framework of a legislative amendment he proposed in early 1991. The amendment was approved by the House of Representatives on June 20, 1991. Within the Middle East, Israel's Defense Minister Moshe Arens also suggested a complete ban on the transfer of conventional arms to the region. In a number of meetings with foreign dignitaries, as well as in a meeting with participants in a seminar on "Arms Control and the New Middle East Security Environment" held by the Jaffee Center for Strategic Studies in January 1992, Arens argued that the only feasible approach to the matter would be to install a complete moratorium on the transfer of such weapons to the region: "I suggested to Secretary Baker when he was here on his first visit after the Gulf War that maybe an agreement could be reached with the arms exporters that there would be a cessation of sales of weaponry. As defense minister of Israel, I would be ready to agree to that."

Clearly, the main appeal of such proposals was that their implementation did not require the cooperation of the recipients-- some of whom were, at best, only now beginning to negotiate with one another. Also, initiatives for absolute bans allow for quick implementation, avoiding the endless debate as to which categories of weapons transfers should be banned and which should be permitted. In addition, a complete ban might be easiest to verify, since **any** transfer identified would constitute a clear violation of the ban.

Yet by 1992 and early 1993 such proposals seemed completely unacceptable to almost all supplier and recipient states. Competing with their interest in arresting proliferation, most suppliers had other interests--to be elaborated below--that propelled them to continue transferring arms to the region. Meanwhile, most Arab states rejected proposals to ban such transfers, arguing that in light of Israel's advanced indigenous production capacity, such a ban would favor it.

The reference to conventional weapons in the Bush initiative was more modest than the Mulroney-Fascell-Arens proposals, and its timing was partly designed to head-off the Fascell amendment. The initiative called for the convening of representatives of the five permanent members of the UN Security Council (the P-5) to discuss the formulation of guidelines for restraining conventional arms transfers to the Middle East. The Bush initiative noted that during the 1980s, the US, the Soviet Union, France, Britain and China sold most of the weapons supplied to the region. It called upon these suppliers to abide by guidelines for responsible arms transfers; to avoid destabilizing arms sales; and to adopt strict internal controls on the end-use of all weapons and other items supplied.

As a consequence of the Bush initiative, representatives of the P-5 met in Paris in July 1991. There they committed themselves to adopt efficient measures for arresting the proliferation of weapons, and to implement "effective measures of nonproliferation and arms control in a fair, reasonable, comprehensive and balanced manner on a global as well as on a regional basis." In a post-meeting communique, the five also undertook to avoid weapons transfers that might prove destabilizing. Their statement also recognized that "indiscriminate transfers" of weapons and technology contributed to eroding regional stability, and noted their countries' particular responsibility to prevent such risks.

In their statement, the P-5 also expressed their awareness of their special role "in promoting greater responsibility, confidence and transparency in this field." Accordingly they took upon themselves to practice self-restraint in arms sales by adopting appropriate laws and regulations; to consult and exchange information regarding pending arms exports to Middle East states; and to engage in additional meetings designed to formulate specific guidelines for weapons transfers.

Yet even at their second meeting, in London on October 17-18, 1991, the P-5 failed to agree on fixed criteria for judging which arms transfers should be regarded as eroding regional stability, and which should be seen as consistent with the recipients' legitimate requirements for defense and deterrence. It thus seems that the restraints envisaged by the Bush initiative would have to be implemented by the major suppliers on an ad hoc basis. Within this context, judgments were less likely to be made on the basis of the weapons systems involved, since decisions as to which should be considered offensive and which defensive could be made with ease only at the two extreme ends of the spectrum. Rather, such judgments were more likely to be made on the basis of the nature of the recipient's political regime and its stated and inferred intentions.

Meanwhile, the concluding statement of the summit held in London in July 1991, by the leaders of the seven largest industrial states (the G-7), called for "preventing the creation of disproportional arms arsenals" and avoiding arms transfers that might exacerbate existing tensions. In this context, the G-7 decision was sharper than the parallel reference in the Bush initiative. It noted that

> the principle of action requires all of us to take steps to prevent the building up of disproportionate arsenals. To that end all countries should refrain from arms transfers which would be destabilizing or would exacerbate existing tensions. Special restraint should be exercised in the transfer of advanced technology weapons and in sales to countries and areas of particular concern. A special effort should be made to define sensitive items and production capacity for advanced weapons, to the transfer of which similar restraints could be applied. All states should take steps to ensure that these criteria are strictly enforced. We intend to give these issues our continuing close attention.

The third meeting of the P-5, held in Washington on May 28-29, 1992, seemed to make little progress in resolving these inherent difficulties. Although the P-5 meetings were envisaged by the Bush initiative as being confined to efforts to arrest conventional weapons proliferation, the statement issued at the end of the third meeting addressed mainly the requirements of preventing the spread of mass destruction weapons.

Notably, the Bush initiative had contained a commitment to the effect that the guidelines adopted by the suppliers would permit the region's states "to acquire the conventional capabilities required for legitimate deterrence and defense against military aggression." In this spirit, the P-5 confirmed during their July 1991 meeting that Article 51 of the UN charter reserved the right of self-defense to all states, and noted that this implied the right to acquire arms for this purpose. The concluding statement of the P-5 also stipulated that "the transfer of conventional weapons, conducted in a responsible manner, should contribute to the ability of states to meet their legitimate defense, security and national sovereignty requirements and to participate effectively in collective measures requested by the United Nations for the purpose of maintaining or restoring international peace and security."

By early 1993 the future of the P-5 talks had become increasingly cloudy. First, it was not yet clear whether the incoming Clinton administration would regard these talks as a productive avenue for arms control. Secondly, the three advanced industrial members of the P-5--the United States, France, and Britain--had become engaged during the second half of 1992 in rather fierce competition to supply arms to the Middle East, particularly the Gulf region. Meanwhile, Russia and China had adopted a similar competitive pattern with respect to Iran. Finally, following the announced sale of F-16 advanced aircraft by the US to Taiwan in mid-1992, China withdrew from participation in the P-5 talks.

Making Arms Transfers and Weapons Arsenals Transparent

The Bush initiative proposed limited transparency on conventional arms transfers. It would be restricted to the relationship among the arms suppliers. President Bush called upon the principle suppliers to adopt consultation mechanisms, allowing them to notify each other of pending arms sales prior to implementation. He also suggested that they hold regular discussions regarding arms transfers; that they consult each other when one of them suspected that a transfer might constitute a violation of the agreed guidelines; and that they provide each other with an annual report of all transfers made.

Indeed, the only operative step resulting from the Bush initiative and the P-5 meetings was the decision of the P-5 to implement the principle of transparency with regard to conventional weapons sales to the Middle East. Yet by 1993 even this agreement remained precarious. After their first meeting, the five were reportedly committed to informing each other of significant arms sales to the Middle East **at the contract formulation stage**. Such prenotification was designed to provide an opportunity to raise objections about a pending sale, and to cancel it if the five agreed that it would destabilize the region.

The US continued to insist on prenotification, while the other four parties preferred the provision of appropriate information at the delivery stage of each transfer. Britain, France and Russia eventually accepted Washington's position, but China continued to reject the principle and practice of prenotification.

A more comprehensive transparency proposal--to establish an international arms transfers register in which each transfer of conventional arms from one state to another would be recorded--was first advanced in the aftermath of the Gulf War by Britain's Prime Minister John Major. The suggestion was based on the hope that the transparency on arms transfers gained by the register's establishment would provide the international community with early warning regarding the accumulation of arms by diverse states.

The idea of creating such a register was also included in the Mitterand arms control initiative. The G-7 meeting in London also endorsed the Major proposal and decided to present it, following the insertion of some amendments, to the November 1991 meeting of the UN General Assembly. On December 9, 1991 the Assembly adopted the G-7 proposal and established the register.

In contrast to the P-5 decision to prenotify members with respect to pending arms sales to Middle East states, the initiative endorsed by the G-7 and adopted by the UN General Assembly established a mechanism in which **all** international arms transfers would be registered--but only at the delivery stage of the sale. Thus it did not provide or reinforce a mechanism for preventing such sales. Nor did the register contain a verification system for assuring that suppliers and recipients were indeed complying with the requirement that they register all significant arms transfers. And even if compliance were obtained, at best the register might help create an "embarrassment factor" with respect to conventional arms transfers. Hopefully, some transfers might be avoided if the recipients and/or suppliers knew that they would inevitably be made public.

Finally, the G-7 proposal was less inclusive than Prime Minister Major's original suggestion: registration requirements were limited to main weapons platforms such as tanks, armored personnel carriers (APCs), armored fighting vehicles (AFVs), artillery, combat aircraft, combat helicopters, warships, submarines and surface-to-surface missiles. Thus, at best, the register could prevent surprises regarding the accumulation of arms by different states by increasing international awareness regarding such accumulation. Presumably, this might reduce the odds of strategic surprise, and might provide time to react regarding such accumulation.

As noted earlier, by November 1991 the UN General Assembly had adopted the G-7 proposal with minor changes. The UN stipulated that recipients and suppliers of arms were to register relevant arms transfers beginning one year after the resolution's approval. Accordingly, such "registrations" were designated to begin by November 1992.

Additional ideas aimed at increasing transparency were advanced by President Mitterand. In his initiative, the French president proposed to establish a data base with respect to existing arms arsenals worldwide. He also noted the need to establish regional military balances and to encourage the exchange of related military data. The idea gained the support of the G-7 London meeting and was further crystallized during the G-7 July 1991 meeting. Consequently, their statement included a commitment to "urge greater openness about overall holdings of conventional weapons. We believe the provision of such data, and a procedure for seeking clarification, would be a valuable confidence and security building measure." Yet by 1993 not a single step had been taken to establish the proposed international data base on military forces and weapons arsenals.

Limiting Defense Expenditures

The possibility of utilizing economic leverage in order to limit proliferation of conventional arms in different parts of the world, was raised for the first time by the leaders of the G-7 during their mid-July 1991 meeting in London. In their concluding statement, they defined the reducing of defense expenditures as a key element of sound economic policy. Indeed, their decision included a detailed reference to the relationship between the two factors:

> We believe that moderation in the level of military expenditure is a key aspect of sound economic policy and good government. While all countries are struggling with competing claims on scarce resources, excessive spending on arms of all kinds diverts resources from the overriding need to tackle economic development. It can also build up large debts without creating the means by which these may

be serviced. We note with favor the recent report issued by the United Nations Development Programme (UNDP) and the recent decisions as to by several donor countries to take account of military expenditure where it is disproportionate when setting up aid programs, and encourage all other donor countries to take similar action. We welcome the attention which the managing director of the International Monetary Fund (IMF) and the president of the World Bank have recently given to excessive military spending, in the context of reducing unproductive public expenditure.

Unfortunately, not a single step was taken after this proclamation was adopted in order to translate it into action. Indeed, any such attempt would have proven extremely difficult. For it is far from clear what criteria the G-7 would have been able to apply in trying to determine that a state's defense expenditures were excessive. The fierce debates taking place within the seven about their own defense budgets were indicative of the problems entailed.

Surface-to-Surface Missiles

Efforts to control the proliferation of surface-to-surface missiles in the Middle East encompassed a number of diverse measures:

Demand-side Nonproliferation

The Bush initiative called upon recipients of ballistic missiles and technology in the Middle East to adopt short-term as well as long-term measures to make the region free of such weapons. For the short term, the initiative called upon all Middle East states to freeze existing surface-to-surface missile arsenals by refraining from acquiring, producing, and testing such missiles. For the long term, the initiative defined the elimination of ballistic missiles as the final objective of arms control in this realm. Later, these pleas won endorsement at the July 1991 P-5 meeting in Paris. So far, however, none of the region's states have responded to the missile freeze or to the missile-free-zone proposals.

Supply-side Nonproliferation: The MTCR

The Missile Technology Control Regime (MTCR) was established in April 1987 by the US, Canada, France, England, Germany, Italy, and Japan. It comprises a set of guidelines devised by the principal advanced industrial states for limiting the transfer of ballistic missiles, and missile development and production technologies, in order to arrest the global spread of surface-to-surface missiles. Notably, the MTCR's existing guidelines refer only to missiles with a range of over 300 km and a warhead with a weight of over 500 kilograms. Thus, they remain largely irrelevant to preventing the proliferation of short-range ballistic missiles--which, due to the close proximity of capitals and major strategic assets in the Arab-Israel conflict arena--are the most significant category in the Middle East context.

Possibly for this reason, both the Bush initiative and the concluding statement of the July 1991 Paris meeting of the P-5 avoided any reference to the stipulations of the MTCR. The Bush initiative merely called upon the suppliers of missile technology to "step up efforts to coordinate export licensing for equipment, technology and services that could be used to manufacture surface-to-surface missiles," and to ensure that such "export licenses would be provided only for peaceful purposes." In contrast, the Mitterand initiative included a call upon potential suppliers to strengthen their efforts to prevent ballistic missile proliferation by complying strictly with the stipulations of the MTCR agreement. A similar plea was included in the statement published by the G-7 leaders at the conclusion of their meeting in London in mid-July 1991. The seven also welcomed the recent decision of a number of states to adopt the MTCR restraints and expressed their support for the declaration adopted by the MTCR conference, held in Tokyo in March 1991, calling upon all states to adopt the MTCR guidelines. At the same time, the G-7 noted that they had no intention of inhibiting cooperation "in the use of space for peaceful and scientific purposes."

Meanwhile, during 1991 the Bush administration exerted significant pressure on China and Israel to accept the MTCR guidelines. The regime received a significant boost when the two countries yielded to such US 'persuasion,' in November 1991 and January 1992, respectively. By early 1993, however, the two countries had yet to be accepted as members of the MTCR regime. They were thus expected to adhere to the limitations stipulated in the MTCR agreement without enjoying the benefits thereof.

Deterrence and Forceful Prevention

Although the principle of preventing the proliferation of ballistic missiles in the Middle East by deterrence and by the actual use of force did not become part of the declaratory policy of any regional or extra-regional power, in 1991-1992 it seemed to have been embraced by the Bush administration. First, it was adopted in the context of the relevant UN resolutions stipulating the dismantling of Iraq's surface-to-surface missile force in the aftermath of the Gulf War. Next it was reflected in US efforts to prevent the transfer of 500 km-range Scud C missiles from North Korea to Syria and Iran. Thus in October 1991 US sources "informed" the media that Israel intended to intercept a Korean ship carrying such Scuds to Syria. Most likely, the leaks originating from Washington were intended to deter the Koreans from delivering these Scuds, after a first shipment of Scud C launchers had already reached Syria. Notably the Bush administration refrained from negative commentary regarding the possibility that Israel might intercept such a shipment. Thus the principle of forceful prevention was first implicitly endorsed.

It nevertheless remains unclear whether Israel had indeed intended to conduct such an interception, particularly since the international legal grounds for such an act would have been quite shaky, and the strategic implications might have been quite significant, ranging from Syrian reprisals against ships bound for Israeli ports to a full-scale military confrontation. In any case, Washington's deterrence exercise succeeded, and the Korean ship turned around, heading to an unknown destination, probably Iran.

The second episode in this context occurred in March 1992, when US intelligence was said to be tracking a ship carrying Scud C missiles heading from North Korea to Syria or Iran. This time, Washington leaked **its own** intention to intercept the shipment. The international legal grounds for such an interception remained shaky. Bush administration sources argued that it could be conducted in the framework of the UN Security Council resolutions imposing an embargo on Iraq. But it was far from clear how the respective UN resolutions could be interpreted in a fashion allowing the interception of a shipment clearly not bound for Iraq. At any rate, by mid-March the North Korean ship had succeeded in evading US surveillance, and arrived safely at the

Iranian port of Bandar Abbas. Later it became known that the Scud Cs had reached their Syrian destination.

These efforts to intercept Korean missile shipments to the Middle East had far-reaching implications. Primarily they indicated that the US had reversed its previous opposition to preventive nonproliferation by force, or, at a minimum, that it was prepared to attempt to deter arms transfers by threatening to use force. In an earlier context, such opposition had clearly been reflected in June 1981, when the Reagan administration sanctioned Israel for bombing the Osiraq nuclear reactor in Iraq. In the case of the Korean ships, the principles involved in post-Gulf War efforts to disarm Iraq's missile and nonconventional arsenals and production capacity were expanded to allow pre-war prevention of ballistic missile transfers to Syria. By early 1993, however, it was far too early to assess what attitude the incoming Clinton administration would adopt with respect to reliance on forceful prevention against ballistic missile proliferation.

Nuclear Weapons

The agenda for nuclear nonproliferation in the Middle East comprised a number of initiatives--some intended to provide a cap on the quest for nuclear arms in the region, others directed at long-term efforts to make the region free of nuclear weapons.

Production Freeze

The Bush initiative included the first official proposal for freezing existing nuclear capabilities in the Middle East, by calling upon the region's states to implement a verifiable ban on the production and acquisition of weapons-usable nuclear materials. Such materials were specified to include only enriched uranium and separated plutonium. The ban was to be implemented after the measures taken to disarm Iraq's nuclear capability were completed.

The freeze proposal was endorsed by the P-5 meeting in Paris in mid-July 1991. The concluding statement of the meeting called for "a ban on the importation and production of nuclear weapons usable materials." The formula adopted by the P-5 was wider in scope than that found in the Bush initiative, since it did not limit the materials to which the freeze would apply to separated plutonium and enriched uranium only, and could thus apply to other weapons-related material as well.

Notably, the Bush proposal did not apply to past efforts to produce plutonium and enriched uranium in the region. Neither did it address the long-standing ambiguity surrounding Israel's activities in the nuclear realm. In the latter respect, it contrasted sharply with another proposal to end the production of nuclear weapons-grade material in the Middle East, developed by a number of senior Egyptian analysts. The latter proposal was first communicated informally to a number of Israeli analysts in the immediate aftermath of the Gulf War. Later it found explicit expression in an article published in *Al-Ahram* on April 28, 1991 by Ambassador Salah Bassiouny, then director of the National Center For Middle East Studies in Cairo. It was later also expressed by Abdel Monem Said Aly, of the Al-Ahram Center for Political and Strategic Studies, in a paper he delivered at a conference held in Moscow in October 1991.

The Bassiouny production freeze proposal differed in one key respect from the proposal advanced by President Bush: it contained a "transparency" stipulation, requiring that as a first stage toward implementing the freeze Israel should declare that it possessed a nuclear stockpile.

In informal communications, US officials rejected this notion, arguing that verifying a freeze required only that the absence of further production was assured. Accordingly, they suggested that verification of such a freeze focus on whatever production facilities (if any) may exist, and not require the declaration of present inventories and presumed past activities. Concurrently, some Israelis feared that Egypt's quest for nuclear transparency might be merely designed to get Israel's nuclear potential 'out of the closet' in the hope that the resulting international pressure might compel it to sign the NPT. In addition, Americans and Israelis shared a deep concern that the suggested transparency might create significant domestic pressures within Arab states to emulate Israel's advantage in this realm, thus actually stimulating a nuclear arms race in the region and defeating the purposes of arms control in the Middle East. This concern seemed to be accepted by influential Egyptian officials who disassociated themselves from the Bassiouny initiative.

Both the Bush and the Bassiouny freeze proposals appeared to accept that existing political circumstances in the region would not allow the implementation of far-reaching measures to prevent nuclear proliferation in the Middle East, and that Israel would not sign the NPT and accept full-scope IAEA safeguards, and/or agree to implement a verifiable transformation of the region into a nuclear free zone (NFZ), until some record of stable peace in the Middle East had been established over time. Since such "all-or-nothing" approaches did not advance the cause of arresting nuclear proliferation in the region, interim freeze proposals seemed to be the only realistic alternative to an uncontrolled nuclear arms race in the Middle East.

Adherence to the NPT

The Bush initiative called upon all Middle East states to join the 1968 Nuclear Non-Proliferation Treaty (NPT) and to place all their nuclear facilities under safeguards of the International Atomic Energy Agency (IAEA). The trend towards wider adherence to the NPT was reinforced by the aforementioned decisions of France, China, and South Africa to sign the 1968 treaty.

The statement concluding the July 1991 P-5 meeting mentioned the NPT only indirectly, by voicing support for existing arms control agreements in the nuclear realm. Yet it also contained a direct call to the region's states to allow the application of IAEA safeguards to all their nuclear facilities.

In contrast, the statement made following the G-7 July 1991 meeting in London already reflected the new awareness regarding the scope of Iraq's nuclear activities--resulting from the post-war UN inspection visits--and the ramifications of these revelations for the credibility of existing nuclear nonproliferation measures and mechanisms. Accordingly, the G-7 statement included a renewed plea to join the NPT and to place all nuclear facilities under IAEA safeguards, as well as a renewed call upon the suppliers of nuclear material and technology to implement all guidelines and stipulations of the Nuclear Suppliers Group. In addition, the statement contained a commitment to maintain and reinforce the NPT beyond 1995, when the treaty formally expires unless renewed; to strengthen and improve the IAEA safeguard system; and to adopt new measures in the framework of the Nuclear Suppliers Group, intended to ensure adequate export control on dual-use items.

Within the region, during 1992 Egypt renewed its demand that Israel sign the NPT. Official government spokesmen argued that Israel should initially provide a political statement regarding its intention to sign the Treaty, and should follow it with legally binding action, i.e., its actual signature. By the end of the year, Egypt had intensified its efforts to obtain an Israeli signature by defining it as a precondition to its own willingness to sign the Chemical Weapons Convention. Indeed, Cairo became active in mobilizing other Arab governments to resist signing the CWC as long as Israel did not sign the NPT.

Establishing a Nuclear Free Zone

The transformation of the Middle East into a nuclear free zone (NFZ) was proposed, in different versions, by both Egypt (since 1974) and Israel (since 1980). On a number of occasions the UN General Assembly adopted the idea, approving by large majorities a version similar to the one proposed by Egypt. The main difference between the Israeli and Egyptian versions concerned the mechanism by which a nuclear free zone should be established in the Middle East.

Egypt's draft resolutions called for the establishment of a Middle East NFZ without elaborating a mechanism for its establishment. Indeed, its proposal did not even suggest that a formal agreement creating such a zone should be negotiated among the region's states. Rather, it implied that the region's states should simply comply with the constraints defining the creation of such a zone. Thus, it did not envisage that the establishment of an NFZ in the Middle East might require a transformation of the political relations among the region's states.

In contrast, the Israeli draft resolution, first proposed on October 31, 1980, called "upon all states of the Middle East and non-nuclear weapon states adjacent to the region, which are not signatories to any treaty providing for a nuclear weapons free zone, to convene at the earliest possible date a conference with a view to negotiating a multilateral treaty establishing a nuclear weapon free zone in the Middle East."

The Israeli focus on the negotiation mechanism seems to have been quite intentional; primarily, it resulted from the conviction that Israel should not surrender the deterrent effect of its nuclear potential unless Arab willingness to negotiate with Israel were to provide sufficient evidence of Arab agreement to establish permanent peaceful relations with the Jewish state. Thus the negotiation process was seen as an essential part of the effort to build mutual confidence among the region's states without which an NFZ could not be viable.

The second distinction between the Israeli and Egyptian NFZ proposals concerned their different approaches to the NPT and to IAEA safeguards. The Egyptian NFZ proposal suggested that pending the establishment of such a zone in the Middle East, the region's states should adhere to the stipulations of the NPT and subject all their nuclear facilities to IAEA safeguards. The Israeli approach to these matters took the opposite view, presenting the creation of an NFZ as a substitute to the NPT. The latter approach seemed to be based on the view--reinforced by the experience with Iraq--that the IAEA safeguard system, designed to verify compliance with the NPT, was highly deficient. Consequently the Israeli approach seemed to suggest that if nuclear proliferation in the region was to be arrested, credible and intrusive verification measures had to be negotiated by the region's states in the course of establishing an NFZ.

The Bush initiative also included a commitment to continue supporting the establishment of an NFZ in the Middle East. In contrast, this avenue to nuclear nonproliferation was not even mentioned in the Mitterand initiative or in the concluding statements following the July meetings of the P-5 and the G-7.

Chemical Weapons

The May 1991 Bush initiative called for the rapid conclusion of negotiations of the Chemical Weapons Convention (CWC). The initiative also called upon all Middle East states to become original signatories of the convention and, prior to signing, to implement appropriate clauses of the convention as a confidence-building measure.

The Mitterand initiative also called for a total ban on chemical weapon arsenals, as well as for steps to destroy existing stockpiles. With minor changes, the July 1991 P-5 meeting repeated the formulation of the Bush initiative, suggesting that all Middle East states sign the CWC as soon as its formulation was completed. The July 1991 G-7 statement defined the objective in this realm as an efficient and complete ban on the existence of chemical weapons, and calls for the rapid and successful conclusion of the negotiations of the CWC. It also urged all states

112

to sign the treaty as the most efficient mode for preventing chemical weapons proliferation. The seven also announced their intention to become original signatories of the CWC and called upon all states to do the same.

Referring to the need to halt chemical weapons proliferation, the G-7 statement also called upon all suppliers to strengthen mechanisms for controlling the export of chemical materials. In this context, they welcomed the measures taken by the Australian Group and by other states "on the control of exports of chemical weapons and precursors and related equipment." The seven also stated their desire to achieve "increasingly close convergence of practice between all exporting states."

The G-7 statement included a ban on the use of chemical weapons, which it defined as "an outrage against humanity." It further contained a commitment to "give immediate consideration to imposing severe measures against [the country making use of such weapons] both in the UN Security Council and elsewhere."

Meanwhile by June 1992, after lengthy negotiations had produced a German-orchestrated compromise, the detailed formulation of the CWC was completed. Subsequently approved by the Conference on Disarmament and by the UN General Assembly, the Treaty was presented for signature in a conference held in Paris in mid-January 1993.

The CWC called for a ban on the use, as well as the production and stockpiling, of poison gas. It also provided for on-site inspection of declared facilities and challenge inspection of any site in which the making or storing of chemical weapons was suspected. The accord was expected to win endorsement by the UN General Assembly by the end of 1993.

In a conference held in Paris in January 1989, the Arab delegations presented a unified position, linking their own acceptance of the CWC with Israel's acceptance of the NPT. This position seemed to be based on the notion that chemical weapons provide Arab states with a counter-deterrent to Israel's nuclear potential. Thus, in the Arab view, the pursuit of such weapons and of the means of delivering them should not be abandoned until Israel had accepted similar constraints with respect to its nuclear potential. We have noted that during 1992 Egypt became the spearhead of the Arab refusal to sign the CWC as long as Israel did not sign the NPT. In so doing, it rebuffed growing pressures by the Bush administration. Its success was reflected in the fact that all the non-Mahgreb Arab states refrained from participating in the January 1993 signing ceremony in Paris.

By contrast, in a speech delivered by Foreign Minister David Levy to the UN General Assembly in October 1991, Israel announced its intention to sign the CWC. At the time Levy indicated that Israel's signature would be made contingent on the consent of all the region's states to comply with the CWC and to accept intrusive verification measures. But the new Israeli government that took office in the summer of 1992 decided to drop these preconditions. Thus on September 24, 1992 the Israeli Cabinet decided that Israel would become an original signatory to the CWC and on January 13, 1993 Foreign Minister Peres signed the Treaty in Paris.

Biological Weapons

The May 1991 Bush initiative called for strengthening the 1972 Biological Weapons Convention (BWC) through the "full implementation of existing BWC provisions and an improved mechanism for information exchange." The initiative also called upon Middle East states to adopt confidence-building measures in the biological weapons realm. Consistent with its generally wider scope, the Mitterand initiative went a step further, calling for the destruction of existing biological weapons stockpiles.

While the July 1991 P-5 statement did not contain a specific reference to biological weapons, the statement concluding the G-7 meeting in July called for an efficient and total ban on the existence of such weapons. The seven also expressed the hope that the September 1991 Biological Weapons Review Conference would strengthen the confidence-building measures included in the BWC, and would examine measures designed to verify that BWC signatories were indeed complying with the convention's stipulations.

The Bush initiative and the decisions of the G-7 also contained expressions of discontent with the existing formulation of the BWC. This was reflected in the concluding sentence of the G-7 reference to this topic: "We each believe that a successful Review Conference leading to strengthened implementation of the BWC, would make an important contribution to preventing the proliferation of biological weapons."

Yet it was not very likely that the BWC could be significantly improved. The ease with which biological weapons can be produced renders any ban on production almost impossible to verify. Not surprisingly, in September 1991 the head of the US delegation to the Biological Weapons Review Conference stated that the Bush administration had concluded that it was impossible to verify compliance with BWC stipulations. Thus the ambiguous nature of US efforts in this realm: on the one hand Washington continued to urge adherence to the BWC; on the other, it admitted that the treaty remained inherently deficient.

The Multilateral Negotiations Process

As noted earlier, the multilateral negotiations on Arms Control and Regional Security in the Middle East opened in Moscow in late January 1992. The first organizational meeting held there, as well as subsequent meetings of the working group held in Washington and in Moscow (in May and September 1992, respectively), were orchestrated by the Bush administration, although Russia officially cosponsored the talks and European representatives as well as other 'outsiders' were also present. US navigation of the Washington and Moscow meetings seemed to have been based on the Bush administration's assessment that the political conditions in the Middle East were not yet ripe for gaining the cooperation of the region's states in serious efforts to stop the spread of conventional and nonconventional weapons. The US had evidently concluded that the bilateral talks on Arab-Israeli peace must progress substantially before the parties might be ready to consider far-reaching nonproliferation measures. Indeed, the Bush administration seemed to have accepted the proposition that premature discussion of some of the sensitive issues involved in the nonproliferation agenda, particularly in the nuclear realm, might make the region's states even more nervous, thus possibly hindering the bilateral talks.

Accordingly, the US refrained from introducing its own May 1991 Bush initiative for discussion at the multilateral talks. Instead, it conducted the May and September meetings largely in seminar form, focusing on the US and Soviet experience in negotiating arms control and confidence-building measures.

This approach to the process was reflected clearly in the

opening address by Secretary of State James Baker at the first Moscow meeting, in late January 1992. In his statement, Baker focused almost exclusively on the need to apply confidence-building measures in the Middle East:

> In the first instance, we envision offering the regional parties our thinking about potential approaches to arms control, drawing upon a vast reservoir of experience stemming from attempts to regulate military competition in Europe and other regions. From this base, the group might move forward to considering a set of modest confidence-building or transparency measures covering notifications of selected military-related activities and crisis-prevention communications. The purpose would be to lessen the prospects for incidents and miscalculation that could lead to heightened competition or even conflict.

In a subsequent address delivered in August 1992 at Tel Aviv University, State Department Director of Policy Planning Dr. Dennis Ross articulated his understanding of the Bush administration's approach to the process. Ross emphasized that, while urging the parties to define ambitious goals and objectives for the process, the administration was advocating a careful, step-by-step and "brick-by-brick" approach toward the realization of these goals. He also made clear that Washington believed that the Middle East arms control process must be structured similarly to the manner in which US-Soviet arms control proceeded: beginning with modest confidence-building measures and dealing with core strategic systems at the very end of the process.

Egypt, however, argued that the realm of nonproliferation of mass destruction weapons must not be ignored. Hence the Bush administration urged the region's states to adopt a two- track approach: to define long-term objectives in the realms of disarmament, arms control and confidence-building, while at the same time suggesting ways to achieve the phased implementation of specific confidence-building measures. Accordingly the multilateral talks held in Moscow in September 1992 ended in agreement that at their next meeting, the parties would introduce papers articulating their positions in both realms.

Subsequently, Israel undertook to define its "visionary goals" for the arms control process in the Middle East. In a speech delivered on the occasion of signing the CWC in Paris on January 14, Foreign Minister Shimon Peres announced that "in the spirit of the global pursuit of general and complete disarmament, and the establishment of regional and global arms control regimes, Israel suggests to all the countries of the region to construct a mutually verifiable zone, free of surface-to-surface missiles and of chemical, biological and nuclear weapons." He stressed that

> arms control negotiations and arrangements should be mutually agreed upon and include all the states of the region. Implementation and verification mechanisms, the establishment of comprehensive and durable peace, should be region-wide in their application. Priority in this process ought to be assigned to systems whose destabilizing potential and effects have been proven through their use in wars and have inflicted mass casualties.

Within this context, Israel called upon the region's states "to install mutual challenge inspections once peace has been established and endured the test of time."

Finally, it should be noted that the modest launching of the Middle East multilateral negotiations on arms control and regional security was also affected by the absence of key regional powers. Syria refused to participate in the Moscow conference, as well as in the two subsequent meetings of the working group, arguing that some progress in bilateral efforts to resolve its dispute with Israel must be achieved before Syria could take part in any discussions about regional arms control. Although by early 1993 Syria had yet to agree to take part in the multilateral talks, Egyptian officials told their Israeli counterparts in September 1992 that they hoped to obtain Syria's participation when the talks reconvened in 1993.

No less important, key proliferators such as Iraq, Iran and Libya were not even invited to take part in the Moscow-Washington-Moscow talks. This merely underscored the embryonic nature of the process, and its limited potential, by early 1993, to produce substantive results.

Summary and Assessment

Following the Gulf War, unprecedented efforts were made to launch an arms control process in the Middle East. This period may turn out to have constituted a major turning point in this regard. This was due to the cumulative effect of a unique configuration of factors and circumstances that encouraged such a process in the post-Gulf War regional environment. As a result, for the first time since the early 1950s the leading powers, following America's lead, conducted discussions aimed at limiting the flow of arms to the region. And for the first time in the region's history, a number of the region's states convened to conduct multilateral discussions on the possible application of arms control and confidence-building measures in the Middle East.

Yet the region's arms control process was still in an embryonic stage. The major external arms suppliers (the P-5) had yet to agree to clear criteria for arresting the spread of arms in the Middle East. By 1993 they had not yet defined how "offensive" or "destabilizing" systems might be identified. Nor could they reconcile their commitment to arms control with competing interests such as the support of local allies and the earning of hard currency. Indeed, in late 1992 US conduct based on such competing interests threatened even the future of the P-5 talks, as China responded to the proposed sale of F-16 combat aircraft to Taiwan by warning that it intended to boycott these talks. By early 1993 it became clear that the P-5 had reverted to full-scale competition over satisfying the demand for arms in the Middle East and the Gulf region, as huge arms deals were concluded by the US with Saudi Arabia, by Russia with Iran, and by France with members of the GCC.

Such supply-side forces were matched by the resistance to an arms control process among many of the region's states. As long as the Middle East remained engulfed in unresolved conflicts, its states continued to resist steps which they feared might adversely affect their capacity to deter threats. Thus Syria and Israel remained reluctant to assume any obligations that might weaken them while they negotiated a possible resolution of their conflict. Syria refrained from taking any part in the multilateral talks, arguing that progress must first be made in the bilateral efforts to resolve remaining Arab-Israeli disputes. In turn, the US refrained from presenting its own May 1991 'initiative' for discussion in the multilateral talks. And until 1993, Israel resisted discussion of efforts to control the spread of mass destruction weapons, presumably because any discourse affecting the deterrent capacity of the region's states seemed premature until more progress was registered in the bilateral Arab-Israeli talks.

Saudi Arabia feared that any effort to arrest arms transfers would primarily affect US supplies to the kingdom while its hostile neighbors, Iran and Iraq, remained largely immune to such controls. Meanwhile Iraq, Iran and Libya were completely removed from current discussions; none of the three was regarded as a potential willing participant in a regional arms control regime. In light of their role in the region's proliferation trends, efforts to establish a Middle East arms control regime would remain meaningless as long as they did not participate.

7. The Palestinian Struggle
David Tal

By its fifth year, the Intifada had changed its character almost completely. On the one hand, widespread demonstrations and riots were far less frequent, and most Palestinians had returned to work in Israel. The initial attempt by the Intifada leadership to dissociate the population from the civil administration had also failed. Yet on the other hand, the Palestinians had not given up their struggle. Sporadic riots and disorders continued to occur, reflecting the fundamental evolution that had taken place in the local population's attitude toward the IDF: there was no fear of confronting Israeli soldiers and even clashing with them. Furthermore, and of far more serious consequence, during the last months of 1992 and early months of 1993 there was a sharp escalation in cases of spontaneous individual Palestinians attacking and knifing Israelis in the Territories as well as in Israel proper (see Table I).

Escalation of the Armed Struggle
The peace process did not bring calm. On the contrary, Palestinians either were frustrated by lack of progress in the process, or rejected the process in the hope that armed attacks would force a break in the talks (see tables II, III, and IV).

The Internal Front
The killing of Palestinians by Palestinians became a burning issue for Palestinians. Between January 1991 and December 1992, the number of Palestinians executed by Palestinians was almost double those killed by the IDF (see Table IV).

Israeli Response
To counter the increase in activity by hard core militants, both the Israel Police and the IDF developed undercover units. These concentrated mainly on tracking armed Palestinians, and relied heavily on intelligence work.

In December 1992 an exceptional countermeasure was invoked: 414 Palestinians, affiliated with Hamas and the Islamic

Jihad, were temporarily deported to Lebanon. The deportation came in response to a series of lethal attacks carried out by Hamas operatives in early December that resulted in the deaths of six IDF soldiers. These deportations reversed a trend of decline in Israeli reliance on this measure. Use of punitive sealing and demolition of homes remained low (see tables V and VI).

Border Infiltrations

Lebanon continued to be the main base and point of departure for terrorist units headed toward Israel. The reduction in infiltration attempts by Palestinians through the Lebanese border is explained by the restrictions imposed upon the Palestinians in the refugee camps in the Tyre-Sidon region by the Lebanese Army, as well as by the internal struggle within the refugee camps between advocates of Arafat's political line, and their opponents. Palestinian energies were also spent on the internal struggle by the PLO against Abu Nidal's Fath--Revolutionary Council (FRC) during 1991-1992.

During 1991-1992 there were several attempts to infiltrate Israel from Jordan. This stemmed from the growing power of the Muslim Brothers in Jordan, along with the presence of Palestinian Islamic Jihad factions there. Thus nearly all the infiltration attempts from Jordan were committed by Hamas or Palestinian Islamic Jihad. During 1992 the Jordanian authorities increased their efforts to curb this fundamentalist activity, with apparent success (see Table VII).

Table I

Incidents of Riots and Disorder, by Region

	West Bank	*Gaza Strip*	*Total*
1988	18,223	4,827	23,050
1989	34,578	8,033	42,611
1990	57,882	8,061	65,943
1991	29,682	3,730	33,412
1992	28,154	3,569	31,723

Table II

Terrorist Activity Since Beginning of Intifada

	Bombing	*Shooting*	*Stabbing*	*Grenades*	*Fire-bombs*
1988	122	42	50	29	1,787
1989	126	112	126	63	1,286
1990	227	169	137	157	1,162
1991	212	299	127	122	1,448
1992	181	512	111	95	1,280

Table III

Terrorist Activity in 1991-1992, by Region

	West Bank		Gaza Strip		Israel	
	1991	1992	1991	1992	1991	1992
Bombing	148	101	48	61	16	19
Shooting	222	258	72	246	5	8
Grenades	66	35	49	59	7	1
Firebombs	1,140	783	153	391	155	106
Stabbing	40	23	58	62	29	26

Table IV

Fatalities by Terrorist Attacks in the Territories

	Israelis		Palestinians	
	Soldiers Killed	Civilians Killed	Killed by IDF	Killed by Palestinians
1988	4	10	257	19
1989	8	24	250	138
1990	7	16	119	184
1991	4	20	82	193
1992	19	22	127	239

Table V

Punitive Sealing and Demolition of Homes

	West Bank		Gaza Strip	
	Sealing	*Demolition*	*Sealing*	*Demolition*
1988	37	95	12	42
1989	32	56	35	46
1990	73	34	24	51
1991	17	16	12	9
1992	14	1	4	3

Table VI

Deportations by Region

	West Bank	Gaza Strip
1988	22	11
1989	16	10
1990	-	-
1991	-	8
1992	252	162

124

Table VII

Border Infiltration Attempts:
January 1991-December 1992

	1991	*1992*
Lebanon	16	2
Jordan	7	1
Egypt	1	-

PART II

MAIN MIDDLE EAST ARMIES

8. Introduction

Amos Gilboa

Two central strategic events have shaped recent developments in the region's principal armed forces, in both the conventional and the nonconventional spheres: the Second Gulf War and its aftermath, and the collapse of the USSR and the Soviet Bloc.

The Gulf War

The Second Gulf War lent added weight to a series of quantitative and qualitative lessons that were present even earlier. We must distinguish, however, between the act of recognizing these lessons, and their application to the day-to-day task of force-building. By late 1992 many lessons had been applied only partially, and others not at all, due to budgetary constraints.

The obvious lesson to be derived from the war for regional air forces, was that the strongest military asset is a large, high quality air arm with a medium- and long-range capacity, and night-fighting and PGM capabilities. The Arab effort in this regard centered upon building such air forces, that would be on a par with that of Israel.

Syria, for example, began even before the Gulf War to negotiate for supply of MiG-29s--comparable to the American F-15 and F-16, though with inferior ergonomics--and the Su-24, which parallels the British Tornado, with the exception of night-fighting capability. Damascus did not consummate the deal with Moscow, however, due to financial constraints stemming from the Russians' refusal to supply credit as in the past. Similarly, Saudi Arabia sought American F-15Es; these offer a virtual qualitative quantum leap in terms of range, night-fighting capabilities, aerial combat and versatility for a ground attack role. In October 1992 the US Congress approved the administration's request to sell Riyadh 72 F-15XPs, which are inferior to the F-15E mainly with regard to ground attack capability.

In addition, Egypt concluded arrangements to receive additional F-16s of the advanced D Model. Egypt and Saudi Arabia were buying LANTIRN airborne night-vision kits, as well as smart bombs identical to those supplied by the US to Israel: Egypt was getting the GB4-15, a remote-control TV-guided air-to-surface bomb; and both were receiving the Maverick fire-and-forget TV-guided bomb, the AIM-9 air-to-air missile, and a variety of cluster bombs.

Turning to air defense, the lessons drawn by the Arabs and Iran from the Gulf War centered on the need to obtain higher quality weapons systems that an adversary could not easily neutralize electronically--as the US did in the war, and the IDF presumably could do. Thus Syria and Iran sought to acquire Russian SA-10 missile batteries that are considered comparable to the American Patriot. By late 1992 Syria was still unsuccessful in this regard.

Arab military commanders who took part in the Gulf War noted the success of attack helicopters--particularly the Apache--against stationary and mobile armor: these demonstrated considerable night-fighting and all weather versatility, and featured Hellfire missiles that penetrated the T-72, and could, the Arabs assessed, penetrate the Israeli Merkava as well. Supply of Apaches to Saudi Arabia was scheduled to begin in 1993; a transaction with Egypt was to be signed in 1993.

Looking to long-range capabilities, all the Arab armies, and Iran, appear to have concluded that they require versatile (conventional and nonconventional warhead) long-range surface-to-surface missiles. By late 1992 Iran and Syria had already obtained such missiles; Saudi Arabia, Libya and Algeria all sought them. Their deployment was being worked into Arab and Iranian combat doctrine, and they were likely to constitute a central component of the conventional (at a minimum) weapons arsenal used in a new war.

The Second Gulf War hastened the integration of a number of additional elements into Arab combat doctrine. One was night-fighting capability by ground forces. The Syrian Army, for example, was particularly weak in this regard; it concluded that it needed to develop a ground night-fighting capacity, and was expected to absorb modern night-fighting systems in 1993. Another new key element concerned precision-guided munitions. Here the Arab armies developed something of an obsession, centering on two issues. On the one hand, they sought to acquire PGMs. On the other, they invested considerable efforts--with Syria in the lead--in developing a defensive capability against

PGMs. Additional Arab attention--particularly Iraqi--was now devoted to EW and reliable communications equipment. Finally, by early 1993 there were indications of a growing interest in aspects of close air-ground coordination.

The Collapse of the USSR and the Eastern Bloc

Beyond its political-strategic ramifications for the Middle East, the Soviet Union's collapse generated a series of new constraints upon the Arab armies. One key development touched on military acquisitions. Instead of the very convenient credit terms that in effect constituted long-term loans, and that characterized arms supply contracts since the USSR became the Arabs' primary supplier of weapons systems beginning in the 1950s, Russia now insisted on tough commercial conditions: hard currency payments, large downpayments, and strict debt repayment. The brunt of these new demands fell particularly hard upon Syria.

This was countered to some extent, however, by the increased availability, in large quantities and at low prices, of a variety of Eastern Bloc weapons systems. By late 1992 the T-72 tank was being sold for $250,000-500,000--compared with some $3 million for a comparable-quality western tank. Both Syria and Iran took advantage of this development. Egypt, too, considered acquiring diverse parts and systems from Eastern Europe.

Those hastening to purchase Soviet weaponry had, on the other hand, to consider problems that might arise in future due to lack of spares and poor maintenance standards. One result was for potential customers, particularly the Syrians and Iranians, to delay concluding arms deals while they weighed the new pros and cons.

Into this supply gap rushed the Chinese and the North Koreans, who had virtually no political inhibitions and considerable financial motivation regarding supply of advanced systems, including components for nuclear and missile delivery systems. Egypt had been a constant customer of the PRC for years. Now countries like Iran, Syria and Algeria turned to the Far East as well.

Finally, traditional western suppliers such as France and Britain also sought to fill the partial gap in the sophisticated weapons market left by the Soviets.

Force-building: Quantity and Quality

Thus 1991 and 1992 represented a growing momentum in force-building efforts, particularly for Syria, Saudi Arabia, Egypt and Iran. This contrasted sharply with the slowdown that characterized the late 1980s, mainly with regard to Syria (and with the prominent exception of Iraq). In addition to the two principal inputs to this process discussed above--the Second Gulf War and the demise of the Soviet Union--a number of additional developments were specific to each country. Thus Saudi Arabia was spurred on in its force-building efforts by the dramatization of the Iraqi threat, and by a new awareness of the growing danger posed by Iranian force-building. Syria, on the other hand, came into a windfall of additional financial resources from the Saudis and Gulf emirates, enabling Damascus to spend an additional $1.5 billion on new arms. Egypt, too, benefited financially from the war, as large debts were wiped off the books, and 700 surplus American tanks were supplied at shipping cost.

The main characteristic of this momentum, in terms of both current arms supplies as well as those being contracted for, was the dual emphasis on quality multiplied by large quantities. All the sophisticated arms systems that were unveiled in the course of the Gulf War were quickly placed on the Arab arms acquisition agenda. Saudi Arabia led the pack, with primary emphasis on the air component: advanced F-15, F-16 and Tornado combat aircraft, and Apache attack helicopters. Herein lay the primary disruptive element with regard to the Arab-Israel military balance.

Arab ground forces as well were placing a new emphasis on large quantities of high-quality weapons systems. Syria received hundreds of advanced T-72 tanks and Eastern Bloc self-propelled guns during 1992, along with the better part of a purchase of North Korean Scud C 500 km-range surface-to-surface missiles. Iran also purchased Scud Cs. Egypt took possession of several dozen M-1 A1 tanks during 1992, and commenced assembly of additional hundreds. And Saudi Arabia planned to acquire several hundred M-1 A1s and/or the more advanced M-1 A2s, in the coming years, as well as hundreds of Bradley Fighting Vehicles. First shipments of advanced American MLRS units were also scheduled to arrive in Saudi Arabia by the end of 1992.

This rapid expansion was accompanied and reinforced by a growing Arab ambition to undertake indigenous production of principal weapons systems. Egypt, in particular, was moving from assembly (and possibly production) of advanced tanks to production of Scud missiles. Iran was acquiring an indigenous capability to produce Scuds, and was seeking a similar capacity for tanks as well. By the end of 1993 Syria would probably also be able to produce its own Scud Cs, and to begin assembling tanks and artillery. Only Jordan and Iraq lagged behind--the one due to economic difficulties, the other because of the international embargo.

In summarizing developments with regard to ground force-building, we note that the Arab and Iranian armies were placing new emphasis on armor and mechanization, and reducing infantry cohorts. Iraq, in particular, struck over 20 infantry divisions from its order-of-battle in the course of post-war reorganization and rebuilding. Commando units, or elite infantry, were however still being cultivated. The Syrian order-of-battle anticipated the addition of a new armor division, while Saudi long-range plans developed in 1992 called for a doubling of army manpower. Iran for its part was planning to double or even triple its armor formations, to reach an order-of-battle of some 5,000 tanks.

Additional qualitative force-building components in the Arab armies included, first and foremost, a new emphasis on career military personnel. Jordan canceled conscription, and by 1993 its armed forces would comprise only standing army personnel. The Iraqi Army, in its rebuilding efforts, was favoring trusted career personnel. In Saudi Arabia, too, efforts were being made to recruit quality manpower, particularly with academic training--albeit with limited success in 1992. Further, the Jordanian, Egyptian and Saudi armed forces were carrying out joint maneuvers with the US and other western forces. Finally, the Egyptian Air Force's move to adopt western combat doctrine was of note, particularly with regard to enhanced pilot independence and initiative.

The Security Burden

The overall economic burden of security remained high in Iran and the principal Arab states in 1992--but lower than the record levels of the 1980s. Indeed, 1992 levels of defense spending were more or less on a par with those of 1990 and 1991. In Syria, for example, 30 percent of the budget was devoted to defense in 1992, compared with 35 percent in 1990. In 1992 this constituted 8.5 percent of GNP--down from 16 percent in 1985. The large infusion of funds to Syria in the aftermath of the Second Gulf War provided new resources for acquisition and force-building, but on a one-time basis: Syria's fundamental economic problems remained, and continued to require a reduction in the armed forces' routine activity.

Egypt spent some 15 percent of its budget on defense in 1992, constituting 4.5 percent of GNP (as against 7 percent of GNP in 1985). We have noted that Egypt, like Syria, benefited financially from the Second Gulf War, as some 50 percent of its debts were erased; this provided temporary relief for the economy, yet here too the basic problems remained, and the Egyptian Army was also forced to cut back on routine activities.

Jordan's defense outlay of 20 percent of the overall budget in 1992 was down from 28 percent a year earlier. At 9 percent of GNP, Jordan also registered a reduction from the 1980s (12 percent). In contrast to Syria and Egypt, Jordan suffered financially from the Gulf War, losing all inter-Arab aid, and witnessing a freeze in American aid. This brought about a freeze in acquisition plans for major weapons systems. In contrast, the Saudi Arabian defense budget was not decreasing--$14.5 billion (30 percent of the overall budget) in 1992, up from $14 billion two years earlier. In real terms, however, the Saudi budget was still lower than those of the mid-1980s. Saudi acquisitions from the United States from the end of the Second Gulf War to autumn 1992 exceeded $25 billion. Finally, Iran's 1989 Five-Year Plan called for 18 percent of the budget to be devoted to defense, and $2 billion to procurement.

Thus, with the exception of Saudi Arabia and Iran, the region's principal military powers were not likely to increase their military budgets in the coming years. Indeed, during the first years of the 1990s they reduced those budgets. Still they did not, for the most part, seriously delay acquisition of major new weapons systems.

The Nonconventional Dimension

By 1992 at least two Arab states--Iraq and Algeria--as well as Iran were clearly seeking to attain a nuclear weapons capability, and to be able to mount nonconventional warheads on long-range (by Middle East standards) missiles. Iraq and others had already attained chemical warhead capabilities. Egypt confined itself to the chemical and missile spheres, though it retained an advanced technological potential in the nuclear field. Saudi Arabia appeared interested only in long-range missiles.

Iraq was of course a special case. Prior to the Second Gulf War it was moving forward in all three fields, and was within no more than 2-3 years of attaining a military nuclear capability. Despite the obvious setback it suffered in and since the war, Iraq retained a pool of know-how and scientific and technical manpower--and possibly components and capabilities that it succeeded in concealing from the international inspectors--that rendered it the region's principal potential nuclear threat, if and when UN enforcement efforts were to wane or cease altogether. Meanwhile, it was Iran that stood out in 1992 as the country investing the most concerted effort to attain a military nuclear capability--possibly by the end of the 1990s.

9.   The Egyptian Armed Forces
Amos Gilboa

Following the 1973 Yom Kippur War, Egypt detached itself from the Soviet Bloc, and commenced an extended process of reorientation toward the West, primarily the United States. The reasons for this shift were essentially political and economic, but they also comprised a determination to rearm the Egyptian Armed Forces with western weaponry.

The most significant advance in this process was registered in 1979, when Egypt signed a peace treaty with Israel. In seeking to reinforce Cairo's moderate trends, the US made available military assistance that, over the years, approached in content and financial scope America's military aid to Israel. And the American arms market was opened to the Egyptians. Since the early 1980s the Egyptian Armed Forces have undergone a continuous process of reorganization, based on two five-year plans, with two primary objectives: modernization, including mechanization and mobilization of land forces; and westernization of weapons systems.

By 1992 the Egyptian Armed Forces presented a radically different profile from that of ten years earlier. The most significant breakthrough was by the air force. Ground forces, assigned a lower priority, registered a more gradual improvement.

Air Force

Egypt was the first of the Arab countries to recognize that a modern air force with high quality aircraft was a key requisite for fielding a modern force capable of both offensive and defensive operations. Hence the priority assigned to air force acquisition in allocating American aid funds--in recent years, some 80 percent of the annual $1.3 billion grant. In the vanguard was the F-16 combat aircraft, some 80 of which had been acquired by 1992, with two additional packages of 46 F-16Ds in the pipeline beginning in 1992. The obvious goal was to reach a strength of about 190 F-16 high quality aircraft; the only constraint upon this effort appeared to be financial.

Alongside the F-16, Egypt was also acquiring its European equivalent, the Mirage 2000; some 20 had arrived by 1992, with completion of the deal--for 40 all told--held up, again, by financial constraints. The Egyptian Air Force continued to deploy a number of older western models, too--32 Phantom F-4s, 43 Alpha Jet trainers capable of a ground support role, and some 64 Mirage Vs--as well as about 250 aging, but well maintained, Eastern Bloc and Chinese MiG-19s and 21s. Thus by 1992 the Egyptian Air Force order-of-battle numbered some 520 combat aircraft, half western and half former Eastern Bloc in origin. Some 110 unserviceable aircraft were mothballed. As for the air force helicopter fleet, plans were laid to acquire American Apache attack craft to replace French Gazelles; the transport fleet remained based on aging Soviet Mi-8s and the Westland Commando.

The revolution in the Egyptian Air Force was not confined to acquisition of western combat aircraft. It also found expression in a series of additional changes that, taken together, generated a significant new quality dimension. First and foremost was the adoption of western combat doctrine with regard to all aspects of command and control, attack, support and aerial combat roles, training, etc., with the key objective of producing a pilot who displays independent initiative. Secondly, the Egyptians acquired advanced ordnance, avionics, and accessories. They also purchased advanced support aircraft, such as the early-warning Hawkeye, and RPVs and mini-RPVs for real-time intelligence missions. Training in a wide variety of American facilities was expanded. All told, in 1992 Egypt deployed a quality air arm with night combat capabilities, and with plans for further expansion in coming years.

Air Defense

The Egyptian Air Defense arm did not in recent years receive the same priority as the air force. This, in marked contrast to the past, when the opposite priority prevailed. Thus air defense continued to rely primarily on Eastern Bloc stationary SA-2 and 3 batteries, and mobile SA-6s. These have been supplemented with French Crotales and American Hawks, along with western short-range batteries: Chaparrals, and Skyguard combination SAM and AA gun systems. In 1992 the Egyptians showed an interest in possible acquisition of newer SA systems that had served the East German Armed Forces, and were being phased out by the unified German military establishment.

Ground Forces

From the Yom Kippur War until the late 1970s the Egyptian Army comprised 10 divisions: five infantry, three mechanized and two armored. By 1992 the ground forces order-of-battle numbered fully 12 divisions, of which seven were mechanized, four armored and only one infantry. These figures fully reflected the gradual but profound changes instituted in Egyptian ground forces--from an infantry army to a mobile, mechanized and armored force.

Armor. In the 1970s the Soviet T-62 was the vanguard of Egyptian armored force, although in terms of quantity the Egyptians held more T-54/55s. As with the air force, here too the peace treaty with Israel marked the beginning of a transition to western weapons systems. The first stage was the acquisition of some 850 M-60 A3s, around which two new armor divisions were formed. In parallel, and with British assistance, the T-55s were upgraded by converting their 100mm guns to 105mm. More recently, as a "bonus" from the Gulf War, the US gave Egypt 700 M-60 A1s; during 1992 these began to replace unimproved T-55s, after upgrading to M-60 A3 level

All told, in 1992 the Egyptian armor orbat numbered some 3,200 tanks--half western and half Soviet Bloc (some upgraded). The Egyptians still did not have a high quality tank, but this was about to change, along with a growing predominance of western armor and the phasing out of the last unimproved T-54/55s. Thus in 1991-92 Egypt undertook to acquire 525 M-1 A1s from the US, and to establish its own plant to assemble most of them on Egyptian soil, with many imported American components. The tanks would be absorbed into the Egyptian order-of-battle by the end of the third five-year plan in 1998. By early 1993 several dozen of these tanks had been delivered, for orientation purposes.

APCs. Here too, radical changes took place. In the late 1970s Egyptian mechanized infantry still used Eastern Bloc APCs-- primarily the BTR-50. By 1992, of 4,400 APCs in the order-of-battle, half were of western origin: some 2,000 American M-113s provided the backbone of the mechanized divisions, along with another 250 wheeled Spanish BMR-600s.

Anti-tank deployment was also revised. The stand-by Sagger missile was supplemented gradually by the jeep-mounted American TOW. They joined the veteran Milan and the Egyptian-made, British-origin Swingfire.

Artillery. Here developments were slow. Most artillery pieces were still towed, reflecting the heavy cost of self-propelled units, and the Egyptian investment in indigenous production of both artillery weapons systems and their ammunition. Hence the Egyptians also emphasized investment in auxiliary support systems. All told, in 1992 the Egyptians deployed some 2,200 artillery pieces, of which only 200 or so were American M-109 SPs.

Thus between 1978 and 1992 the Egyptian Army became a mobile armored force, reduced in numbers from 600,000 to about 320,000. Westernization was prominent but gradual, and would reach "critical mass" with absorption of the M-1 A1 tank. Interestingly, the introduction of so much western weaponry did not generate a parallel evolution in combat doctrine, which remained essentially Soviet. This contrasted sharply with the aforementioned adoption of western doctrine in the Egyptian Air Force, as well as in the navy.

Navy

With eight submarines and more than 90 combat craft, the Egyptian Navy in 1992 was the largest and most advanced in the Arab world. From an essentially Soviet-supplied order-of-battle and combat doctrine, it had undergone a transformation. This process began with the acquisition of Chinese submarines and placement of orders for MFPBs and missile frigates, and proceeded with the purchase of western combat platforms, electronic combat and control systems and the adoption of western combat concepts. In recent years, joint naval maneuvers were held with units of the American, French, British and Italian navies. Most recently, the Egyptian Merchant Marine displayed impressive logistic skills when it transported two divisions to Saudi Arabia during the Gulf Crisis. Future plans called for arming the Chinese-made submarines with advanced Harpoon sea-to-sea missiles.

Thus the Egyptian Navy displayed both offensive and defensive capabilities in its two potential combat arenas: the Red Sea and the Mediterranean.

Military Industries

Egyptian force building relied to a considerable extent on the country's military industries, which in 1992 remained the most advanced in the Arab world. These provided full or partial solutions to armament problems in three spheres: ordnance, auxiliary systems, and some main battle systems. The centerpiece projects included the aircraft industry at Helwan, which assembled the Alpha Jet and (Brazilian) Tucano trainers, and assembled aircraft engines; the tank industry, which (with British collaboration) upgraded T-55 guns from 100 to 105mm, and commenced preparations in 1992 to assemble the M-1 A1; the Kadr plant, which produced the medium-quality Fahd APC; production of British Swingfire AT missiles and launchers; electronics industries that produced all types of communications equipment and several types of radars; and ammunition plants that produced all types of ordnance for Eastern Bloc tanks and artillery, and for light weapons and mortars.

Pride of place was held by missile and rocket production facilities. Here Egypt had developed a solid infrastructure for R&D and construction, which served the now defunct Condor ballistic missile project that was shared with Iraq and Argentina. Current production in this field included Saqr 30 rockets (30 km range), Saqr 80 rockets that could be fired to 80 km ranges from Egypt's Frog launchers, and--according to reports in 1992--Scud missiles for the launchers remaining in Egypt's order-of-battle. The latter effort was apparently being made with PRC and North Korean support; it was not clear whether the project was directed at producing Scud Bs capable of striking at a range of 300 kms, or an extended-range version.

Training, Logistics and Manpower

By 1992 Egyptian training efforts featured, despite serious budgetary drawbacks, both tactical maneuvers and command exercises that concentrated on combined-arms combat, the integrated air-sea-land battle, mobile warfare and special forces missions. Extensive regular joint maneuvers were held with American and British forces. The absorption of western weapons systems was accomplished with a minimum of logistics and maintenance problems.

With regard to manpower, the armed forces succeeded in reducing the percentage of low quality personnel, but experienced difficulty in competing against the civilian market for outstanding university graduates, few of whom joined the standing army. This problem became particularly acute as sophisticated western weapons systems were absorbed. For this reason, as well as for considerations of internal security, the regime made a constant and successful effort to assure the officer echelon a privileged status in Egyptian society, with regard to salaries, benefits and the like.

Gulf War Lessons

Two Egyptian divisions, one armored and one mechanized, took part in the lead assault on Iraqi defenses in Kuwait. While the Iraqis put up a weak defense, the Egyptians nevertheless claimed to have carried out a successful combined-arms operation and to have operated their artillery and engineering units efficiently. In contrast, American sources assessed the Egyptian performance as middling.

Whatever the merits of the Egyptians' combat operation in the Gulf, their transfer of two divisions to Saudi soil was judged an impressive logistics operation. This points to the first Egyptian lesson from the Gulf experience: the importance, for the leading Arab military power, of a force projection capability throughout the Middle East.

Secondly, the Egyptians' experience (unlike that of the Syrians, for whom this was new) reinforced what they had already internalized regarding modern combat doctrine: the importance of the mobile combined-arms battle, featuring numerous special task forces and heavy air support; real-time intelligence; proper use of air PGMs; the advantages of night-fighting capabilities, including thermal target acquisition and tank and Apache helicopter night-vision firing; and the failure of (Iraqi) static defense that relied on prepared fortifications and obstacles in the face of air superiority and maneuver by armor and mechanized formations.

The Nonconventional Dimension

By 1992 Egypt had a broad infrastructure of R&D and personnel in the nuclear field, including a proven capacity to produce laboratory quantities of heavy water and the possession of a "hot" laboratory capable of separating plutonium at laboratory levels. In 1992 the Egyptians planned to enlarge the capacity of their small veteran research reactor at Inshass, and to purchase another research reactor from Argentina, with a 22 megawatt capacity. There were scattered reports of contacts with Canada and with the PRC for the acquisition of 600 and 300 megawatt reactors, respectively. All these activities were restricted to the civilian field; no Egyptian military nuclear effort was evident. Egypt's considerable efforts to address Israel's and Iraq's perceived nuclear capacities (the latter not usually publicly acknowledged by Cairo due to inter-Arab sensitivities) were played out strictly in the diplomatic arena.

Turning to chemical weaponry, Egypt was the first Arab state to produce and employ such arms, back in the 1970s in Yemen. In 1992 the Egyptians retained chemical production capabilities, but apparently did not maintain actual chemical weapons in their order-of-battle, sufficing instead with a defensive capacity against chemical attack. In the realm of biological weapons, too, Egyptian efforts apparently did not exceed a research capacity.

Concluding Assessment

In 1992 the Egyptian Armed Forces concluded ten years of modernization, based primarily on cooperation with the United States. A third five-year plan was to commence in 1993. The most prominent changes took place in the air force, followed closely by the navy; they featured not only the introduction of western weapons systems, but western combat doctrine as well. In contrast, while the Egyptian ground forces did acquire an enhanced capability to conduct combined mobile operations, the more significant evolution--acquiring large quantities of quality western weapons systems and adopting western combat doctrine-- would only commence in earnest in 1993, with absorption of the first M-1 A1 tanks.

Finally, the production and assembly capacity of Egypt's military industries added a unique dimension to Egyptian force-building efforts. In this regard, the production of surface-to-surface missiles was possibly the most significant, and dangerous, development in 1992.

10. The Iranian Armed Forces
Amos Gilboa

During the five years from the end of the Iran-Iraq War to 1993, the Iranian Armed Forces were effectively licking their wounds. They were incapable of posing a threat to Iran's close neighbors. But from 1990 on, a number of processes commenced that were designed to give Iran "decisive strategic capabilities" by the second half of the 1990s--assuming, of course, the absence of outside intervention or new domestic constraints.

In this chapter we shall present and assess the Iranian force-building process and its ramifications, and Iran's order-of-battle as of late 1992.

Primary Force-building Directions

The key directions of Iran's force-building plans for the 1990s rested on the country's financial and manpower resources, on the one hand, and on the main lessons derived from the Iran-Iraq War with regard to Iran's military weaknesses, on the other. Those lessons pointed to a glaring inferiority in the air; the requirement for a significant surface-to-surface missile force (Iran ended the war with a few Scud B launchers and no missiles); and an inferiority in armor--Iran ended the war with 200 tanks, against Iraq's 4,000.

These lessons, in the order presented above, became the Iranian order of priorities for force-building. All acquisition programs were adjusted accordingly, and--an obvious lesson derived from the embargo on weapons sales to Iran--were accompanied by an unequivocal requirement that every transaction involve the transfer of self-production capabilities to Iran. Beyond these conventional force-building requirements loomed the transparent design that Iran enter the next millennium as a nuclear mini-power.

Air Force

By the end of 1992 the air force's active orbat of combat aircraft comprised some 195 planes, including 105 American F-

14s, F-5Es and F-4D/Es, organized in 12 combat squadrons, and about 65 Eastern Bloc quality aircraft, organized in two MiG-29 squadrons and one Su-24 squadron. In mothballs or inactive were another 200 planes or so: about 95 American aircraft that served for cannibalization purposes to keep the 105 aforementioned planes running, and some 115 planes that had arrived from Iraq during the 1991 Gulf War (two squadrons of Su-24s, two squadrons of Mirage F-1s, and a reduced squadron of MiG-29s).

The Iranian objective was to build an air force comprising about 300 advanced multi-role combat aircraft, with the MiG-29 and 31 (the latter not yet supplied outside of Russia) and Su-24 at the heart of the force. We have noted that over one-third of this number were already in Iranian hands by late 1992 (65 in combat squadrons and several dozen from Iraq). Thus the forecast for at least the coming five years postulated, first, absorption of the Iraqi planes, followed by absorption of additional MiG-29s and Su-24s remaining to be supplied from a $10 billion deal signed with the USSR in 1989. During 1992 discussions began regarding acquisition of MiG-31s. As for the Mirage F-1s from Iraq, the Iranian intention to base the air force on Russian weapons systems appeared to rule out their absorption into the active fighting force; rather, they were probably destined to serve as bargaining cards, to extract alternative compensation from Iraq at an appropriate time.

If despite economic difficulties, Iran were to succeed in its air force building effort--and we recall that this is its highest priority--then during the second half of the 1990s the Iranian Air Force would be one of the strongest in the Gulf theater, with operational capabilities (using mid-air refueling) throughout the Fertile Crescent and Gulf region.

Air Defense

The 1989 major transaction with the USSR also comprised several mobile SA-6 batteries, along with stationary long-range SA-5 batteries. During 1992 the Iranians negotiated to acquire the SA-10, which is roughly parallel to the American Patriot. SA-2 batteries and radars were acquired from China. Thus, like the air force, the Iranian Air Defense would rely on eastern weapons systems, with the SA-10 the central system.

Surface-to-Surface Missiles

Here too Iran appeared to be in the early stages of a radical buildup. We have noted that it ended the war with Iraq without any missiles in its order-of-battle. By late 1992 it had acquired, from the PRC and North Korea, at least 300 Scud Bs and an unknown number of launchers, a number of Scud Cs with a 500 km range, and several dozen CSS-8 150 km range missiles. Negotiations were progressing with North Korea to purchase Nodong 1,000 km range missiles, once development was completed in 1993.

In these missile dealings Tehran was successful in obtaining transfer of the appropriate technologies for its own production efforts. The PRC transferred rocket and missile (apparently the CSS-8) technology. In 1993 the Iranians hoped to operate Scud B and C production lines based on North Korean technology. Nodong technologies were also likely to be transferred. Thus it was clearly possible to envision an indigenous Iranian capability to produce missiles with ranges of 1,000 km, and then to extend this range even further. The distance from Tehran to Tel Aviv is 1,600 km.

Ground Forces

In 1992 the Iranian ground forces numbered some 385,000 personnel, of whom about 195,000 were professional and regular army, 150,000 Revolutionary Guards, and 30,000 Basij militia volunteers. The Basij comprised hundreds of thousands of personnel during the Iran-Iraq War, but most were released soon thereafter. Iran did not have any standardized reserve service.

The army fielded 10-12 divisions, of which four were armor, seven infantry and one special forces. The Revolutionary Guard order-of-battle was less structured, and included 28-30 divisional frameworks, of which two were armor, two mechanized and the remainder infantry. All these forces together deployed some 700-800 tanks, including several dozen Polish T-72s and a few T-62s, and 700 APCs, of which 100 were BMP-1s; the remainder of Iranian armor was a general mixture of outmoded eastern and western models. Similarly, the 1,500 to 2,000 artillery

146

pieces were primarily towed 122 and 130mm models from the PRC, North Korea and the USSR.

The obvious asymmetry between the large number of divisional formations and the small quantities of weapons platforms represented the gap between standards and reality. The situation was particularly serious with regard to tanks and APCs. Revolutionary Guard armor divisions deployed a few dozen tanks, and mechanized divisions a total of around 100 APCs. The regular army divisions were only slightly better off. All divisions, but particularly those of the Guards, also suffered serious manpower deficiencies, due apparently to recruiting and organizational difficulties (the country, with a population of at least 55 million that until recently grew at a rate of 3.8 percent per annum, could hardly be considered manpower-deficient). The only branch that appeared to be relatively well off was artillery, although it lacked any significant numbers of SP artillery.

The long-term Iranian objective was to build a force of 5,000-6,000 tanks, most medium and high quality, about 2,000 self-propelled artillery pieces, thousands of APCs, and thousands of tank and APC transporters. During 1991 and '92 the Iranians negotiated acquisition of these items with Russia, Poland, Hungary, Czechoslovakia and others from the former Eastern Bloc. In late 1992 an extensive deal was reached with the Russians for the supply of large quantities of advanced tanks and APCs, beginning in 1993.

The division of labor between the army and the Revolutionary Guards assigned the former the task of defending the country's borders. Hence it received priority in weaponry and trained manpower. During 1992 the army held several extensive combined-arms maneuvers; it was impossible to assess their professional level. The Guards, with responsibility for internal security, export of the revolution and special operations, received a certain priority in terms of overall service conditions, and enjoyed high prestige. Recruits had to pass rigorous tests of loyalty and piousness, rather than professional military standards. But even the standing army tested for religiosity at the conclusion of courses.

Navy

The Iranian Navy in 1992 remained essentially the force built by the Shah, based on advanced western craft: primarily three destroyers and five frigates/corvettes. It was not depleted by the war with Iraq, where it displayed clear naval superiority over the Iraqi Navy. Over the years, the embargo created a spares problem, with North Korea and the PRC supplying what they could.

Despite the lack of priority attributed to naval force-building in the overall Iranian plan, a deal was made with Russia to supply two or three Kilo-class submarines--the most advanced non-nuclear submarine available--and Iranian crews were trained at a Russian base in Latvia. The first of these submarines was delivered in the fall of 1992, midst considerable controversy provoked by American objections to the deal. These craft gave Iran the potential to blockade the Straits of Hormuz, and to interfere with shipping lanes in the Gulf of Oman and the Indian Ocean--a threat of considerable import for the Saudis and Americans. Iran was also scheduled to receive from the PRC MFPBs armed with C-801/2 sea-to-sea missiles, as well as Silkworm shore-to-sea missiles.

Nuclear Capabilities

During 1992 a number of reports appeared to indicate that Iran was taking serious steps to acquire a military nuclear capability by the end of the decade. New infrastructure projects included expansion of nuclear research centers in Tehran and Ispahan, and construction of a new center at Kazvin. These centers apparently were engaged in plutonium separation, as well as in research into diverse methods of enriching uranium. At the Tehran center, the PRC constructed a small (27 kilowatt) research reactor. Iran and India began negotiating in 1991 for the supply of a 10-15 megawatt reactor based on natural uranium and heavy water. Negotiations also took place with Pakistan and Argentina for the construction of additional research reactors.

Iran was also seeking to refurbish two power reactors ordered by the Shah that were damaged in the war with Iraq. A deal was made with the PRC in June 1990 for construction of a

300 megawatt power reactor. After more than two years of delays due to American pressure on Beijing, the deal was said to be finally sealed and ready for execution in September 1992. Similar American pressure appeared to be more effective in keeping Moscow from carrying out a transaction signed in 1990 for the supply of two 440 megawatt power reactors.

Iranian nuclear scientists, engineers and technicians were being trained primarily in Western Europe, Pakistan, the PRC, Argentina, and in Iranian universities and nuclear research facilities. Considerable effort was invested in persuading Iranian nuclear experts who had fled the Khomeini regime to return, while Iranian emissaries conducted 'executive search' missions for nuclear experts from the former Soviet Bloc. Here some initial success may have been registered. In contrast, there appeared to be no foundation to reports during 1992 that several nuclear warheads had found their way to Iran from the Muslim republics of the former Soviet Union.

Iran did not deny having nuclear ambitions, but qualified them as legitimate and confined to peaceful purposes. An IAEA mission in early 1992 reported "nothing suspicious" in the Iranian nuclear program. It was difficult not to recall the Iraqi precedent, and the attendant lesson: IAEA inspections cannot uncover military uses of nuclear facilities if the location of the facilities is not known.

11. The Iraqi Armed Forces
Amos Gilboa

In the 1991 Gulf War the Iraqi Armed Forces absorbed a terrible blow--perhaps the most serious thrashing ever to an Arab army--but did not break. The army's basic structure survived, along with its command and control network.

The second half of 1991, and 1992, witnessed two central recovery processes: the armed forces were rebuilt and reorganized around existing resources, in view of the international embargo that prevented replenishment of munitions stocks; and, in parallel, the army was deployed, and with considerable success, for internal security tasks. At the same time, a national effort was mounted to retain as much as possible of Iraq's residual nonconventional capabilities, particularly in the nuclear and medium-range ballistic missile realms.

In this chapter we shall present and analyze Iraq's military strengths as of early 1993, the rebuilding process and its objectives, and assess the armed forces' current and future capabilities.

Ground Forces' Orbat and Strength

One of the principal problems confronting any attempt to determine the Iraqi order-of-battle, and particularly the strength of its main weapons systems, is that of Iraqi losses in the war. By late 1992 no reliable figures were available, and it remained difficult to determine what weaponry had been destroyed, abandoned or assumed lost, and what had been restored to serviceability. Our figures reflect the active inventory of the Iraqi orbat that can be ascertained on the basis of a variety of sources.

In summer 1992 the Iraqi order-of-battle numbered 28-30 divisional frameworks, as against 67 prior to the war. These comprised six armor divisions (nine before the war), four mechanized (five previously), and 18-20 infantry (52). The army counted some 400,000 troops on active duty. They deployed about 2,500 tanks, including several hundred T-72s (5,500-6,000 before the war), 3,000-3,500 APCs (6,000), and some 1,500 artillery pieces, most towed and a few SP (4,500 before the war, of which 500 SP).

Refurbishing and Reorganizing the Ground Forces

The ground forces' order-of-battle and strengths reflected the objectives and significance of Iraq's reorganization efforts. As long as the embargo held, the army had to be adapted to existing resources, and its size reduced. In the short term, it had to be made ready to deal with internal security problems and to defend the country's borders.

Reorganization meant, first of all, the release of hundreds of thousands of reservists, the dismantling of divisions, dispersal and amalgamation of formations and, overall, drastic reduction of the order-of-battle. Here the emphasis was on reducing the infantry orbat, while preserving the armor and mechanized components. In so doing the Iraqis finally applied, under duress, one of the key lessons of the Iran-Iraq War, which had hitherto been neglected. A key priority was to fill the large gaps in the manpower standard of divisions that remained--again, with priority assigned to armor and mechanized units. The Iraqis' organizational skills enabled them to absorb new cohorts of recruits quickly and systematically.

The army's training infrastructure, including divisional training bases, was barely damaged in the war. It quickly and efficiently set to work producing skilled technical personnel, commanders and soldiers with field skills. Here particular emphasis was placed on permanent serving personnel. Economic inducements--salaries 150 percent higher than in government service, living allowance grants, etc.--reflected the regime's determination to reform a large and loyal cadre of professional soldiers despite the country's drastic economic circumstances.

This process quite naturally awarded top priority to the rapid rebuilding of the Republican Guard, which remained the quality backbone of Saddam Hussein's regime. The Guard was restored to its previous armor and mechanized strength: three armor and one mechanized division, at full standard. But its infantry divisions were reduced to three. In parallel, steps were taken to establish a "Special Republican Guard"--a new force dedicated to internal security tasks, that numbered ten infantry battalions by mid-1992, and was still growing.

That this rebuilding process went ahead despite the embargo reflects the fact that the army remained intact, with strong foundations upon which force-building could recommence. On this basis the Iraqis were able, after rebuilding their technical and maintenance infrastructure and reopening military industries that survived the war, to cannibalize diverse weapons systems, some of which had become inoperable during the war; restore other systems damaged in the war; carefully (but painfully) dig into spare parts stores that survived the war--all this, under a rather drastic austerity regime.

Training, Combat Readiness and Deployment

In almost every speech he made in 1992, Saddam Hussein reiterated his three top priorities for restoring the army: training, training and training. He coined this motto with the objective that individual field skills become virtually reflex actions. Indeed, individual and team training was at the center of army instruction activities as new units were systematically readied. Every formation that completed its rebuilding process underwent a series of fundamental (up to battalion level) maneuvers. By late 1992 maneuvers had reached brigade level; an initial corps-strength exercise was held in early 1993.

The Iraqis undoubtedly drew lessons from the Second Gulf War (1991), just as they did from the First (Iran-Iraq) Gulf War. These presumably included the need to create combat depth and to improve the balance between infantry and armor/mechanized contingents, as well as requirements for concentrated deployment of combat helicopters, acquisition of long-range artillery, armor force maneuverability, etc. Most of this, however, is supposition; the only reliable information in this regard points to three clusters of lessons: the need for younger and more skilled NCOs and officers with better field skills; improved deployment against PGMs and EW systems; and sharper application of tactical lessons gleaned from the Iran-Iraq War.

All these efforts to enhance training and force-building undoubtedly would continue to suffer from the exigencies of current internal security tasks. Here as elsewhere, the Iraqis systematically set about reducing damage to a passable minimum, so that current security would have the least possible drag effect on force-improvement efforts. Thus for example, the Republican Guard was not used against the Kurdish and Shi'ite rebellions unless absolutely imperative, while those units that were deployed were rotated regularly.

In summer 1992 an enhanced effort was commenced to suppress the Shi'ite rebels in the marshes of southern Iraq. Relatively large units, particularly infantry, were deployed, and engineering units set about building dikes to drain the marshes. In contrast, activity against Kurdish rebels in the north was limited. UN-sponsored air activity out of southeast Turkey constituted a central deterrent against Iraqi military efforts in the north.

The Iraqis' basic deployment situated about half the order-of-battle opposite the Kurds and along the border with Iran; the Republican Guard was deployed in and around Baghdad; and the remaining army formations were deployed in the south, and facing Saudi and Syrian forces.

Air Force and Air Defense

Of the 700 aircraft in the Iraqi order-of-battle on the eve of the Gulf War, there remained after the war around 400. This constituted a loss of close to half of Iraq's air power. Worse, the Iraqi Air Force was left with almost no Su-24s and only about 40 Mirage F-1 quality combat planes, and with few MiG-29s (most of which were transferred to Iran during the war, and remained there). Thus about half the remaining air orbat comprised outdated MiG-21s, and the other half medium quality MiG-23s and Su-7/20/22s.

An additional setback until the spring of 1992 was the fact that Iraqi Air Force planes were not flying at all, in accordance with the ban on all but helicopter flights. The Iraqis found a variety of compensatory means, such as extensive use of simulators, and training by Iraqi pilots in foreign countries. In April 1992, after Iranian planes bombed a Mujahidin i-Khalq Iranian rebel base inside Iraq, the Iraqi Air Force took to the skies despite the ban, observing only the prohibition on flights north of the 36th parallel, and was not challenged by the international coalition. The return to training and a normal routine in air force squadrons was an important turning point. It was accompanied by the repair and restoration of air bases damaged in the war, including those at H-2 and H-3 in western Iraq. Beginning in summer 1992, the air force even took part in combat against the Shi'ite rebels in the southern marshes, withdrawing north of the 32nd parallel only after clashes with the US-led international air contingent there.

The Iraqis were more fortunate in preserving most of their helicopter force during the Gulf War, largely through successful camouflage operations. Out of some 350 combat and transport helicopters, about 300 survived the war; 100 combat, and 200 transport. Adding in light helicopters, the Iraqi post-war orbat reached around 400. These played a major role in counter-insurgency activities against Kurds and Shi'ites during 1991.

Iraqi Air Defense suffered heavy blows in the war, but did not collapse. By late 1992 it was reorganizing, based on existing resources, despite the embargo. Command and control systems were particularly hard hit in the war. The most central facilities were restored, but peripheral facilities were still functioning on an improvised basis in late 1992. The detection and early warning system was also badly hit, and by late 1992 had still not been restored. Thus Iraqi monitoring of aerial activity was based on ground observation, together with a few radar stations the Iraqis had succeeded in restoring to serviceability.

Finally, the SA missile alignment was eroded during the war by about half--from 200 heavy and light batteries, to 100 or so. As with ground forces, here too extensive organizational efforts were made to regroup and disperse units; the Iraqis managed to render operative (before returning them) four Improved HAWK batteries taken from the Kuwaitis. The greatest problem encountered was that of spares, particularly with regard to western systems such as the Roland.

In the winter of 1992-1993 the air defense alignment was again eroded--this time by American aircraft attacks on units deployed south of the 32nd parallel. While it was difficult to estimate damages, the Iraqi recovery program was undoubtedly affected.

The lessons drawn by the Iraqis in the air arena from their encounter with the world's largest and most qualitative air power are not known. Throughout the Gulf War as well as the clashes over the 32nd parallel in 1992 and 1993, the Iraqis essentially

154

avoided directly confronting the coalition in the air. In any event, whatever lessons may have been drawn could not be applied with any effect until the embargo was lifted.

The Nonconventional and Missile Dimension

A portion of Iraq's nonconventional capabilities was destroyed in the war; an additional portion was in the process of destruction at the hands of the post-war international inspection teams. Nevertheless it was fair to assume that the Iraqis would continue to possess certain capabilities. Their policy in this regard was two-pronged. On the one hand, they allowed the UN to destroy what it and western intelligence could discover, yet without volunteering any information; on the other, they patiently awaited the day when the inspection regime would end, or at least be reduced in scope and determination, so they could renew their R&D and production efforts. And they sought to hasten this day by harassing the inspection teams.

In the nuclear realm, international efforts uncovered an Iraqi program to produce a nuclear weapon by 1992-93. Toward that end Iraq employed three tracks for obtaining fissile material: centrifugal, electromagnetic, and chemical. Most of the components of this program were destroyed, but serious questions remained unanswered: How much fissionable material had the Iraqis secreted away? Where was it concealed, and could it be uncovered? Did Iraq indeed possess an unacknowledged underground nuclear facility for plutonium production, as alleged repeatedly by David Kay, who headed nuclear inspection teams sent to Iraq in 1991? Clearly beyond doubt was the ongoing presence in Iraq of thousands of nuclear scientists and technicians, whose collective knowledge and experience was now Iraq's greatest asset. All these questions and assumptions informed the assessment that the moment international controls were fully or partially removed, Iraq would renew its efforts to produce nuclear weapons.

In the realm of chemical weapons, both UN and outside sources assessed that the Iraqis had delivered for destruction nearly all their stores of finished weapons systems as well as bulk chemicals. Conceivably this could be explained by a lower level of sensitivity on the part of the Iraqis. Of particular interest was the revelation that Iraq had indeed possessed chemical warheads for its surface-to-surface missiles; by the fall of 1992, 76 had been destroyed. It was less clear whether the Iraqis continued to possess additional chemical warheads that remained undeclared. All told, some 60,000 tons of chemical weapons were uncovered. The process of concentrating them in destruction sites began in July 1992, and destruction was expected to extend throughout 1993 and possibly beyond.

The UN inspection teams were less successful in uncovering biological weaponry. Yet it seemed likely that large quantities of biological weapons were hidden in Iraq, and remained virtually undetectable.

Turning to surface-to-surface missiles, Iraq appeared to have retained considerable capabilities. It possessed about 20 mobile launchers prior to the war. Of these, one may have been destroyed in the war. The UN inspectors destroyed six after the war, and the Iraqis claimed to have destroyed eight themselves--a claim that could not be validated. Thus estimates of the residual Iraqi arsenal ranged from five to 13 mobile launchers. As for stationary launchers, UN teams destroyed several dozen in western Iraq after the war. Incidentally, these launchers had not fired a single missile during the war; all missiles were fired from mobile launchers, which used the stationary sites for aiming purposes.

In assessing Iraq's arsenal of missiles, the point of departure was the 800 Scud Bs supplied to Iraq by the USSR. After the war, UN inspection teams destroyed 62 missiles. If we add to these the missiles fired by Iraq in the first and second Gulf wars, as well as missiles used for test-firings, we reach a total of about 600 missiles expended. Conceivably, a portion of the remaining 200 or so were cannibalized in the course of extending missile ranges (thereby producing the al-Hussein and other hybrids). But it seemed certain that some additional missiles were hidden in Iraq. There appeared to be no basis for claims that Iraqi missiles were stored in Jordan.

Concluding Assessment

In contrast with the huge and clumsy army, saturated with infantry but also rich in weaponry, that Iraq fielded on the eve of the 1991 Gulf War, the post-war force was considerably smaller.

It drastically reduced its infantry component, restored its armor contingent, reestablished a training regimen, enhanced its professional manpower contingent, and learned to function under an austerity regime imposed by the international embargo. Acquisition of new main weapons systems was prevented by the embargo; this was particularly critical for Iraq's air arm.

The army continued to suffer morale and discipline problems, but it was capable of shouldering the two missions it was assigned: dealing with the Kurdish and Shi'ite internal insurrections, and defending the country's borders--particularly that with Iran. By late 1992, and into 1993, the armed forces did not appear capable of carrying out operations at the divisional or corps level, or initiating large scale military operations against a regular army. It would concentrate on developing the existing order-of-battle with the aim of producing a flexible, well-trained force, capable of lower-echelon operations. Considering its inbuilt limitations and the constraints imposed by the Iranian and domestic threats, the Iraqi Army did not appear to pose a near-term threat to either Israel or its immediate neighbors.

If and when, however, the international embargo were canceled or reduced in scope due to new political circumstances, the Iraqi Armed Forces would be at a favorable point of departure for quickly developing an enhanced order-of-battle, with improved strength, primarily in the air and air defense arms. (The Iraqi Navy, incidentally, which was completely destroyed in the war, would have to be built entirely anew.) Were this to happen, and given Saddam Hussein's ongoing political ambitions and the likelihood of quick new Iraqi progress in the nonconventional field, then Iraq would again project a threat both to the Gulf region and to Israel.

12. The Israel Defense Forces
Amos Gilboa

The Second Gulf War did not alter the IDF's guiding security concept. But it did call into question several of that concept's component principles.

For one, it became clear that the IDF did not possess an appropriate countermeasure for the threat of surface-to-surface missile attack, particularly an attack carried out from a distance of several hundred kilometers. The Israeli rear, with its dense population concentrations, remained exposed. It also was evident that, in the event of missile attack from a non-confrontation state, i.e., one that did not directly border on Israel, the IDF could not apply its traditional security approach that dictated transferring the war quickly to enemy territory. It was hardly feasible to send armor divisions to the suburbs of Baghdad. Iraq could only be reached quickly by air power, and to do so Israel would have to risk violating the air space of neighboring Arab states, hence risk war with them too.

Further, due to the large distances involved, the capacity of the Israel Air Force to deliver a substantial blow to Iraq was also constrained. Inevitably, the argument was raised in Israel's security establishment that the air force's deterrent profile against distant enemies had been sharply reduced.

All these considerations raised basic questions concerning a series of new requirements: acquisition of long-distance intelligence, defense of the civilian rear, interception of surface-to-surface missiles, and effective punishment of distant enemies. Meanwhile, intelligence assessments anticipated an expansion of strategic (conventional and nonconventional) threats to Israel over the course of the coming decade, particularly from countries on the more distant periphery: efforts by Iran, Libya and Algeria to acquire medium-range missiles, some with a capability of pinpointing Israeli strategic targets; and efforts, particularly by Iran, to acquire a military nuclear capability. Syria too sought to build a medium-range missile force.

On the other hand, the near and medium-term assessment of the Israeli security establishment forecast, at least through 1994, a reduced threat of Arab war against Israel. This perception applied to the formation of a new Arab coalition, which seemed highly unlikely, as well as to Israel's single most dangerous neighbor, Syria. As for a coalition, the notion of an "Eastern Front" confronting Israel, with an Iraqi expeditionary force as its necessary linchpin, was moved to the back burner by events in the Gulf, for several years at least. Iraq's defeat, the international embargo placed upon it, and the resultant setback suffered by Baghdad's nonconventional plans--all contributed to this turn of events. Syria, with neither Russian support nor an Iraqi backup, now embraced the political option.

Hence the benign Israeli assessment for the near future, and the consequent decision in Israel to take a calculated risk and invest most available resources in an IDF force-building program that was premised upon a quantum leap in qualitative weaponry. Lieutenant General Ehud Barak, who succeeded to the post of chief of staff in April 1991, placed central emphasis on a five-year force-building plan. Thus 1992 was the first full year of the plan's implementation, and of the "shake-up" in the IDF that many had long hoped for.

The Five-Year Plan: Concepts and Principles

The IDF plan was designed to provide answers to two types of threat: strategic and battlefield. The operational concept behind the plan was based in part on the official lessons drawn from the Gulf War. It held that in a future war, the IDF must achieve decisive victory quickly, and with a drastically lower ratio of attrition (in personnel and equipment) than that of the 1973 Yom Kippur War. It must wage continuous warfare--daytime, nighttime, all-weather and in the enemy rear. This meant generating a destructive capacity that would inflict heavy damage on the enemy and strike at his morale, at an early stage in the fighting.

The new concept also called for close integration between land and air forces. Attack-and-destroy tasks would be awarded to whichever force could best accomplish the task, as battlefield conditions developed. It was assumed that a war would involve not only combat echelons, but the rear as well. In any event, the victory would be decided by the offensive, and this remained the basis for force-building.

Against strategic threats, the IDF's long-term answer, as defined publicly by senior security planners, included rear echelon reorganization, long-term intelligence, early warning, a capacity to destroy surface-to-surface missiles (the Arrow anti-missile missile and accompanying systems), and long-distance airborne retaliation. The battlefield long-term formula placed central emphasis on ground and airborne PGMs and C^3I support systems, enhancement of existing armor and infantry capabilities, improvements in the IDF command echelon, and a sharpening of the "operational edge:" the battalion, the squadron and the brigade.

The concept behind these new emphases was two-pronged. First, the IDF's existing menu of weapons systems appeared to have reached a dead end. Theater conditions left little room for maneuver. The Arab armies deployed more or less the same principal weapons systems as Israel. Yet budgetary constraints prevented replacing all the IDF's tanks and aircraft with a new generation, while adding more and more of the same tanks, artillery and planes would not contribute substantively to victory. Indeed, a "victory" in which the IDF suffered, say, 2,000 tanks damaged or destroyed, would be a pyrrhic triumph.

Secondly, Israel's future qualitative edge would have to be based on indigenous, "blue and white" development and production of force-multiplier support and munitions systems. Israel enjoyed certain unique technological opportunities--some already on the shelf, others in the R&D stage--that had remained hitherto unexploited due to budgetary constraints.

Generating these new operational capabilities and upgrading weapons systems deployed by existing formations, with emphasis on the tank, required huge investments. The five-year plan offered two solutions to the budgetary problem. First, a comprehensive effort was made to streamline all systems that did not contribute directly to security, or, in the words of the chief of staff, to cut back on "everything that doesn't shoot." Here a certain risk would have to be taken--that IDF routine activity, including training, would not be adversely affected. All assets were to be brought to bear on those operational capabilities that could ensure a more effective IDF performance on the future battlefield--while always maintaining readiness to rebuff a surprise attack.

A second solution was to increase the IDF's budget if and as Israel's GNP increased. From the early 1980s, and particularly during the mid-'80s, the share of the defense budget in Israel's overall national economy declined. In 1985, for example, the defense budget constituted 45.7 percent of the overall budget, and 11.1 percent of GNP. By 1991 it had dropped to 28.1 percent of the budget, and 8.8 percent of GNP.

Both solutions were also based on the assumption that US military aid to Israel of $1.8 billion annually would continue, and that Israel would be permitted to convert close to $500 million of this to shekels for financing indigenous R&D and acquisitions.

In fact, by 1992 the financial side of the plan had already become problematic. The 1992 defense budget dropped to 24.6 percent of the total, and 8.2 percent of GNP. The plan was structured to absorb annual fluctuations, but revisions were obviously needed. And even more emphasis was now placed on generating funds through economies within the defense establishment; about NIS 3.5 billion would have to be generated by 1996. To reach this goal, the order-of-battle was cut in several sectors, reservists' training exercises were reduced, and training facilities closed. To reduce damage, greater reliance was placed on simulators and single-day exercises, particularly for reserve officers. The standing army was largely unaffected by these cutbacks.

Another step was to reduce reserve duty by half: from nine million days per annum in 1991, to some four million by 1996. Reservists in excess of T.O.M. were cut; the maximum age for combat reservists was reduced to 45; and new and larger cohorts of conscripts enabled further reductions in reserve call-ups. In the West Bank and Gaza, special regular companies were trained for crowd control duties, replacing reserve units.

The professional army was also cut. Rear echelon headquarters manpower standards were sliced by 15 percent, with the goal of releasing some 3,000 professional soldiers and 1,000 civilian employees of the IDF by 1996. About 1,000 professionals and civilian employees were released in 1992 alone. The IDF "standard of living" was also lowered. Travel missions abroad were canceled, and attache offices eliminated. Consumption of water, fuel, food, vehicles and telephone services was conspicuously reduced. Professional soldiers' salaries and perks were not touched, however.

Additional steps included cuts in reserve stocks of all types, and organizational changes in diverse staff headquarters.

For example, the Training Branch of the IDF was scaled down. The National Security College was combined with the Command and Staff College. The Youth Corps was absorbed by the Education Corps, thereby saving NIS 30 million annually. And Ground Corps Headquarters and service units were streamlined.

Taken together, these economy steps were painful. The reduced orbat, the cutbacks among professional officers, and reductions in training all took a certain toll on IDF performance. To cushion the worst effects, it was decided to restrict the reduction in training of any given reserve unit to two years. Extra severance pay and a major effort at fairness helped ease the release of long-time serving personnel.

In parallel, the reduction in manpower was exploited as a springboard for improvement. The induction of ever larger cohorts of new recruits--including thousands of immigrants from the former Soviet Union who tended to test well as officer material--enabled the IDF to exempt lower quality manpower that was previously conscripted. At the same time, standards for officers training could be raised, as could those for officers and NCOs who sought employment in the professional army, and company and battalion commanders could now be offered incentives, such as university studies, to sign on for extended periods of time.

For the first time in its history, the IDF was exposed to the notion of economic planning. All command echelons were given incentives to address unit activities, such as operations and training, in terms of quantitative economics, and to decentralize control of systems and authority to lower levels. Overall, the idea was to maximize exploitation of valuable resources, reduce and enhance expensive manpower, and enhance exploitation of relatively inexpensive conscript manpower.

Ground Forces

The IDF ground forces main order-of-battle in 1992 comprised 12 armor and four territorial divisions; about 3,850 tanks, of which 870 were high quality Merkava Mark I/II/IIIs; some 8,000 APCs of all types, including 5,000 M-113s; about 1,300 artillery pieces, including heavy mortars; and 13 independent brigades of mechanized infantry/paratroopers.

Alongside certain cutbacks in this orbat, emphasis was placed on quality upgrading of existing systems. Thus the first Merkava Mark IIIs were deployed, while an upgrading process for existing tanks involved improved armor, firepower, fire control and night-vision equipment, along with advanced munitions. Infantry units also received new APCs, along with night-vision accessories for weapons systems, and support systems to increase mobility. Artillery units received enhanced munitions, fire control systems, etc.

One of the central lessons drawn from the Second Gulf War concerned the importance of artillery fire, and the saturation efficiency displayed by the American MLRS. The IDF five-year plan envisioned acquiring this weapons system. In addition, it was decided to upgrade the M-109 SP artillery piece, the backbone of the Artillery Corps, rather than enter into an expensive project of producing an Israeli rapid fire SP artillery piece mounted on a Merkava chassis, the Sholef.

In a parallel development, the field corps headquarters was strengthened in 1992, giving it more authority vis-a-vis each individual field corps--infantry/paratroops, artillery, armor, signals and engineering. A host of tasks, ranging from manpower and combat doctrine to responsibility for maintenance and combat medicine, were transferred to the combined field corps headquarters. Training exercises were fine-tuned to emphasize integration of new weapons systems, combined arms operations with the air force and particularly with attack helicopters, night combat, improved infantry field skills, use of simulators, and training of the command echelon.

Air Force

The Israel Air Force order-of-battle in 1992 comprised nearly 700 combat aircraft: some 65 F-15s, 174 F-16s of several varieties, about 140 Phantom F-4s (including the upgraded "Phantom 2000" or Kornas), and 315 Kfirs and Skyhawks. Additional combat aircraft of diverse outmoded types were mothballed. Further, the orbat comprised about 224 helicopters, of which 91 were combat helicopters, including some 18 Apaches.

Following the Gulf War the IAF received 10 used F-15s and a number of transport helicopters from the US. In the summer of 1991 the IAF began absorbing the first of 60 C and D type F-16s, a process that would continue into the first half of 1993. Conversion of the Phantom fleet to the Kornas would continue, as would additional upgrading programs. During 1993 too, the Air Force would decide between the Improved F-16 and the F-18 as its main combat aircraft for the year 2000. With older aircraft being mothballed, within a few years the IAF would be equipped with three or four high quality aircraft: the F-15, F-16, Kornas and possibly the F-18.

Also in 1993, the IAF helicopter fleet was expected to undergo major expansion. In accordance with Gulf War commitments, the US would supply 24 Apaches gratis, and in 1994 would add 10 Blackhawk combat transport helicopters. These gifts would considerably relieve the budgetary pressure on acquisitions from US defense aid funds to Israel. Further, both the Apache and the Blackhawk offered integrated solutions to some of the key lessons of the Gulf War: the important role of the AT helicopter in the land battle, and the Apache's capacity to maintain a continuous all-weather and night-fighting combat profile.

The guiding concept in the IAF's force-building program held that the addition of more aircraft and equipment merely hindered operations and their budgeting. Moreover, once the combat plane orbat was allowed to grow, it would have to be fed, with more acquisitions required every few years to replace aging aircraft. On the other hand, the air force remained the IDF's primary instrument of deterrence. It most characterized the IDF's offensive ethos. The Gulf War had proven the importance of both air superiority and the capacity of the air arm to achieve massive destruction of enemy infrastructure and ground forces. Further, Arab air force-building plans could not be ignored.

Hence IAF force-building would be based on the maintenance, even increase, of the qualitative gap between it and Arab air forces, in four key sectors: manpower, indigenously-produced technology to enhance fire-power and maneuverability, combat tactics, and organizational efficiency. Meanwhile the IDF's overall budget-cutting process hit the air force as well, beginning with a reduction in flight hours. While this produced immediate savings (one flight hour of an F-16 costs $9,000; of an F-15, about $17,000), it also negatively affected training and motivation levels. Hence a happy medium had to be found.

Turning to air defense, after the Gulf War, Patriot SA missile batteries were permanently integrated into the IDF orbat. By 1993 three batteries had been operationalized, with one more to be acquired. Arrival of the Patriots necessitated organizational changes in the air defense alignment.

Navy

By early 1993 the main order-of-battle of the Israel Navy comprised three outmoded submarines, 21 MFPBs of various models, and 46 patrol boats. Post-Gulf War acquisitions involved mainly new and faster patrol boats of the Dabur and Dvora models. Upgrading of existing boats included installation of night-vision systems, advanced munitions, and electronic systems. Of special note was the combat integration of the Barak shipborne missile--a versatile system capable of neutralizing and destroying, at long ranges, missiles, aircraft, drones and smart bombs, as well as surface vessels and terrorist speedboats.

By the end of 1993 the navy would absorb the first of three Sa'ar 5 MFPBs being constructed in the US. Also in progress was construction of two Dolphin-class submarines in Germany--a project that had been cut due to budgetary constraints, then reinstated as part of German aid to Israel after the Gulf War. The first submarine was scheduled for delivery in 1997.

The navy's central operational activity was sealing off the Israeli coast against terrorist incursions from the sea. In 1991-92 it did this with remarkable success.

Current Security Activities against Terrorism

During 1992 IDF anti-terrorist activity in the West Bank and Gaza focused on three key components: intensive operations by special and undercover units; enhanced intelligence capabilities, including airborne intelligence; and the institutionalization of regular companies dedicated to permanent anti-Intifada operations, instead of reserve or combat infantry units. Success in these endeavors enabled the IDF to reduce its manpower deployment in the Territories, reduce collateral damage to training schedules due to Intifada duty, and take the initiative in pursuing hard core terrorist groups. Constant search and pursuit missions by undercover units in the heart of Palestinian population concentrations produced results: many terrorist units were eliminated, while other hastened to give themselves up.

Yet the IDF and other security forces continued to face serious challenges in the Territories in 1992. The Intifada continued to deteriorate from "cold" weapons to use of firearms against Israelis. New terrorist units cropped up to replace those that were eliminated. Neither intelligence nor operational solutions could be found for the phenomenon of Palestinians wielding knives and axes on Israeli streets on a completely individual basis. And terrorist acts launched from the Territories into Israel proper, multiplied.

The IDF was more successful in the Southern Lebanon Security Strip, where it prevented all terrorist penetrations into Israel. Here Hizballah was the principal aggressor. Throughout the year the IDF carried out preventive air and land penetrations into Lebanon against Hizballah bases and units. In one instance, in February 1992, Hizballah Secretary General Abas Musawi was killed by a helicopter ambush on his motorcade.

In the course of 1992 the IDF-Hizballah confrontation appeared to take on a certain dynamic, with its own "rules of the game." Hizballah would attack IDF or SLA units in the Security Strip. The IDF response, particularly in the air, produced Hizballah Katyusha rocket attacks, mainly on the Security Strip. A particularly heavy IDF response produced Hizballah rocket attacks on northern Israel. These attacks escalated in November 1992, and sharpened IDF awareness of the ongoing problem of dealing with rocket attacks on Israeli population centers, and of the potential for escalation in the Israel-Hizballah confrontation.

The problems in the north were illustrative of the near constant burden of routine security activities on all three regional commands--northern, central and southern. Counter-terrorism activity had become the principal yardstick for measuring command success. This apparently unavoidable outcome of the war with terrorism inevitably affected the IDF's capacity to ready itself for the more existential threats presented by the Arab armies and Arab and Iranian force-building efforts.

The Strategic Response

The Rear Command

In December 1991 a key lesson of the Second Gulf War was applied when the government approved the addition of a Rear Command to the IDF's three regional commands. The Rear Command, responsible for defending the rear echelon in war and in peace, was assigned two principal objectives. First, it would free the hands of the other three regional commanders at the warfront so they could concentrate on winning the battle there, without concerning themselves with the rear. Thus the Rear Command became responsible for defense of the country's densely populated urban centers, along with about 90 percent of Israel's strategic targets. Secondly, it would take integrated command over all emergency services, such as Magen David Adom (the Israeli version of the Red Cross), the fire and police departments, local councils, and emergency economic services, through a single organization responsible for preparing the rear echelon for war. It would define combat doctrine, training and organizational needs, and allocate resources.

One of the Rear Command's first activities was to define building requirements that would provide a proximate "sheltered expanse" in dwellings and offices, to replace the traditional bomb shelter, which was now judged to be too distant for most people to reach in the limited early warning time provided by missile attacks. A second step was to renew the public's supply of chemical protective equipment.

The initial organization of the Rear Command would continue for several years. The decision to relegate this task to the IDF had, at least temporarily, closed the discussion as to whether the army or a civilian body should properly take charge of rear defense activities. But not all areas of controversy were resolved. The new command's territory did not, for example, include areas near Israel's borders. Hence when Kiryat Shmona, high in northern Galilee, was subject to Hizballah rocket attacks, it was virtually left to its own devices by the busy Northern Command. And the many civilian institutions now brought under Rear Command authority would of course fight for priorities in allocation of scarce resources.

An Anti-Missile Defense System

The Gulf War also gave impetus to Israel's project of developing the Arrow anti-missile missile and its support systems. In June 1991 Israel and the US signed a memorandum of agreement to cover the second R&D phase. It called for 11 test firings over 45 months, at a cost of $270 million, of which the US SDI project would fund 72 percent. It was only with the fourth and fifth test firings, in late 1992 and early 1993, that the Arrow Project began to show prospects for success. The IDF, while recognizing the need for an effective anti-missile weapons system, insisted that its performance must render successful missile interception a high probability, while its cost--including that of support radar and infrastructure systems--be affordable to Israel. The IDF also demanded that the Arrow system be operational by the late 1990s, in time to counter anticipated theater missile threats.

Intelligence Satellite

The Gulf War also sharpened Israel's requirement for satellite photo intelligence. This found expression in statements by the intelligence establishment, and by Defense Minister Arens before he left office in July 1992, when he noted that Israel hoped to achieve this goal soon. An IDF satellite intelligence capacity would contribute to long-range collection capabilities, as well as to Israel's deterrent profile.

Strategic Cooperation with the US

Israel's strategic relationship with the United States was long recognized as a central element in its overall strength and its deterrent profile. The relationship was enhanced in the aftermath of the Second Gulf War in a number of ways. The US displayed a greater readiness to share advanced technology, by way of maintaining Israel's qualitative edge; it would seek to maintain the annual $1.8 billion defense aid allotment, including $475 million of convertible funds, at least for the near future; and agreement was reached to preposition inside Israel some $200 million worth of American ordnance, and particularly ammunition, thereby aggrandizing the IDF's potential wartime reserve stocks.

Concluding Assessment

The IDF of late 1992-early 1993 was an improved force, compared to that of the pre-Gulf War period, in its capacity to deal with operational and, to some extent, strategic threats posed by Arab armies. Armor, and to a lesser extent infantry formations, were enhanced, as was air force integration into the ground battle. The five-year plan provided a clear sense of direction regarding qualitative force-building, and in calling for removal of outmoded weapons systems from the order of battle, upgrading of existing systems, and introduction of new, smart systems capable of increased and more accurate destruction at greater distances. Armor formations would continue to constitute the IDF's backbone in terms of assault maneuvers and conquest of territory--but no longer in terms of destruction of enemy ordnance and units.

The five-year plan was flexible, and was updated annually. Hence it constituted, in effect, a permanent or revolving long-term development scheme, that determined allocation of assets and annual training activity for the IDF. This appeared to be successful in giving greater stability to combat units. Meanwhile, however, the IDF remained in a constant struggle to allocate scarce resources efficiently. New budget cuts for 1993 compelled the General Staff once again to announce cutbacks: in long-term projects, the order-of-battle, current security activities, reserve stocks, and training.

Thus the basic dilemma of allocating scarce resources among the three main force-building efforts--upgrading existing systems, PGMs, and strategic capabilities--was likely to become ever sharper with the passing years. So would the need to find reasonable trade-offs between "current" cutbacks in training, reserve duty and the like on the one hand, and "future" investments in quality weapons systems, on the other, particularly if in future the general staff were to invest less energy and determination in advancing its long-range planning strategy.

But scarcity of budgetary resources was not the only source of uncertainty for IDF planners. The peace process was taking place in a 'window of opportunity' generated by global and regional developments. What if that window were to close? Iraq, for example, might reestablish itself as a major potential antagonist. Iran, or perhaps some other periphery state, might project a strategic challenge sooner than anticipated.

Within the IDF, the key dilemmas appeared to be primarily organizational. In particular, the new economic orientation for evaluating performance, which the US Army had first introduced during the Vietnam period, would enter firmly into IDF 'organizational culture' only over time. Nor was it certain that this businesslike approach was the right one for an army like the IDF, which had to remain focused on the key objective of winning wars.

Similarly, the new direction in manpower planning was to focus on a large regular or conscript army, with fewer professional soldiers and fewer reserves. Obviously, this produced budgetary savings. But the IDF's main challenge would come from Arab armies and regional technological innovations, and not from current security tasks in the Territories or the Security Strip, or protection of the rear echelon. Did this not require a larger professional army, one with experience that could not be quantified in budgetary terms?

Another dilemma faced by the IDF in recent years was its increasing exposure to public media and political criticism. Training accidents--never absent from any army's routine--became the focus of sharp public scrutiny in 1992, despite IDF successes in actually reducing their scope. Israel's armed forces were no longer, as in the past, immune to public criticism.

Finally, we have noted already the prevalent assessment in 1992-1993 that the near-term danger of war was low, thereby enabling the IDF to take advantage of the peace process by initiating basic reforms to prepare it for more distant dangers. But IDF planners were also accompanying the peace process itself quite closely--planning and preparing for the hoped-for day when they would be called upon to offer their special input to the process: security arrangements.

13. The Jordanian Armed Forces
Amos Gilboa

Between 1990 and 1993 the Jordanian Armed Forces were stagnant. Force-building and weapons system enhancement were at a standstill. The country's dire economic straits did not permit it to devote assets to any significant buildup. Nevertheless during 1992 the armed forces commenced a process of genuine internal change.

Order-of-battle and Force Strength

The Jordanian Army order-of-battle stood in 1992 at four regular divisions--two armor and two mechanized. These were reinforced by reserve formations, which were first deployed for defensive purposes during the 1991 Gulf War, and three regular independent brigades--special forces, and infantry. The air force deployed 103 combat aircraft--F-5s and Mirage F-1s. Air Defense relied on 14 HAWK SA missile batteries, and several dozen low altitude SA missile launchers of Soviet make (SA-8, 13 and 14), integrated at the divisional level.

Clearly the most backward of the Jordanian Armed Forces branches was the air force. All acquisition plans--e.g., for Mirage 2000s--were frozen. Nor did the army renew its armor contingent, or even plan to acquire a high quality tank. But the armor corps could rely on highly trained crews and a high command level, as well as the fact that its platforms were not appreciably inferior to most of those in the regional theater. Hence Jordanian armor continued to constitute a potentially important factor in the regional military balance.

Two additional factors added a quality dimension to the Jordanian ground forces. For one, artillery was advanced and modern, and equipped with quality French fire-control systems. Then too, each division had its air defense brigade, based on the aforementioned Soviet SA batteries, and Shilka radar guidance. Thus despite the absence of a good air force, Jordan retained reasonable defensive capabilities.

Like the other Arab armies, the Jordanians derived lessons from the Gulf War. One touched on the need to improve mobility and transport capacity; another, on the requirement for enhanced infantry and anti-tank capabilities in the defense of mountain passages. On a broader scale, even before the Gulf War the Jordanians had noted the success of PGMs, and were negotiating with the US the acquisition of Hellfire AS missiles for their Cobra helicopters (negotiations were frozen as a result of the events of the war). Finally, in view of their inability to acquire primary weapons systems and advanced ordnance, the Jordanians focused on the need to acquire diverse support systems such as force multipliers, along with spares.

Changes in Force Structure

Perhaps most important were the changes in force structure and personnel management that the Jordanian Armed Forces initiated in late 1991 and during 1992. Here the primary impetus was apparently political.

The point of departure for these changes was the regime's order of priority in ranking its army's broad strategic objectives. Prior to 1991, this began with the defense of the country's borders, followed, in declining order of priority, by the security of the Hashemite regime, and integration into an Arab anti-Israel war coalition. Now, in the wake of the riots of the late 1980s, coupled with the rise of an extremist Islamic movement and its entry into parliament, the Jordanian leadership recognized that regime security must take priority in formulating the army's objectives.

The Gulf War only reinforced this perception. While the army deployed in accordance with its defense plans against Israel, the pro-Saddam enthusiasm that swept the street, with its heavy pro-Palestinian and pro-Islamic overtones, was a source of great concern to the Hashemite regime.

Terrorist activity and incursions from Jordan against Israel in 1991 also contributed to this reappraisal of the army's objectives. Nearly all these activities were carried out by Jordanian Army soldiers of Palestinian origin and/or Islamic fundamentalist persuasion. The internal dilemma posed by these attacks was further sharpened by the fact that most of them were foiled at an early stage by the Hashemite security services.

It was against this backdrop that the regime decided in the fall of 1991 to adapt the internal ethnic composition of the army to its new principal mission: regime security. Thus compulsory military service was suspended, and steps were taken to remold the army as a standing professional force in its entirety. Publicly, the regime cited dire economic conditions as justification for this streamlining move; these undoubtedly existed, but they were not the primary consideration. In early 1992 the regime claimed that the armed forces numbered some 130,000 men, and that its goal was to bring about a reduction to 100,000 (outside estimates had placed the total force contingent at 100,000 or less, without reserves, even before the planned reduction).

In fact, the army had been an entirely professional body prior to 1976. The compulsory service law passed that year generated two parallel trends: a strengthening of the Palestinian contingent in the armed forces, vis-a-vis the bedouin; and an overall force expansion. Now the regime began reversing these trends. During late 1991 and throughout 1992 it first reduced the number of draftees in service, then froze the induction of new cohorts, and finally ordered early release for serving conscripts. The process was expected to be completed by early 1993, at which point the entire army would be based on professional manpower. Nevertheless the regime avoided actually revoking its compulsory service laws--it merely suspended them--presumably to avoid the embarrassment of admitting the failure of its effort to integrate Palestinians, and in order to be able to reinstitute the draft, if necessary, without recourse to new legislation.

Alongside this force-restructuring plan, the regime took additional steps to ensure the loyalty of the armed forces. For one, plans were weighed for reforming the Peoples Army. This militia force saw "action" during the Gulf War, where it reinforced the regime's impression that it was unreliable and disloyal, and should not be issued weaponry, as mandated by standing orders. Hence two alternatives were considered: either introducing far-reaching alterations to improve loyalty, or dismantling the force and replacing it with a smaller National Guard. Beyond this, the regime resolved to give higher priority in terms of manpower and asset allocation to its internal security force.

A number of steps were also taken in 1992 to effect a broad reorganization of the armed forces. The structure of general staff headquarters was altered. Three arms--ground, air, and naval--were established, and subordinated to the ground forces chief of staff (formerly the chief of the general staff of the armed forces), who in turn was subject to a new superior command echelon, commander of combined forces (filled by Fathi Abu Taleb, formerly chief of the general staff, and now promoted to fieldmarshal). The restructuring effort brought about the integration of diverse administrative functions and the streamlining of control and coordination. A number of general staff frameworks were dismantled. And combat units would now receive priority in manpower and logistics allocations.

Concluding Assessment

Economic circumstances have caused the Jordanian Armed Forces to stagnate in terms of force-building and modernization with principal weapons systems. Even limited American military aid of some $50 million annually was frozen after the Gulf War, and was expected to be renewed in 1993 at a lower rate--$27 million. Yet the Jordanians have sought successfully to maximalize their limited assets. They have also successfully utilized loans from France and England totaling some $600 million.

The regime's primary objective in 1992-93 was to field a quality force, essentially professional in structure, and loyal to the king. Consequently force size was reduced in favor of efficiency, organizational modernization, and professionalism in manpower. While no new platforms were acquired, force-multipliers like night-vision equipment and fire control systems were among the most advanced in the Arab world. The air force, on the other hand, was among the most obsolete in the region. Only an unanticipated injection of outside aid could enable Jordan to set about renewing its main combat platforms, beginning with the air force's suspended Mirage 2000 deal.

The overall combat concept of the Jordanian Armed Forces remained essentially defensive. Their capacity to accomplish their defensive missions was certainly adequate.

14. The Saudi Armed Forces
Amos Gilboa

The Iraqi invasion of Kuwait and the ensuing Gulf War found the Saudi Armed Forces in the throes of a force-building program that involved large and extended acquisitions of weaponry. Underlying this dynamic was a Saudi (and American and British) assessment that during the first half of the 1990s the Peninsula was not likely to confront primary threats from its strong neighbors to the north, Iran and Iraq.

The Gulf Crisis revealed the Saudis' security weaknesses, both strategic and tactical: armed forces incapable of defending the country and its oil resources against an enemy like Iraq, and relatively unimpressive battlefield performances, on land as in the air. In this chapter we shall present and analyze the lessons drawn from the war experience by the Saudis, resultant changes in order-of-battle and force levels, and new directions and problems in force-building.

Lessons of the War

The Saudi Armed Forces were the only Arab force that took an active part in combat on all fronts: land, air and sea. The Saudi Air Force carried out some 11,000 sorties, including bombing, interception and escort missions. It downed two Iraqi aircraft and lost two F-15s. American sources assessed the performance of Saudi pilots as "not bad;" training in the US appeared to have contributed considerably to Saudi capabilities. However the Americans hastened to add that the Saudi aircraft performed in a sanitized atmosphere provided by American C^3I capabilities, and that on their own the Saudis would not have managed well.

Saudi ground forces took part in a series of confrontations during the war: artillery battles, the Hafji fighting, and the invasion of Kuwait. General Schwartzkopf's assessment of the Saudi Army's combat capabilities was scoffingly low. Saudi National Guard units, deployed in brigade formations, received a somewhat higher mark. Indeed, the Saudis themselves concluded that their army's performance was poor, particularly with regard to individual field skills, team coordination, officer performance and lack of administrative coordination.

Thus the primary tactical lesson drawn from the war by the Saudis was the need to improve soldiers' field skills and officer skills, and to attract qualitative manpower, particularly with academic training, into the standing army. An attempt to implement the latter lesson had already been made in 1989-90; it was renewed after the Second Gulf War, with a variety of inducements added, but initial results appeared to be unencouraging.

The Saudi Navy also participated in the Second Gulf War. It engaged in minesweeping operations in the Gulf, and took part in the naval blockade of Iraq there and in the Red Sea. A Saudi MFPB sank an Iraqi minelayer. And 12 Saudi ro-ro ships assisted in transporting Egyptian, Syrian and even American forces to Saudi soil. Here performance levels were rated by the Americans as medium. The essential conclusion derived by the Saudis from this experience was that their naval force-building efforts had been justified; it remained now to focus on enhancing the force's professional capabilities.

Of even greater significance for the Saudis were the operational and strategic conclusions and lessons they derived from the war experience. First of all, the long-term policy of building one or more military cities facing every threat or potentially hostile front, proved its validity spectacularly against Iraq. The two military cities facing or near Iraq, Hafer al-Batin and Dahran, provided a vital base for the American force concentration in Saudi Arabia. Their logistical, transportation and aviation infrastructures proved adequate to the task. The Saudis thus concluded that they should construct another such military city in the south of the country, and should expand the existing cities yet further.

Secondly, reliance on Arab military forces as a principal concept of Saudi security proved ineffective and, worse, unfounded. Military salvation at a time of crisis would not come from fellow Arabs. Hence there was neither potential reward in, nor a genuine requirement regarding, entry into security arrangements with other Arab states, particularly of the variety that called for the permanent deployment of Arab forces on Saudi soil. Indeed, it was from the West that military salvation would come. This required that security arrangements be negotiated first and foremost with the United Sates. Still, Riyadh was subject to a series of constraints over this sensitive issue--far more than Kuwait and the emirates, which hastened after the war to sign security pacts with the West.

Finally, there was a perceived need to effect a significant expansion of the Saudi Army and National Guard, and to arm them with the latest, most sophisticated weaponry. This requirement had been formulated even before the war, particularly in the aftermath of the Iran-Iraq conflict, but the Gulf War sharpened it considerably. This brought about the drafting of a long-term plan to double the size and strength of the two services, and of the Saudi air wing as well. The objective was to enable Saudi forces alone to brake the advance of an Iraqi or Iranian surprise attack, until American and other western forces arrived. Yet it was doubtful whether this operational goal could be effected merely by doubling the size of Saudi forces.

Orbat and Force-building

In early 1993 the Saudi Army comprised eight brigades: two armor, four mechanized, one Royal Guard and one special forces. Three of these brigades (one armor, one mechanized and one special forces) were deployed at Tabuq, facing southern Jordan and Eilat; two in the south, facing Yemen; and two in the east, facing Iraq and the Gulf. The National Guard comprised six regular brigades, equipped with American-made APCs and AFVs, along with reserve units.

The Saudi Air Force numbered some 273 combat aircraft (93 F-15s, 72 Tornados and 108 F-5s), about 110 training craft, five AWACS planes, now manned entirely by Saudis, and some 150 helicopters. The Saudi Air Defense comprised 17 stationary HAWK batteries, about 48 Crotale launchers, and six American-operated Patriot batteries. The Saudis deployed 8-12 Chinese-built surface-to-surface missile batteries, with a range of nearly 3,000 km. The Saudi Navy was the highest quality naval arm of any of the Arab countries, and was superior even to that of Iran. It numbered 17 surface ships: nine MFPBs, four American-made missile corvettes, and four French frigates equipped with Harpoon or Otomat sea-to-sea missiles and other advanced weaponry and electronics.

Given the goal of doubling the size of the Saudi forces, the main emphases in long-term acquisitions programs focused on quality aircraft, armor and APCs, enhancement of long-range surface-to-surface missile capabilities, diversification of suppliers, and the requirement that suppliers invest part of payment in Saudi-based projects.

In early 1993 the Saudi ground and air order-of-battle was expected to begin a process of expansion, with the addition of a number of quality main weapons systems: Apache attack helicopters, Patriot SA missiles, American MLRS systems which proved their battleworthiness in the Gulf War, and Bradley APCs. Supply contracts for these systems were signed, but quantities of initial deliveries were not known. In any case, while these systems would clearly upgrade the Saudi forces qualitatively, they would have little effect on overall strength.

Longer term prospects looked more promising. Beginning with the air force, in September 1992 the US administration presented to Congress a long awaited proposal to sell the Saudis 72 F-15XPs--the export version (with air-to-surface attack capabilities reduced) of the F-15E. The proposal had been delayed during the year due to administration considerations involving relations with Israel, as well as to Washington's own arms control efforts in the Middle East. Ultimately it was the domestic economic imperative that provided the justification for declaring the transaction during the US election campaign. Supply of F-15XPs was scheduled to begin within two or three years.

A separate major acquisition deal for advanced aircraft, negotiated as a memorandum of agreement with Britain in the summer of 1988, left the Saudis an option to purchase an additional 48 Tornado attack aircraft. They began activating the option with an initial deal reached in February 1993. The Tornado purchase was part of al-Yamama 2, a major Saudi acquisition program that also comprised separate options for 40-50 Blackhawk helicopters, trainer aircraft, airbase construction, and an additional six minesweepers.

Taking all the Saudi acquisition plans together, the picture for the future was of the strongest and highest quality air force in the Gulf theater, comprising some 400 high quality aircraft of diverse types (F-15, F-16/18, Tornado) and 48 Apache attack helicopters. All acquisition plans also called for purchase of large quantities of the most advanced munitions.

Turning to armor, by the end of 1992 the Saudis confronted a dilemma: the American M-1 A2 production line was about to be shut down. This implied higher support expenses and possibly problems obtaining spares in future. The Saudis held a series of discussions with a variety of American sources and consultants in their search for a solution. One possibility was to acquire the M-1 A1, and add their own improvements. Another might be to acquire the British high-quality tank, Challenger. Meanwhile they ordered several hundred additional M-1 A2s. One way or another, the Saudis planned in the near future to equip their two armor brigades with new high-quality tanks, and to establish an additional five armor/mechanized brigades in the more distant future. They also planned to double the National Guard standing contingent to 12 brigades. To this end, they contracted to acquire 1,100 LAV armored vehicles from the US (first shipments arrived from the US and Canada in 1992), and several hundred TOW launchers.

During the Second Gulf War, the Saudis apparently intended and even made preparations to fire their Chinese-made missiles against Iraq, though they never did so. In any event, the war prompted them to seek at least to double their SS missile strength.

Systemic Constraints

By early 1993 the Saudi order-of-battle numbered 105,000-110,000 soldiers: 40,000 or so in the standing army, about 55,000 (not including reserves) in the National Guard, and some 10,000-15,000 in the Border Patrol and Coast Guard, which were under the command of the Ministry of Interior. In order to double this strength within a few years, the Saudis had to recruit about 100,000 more soldiers. As a variety of inducements and incentives for volunteers proved insufficient, the situation appeared to require a compulsory conscription law. Yet internal concerns--the opposition of tribal and religious leaders, and fear of disrupting domestic stability--evidently constrained the conscription initiative. Even if the Saudi royal family succeeded in overcoming this opposition and passing the law, it might be difficult to enforce. This cast doubt on the Saudis' capacity effectively to absorb the new main weapons systems they had ordered.

In parallel, there were also strong currents of domestic opposition to accepting the permanent presence of western troops on Saudi soil, and even to signing security agreements with the West. These issues were discussed at length with the United States throughout 1991 and 1992. Three primary alternative options were examined: prepositioning of US weapons systems in Saudi Arabia, establishing a routine of joint maneuvers, and enhancing the American naval presence off the Saudi coasts. But by late 1992 no strategic cooperation agreements had been signed in this regard.

Concluding Assessment

In conclusion, a number of strategic trends and counter-trends are worthy of reiteration. On the one hand, Saudi force-building plans were impressive from both a quantitative and a qualitative standpoint. They were designed to render the Saudi Armed Forces the best, from the standpoint of qualitative weapons systems, in the Middle East. On the other hand, it was very doubtful whether the Saudis would succeed fully in realizing these impressive force-building plans. Even if they did succeed, at least partially, Saudi Arabia would still be hard put to defend itself against an enemy like Iran or Iraq. But in a different context--as part of some hypothetical future Arab military coalition against Israel--the Saudis could be capable of dispatching a well equipped, lethal expeditionary force to Israel's southern front, as well as posing a threat to all of Israel's airspace.

15. The Syrian Armed Forces
Amos Gilboa

Throughout 1992 Syria continued to pursue three central force-building processes that commenced with the outbreak of the Gulf Crisis in 1990: strengthening its armor forces, enhancing the overall qualitative dimension of its ground forces, and building a long-range attack arm. In this chapter we shall present and analyze these processes, assess the capabilities of the Syrian Armed Forces, and look at the role of "strategic parity" in light of Syria's participation in the peace process.

Gulf War Lessons

The war constituted a turning point for the Syrian Armed Forces. Prior to the outbreak of the Gulf Crisis, the army was at a low level of readiness. As a consequence of Syria's ongoing poor economic situation, all primary and auxiliary weapons system acquisition plans had been frozen, and force-building efforts had ceased.

Syria's participation in the war--it despatched the 9th Armor Division from the Golan front--altered this negative state of affairs. The beginnings of a rapprochement with the US were effected, relations were improved with Western Europe, and Syria's inter-Arab isolation came to an end. In practical terms, these developments produced a $1.5 billion Saudi grant, together with convenient loans of several hundred million dollars from Western European banks. Of particular significance was the total absence of strings attached to the Saudi grant. Previous Saudi financial aid had been linked to specific projects, and was closely supervised. Moreover, developing international political and economic conditions afforded the Syrians the opportunity to obtain easily available and cheap weapons systems from the now defunct Eastern Bloc.

Syria's armor division participated in the conquest of Kuwait in the back-up echelon, and did not engage in active combat. But its commanders were heavily exposed to western weapons systems and combat doctrine, as they participated in general discussions and diverse command briefings with the

Americans and others. They were particularly impressed on the tactical-operational level with the use of PGMs, the neutralizing of Iraq's air defenses with massive air attacks supported by intelligence and electronic auxiliary systems, and, correspondingly, the supreme importance of advanced quality aircraft in large numbers.

Of even greater importance for the Syrians than these lessons per se was apparently the realization that, if the Americans could succeed with these weapons systems and combat doctrine, then so could Israel, which possessed the same systems and doctrine. In other words, what took place in Lebanon ten years earlier in the air and air defense realms, could be repeated in the event of another round with Israel. If the Syrians had assumed that during the decade since their stark defeat at the hands of the Israel Air Force they had successfully plugged the gaps in their air defenses, the 1991 Gulf War forced them to face up to a different reality.

At the strategic level, the war provided an object lesson for the Syrians of the importance of medium-range surface-to-surface missiles, and of Israel's special sensitivity to attacks upon its population centers. Particularly encouraging was the extreme difficulty experienced by the US--hence Israel too, in future--in destroying mobile surface-to-surface missile batteries that are continually being moved and concealed.

The Syrians' principal difficulty during the 1991-1992 force-building period was in adapting the new program to Syria's proper order of priorities: an advanced air force and air defense, an SS missile arm, and qualitative improvements in the army. The Saudi grant was spent in its entirety on army acquisitions, and fell short of advancing air acquisitions. Thus the main force-building effort was concentrated in the army, in SS missile acquisition and in stocking up on spares; the air force and air defense were kept waiting.

Ground Forces' Orbat, Strength and Force-building

As a result of the 9th Armor Division's sojourn in Saudi Arabia, the Syrians cast about for a replacement formation. Their solution was to plan to convert a reserve armor division to active duty status. This in effect would add an additional division to the order-of-battle in 1991. Thus by 1992 the ground forces orbat comprised, as main units, two armor corps headquarters, 11 four-brigade regular divisions (seven armor, three mechanized and one special forces), one reserve armor division being established, two independent infantry brigades, and seven independent commando formations.

Moreover, during the second half of 1991, and throughout 1992, the ground forces absorbed a very large quantity of advanced mobile weapons systems: 400 Improved T-72 tanks from Russia and Czechoslovakia, and 300 SP artillery pieces from Bulgaria. This large a scope of transactions carried out in such a short period of time was without precedent for the Syrian Armed Forces. It constituted a qualitative as well as quantitative quantum leap: Syria's T-72 orbat grew by almost 40 percent, and its SP artillery pieces were doubled.

If the T-72 deal seemed a natural development, the purchase of SP artillery aroused unusual interest. The Syrians had always been complacent about their towed artillery--particularly 130mm medium and D-30 122mm field guns. Even after the purchase of 300 self-propelled artillery pieces from Bulgaria, most Syrian artillery was still towed. The question now arose, whether this new direction reflected Syrian considerations of developing a clear offensive option on the Golan. Future purchases would be the best indicator.

By the end of 1992 the Syrian order-of-battle comprised about 4,800 tanks (some 1,500 T-72, 1,000 T-62, and over 2,300 T-54/55), some 5,000 APCs, of which 2,450 were BMP-1s, and around 2,400 artillery pieces (400 SP). Speculation as to the deployment of the newly arriving T-72s centered on a number of possibilities. One particularly appealing option was to equip most of the armor divisions with T-72s, convert the reserve armor division to a regular formation with the tanks made available by the absorption of T-72s in regular divisions, and gradually set up new armor brigades on the basis of tanks made available.

Night-fighting capabilities were always a weak point with the Syrian Army. Indeed, it was one of the most backward Arab armies in this regard. In the aftermath of the Gulf War the Syrians launched a concerted effort to locate such systems among both eastern and western suppliers. By late 1992 no transactions were known to have been completed--apparently due to the high prices asked for the large quantities required by the Syrian Army; but they were almost certainly in the pipeline for 1993.

Ground Forces' Manpower, Training and Maintenance

In late 1992 the Syrian Armed Forces numbered some 400,000 personnel, of which slightly more than 300,000 were in the army. The latter apparently suffered some difficulties in this regard, and manpower gaps were conspicuous. High school and university graduates continued to be integrated into the regular army as NCOs rather than officers, as a matter of policy. But it was difficult to judge the qualitative level of the Syrian soldier. The impression left on the Americans by the Syrian armor division in the Gulf was extremely poor. Yet this must be taken with a grain of salt, since the division's officers and NCOs were known to have shown little enthusiasm for their task.

With regard to training, there were also few surprises. Maneuvers and exercises--for commanders at all levels, live fire armor corps exercises at the brigade level, a divisional exercise, etc.--proceeded according to routine, although budgeting constraints had a debilitating effect on training levels. It stands to reason that in the course of their division's sojourn in Saudi Arabia, the Syrians noted the simple methods used by the Iraqi Army to counter diverse smart bombs. Given that the Syrians assumed that Israel deployed similar weaponry to that of the Americans--an impression driven home by post-war statements of senior Israeli military officials--they presumably hastened to work into their training and instruction programs the lessons of passive defense against PGMs. Meanwhile maintenance continued to present difficulties to the Syrian Army, although weapons system serviceability was satisfactory.

Surface-to-Surface Missiles

Negotiations with North Korea and the PRC for the purchase of medium-range surface-to-surface missiles took place even before the Gulf Crisis. Indeed, a deal signed with North Korea before the crisis included the acquisition of several dozen Scud Cs, and a small number of launchers, as well as the transfer of technology for indigenous production of the missile. The Scud

C has a range of 500 km, a 700 kg warhead, and a CEP of one km (according to some claims, 500 meters). The deal was carried out during the second half of 1991 and throughout 1992, and most components were supplied, although by late 1992 the production line had not yet been set up. In July 1992 the Syrians carried out their first test firing--an indication of the advanced state of their preparations. Yet by late 1992 the missile had not yet become part of the operational order-of-battle.

The primary ramification of the successful absorption by Syria of the Scud C was clear. Syria had obtained a capability to strike at most of Israel, including key strategic targets, without having to deploy launchers on the Golan, but rather in more protected and secluded areas north of the Damascus region. This gave their launchers and attendant systems greater survivability. Once the production line was established, the only remaining challenge for the Syrians would be production capability, and quantities of new missiles placed on reserve. Syria would be independent in this regard, and free of any residual dependency on supply of missiles from Russia or elsewhere.

One key question remained unanswered: would Syrian missiles be designated as a deterrent against attack by the Israel Air Force on strategic targets in Syria, and thus be launched only in the event of such an attack, or would they be fired as an integral part of a Syrian offensive war plan? In any case, by the end of 1992 the Syrian missile orbat comprised 18 Frog rocket launchers, 18 SS-21 launchers, 18 Scud B launchers, and a small number of Scud C launchers. Moreover, a deal with the PRC for M-9 missiles was still in the cards. In this regard it was not clear whether Syria would suffice with its Scud C capability; nor was it certain whether American pressure on Beijing would scuttle the M-9 deal.

Finally, there remained the option for Damascus to mount chemical warheads on its Scuds. The Syrians are known to have developed a chemical warhead in the late 1980s. Western intelligence sources reported that a test firing of a chemical warhead was conducted in the spring of 1992. If so, then clearly the Syrians were not neglecting this aspect either.

Air Force and Air Defense

Paradoxically, it was in the sectors of highest priority that the least force-building progress took place. In extensive deliberations with the Russians that commenced prior to the Gulf War regarding a major long-term arms program, emphasis was placed on acquisition of two squadrons of MiG-29s and one of Su-24s. The Syrians envisioned in these planning sessions a total force of some 150 MiG-29 and Su-24 high quality aircraft. By late 1992 there were no indications that a deal had been reached. The primary obstacle was the Russians' new and stringent conditions of payment: a large hard currency advance, payments during actual delivery, and a demand that Syria pay its old debts to the former Soviet Union. Of course the Syrians recognized that, unlike in the case of tanks and SP artillery which could be found elsewhere in the former Eastern Bloc, no supplier could replace the Russians when it came to MiGs and Sukhois.

Thus by late 1992 the Syrian Air Force deployed about 530 combat aircraft: 20 MiG-29s, 20 Su-24s, 100 Su-20/22s, 40 MiG-25s, 130 MiG-23s (of which 50 Improved), and over 220 MiG-17/21s.

Nor were the Syrians any more successful in striking a deal with the Russians in the air defense sphere. Again the reason was financing. The Syrians sought SA-10s, similar to the American Patriot anti-aircraft missile. Thus the Syrian air defense alignment continued to rely on an extensive, dense deployment of relatively outmoded missiles: about 170 SA-6 and SA-8 mobile batteries and fixed SA-2s and SA-3s, and a few brigades of SA-5 batteries, with a range of several hundred kilometers.

Navy

The Syrian Navy, which is defensive in orientation, did not undergo any major developments in 1992. It continued to deploy two frigates, 19 MFPBs, three submarines and a variety of lesser craft. Operational emphasis was placed on coastal defense, backed up by shore-to-sea missiles, naval helicopters, massive coastal fortifications and an adequate detection capability. The three submarines offered some offensive capacity, but their serviceability was poor. Discussions with the Russians over the acquisition of an additional three submarines appeared to be dormant, due to the low priority Damascus assigned to this option.

Russians in Syria

Following the collapse of the Soviet Union, and in view of Russian demands that Syria pay in hard currency not only for arms acquisitions but for the services of Russian advisors as well, the Syrians concluded in early 1991 that they should commence gradually reducing the scope of the Russian advisory staff on their soil. The cutback began in 1991; by mid-1992 there apparently remained just over 1,000 advisors. As this reduction became increasingly comprehensive, it was certain to have at least a short-term effect on the readiness of the Syrian Armed Forces. Ultimately the Syrians seemed likely to continue to employ some advisors on a personal contract basis.

As for the presence of Russian military units in Syria, little significant change was registered. The Russians retained a permanent naval deployment at the port of Tartus, with four auxiliary ships, and regular ship visits. Additional Russian non-naval units also continued to be deployed in Syria, where they served Russian purposes.

The Nonconventional Dimension

During 1991 and 1992 the Syrians initiated an effort to develop nuclear capabilities. This program, still in its infancy and devoid for the time being of military significance, comprised the establishment of a nuclear research infrastructure, the Center for Scientific Study and Research near Damascus; training of scientific and engineering cadres in Europe, the PRC, Pakistan and India; acquisition of nuclear components, primarily from Belgium, Germany, France and Britain; a contract with the PRC to establish a small, 30 kw capacity nuclear research reactor based on enriched uranium; and initial contacts regarding construction of larger reactors, with up to 10 megawatt capacity.

Notably, this was not a high-priority effort with the Syrians. The real danger involved the possibility that at some point in the future, Syria's close collaboration with Iran would involve the transfer to Syria of technology, materials and expertise.

187

As for other nonconventional areas, we have already noted Syria's capacity to deliver chemical weapons by means of missiles and bombs. By 1992 Syria had for several years also possessed the ability to produce biological weaponry.

Concluding Assessment

Despite the growing Syrian rapprochement with the US, as well as the collapse of the USSR, the Syrian Armed Forces were continuing to base their force-building program on Soviet weaponry in all major categories. Thus one key problem was obviously an exaggerated dependency with regard to spares and ammunition. This was particularly true in the Syrian case, insofar as the country had no significant military industrial capacity beyond R&D institutions and production facilities for a few auxiliary systems.

In this sense, the anticipated establishment of a production line for Scud C missiles was a notable exception. It could be seen either as a unique phenomenon--one that reflected the tremendous importance the Syrians attached to self-production of surface-to-surface missiles--or as the harbinger of a broader process that reflected lessons drawn by the Syrians from the relative success of the embargo that had been placed on Iraq under radically different international circumstances. By 1993, preliminary indications pointed to the second possibility.

During 1992 the army executed a qualitative and quantitative quantum leap, by absorbing quality tanks and SP artillery. The accelerated pace of absorption and the organizational changes required thereby undoubtedly reduced Syrian Army readiness in the short term. This effect was amplified by the cutback in Russian advisors. However, once this absorption stage was completed--a period of one or two years at least--the army's strength and quality would increase.

An armor/mechanized order-of-battle of 11/12 divisions, of which 50 percent were equipped with the T-72, meant that Syria's defensive capability would be enhanced considerably. In wartime the army would be able to plug weak points on the flanks of the Golan deployment, at the Jordan and Lebanon borders, and simultaneously to carry out a main offensive based on hundreds of quality tanks. With improved offensive capabilities overall, the

Syrians could also launch main attack efforts from Lebanon. An enhanced orbat would enable Syria to increase its deployment inside Lebanon beyond the scale of two divisions of recent years, without reducing strength on the Golan. (Even if the Syrians decided, for political reasons, to remove their units from most of Lebanon, they would undoubtedly seek to retain them in the Lebanese Biqa' for the foreseeable future.)

It is all the more striking, against the backdrop of the enhancement of Syria's ground forces and surface-to-surface missile potential, that the Syrian Air Force and Air Defense did not yet commence the qualitative force-building program that the Syrians envisaged. This imbalance would presumably soon be rectified. In any event, the Syrian Armed Forces continued to constitute the most serious threat to Israel. Yet the Syrian political and military leadership understood that its armed forces alone could not, under existing international conditions, stand against Israel's main force. To do so, they would need additional Arab force components, from Iraq and Jordan for example, as well as the equivalent of the security guarantees Damascus received in the past from the Soviet Union. In early 1993 both of these possibilities appeared unlikely.

This is not to imply, however, that in 1992 and early 1993 Syrian operational thinking completely rejected the option of a surprise, limited military action on the Golan, following which the Syrian Army would dig in and exploit its impressive defensive capabilities. Yet even in this instance, the Syrians presumably understood that, unless reinforced by additional Arab armies, they would suffer an obvious disadvantage vis-a-vis Israel. Nor had the Syrians forgotten or neglected the lesson they drew from the Gulf War: that the Israeli arsenal comprised the same weapons systems as the American, and that Israel would not hesitate to use them, quickly and efficiently, against a Syrian force attacking on its own.

In short, President Asad and the Syrian leadership presumably recognized in 1992 that, given international, inter-Arab and Syrian economic circumstances, Syria would not soon achieve its much vaunted 'strategic parity' with Israel.

PART III

REGIONAL MILITARY FORCES

Introductory Note

In Parts III and IV the definition of high quality tanks includes the following tanks (mentioned in the text): T-72/improved T-72; Chieftain in Jordan and Oman (but not Chieftain Mk.5 in Iran and Kuwait); M-60 A3; Merkava. Similarly, the high quality interceptors include F-14, F-15 and MiG-25. High quality strike and multi-role aircraft include F-16, F/A-18, Mirage 2000, Tornado, MiG-29 and Su-24. Short range SAMs include all models which normally fulfill the task of providing air defense to ground forces, though these weapons systems may also be part of the Air Force or Air Defense Force. Defense expenditure figures include foreign military grants. Arms transfers to and from Middle East countries cover transfers during the most recent three years; numbers of weapons systems mentioned include systems in service and in storage; and bombers are included in numbers of total combat aircraft.

Uniqueness of 1992

We have included in the chapter on Israel data regarding the Arab and Jewish population, the Jewish settlements, and the area of the administered territories occupied by Israel in 1967. Since this is the first time we cover these data, we offer comparative figures with respect to 1967 and 1977.

Several countries have begun major armed forces reorganization efforts, and many new weapons systems have been ordered. In cases where these weapons are understood not to have reached their destination by Jan. 1993, they are to be found under "on order."

The Gulf War generated major population shifts, mainly involving the foreign work force in the Arabian Peninsula, and specifically Kuwait. Our information is incomplete.

Finally, arms and personnel from or in what is today Russia, are listed under USSR if they are correct up to late 1991. More recent information is listed under Russia. In the Glossary, countries of origin of items listed are those that originally produced the items, even in instances where the country has ceased to exist (e.g., USSR, Czechoslovakia).

Acknowledgements

In addition to my colleagues at JCSS, I wish to thank a number of persons for their comments and assistance during the process of collecting and collating the data for Part III: Ofra Bengio, Uzi Rabbi and Yehudit Ronen of the Dayan Center for Middle Eastern and African Studies, Tel Aviv University; and JCSS researchers and research assistants whose aid was particularly valuable--Anat Kurz, David Tal, Maskit Burgin, Moshe Grundman, Yiftah Shapir and Alexandra Meir, and especially Yoel Kozak, Michal Harel and Anat Henefeld. Withal, I alone bear responsibility for any inaccuracies.

Z.E.

1. ALGERIA

BASIC DATA

Official Name of State: Democratic and Popular Republic of Algeria

Head of State: President of the High State Council Ali Kafi

Prime Minister: Belaid Abd al-Salam

Minister of Defense: General Khalid Nezzar

Chief of General Staff: Major General Abd al-Malik Guneizia

Commander of the Staff of the Ground Forces: Major General Khalifa Rakhim (also Deputy Chief of the General Staff)

Commander of the Air Force: Brigadier General Muhammad al-Mukhtar Bouteimine

Commander of the Air Defense Force: Brigadier General Achour Laoudi

Commander of the Navy: Captain Abd al-Majid Taright

Area: 2,460,500 sq. km.

Population: 27,160,000

ethnic subdivision:

Arabs	21,320,000	78.5%
Berbers	5,269,000	19.4%
Europeans	272,000	1.0%
Others	299,000	1.1%

religious subdivision:

Sunni Muslims	26,888,000	99.0%
Christians and Jews	272,000	1.0%

GDP:

1987--$64.5 billion

1988--$54.1 billion

Balance of Payments (goods, services & unilateral transfer payments):

year	income	expenditure	balance
1989	$10.57 bil.	$ 11.10 bil.	-$530 mil.
1990	$13.80 bil.	$ 11.50 bil.	+$2.30 bil.

Defense Expenditure:
    1989--$974 million (unconfirmed)
    1991--$875 million
Foreign Military Aid and Security Assistance Received:
    financial aid from:
        USA--$150,000 grant (for military training)
    military training:
        foreign advisors/instructors from--Bulgaria, a few Germans
            (former GDR) on individual contracts, USSR/Russia
        trainees abroad in--USSR before end of 1991; training in
            Russia (unconfirmed)
    arms transfers from:
        Brazil (ARVs)
        Britain (radars, target drones, naval vessels)
        Canada (aircraft training simulators)
        France (ARVs, ATGMs)
        PRC (combat aircraft, patrol craft)
        USSR before end of 1991 (tanks, combat aircraft, SAMs),
            Russia (air force and AD equipment)
Foreign Military Aid and Security Assistance Extended:
    military training:
        foreign trainees from--Morocco
    facilities provided to:
        Palestinian organizations (training camps)
Cooperation in Arms Production/Assembly/R&D with:
    Argentina (small nuclear research reactor); Britain (naval
    vessels); Italy and Tunisia (diesel engines); France (trucks);
    PRC (nuclear reactor under construction)

INFRASTRUCTURE
Road Network:

length:	80,000 km
paved roads	60,000 km
gravel, crushed stone and	
earth tracks	20,000 km

    main routes:
        Algiers--Oran (Wahran)
        Algiers--Sidi-bel-Abbes

Oran--Oujda (Morocco)
Sidi-bel-Abbes--Bechar--Tindouf--Atar (Mauritania)
Bechar--Adrar--Gao (Mali)
Algiers--Laghouat--Tamenghest   (Tamanrasset)--Agadez
(Niger)
Algiers--Setif--Constantine
Constantine--Biskra--Touggourt
Constantine--Tebessa--Sousse (Tunisia)
Algiers--Annaba--Tunis (Tunisia)
Annaba--Tlemcen

Railway Network:

length:	3,890 km
standard gauge	2,632 km
narrow gauge	1,258 km

main routes:
Algiers--Mostaganem--Oran
Mostaganem--Sidi-bel-Abbes--Bechar--Kenadsa
Sidi-bel-Abbes--Oujda (Morocco)
Algiers--Constantine--Annaba--Tunis
Algiers--Laghouat
Constantine--Biskra--Touggourt
Annaba--Tebessa--Tunis

Airfields:

airfields by runway type:

permanent surface airfields	53
unpaved fields and usable airstrips	92

airfields by runway length:

over 3660 meters	3
2440--3659	30
1220--2439	66
under 1220	46
TOTAL	145

international airports: Algiers, Annaba, Constantine, Oran
major domestic airfields: Adrar, In Amenas, Bechar, Biuskra,
Borj Omar Driss, Ghardaia, El Golea, Laghouat, Ouargla,
El Oued, Illizi, In Salah, Tamenghest, Timimoun Tindouf,
Touggourt

under construction--Ayn Guezzem, Batna, Bordj Bajdi Mokhtar, Setif

Airlines:

companies: Air Algerie (international and domestic)

aircraft:

Airbus A-310-200 (2 possibly on loan from Libya)	4
Boeing 767-300	3
Boeing 737-200/737-200C	16
Boeing 727-200	11
Fokker F-27-400M	8
Lockheed L-100-30	2

Maritime Facilities:

harbors--Algiers, Annaba, Arziw, Bejaia, Beni Saf, Jijel, Ghazaouet, Mostaganem, Oran, Skikda (Philippeville)

anchorages--Cherchell, Collo, Dellys, Nemours, Tenes (Port Breira)

oil terminals--Algiers, Annaba, Arzew, Bejaia, Oran, Skikda

Merchant Marine:

vessel type	number	DWT
passenger	5	
liquified gas carrier	9	
general cargo/container	27	
tanker	6	
bulk carrier	9	
ro/ro	12	
chemical tanker	2	
product tanker	2	
bunkering tanker	4	
TOTAL	76	1,041,490

Nuclear Capability:

a small nuclear research reactor (from Argentina); a nuclear reactor of 15 MW probably upgradable to 40 MW under construction (from PRC); basic R&D; known Algerian facilities are subject to IAEA safeguards

Defense Production:

army equipment:

production under license--diesel engines (with Italy and Tunisia); trucks (in collaboration with France); small arms

aircraft and air ammunition:
> production under license--Czech transport aircraft and four passenger light aircraft

naval craft:
> tugs; landing craft, gunboats and patrol boats under construction (under license from Britain) at Mers al-Kebir

ARMED FORCES

Personnel:

military forces (figures for reserves and total unconfirmed)--

	regular	reserves	total
army	170,000	150,000	320,000
air force	9,500	-	9,500
air defense	12,000	-	12,000
navy + coast guard	7,000	-	7,000
TOTAL	198,500	150,000	348,500

para-military forces--

gendarmerie	30,000

Army:

major units (the Army is undergoing reorganization; not all units are fully manned):

unit type	divisions	brigades
armored/tank	2-3	1
infantry, mechanized	-	6
motorized infantry	-	5
airborne/special forces		1
TOTAL	2-3	13

+ several independent batallions

small arms:

personal weapons--
7.62mm AK-47 (Kalashnikov) AR
7.62mm AKM AR
7.62mm SKS (Simonov) SAR

machine guns--
14.5mm ZPU 14.5x4 HMG (employed in anti-aircraft role)
12.7mm D.Sh.K. 38/46 (Degtyarev) HMG

7.62mm SG-43/SGM (Goryunov) MMG
7.62mm RPD (Degtyarev) LMG
7.62mm PK/PKS (Kalashnikov) LMG
7.62mm (0.3") BAR LMG (possibly phased out)
light and medium mortars--
   82mm M-43
light ATRLS--
   RPG--7   ca.1000

tanks:

model		number
high quality		
T-72		300-400
medium quality		
T-62		330
T-55/T-54 (some in storage)		500-540
	(sub-total	830-870)
low quality		
AMX-13		50
PT-76		70
	(sub-total	120)
TOTAL		1250-1390

APCs/ARVs:

model		number
high quality		
BMP-2		100-200
BMP-1		800
Engesa EE-9		50
	(sub-total	950-1050)
others		
AML-60		150
BRDM-2		200
BTR-40/50/60		500
BTR-152		250-300
M-3 (Panhard)		50
	(sub-total	1150-1200)
TOTAL		2100-2250

artillery:

self-propelled guns and howitzers--	number
122mm M-1974 SP howitzer	90
towed guns and howitzers--	
152mm howitzer	70
130mm M-46/M-59 gun	+
122mm D-30 howitzer	160
122mm M-1938 howitzer (possibly phased out)	+
85 mm M-1945/D-44 field/AT gun	
mortars, heavy, over 160mm--	
160mm M-43 mortar	+
mortars, heavy, under 160mm--	
120mm M-43 mortar	
TOTAL (guns and mortars)	420
MRLs--	
240mm BM-24	40-50
140mm BM-14-16	170
122mm BM-21	200
TOTAL (MRLs)	410-420

anti-tank weapons:

missiles--	launchers
AT-1 (Snapper)	100
AT-2	100
AT-3 (Sagger)	1000
AT-4 (Spigot)	+
AT-5 (Spandrel; mounted on BMP-2 APC)	+
BRDM-2 carrying AT-3 (Sagger)/AT-5 (Spandrel)	+
MILAN	ca.200
guns--	number
85mm M-1945/D-44 field/AT gun	80
76mm AT gun	40
107mm B-11 recoilless rifle (unconfirmed)	50
TOTAL	170

surface-to-surface missiles and rockets:

model	launchers
FROG-7/FROG-4	30-35

army anti-aircraft defenses:

	launchers
missiles--	
self-propelled/mobile	
SA-6 (Gainful)	60
SA-8 (Gecko)	10
SA-9 (Gaskin)	+
SA-13 (Gopher, unconfirmed)	+
man-portable	
SA-7 (Grail)	+
SA-14 (Gremlin, unconfirmed)	+

	number
short-range guns--	
57mm ZSU 57x2 SP	50
23mm ZSU 23x4 SP (Gun Dish)	130
23mm ZU 23x2	50
57mm M-1950 (S-60)	+
37mm M-1939	145
TOTAL	375+

Air Force:

aircraft--general:	number
combat aircraft	295
transport aircraft	67
helicopters	66

combat aircraft:

interceptors--	
high quality	
MiG-25 A/B/U (Foxbat)	25
others	
MiG-23MF (Flogger G)	70
MiG-21 MF/bis/U (Fishbed)	110
(sub-total	180)
Total	ca. 205
strike and multi-role aircraft--	
medium quality	
MiG-23/27 (Flogger B/D)	50
Su-20 (Fitter C)	20
(sub-total	70)

others
    Su-7 BM/U (Fitter A, in storage)   20
  Total   90
TOTAL   295
on order: MiG-29 (Fulcrum), Su-24 (Fencer, possibly delivered)

transport aircraft (including tankers):
An-12 (Cub)   6
An-24 (Coke)/An-26 (Curl, possibly civilian)   ca. 10
Beechcraft Queen Air/Beechcraft King
    Air/Beechcraft Sierra 200/Beechcraft
    Super King Air T-200T
    (T-200T employed in maritime patrol role)   12
C-130H & L-100-30 Hercules   17
Fokker F-27 Mk 400/Mk 600
    (employed in maritime patrol role)   3
Gulfstream III   3
IL-76 (Candid, including 1-2 tankers)   4
Mystere-Falcon 900 (unconfirmed)   2
TOTAL   67

training and liaison aircraft:
with ground attack/close air support capability--
    CM-170 Fouga Magister   20
    L-39 Albatross   24
        (sub-total   44)
others--
    Beechcraft T-34C (Turbo Mentor)   6
    Yak-18 (Max)   16
        (sub-total   22)
TOTAL   66

helicopters (some in storage):
attack--
    Mi-24/Mi-25 (Hind, number unconfirmed)   36
heavy transport--
    Mi-6 (Hook, not serviceable)   4

medium transport--		
Mi-8/Mi-17 (Hip)		12
SA-330 Puma		5
	(sub-total	17)
light transport--		
Alouette II/III		6
Bell 206		3
	(sub-total	9)
TOTAL		66

on order: French helicopters

advanced armament:

air-to-air missiles--
AA-2 (Atoll)
AA-6 (Acrid)
AA-7 (Apex, unconfirmed)
air-to-ground missiles--
AT-2 (Swatter)
AT-6 (Spiral)
AS-10 (Karen)
AS-14 (Kedge)

anti-aircraft defenses:

long-range missiles--

model	batteries
SA-2 (Guideline)/SA-3 (Goa)	41

military airfields: 15

Ain Ousira, Algiers, Balida, Bechar, Biskra, Boufarik, Oran, Ouargla, Tindouf, 6 additional

aircraft maintenance and repair capability:
for all models

Navy:

combat vessels:

submarines--	number
K class (Kilo)	2
R class (Romeo)	2
Total	4

MFPBs--	
Ossa I	2
Ossa II	10
Total	12
missile corvettes--	
Nanuchka II	3
gun corvettes--	
C-58	1
ASW vessels--	
Koni class frigate	3
SO-1 large patrol craft	6
Total	9
mine warfare vessels--	
T-43 class minesweeper	1-2
gunboats/MTBs--	
Kebir class (Brooke Marine, incl, coast guard)	12
patrol craft--	
Baglietto Mangusta	6
Baglietto 20 GC	
(possibly with Coast Guard)	10
P-802 (possibly with customs service)	2
P-1200 (possibly with customs service)	3
Chinese 25 meter patrol boat (possibly with	
Coast Guard)	6
Total	27
on order: 4 additional Kebir class	
landing craft:	
Polnochny class LCT	1
Brooke Marine 2,200 ton LSL	2
TOTAL	3
auxiliary vessels:	
armed fishing	6
Niryat diving tender	1
Poluchat I class torpedo collecting	1
tankers	4
advanced armament:	
surface-to-surface missiles--	
SS-N-2 Styx	

surface-to-air missiles--
SA-N-4

special maritime forces:
naval commando

naval bases: 5
Algiers, Annaba, Mers al-Kebir, Oran, Skikda

ship maintenance and repair capability:
3 slipways belonging to Chantier Naval de Mers al-Kebir
at Oran; 4 x 4,000-ton dry docks at Algiers; small graving
docks at Annaba; small dry dock at Beni Saf.

2. BAHRAIN

BASIC DATA

Official Name of State: State of Bahrain
Head of State: Shaykh Isa ibn Salman al-Khalifa
Prime Minister: Khalifa ibn Salman al-Khalifa
Minister of Defense: Major General Khalifa ibn Ahmad al-Khalifa (also Deputy Commander in Chief of the Armed Forces)
Chief of the Bahraini Defense Forces: Brigadier General Abdallah ibn Salman al-Khalifa
Commander of the Air Force: Hamed Ibn Abdallah al-Khalifa
Commander of the Navy: Lieutenant Commander Yusuf Muallah
Area: 676 sq. km. (estimate, including 32 small islands)

Population:		550,000
ethnic subdivision:		
Arabs	401,500	73.0%
Persians	49,500	9.0%
Southeast Asians, Europeans	99,000	18.0%
religious subdivision:		
Shi'ite Muslims	385,000	70.0%
Sunni Muslims	165,000	30.0%
nationality subdivision:		
Bahrainis	346,500	63.0%
Alien Arabs	55,000	10.0%
Alien non-Arabs		
Southeast Asians	71,500	13.0%
Iranians	44,000	8.0%
Others	33,000	6.0%

GDP:
1989--$3.58 billion
1990--$3.90 billion

Balance of Payments (goods, services & unilateral transfer payments):

year	income	expenditure	balance
1990	$5.06 bil.	$4.26 bil.	+$800 mil.
1991	$4.48 bil.	$4.64 bil.	-$160 mil.

Defense Expenditure:
    1989--$184.6 million (unconfirmed)
    1990--$193.9 million (unconfirmed)

Foreign Military Aid and Security Assistance Received:
    financial aid from:
        Saudi Arabia (grant)
    military training:
        foreign advisors/instructors/serving personnel from--Britain, Egypt, France, Pakistan, USA
        trainees abroad in--Britain, France, Egypt, Saudi Arabia, UAE, USA; Jordan
    arms transfers from:
        Britain (patrol craft, electronics)
        France (ARVs, helicopters, AGMs)
        FRG (missile corvettes and boats, helicopters)
        Italy (helicopters)
        Norway (ATRLs)
        USA (ATGMs, APCs, combat aircraft, SAMs, helicopters, tanks, landing craft)

Foreign Military Aid and Security Assistance Extended:
    facilities provided to:
        USA (naval facilities, storage facilities, prepositioning of army equipment & intelligence installations); a squadron of British combat a/c--from August 1990 through the Gulf War; 2 Canadian destroyers, from October 1990 through the Gulf War
    forces deployed abroad in:
        Saudi Arabia (part of GCC Rapid Deployment Force); a battalion participated in the 1991 Gulf War

Joint Maneuvers with:
    cooperation with the US-led coalition and participation in the 1991 Gulf War; USA; security agreement with the USA and Britain.

INFRASTRUCTURE
Road Network:
length: 425 km
   paved roads   200 km
   earth tracks   225 km
main routes:
   al-Manamah--Muharraq (airport)
   al-Manamah--Sitrah (oil terminal)
   al-Manamah--Budaiyah
   al-Manamah--Isa Town--Awali
   al-Manamah--Dhahran (Saudi Arabia); 25 km bridge
     causeway
   Awali--al-Zallaq
   Awali--Ras al-Yaman

Airfields:
airfields by runway type:
   permanent surface field   2
   unpaved field   1
airfields by runway length:
   over 3660 meters   2
   1220--2439   1
TOTAL   3
international airport: Bahrain (Muharraq)

Airlines:
companies: Gulf Air (international)--jointly owned by Bahrain, Oman, UAE and Qatar, with headquarters in Bahrain; aircraft listed below
aircraft:
   Airbus A-320-200   3
   Boeing 767-300ER   12
   Boeing 737-200   10
   Lockheed L-1011-200 Tristar   8
   on order: 9 additional Airbus A-320, 6 Airbus A-340,
     Boeing 767-300 ER

Maritime Facilities:
harbors--Mina Salman; Sitrah (ALBA aluminum terminal); Mina Manamah
oil terminal--Sitrah

Merchant Marine:

vessel type	number	DWT
tanker	1	61,401
cargo/container	4	95,501
TOTAL	5	156,902

ARMED FORCES

Personnel:

military forces--

army	5,000
air force	400
navy	600
TOTAL	6,000

Army:

major units:

unit type	brigade	battalion
mechanized	1	
armored		1
TOTAL	1	1

small arms:

personal weapons--
9mm Model 12 Beretta SMG
machine guns--
type unknown
light and medium mortars--
81mm L-16 A1
light ATLRs--
M-72 LAW

tanks:

model	number
high quality	
M-60 A3	81

APCs/ARVs:

model	number
others	
M-3 (Panhard)	90
AML-90	

```
AT-105 Saxon
Ferret (possibly phased out)
Saladin (possibly phased out)
TOTAL                                           200
   on order: 80 M-113 (possibly delivered)
```

artillery:
```
towed guns and howitzers--
   155mm M-198 A1 howitzer                        8
MRLs--                                       launchers
   227mm MLRS                                     7
```

anti-tank weapons:
```
missiles--                                   launchers
   BGM-71C Improved TOW                           60
guns--
   120mm BAT L-4 recoilless rifle
```

army anti-aircraft defenses:
```
missiles--                                   launchers
   man-portable
      FIM-92A Stinger (number unconfirmed)        70
      RBS-70                                    40-50
```

Air Force:
```
aircraft--general:                            number
   combat aircraft                               24
   transport aircraft                           2-3
   helicopters                                26-27
```

combat aircraft:
```
strike and multi-role aircraft--
   high quality
      F-16C/D                                     12
   medium and low quality
      F-5E/F                                      12
   TOTAL                                          24
   on order: 4 F-16C/D in case of attrition
```

transport aircraft:
```
Gulfstream II                                     1
C-130H Hercules (unconfirmed)                   1-2
TOTAL                                           2-3
```

helicopters:		number
maritime attack--		
SA-365 Dauphin		2
medium transport--		
AB-212		10
Bell 412 (with Police)		2
UH-60A Black Hawk (for VIP)		1-2
	(sub-total	13-14)
light transport--		
500MD		2
MBB BO-105		9
	(sub-total	11)
TOTAL		26-27

on order: 8-12 AH-64A Apache, negotiations not finalized

advanced armament:
air-to-air missiles--
AIM-9P Sidewinder
air-to-ground missiles--
AS-15TT anti-ship missile

anti-aircraft defenses:
on order: MIM-23B Improved HAWK SAMs; Cossor SSR and Plessey Watchman air traffic control radars for civilian and military use

military airfields:	1

Muharraq; a second AFB is under construction at Suman

Navy:

combat vessels:	number
MFPBs--	
Lurssen TNC-45	6
missile corvettes--	
Lurssen 62 meter type	2
gunboats/MTBs--	
Lurssen FPB-38 type gunboat	2
patrol craft--	
Cheverton 50 ft. (15.3 meter)	1
Cheverton 27 ft. (8.2 meter)	3

Tracker	3
Fairey Marine Sword	4
Swift FPB-20	2
Wasp 30 meter	1
Wasp 20 meter	2
Wasp 11 meter	3
Total	19

landing craft:

150 ton Fairey Marine LCM	1
Loadmaster 60 ft. (18 meter) LCU	1
Swiftships 390 ton LCU	1
Trompire Ltd. hovercraft	1
US-made landing craft (unconfirmed, surplus from Gulf War)	4
TOTAL	8

advanced armament:

surface-to-surface missiles--
MM-40 Exocet

naval bases: 1

Jufair

ship maintenance and repair capability:

Arab Shipbuilding & Repair Yard (ASRY), a 500,000 DWT drydock engaged in repairs and construction (mainly supertankers; jointly owned by Bahrain, Kuwait, Qatar, Saudi Arabia, UAE-each 18.84%, Iraq--4.7% and Libya-- 1.1%)

3. EGYPT

BASIC DATA

Official Name of State: The Arab Republic of Egypt
Head of State: President Muhammad Husni Mubarak
Prime Minister: Dr. Atif Sidqi
Minister of Defense and War Production: General Muhammad Hussein Tantawi
Chief of the General Staff: General Salah Halabi
Commander of the Air Force: Lieutenant General Ahmad Abd al-Rahman Nasser
Commander of the Air Defense Force: Lieutenant General Muhammad Zahir Abd al-Rahman
Commander of the Navy: Vice Admiral Ahmad Ali Fadil
Area: 1,000,258 sq. km.

Population: 58,987,000

ethnic subdivision:

Arabs	58,043,000	98.4%
Nubians	59,000	0.1%
Greeks, Italians, Armenians	590,000	1.0%
Others	295,000	0.5%

religious subdivision:

Sunni Muslims	55,448,000	94.0%
Copts, other Christians	3,539,000	6.0%

GDP:
1990--$39.45 billion
1991--$29.63 billion

Balance of Payments (goods, services & unilateral transfer payments):

year	income	expenditure	balance
1990	$15.29 bil.	$14.09 bil.	+$1.20 bil.
1991	$16.38 bil.	$13.20 bil.	+$3.18 bil.

Defense Expenditure:
1990--$4.3 billion (unconfirmed) +$700 million grant of US drawdown weapons
1991--$4.1 billion (including US aid)

Foreign Military Aid and Security Assistance Received:
financial aid from:
USA--$1.3 billion grant, and cancellation of a $6.7 billion military debt after the 1991 Gulf War; FRG--$550 million grant, mostly for civilian purposes; Gulf states (including Saudi Arabia)--a grant of ca. $5 billion, for Egyptian participation in the Gulf War; Arab coalition members (mainly Saudi Arabia, Kuwait, UAE)--forgiveness of an Egyptian debt, partly military, of ca. $7 billion after the Gulf War. The "Paris Club" countries--USA, West Europe, Canada, Australia, Kuwait and Japan--forgiveness of about $10.1 billion in debts after the Gulf War (half of Egypt's debt to the "Paris Club"), partly military

military training:
foreign advisors/instructors from--France, USA
trainees abroad in--Britain, France, FRG, USA (over 500 men)

arms transfers from:
Belgium (LMGs)
Brazil (trainer aircraft)
Britain (ATGMs, helicopter parts, radio transceivers, tank guns, torpedoes, naval radars)
France (combat aircraft, ATGMs, helicopters, AAMs, SAMs, radar for AAGs)
FRG (parts for Fahd APCs)
Italy (helicopters, ECM, shipborne SAMs, Skyguard air defense systems, terminally guided aerial bombs)
Japan (training ship)
Libya (10 Czech-made trainer aircraft, a gift)
North Korea (spare parts for Soviet arms; assistance to Egyptian production of SSMs, unconfirmed)
PRC (artillery, supply of spare parts for all Soviet-made systems)
Romania (artillery)

Russia (BMP turrets for Egyptian Fahd APCs)

Switzerland (AAGs)

Turkey (US designed F-16 fighter a/c assembled in Turkey, on order)

USA (APCs, ATGMs, combat aircraft, helicopters, early warning aircraft, radars, SAMs, upgrading kits for SAMs and tanks, UAVs and mini UAVs, fire control systems for submarines, artillery, sonars)

construction aid by:

USA (upgrading of airfields and dry docks)

maintenance of equipment in:

FRG (transport aircraft)

maintenance aid by:

USA (aircraft)

Foreign Military Aid and Security Assistance Extended:

military training:

advisors/instructors in--Bahrain (a few retired personnel), Kuwait, Morocco (unconfirmed), Oman, Qatar, UAE, Zaire; Somalia (unconfirmed)

foreign trainees from--Algeria, Bahrain, Chad, Djibouti, France, Jordan (before the Gulf Crisis), Kuwait, Libya, Morocco, Oman, Pakistan, Qatar, Saudi Arabia, Senegal, Tanzania, Tunisia, Turkey, UAE, Zaire, Zimbabwe, Yemen

arms transfers to:

Chad (small arms)

Djibouti

Kenya (type unknown)

Kuwait (Fahd APCs, Skyguard AA Systems, optronics, gas masks)

Morocco (mortars, APCs)

Oman (APCs, optronics)

Qatar (Fahd APCs, MRLs, optronics, gas masks, MRLs)

Saudi Arabia (engineering equipment)

Singapore (optronics)

UAE (Fahd APCs, air defense systems, optronics, gas masks)

Uganda (type unknown, optronics)

Zaire (Fahd APCs, optronics)

facilities provided to:

USA (airfields at Cairo West, Qena, Inshas); Iraq (naval vessels anchored in Egypt since the Iran-Iraq War)

forces deployed abroad in: 38,500 (one armored division, one mechanized division and Commando units) in Saudi Arabia and UAE between August 1990 and May 1991; by Dec. 1991 all back in Egypt; an expeditionary force, jointly with US forces, to impose peace and protect food distribution in Somalia, 1992-93; 235 troops in UN forces in Somalia, 1993

Cooperation in Arms Production/Assembly/R&D with:

Brazil (trainer aircraft); Britain (ATGMs, radio transceivers, electronics); France (aircraft, electronics, booster for surface-to-surface rockets, helicopters, SP AAGs); FRG (Fahd APCs, company involved in radio transceiver production); Italy (Skyguard AD system); North Korea (SSMs); Sweden (radio transceivers); USA (upgrading M-113 APCs, ammunition, electronics incl. radars and radio transceivers, M-1 A1 tank assembly, upgrading of PRC-made submarines)

Joint Maneuvers with:

France, Italy, Jordan (before the Gulf Crisis), Britain, UAE, USA; cooperation with US-led coalition and participation in fighting the 1991 Gulf War

INFRASTRUCTURE

Road Network:

length:	33,900 km
paved roads	17,900 km
gravel and stone roads	2,500 km
improved earth roads	13,500 km

main routes:

Cairo--Alexandria

Cairo--Tanta--Alexandria

Cairo--Ismailiya

Cairo--Suez

Cairo--al-Mansura--Damietta

Cairo--al-Fayum

Cairo--Asyut--Qena--Aswan
Alexandria--Marsa Matruh--Tobruk (Libya)
Alexandria--al-Alamein--Siwa
Marsah Matruh--Siwa
Ismailiya--Bir Gafgafah--Beer Sheva (Israel)
Kantara--al-Arish--Ashkelon (Israel)
Sharm al-Shaykh--Eilat (Israel)
Asyut--al-Kharga
Suez--Hurghada--Ras Banas--Port Sudan (Sudan)
Suez--Ismailiya--Port Said
Qena--Safaga

Railway Network:

length:	5,110 km
standard gauge	4,763 km
narrow gauge (0.75m.)	347 km

main routes:
Cairo--Tanta--Alexandria
Tanta--Damietta
Cairo--Zagazig--Ismailiya
Cairo--Suez
Suez--Ismailiya--Port Said
Alexandria--Marsa Matruh--Salum
Cairo--Asyut--Aswan
Zagazig--al-Salahiya

Airfields:

airfields by runway type:

permanent surface fields	66
unpaved fields and usable air strips	16

airfields by runway length:

over 3660 meters	2
2440--3659	44
1220--2439	22
under 1220	14
TOTAL	82

international airports: Cairo, Aswan, Alexandria, Luxor
major domestic airfields: Abu Simbel, Asyut, Hurghada, Port
Said, Sharm al-Shaykh

Airlines:

companies: Egyptair (international); Misr Overseas Airways (international, charter and cargo); ZAS (Zarakani Aviation Services, cargo); Air Sinai (domestic, and to Israel); Petroleum Air Service (domestic, to oil fields); Transmed (charter); Cairo AT (cargo)

aircraft:

Airbus A-320	5
Airbus A-300 B4/A-300-600 (including 1 captured by Iraq in Kuwait, and held in Iraq or Iran)	14
BAe-146-200QT	1
Beechcraft Baron	2
Boeing 767-200ER/300ER	5
Boeing 747-300 combi	2
Boeing 737-200/500	12
Boeing 707	3
Cessna Citation II	2
DHC-7 Dash-7	5
Fokker F-27/F-27-500	2
Ilyushin IL-76	2
Lockheed Jetstar	3
Lockheed L-1011	1
MD-87	1
MD-83	1
MD-80	2
Tupolev Tu-154	2

helicopters:

Bell 212 (including on lease)	11

on order: 2 Boeing 767-200ER; 2 MD-83; 2 Airbus A-320, 3 Boeing 737-500; 3 Airbus A-340, delivery 1994, 3 Boeing 777 (letter of intent)

Maritime Facilities:

harbors--Adabiya, Alexandria, Damietta, al-Dikheila, Port Said, Safaga, Suez

anchorages--Abu Zneima, al-Arish, Kosseir, Marsa al-Hamra (al-Alamein), Marsa Matruh, Nuweiba, Ras Banas, Sharm al-Shaikh, al-Tur oil terminals--Ras Gharib, Ras Shukeir, Wadi Firan, Abu Qir

Merchant Marine:

vessel type	number	DWT
passenger	2	
general cargo/container	87	
oil tanker	6	
bulk carrier	14	
passenger/cargo	2	
multi-purpose	4	
bitumen tanker	3	
ro/ro	13	
refrigerated cargo	3	
TOTAL	134	1,486,979

Nuclear Capability:

R&D; a declared policy not to produce nuclear weapons; NPT signatory, installations under IAEA safeguards; a small Soviet-made nuclear research reactor in operation since 1961; a 22 MW research reactor from Argentina on order, delivery 1997

Defense Production:

army equipment:

manufacture--120mm mortars (planned);122mm Saqr 10/18/30 MRLs; Saqr 80 surface-to-surface rockets (with assistance from France); ammunition for artillery, tanks and small arms; mines; rifles; short-range SAMs; conversion of 122mm D-30 howitzers to SP howitzers, still experimental; conversion of 23mm AAGs to Sinai 23 SP AAGs; add-on armor to M-113 APCs; toxic gas (originally with assistance from a foreign company, now discontinued); upgraded Scud B SSMs (with North Korean cooperation); upgrading M-60 A1 tanks to M-60 A3 standard, with cooperation of the USA

production under license--Dragon ATGMs (under development); 130mm artillery pieces; British tank guns; tank tracks; upgrading of Soviet tanks (with British, USA and Austrian assistance); trucks and jeeps (with USA); Fahd APCs (with FRG components and assistance); Soviet design AAGs and small arms;

minefield crossing systems (similar to Viper); MLRs (copy of Soviet models)

assembly--short-range SAMs, AAGs; M-1 A1 tanks, with cooperation from USA

aircraft and air ammunition:

production under license--CBUs (US design); anti-runway bombs; parts for F-16; parts for Mirage 2000; parts for Mystere-Falcon 50 executive aircraft; aircraft fuel pods; aerial bombs

assembly--SA-342 Gazelle helicopters; Embraer EMB-312 Tucano

naval craft:

assembly--US Swiftships patrol boats

electronics:

manufacture--Bassal artillery fire control system; simulators for rifle firing

production under license--AN/TPS-63 radars (assembly, with 30% of components locally produced); radio transceivers (in collaboration with France, Germany, Sweden, USA and Britain); SAM electronics (in collaboration with Britain); fire control system

ARMED FORCE

Personnel:

military forces (not all reserves fully trained; reserves used mainly as fillers for regular units)--

	regular	reserves	total
army	320,000	600,000	920,000
air force	25,000	20,000	45,000
air defense	70,000	60,000	130,000
navy	20,000	15,000	35,000
TOTAL	435,000	695,000	1,130,000

para-military forces--

coast guard--			7,000
frontier corps--			6,000

Army:

major units:

unit type	army corps HQ	divisions	independent brigades/ groups
all arms	2		
armored		4	3
mechanized		7	2
infantry		1	4
airborne			2
special forces			3
TOTAL	2	12	14

+ 6 independent infantry battalions

small arms:

personal weapons--
9mm Aqaba SMG
7.62mm AK-47 (Kalashnikov) AR
7.62mm AKM AR
7.62mm Rashid SAR
7.62mm SKS (Simonov) SAR

machine guns--
14.5mm KPV HMG
14.5mm ZPU 14.5x4 HMG (in anti-aircraft role)
12.7mm D.Sh.K. 38/46 (Degtyarev
12.7mm (0.5") Browning M2 HMG
7.62mm MAG (FN) LMG
7.62mm RPD (Degtyarev) LMG/Suez LMG
7.62mm SG-43/SGM (Goryunov) MMG/Aswan MMG

light and medium mortars--
82mm M-43
60mm (Hotchkiss-Brandt)

light ATRLs--
RPG-2
RPG-7

tanks (some in storage):

model	number
high quality	
M-1 A1	25

M-60 A3	850
(sub-total	875)
medium quality	
M-60 A1	700
T-62	600
T-55 & T-54 (possibly some upgraded)	1050
(sub-total	2350)
TOTAL	3225

on order: 500 M-1 A1 tanks (25 delivered); 700 M-60 A1
tanks listed above, to be upgraded to M-60 A3 standard

note: armored recovery vehicles in service--M-88 A1

APCs/ARVs:

model	number
high quality	
BMP-1	200
M-113 A2	2000
V-150/V-300 Commando	ca. 180
(sub-total	2380)
others	
BMR-600	250
BRDM-2	
BTR-40/50/60/152 (possibly older models phased out)	
Fahd	
OT-62	
(sub-total	2020)
TOTAL	4400

on order: Fahd; Cadillac Gage Commando Scout ARV

artillery:

self-propelled guns and howitzers--	number
155mm M-109 A2 SP howitzer	200+
towed guns and howitzers--	
180mm S-23 gun (possibly phased out)	
152mm M-1943 (D-1) howitzer (possibly phased out)	
130mm M-46 gun/Type-59 gun	440
122mm D-30 howitzer	
122mm M-1938 howitzer (possibly phased out)	

100mm M-1955 field/AT gun
mortars, heavy, over 160mm--
   240mm mortar
   160mm mortar
mortars, heavy, under 160mm--
   120mm M-43 mortar
   107mm (4.2") M-30 SP mortar
     (on M-106 A2 carrier)

TOTAL   2200

artillery/mortar-locating radars--
   AN/TPQ-37
MRLs--
   122mm BM-21
   122mm BM-11
   122mm Saqr 10/18/30/36
on order: 122mm D-30 SP (still undergoing trials, designation AR-122); additional AN/TPQ-37 artillery and mortar-locating radar; 155mm Copperhead projectiles (CLPG, unconfirmed, still in negotiation)

engineering equipment:
   Bar mine-laying system
   EWK pontoon bridges
   GSP self-propelled ferries
   M-123 Viper minefield crossing system/Egyptian Viper-like system, designated Fatah
   MT-55 bridging tanks
   MTU-55 bridging tanks
   Egyptian bridging tanks (on T-34 chassis)
   mine-clearing rollers
   PMP folding pontoon bridges
   PRP motorized bridges

AFV transporters: 1000

anti-tank weapons:
   missiles--   launchers
      AT-3 (Sagger)
      BGM-71C Improved TOW
      BRDM-2 carrying AT-3 (Sagger)
      M-901 ITV SP (TOW under Armor)

MILAN
Swingfire
TOTAL   1600-1800
on order: 180 BGM-71D TOW II launchers
guns--
107mm B-11 recoilless rifle (possibly phase out)

surface-to-surface missiles and rockets:

model	launchers
FROG-7/Saqr 80	+
SS-1 (Scud B)	+
TOTAL	24

on order: Saqr 80, upgraded SS-1 Scud B locally
    produced
number of missiles--
    about 100

army anti-aircraft defenses:

missiles--   launchers

	launchers
self-propelled/mobile	
Crotale	48
MIM-72A Chaparral	50
SA-6 (Gainful)	48
Skyguard AA system (missiles, radars and guns; Egyptian designation Amoun)	18
man-portable	
Ain al-Saqr	
SA-7 (Grail)	

short-range guns--   number

	number
57mm ZSU 57x2 SP	
35mm Oerlikon-Buhrle 35x2 GDF-002	
23mm ZSU 23x4 SP (Gun Dish)	
23mm ZU 23x2	
Skyguard AA system (missiles, radars and guns; Egyptian designation: Amoun)	18
Sinai 23mm AA system	4
TOTAL	2500

on order: 8 additional Skyguard AA systems; Sinai 23
    AA systems, 144 FIM-92A Stinger

CW capabilities:

personal protective equipment
Soviet type decontamination units
stockpile of chemical agents (mustard and nerve agents)
Fuchs (Fox) ABC detection vehicle   12
SPW-40 P2Ch ABC detection vehicle a few

Air Force:

aircraft--general:	number
combat aircraft	
(including about 25% in storage)	515-525
transport aircraft	45
helicopters	197

combat aircraft:

interceptors--	
high quality	
F-16A/B/C/D	
(multi-role, employed as interceptor)	110
Mirage 2000	
(multi-role, employed as interceptor)	18
(sub-total	128)
medium and low quality	
F-7 Shenyang/MiG-21 MF (partly used	
as strike a/c)	200
F-6 Shenyang/FT-6	40-50
(sub-total	240-250)
Total	368-378
strike and multi-role aircraft--	
medium quality	
F-4E Phantom	32
Mirage 5	64
Alpha Jet and Alpha Jet MS-2 (normally an	
advanced trainer; defined in Egypt as	
CAS a/c)	43
Total	139
bombers--	
Tu-16 (Badger)	8
TOTAL	515-525

on order: about 15 additional F-16C/D (batch three; out of an order of 46, delivery in process during 1992-93); additional 46 F-16C/D (batch four, from Turkey, delivery 1994); 20 additional Mirage 2000, possibly suspended due to lack of funds

transport aircraft (older models partly grounded; including tankers):

Boeing 707 (3 to be converted to aerial tankers)	5
Boeing 737	1
C-130H/C-130H-30 Hercules (including ELINT)	24
DHC-5D Buffalo	9
Gulfstream III/IV	3
Mystere-Falcon 20	3
TOTAL	45

note: 12 An-12 presumably phased out

training and liaison aircraft:

with ground attack/close air support capability--
Alpha Jet and Alpha Jet MS-2--listed as strike a/c, above

L-29 (Delfin)	50
L-39 (Albatross)	10
(sub-total	60)

others--

al-Gumhuriya	100
Embraer EMB-312 (Tucano)	54
Yak-18 (Max, possibly phased out)	35
(sub-total	189)
TOTAL	249

on order: 48 L-59E (first deliveries February 1993; intended to be used as CAS/strike, similar to the employment of Alpha Jet)

helicopters:

attack--

SA-342 L/M Gazelle	80

heavy transport--

CH-47C Chinook	15
Westland Commando Mk.2	27
(sub-total	42)

medium transport--
    Mi-8 (Hip)   ca. 50
    UH-60A Black Hawk, for VIP service   2
                           (sub-total   52)
light transport--
    Hiller UH-12E   18
ASW--
    Westland Sea King Mk.47   5
TOTAL   197
on order: 24 AH-64A Apache; 12 additional AH-64A, unconfirmed

maritime surveillance aircraft:
Beechcraft 1900C   8

miscellaneous aircraft:
AEW/AWACS aircraft--
    E-2C Hawkeye AEW   4-5
target drones--
    Aerospatiale CT-20 target drone
    Beech AQM-37A target drone
    Beech MQM-107B target drone
    TTL BTT-3 Banshee target drone   20
UAVs and mini-UAVs--
    R4E-50 Skyeye mini-UAVs   48
    Teledyne Ryan model 324 Scarab   50
on order: 50 additional TTL BTT-3 Banshee target drones; additional Teledyne Ryan model 324 UAVs (unconfirmed); an additional E-2C AEW

advanced armament:
air-to-air missiles--
    AIM-7F/7M Sparrow
    AIM-9 Sidewinder; AIM-9L; AIM-9P
    R-550 Magique
    R-530D Super
air-to-ground missiles--   number
    AGM-65 Maverick   1100
    AGM-84 (air launched) Harpoon
    AM-39 Exocet (unconfirmed)
    AS-1 (Kennel)

AS-5 (Kelt)
AS-30L
HOT
bombs--
   CBU-7A
on order: 282 AIM-7M AAMs; additional 40 AGM-65D,
   40 AGM-65G; guided bombs--20 GBU-10, 28 GBU-12;
   160 CBU-87 and 80 CBU-Mk.20

aircraft shelters: in all operational airfields, for combat aircraft

military airfields: 28

Abu Suweir, Alexandria, Aswan, Beni Suef, Bilbeis, Cairo International, Cairo West, Fayid, Hurghada, Inshas, Janaklis, Jebel al-Basour, Kabrit, Kom Awshim, Luxor, al-Maza, al-Minya, Mansura, Marsah Matruh, Qena, al-Qutamiya, Saqqara, Sidi Barani, Ras Banas, Salahiya, Tanta, al-Zaqaziq, one additional

aircraft maintenance and repair capability:
for all models

Air Defense Force:
radars:

AN/TPS-59	5
AN/TPS-63	19
P-15 Flat Face	+
P-12 Spoon Rest	+
Tiger S (TRS-2100)	15

on order: AN/TPS-63 (to complete total to 42); an additional AN/TPS-59; Trackstar L-band acquisition radar

long-range missiles:

model	batteries
MIM-23B Improved HAWK	12
SA-2 (Guideline) & SA-3 (Goa)	110
TOTAL	122

on order: 188 additional MIM-23B Improved HAWK missiles; MIM-104 Patriot; improvement kits for 12 MIM-23B batteries

Navy:

    combat vessels (some older Soviet vessels may no longer be operational):

	number
submarines--	
R class (Romeo)/Chinese R class	
(4 in the process of upgrading by the USA)	8
MFPBs--	
Hegu (Komar, made in PRC)	6
October	6
Ossa I	6
Ramadan	6
Total	24
gun destroyers--	
Z class	1
missile frigates--	
Descubierta class	2
Jianghu class	2
Total	4
mine warfare vessels--	
T-43 class minesweeper	3
T-301 class minesweeper	2
Yurka class minesweeper	4
Total	9
gunboats/MTBs--	
Hainan class	8
Shanghai II	4
Shershen class MTB (limited serviceability)	6
Total	18
patrol craft--	
Bertram class 28 ft. (8.5 meter)	6
Crestitalia 70 ft.	6
de Castro 110 ton (Nisr class)	3
Swiftships	9
Timsah class	12
Total	36

on order: 6 US-made minesweepers/minesearchers from Swiftships; 2 submarines from FRG (negotiations not concluded); 2 US Knox class missile frigates (negotiations not concluded)

landing craft:

LCM	5
Polnochny class LCT	3
SMB-1 class LCU	2
SRN-6 hovercraft	3
Vydra class LCU	9
TOTAL	22

on order: a US-made landing ship

auxiliary vessels:

Niryat diving support	2
Okhtensky (tug)	4
Poluchat II torpedo recovery	2
training (1 Sekstan, 1 4650-ton, 1 3008-ton and 1 other)	3
Survey vessels	4

advanced armament:

surface-to-surface missiles--
    HY-2/FL-1 (CSS-N-2, Silkworm)
    OTOMAT Mk.2 (also used for coastal defense)
    RGM-84A Harpoon
    SS-N-2 Styx
surface-to-air missiles--
    Aspide
advanced torpedoes--
    Stingray anti-submarine
    Mk.37 anti-submarine torpedo

on order: sub-Harpoon SSMs (for Romeo submarines)

coastal defense: launchers

SSC-2B Samlet coastal defense missile (probably no longer in service)	
OTOMAT coastal defense missile	
SSN-2 Styx converted to coastal defense role	
Total (unconfirmed)	30

special maritime forces:
divers and frogmen
naval bases: 8
Abu Qir (naval academy), Alexandria, Hurghada, Marsa
Matruh, Port Said, Safaga, Suez, Berenice (Ras Banas)
ship maintenance and repair capability:
Alexandria (including construction up to 20,000 DWT),
Port Said

4. IRAN

BASIC DATA

Official Name of State: Islamic Republic of Iran

Supreme Religious and Political National Leader (rahbar): Hojatolislam Ali Khamenei

Head of State (formally subordinate to national leader): President Hojatolislam Ali Akbar Hashemi Rafsanjani

Minister of Defense and Logistics of the Armed Forces: Ali Akbar Turkan

Chief of Staff of the Armed Forces (including IRGC): General Hussein Firuzabadi

Chief of Staff of the Army: Major General Ali Shabazi

Commander-in-Chief of the Islamic Revolution Guards Corps (IRGC): Major General Mohsen Rezai

Commander of the Ground Forces: Brigadier General Abdallah Najafi

Commander of the IRGC Ground Forces: Mustafa Izadi

Commander of the Air Force: Brigadier General Mansour Sattari

Commander of the IRGC Air Force: Brigadier General Mohammad Hussein Jalali

Commander of the Navy: Rear Admiral Ali Shamkhani

Area: 1,647,240 sq. km. (control of Abu Musa Island and two Tunb islands disputed)

Population:		60,000,000
ethnic subdivision:		
Persians	37,800,000	63.0%
Azeris	10,800,000	18.0%
Kurds	1,860,000	3.1%
others (Arabs, Turkmens, Lurs, Bakhtiaris)	9,540,000	15.9%

religious subdivision:

Shi'ite Muslims	55,800,000	93.0%
Sunni Muslims		
(incl. Kurds)	3,000,000	5.0%
Christians, Zoroastrians,		
Jews, Bahais and others	1,200,000	2.0%

GDP (difficulty to calculate due to problems of exchange rates):
1990--$60--$100 billion (estimate)
1991--$60--$100 billion (estimate)

Balance of Payments (goods, services & unilateral transfer payments):

year	income	expenditure	balance
1987	$10.87 bil.	$13.49 bil.	-$2.62 bil.
1988	$10.71 bil.	$10.85 bil.	-$ 30 mil.

Defense Expenditure:
1991--$4-4.5 billion (unconfirmed, difficulty due to exchange rates)
1992--$4-4.5 billion (unconfirmed, difficulty due to exchange rates)

Foreign Military Aid and Security Assistance Received:
military training:
foreign advisors/instructors/serving personnel from--North Korea, Pakistan, PRC (including nuclear technicians), Russia (pilots)
trainees abroad in--France, North Korea, Pakistan (nuclear scientists, aerial staff college trainees), PRC (including pilots)
arms transfers from (currently most deals undergoing renewed negotiations):
Argentina (various items)
Belgium (small arms)
Brazil (APCs, MRLs on order, negotiations in process)
Britain (workshops, spare parts for tanks and ARVs, landrovers, radars)
France (spare parts for MFPBs, artillery ammunition, rubber boats, trucks; helicopters-see Indonesia, below)
FRG (trucks, transport aircraft, allegedly civilian)
Hong Kong (American aircraft and miscellaneous items)

Indonesia (helicopters, French model, assembled or produced under license in Indonesia)

Italy (spare parts for aircraft and helicopters, naval mines via intermediaries)

North Korea (SSMs, artillery pieces, AAGs, small arms, naval mines, midget submarine)

Pakistan (light/trainer a/c, Swedish model assembled in Pakistan, spare parts for combat a/c)

Poland (T-72 tanks on order)

Portugal (ammunition)

PRC (artillery pieces, coastal defense SSMs, combat aircraft, SAMs, tanks, short-range SSMs)

Russia (SAMs, combat aircraft, tanks, APCs, submarines)

South Korea (aircraft spare parts)

Sweden (explosives)

Switzerland (AAGs and fire control)

Taiwan (artillery ammunition, mortars, small arms)

Ukraine (artillery, MLRs)

facilities provided by:

Sudan (IRGC facilities and harbor facilities at Port Sudan)

Foreign Military Aid and Security Assistance Extended:

financial aid to:

Hizb Allah militia in Lebanon--grant estimated at tens of millions per annum; Syria--grant (free oil); Palestinian organizations (Fatah rebels--Abu Musa faction and since late 1989 also PFLP-GC, and $30 mil. annually to Hamas & Palestinian Islamic Jihad)--grant; Sudan--grant and loan, $300 million

military training:

foreign trainees from--Lebanon (Hizb Allah militia); Sudan; Palestinian Hamas and Islamic Jihad

advisors/instructors in--Bosnia (100-200); Lebanon (IRGC personnel with Hizb Allah militia); Sudan (several scores of technicians in the Sudanese Air Force, and IRGC personnel) arms transfers to:

Bosnia (small arms)

Hizb Allah in Lebanon (Artillery, MRLs, small arms, ATGMs, engineering equipment)

PKK (artillery, unconfirmed)

Sri Lanka (small arms)

Sudan (small arms, ammunition, electronic equipment, spare parts for Soviet and Chinese arms)

forces deployed abroad in:

Lebanon--several hundred IRGC revolutionary guards with Hizb Allah, including in Syrian-held Biq'a

Cooperation in Arms Production/Assembly/R&D with:

Czech Republic (artillery, ammunition, ATGMs); German companies (cooperation in production of chemical agents, unconfirmed); North Korea (SSM production and upgrading); PRC (cooperation in nuclear research); India (cooperation in nuclear research); Belgium (cyclotron for nuclear development, private company); Pakistan (cooperation in nuclear weapons-related research and SSM R&D, unconfirmed)

Joint Maneuvers with:

Sudan (naval manueuvers)

INFRASTRUCTURE

Road Network:

length:	138,872 km
paved roads	42,566 km
gravel and crushed stone roads	46,866 km
improved earth tracks	49,440 km

main routes (roads to Iraq not in service):

Teheran--Qom--Yazd--Kerman--Zahedan

Kerman--Shiraz--Bushehr

Shiraz--Ahwaz--Abadan

Bandar Khomeini--Ahwaz

Qom--Isfahan--Shiraz

Qom--Arak--Dezful--Ahwaz--Abadan

Qom--Hamadan

Teheran--Hamadan--Kermanshah--Ilam--al-Kut (Iraq)

Abadan--Basra (Iraq, not in service)

Kermanshah--Qasr-i Shirin--Baghdad (Iraq)
Dezful--Shahabad--Qasr-i Shirin
Shahabad--Kermanshah--Zanjan
Teheran--Zanjan--Tabriz--Jolfa--Nakhichevan (Armenia)
Tabriz--Ardabil--Astara--Lenkoran (Azerbaijan)
Teheran--Mashhad
Mashhad--Ashkhabad (Turkmenistan)
Mashhad--Zahedan--Chah Bahar
Zahedan--Quetta (Pakistan)
Mashhad--Herat (Afghanistan)
Kerman--Bandar Abbas

Railway Network:

length:	4,601 km
standard gauge	4,509 km
1.676m gauge	92 km

main routes:
    Teheran--Qom--Isfahan--Yazd--Kerman
    Qom--Arak--Dezful--Ahwaz--Abadan
    Ahwaz--Basra (Iraq, not in service)
    Teheran--Zanjan--Tabriz--Jolfa--Nakhichevan (Armenia)
    Teheran--Semnan--Mashhad
    Mashhad--Ashkhabad (Turkmenistan)
    Zahedan--Quetta (Pakistan)
    Tabriz--Malatya (Turkey)

Airfields:

airfields by runway type:	
permanent surface fields	80
unpaved fields and usable airstrips	106
airfields by runway length:	
over 3660 meters	17
2440--3659	16
1220--2439	70
under 1220	83
TOTAL	186

international airports: Teheran, Abadan

major domestic airfields: Abu Musa, Ardabil, Bandar Abbas, Bushehr, Chah Bahar, Gorgan, Isfahan, Kerman, Kharg Island, Mashhad, Rasht, Sanandaj, Shiraz, Tabriz, Yazd, Zahedan

Airlines:

companies: Iran Air (international, domestic and cargo); Iranian Asseman Airlines (domestic); Iranian Saha (cargo)

aircraft:

Aerocommander/Turbocommander/ Shrike Commander	11
Airbus A-300 B2	5
Boeing 747-200F/SP/100B/200B	10
Boeing 737-200/200C	4
Boeing 727-200/727-100	6
Boeing 727-100	2
Boeing 707-320C/707F	4
BN-2 Islander	2
Fairchild FH-227B	2
Fokker F-100	6
Fokker F-27	16
Fokker F-28-4000/F-28-1000	4
Mystere-Falcon 20F	4
Piper Chieftain	3

on order: BAe 146, 2 Airbus A-300-600ER, 16 Boeing 737-400, subject to US government approval

Maritime Facilities:

harbors--Abadan, Bandar Abbas, Bandar Anzelli, Bandar Beheshti, Bandar Lengeh (Lingeh), Bandar Shahid Rajai, Bushehr, Chah Bahar, Khorramshahr (not in use), Bandar Khomeini (formerly Bandar Shahpur; also referred to as Bandar Imam)

oil terminals--Bandar Abbas, Bushehr, Bandar Khomeini, Bandar Lengeh, Ganaveh, Kharg Island, Larak Island, Sirri Island

Merchant Marine:

vessel type	number	DWT
general cargo	36	
ro/ro	6	

chemical tanker	4	
refrigerated cargo	3	
bulk carrier	49	
combination bulk carrier	2	
tanker	33	
TOTAL	133	8,671,769

(note: tanker figures do not include leased storage tankers)

Nuclear Capability:

a 5 MW research reactor acquired from the USA in the 1960s; undeclared research and facilities aimed at building nuclear weapons, with assistance from PRC and Pakistan. IAEA signatory; declared installations under full scope safeguards. A 300 MW power reactor and a small research reactor, both from PRC, on order; two 440 MW nuclear power reactors from Russia on order; some cooperation with Turkmenistan; Basic technical assistance and training received from India

Defense Production:

army equipment:

rifles (Heckler & Koch G-3 AR, under license); machine guns (MG-1A1, under license); artillery; MRLs (including 240mm); small arms, mortars, and artillery ammunition; spare parts; trucks (assembly); chemical agents; gas masks; ATRLs (unconfirmed); ATGMs; assembly and production of SSMs (planned, with North Korea, and possibly also Pakistan)

aircraft and air ammunition:

light aircraft (probably still under development); spare parts for aircraft; Zafar 300 attack helicopter, still experimental; SAMs (assembly of Chinese HN-5A and HQ-2, unconfirmed)

electronics:

radio transceivers (copy of USA model)

naval craft and naval ammunition:

250 ton LCU (Foque 101), PBs, mines, 8.4 meter hovercraft

space:

telecommunication satellite under development, to be launched with French cooperation

ARMED FORCES
Personnel:
military forces--

	regular
army	195,000
air force	
(incl. some IRGC)	35,000
navy	
(incl. some IRGC)	20,000
(sub-total, excl. IRGC & Baseej)	250,000)
IRGC	150,000
Baseej	30,000
TOTAL	430,000

Reserves--several hundred thousand, with ability to exceed 1 million men if necessary; only basic training

para-military forces--
IRGC and Baseej can mobilize a large para-military force beyond the regulars and reserve listed above; only partly trained

Army:
major units (including IRGC; most units not fully organized):

unit type	army corps	divisions	independent brigades
all arms	4		
armored		6	1
mechanized		2	
infantry		30	1
paratroop/ special forces/ Commando		2	4
airborne			1
TOTAL	4	40	7

(some divisions undermanned; 10-12 army divisions, 28-30 IRGC divisions; IRGC divisions are smaller in size than army divisions, sometimes equivalent to the strength of one brigade)

small arms:
    personal weapons--
        7.62mm G-3 (Heckler & Koch) AR
        7.62 AK-47 (Kalashnikov) AR
    machine guns--
        12.7mm D.Sh.K. 38/46 (Degtyarev) HMG
        12.7mm (0.5") Browning M2 HMG
        7.62mm MG 1A1 LMG
        7.62mm (0.3") Browning M-1919 MMG
        7.62mm MAG (FN) (unconfirmed)
        7.62mm PK/PKS (Kalashnikov) LMG
        7.62mm RPD (Degtyarev) LMG
    light and medium mortars--
        81mm M-29
        60mm M-19
    light ATRLs--
        3.5" M-20
        RPG-7

tanks:

model	number
high quality	
T-72	scores
medium quality	
Chieftain Mk.3/Mk.5	
T-62	150
M-60 A1	several hundred
T-55/Type 69/Type 59	
low quality	
M-48/M-47	
Scorpion	
TOTAL (limited serviceability)	700-800

    on order: several hundred T-72 M/S from Russia, delivery beginning 1993; some T-72 from Poland (unconfirmed)

APCs/ARVs:

model	number
high quality	
M-113	

BMP-1	100
Engesa EE-9 Cascavel	
others	
BTR-50/60	
MT-LB	
TOTAL	700

on order: hundreds of BMPs-2 from Russia, delivery
beginning 1993

artillery:

self-propelled guns and howitzers--
203mm M-110 SP howitzer
175mm M-107 SP gun
155mm M-109 SP howitzer
towed guns and howitzers--
203mm (8") M-115 howitzer
155mm G-5 gun/howitzer
155mm GHN-45 howitzer
155mm M-114 howitzer

130mm M-46 gun/Type 59 gun	several hundred
122mm D-30 howitzer	several hundred

105mm M-101 howitzer
mortars, heavy, under 160mm--
120mm M-65 mortar
107mm (4.2") M-30 mortar

TOTAL	1500-2000

(approximately 2/3 high quality including several
hundred SP guns & howitzers)
MRLs--
355mm Nazeat
333mm Shahin 2
240mm, Iranian designation Fajr-3
230mm Oghab
122mm BM-21
107mm
on order: 152mm, 122mm SP guns/howitzers, additional
130mm and 122mm pieces

engineering equipment:
    pontoon bridges
    light infantry assault boats
    self-propelled pontoons
AFV transporters: hundreds
anti-tank weapons:
    missiles--   launchers
        AT-3 (Sagger)
        BGM-71A TOW
        SS-11/SS-12
    guns--
        106mm M-40 A1C recoilless rifle
surface-to-surface missiles and rockets:
    SS-1 (Scud B)   10
    SS-1 Scud C variant from North Korea   a few
    CSS-8   +
    on order: Nodong, M-9 (unconfirmed); see also MRLs,
        above
army anti-aircraft defenses:
    missiles--   launchers
        self-propelled/mobile
          Rapier   45
          SA-6 (Gainful)
          Tigercat   15
        man-portable
          FIM-92A Stinger (with IRGC)   some
          RBS-70   50
          SA-7 (Grail)/HN-5A
    short range guns--
    57mm
    37mm
    35mm Contraves Skyguard ADS
    35mm Oerlikon-Bhurle 35x2 GDF-002
    23mm ZSU 23x4 SP (Gun Dish)
    23mm ZU 23x2
    on order: ZSU 23x4 AAGs (unconfirmed)

CW capabilities:
personal protective equipment for part of the armed forces
stockpile of chemical agents
decontamination units

Air Force:
aircraft--general (about 60% serviceable, not counting most of the 115 combat aircraft and 28 transport and civilian aircraft from Iraq that fled to Iran during the 1991 Gulf War; the only Iraqi a/c integrated into the Iranian force are 24 Su-24; all figures include aircraft with Army Aviation and Navy):

combat aircraft (excluding 95 not serviceable)	195
transport aircraft	ca. 120
helicopters (excluding 150 not serviceable)	275

combat aircraft:
interceptors--
  high quality

F-14A Tomcat	20
MiG-29 (Fulcrum; multi-role aircraft employed in interceptor role)	30
(sub-total	50)

  others

F-7 (unconfirmed)/MiG-21 (Fishbed)	25
Total	75

strike and multi-role aircraft--
  high quality

Su-24 (Fencer, including up to 24 Iraqi Su-24)	ca. 35

  medium quality

F-4 D/E/RF Phantom	40

  others

F-5 A/B/E	45
Total	120
TOTAL	195

not serviceable: ca. 35 F-14, 30 F-4, 30 F-5
on order: additional F-7; additional MiG-29; additional Su-24; negotiations regarding other Soviet models

transport aircraft (including tankers):

Aero Commander 690	2
Boeing 747	9
Boeing 737-200	+
Boeing 707 & KC-135 tanker (refuelling; including Boeing 707s in electronic surveillance/EW/CEW role)	9
C-130 E/H Hercules (including 2-3 in electronic surveillance role)	50
Dornier Do-228 (possibly civilian, or employed in maritime surveillance role)	4
Fokker F-27-400M/F-27-600	18
Jetstar	2
Mystere-Falcon 20	14
TOTAL (not all serviceable)	ca. 120

not serviceable: additional C-130 E/H (Hercules)

training and liaison aircraft:

others--

Beechcraft Bonanza F-33	a few
Cessna 185/180/150	45
Mushshak (PAC Mushshak)	25
Embraer EMB-312 (Tucano)	25
Pilatus PC-7 Turbo-trainer	35
Pilatus PC-6	15
T-33	9
TOTAL	154+

on order: additional EMB-312

helicopters:

attack--

AH-1J Cobra	70
Zafar 300 (unconfirmed, probably on trial)	a few
(sub-total	70+)

heavy transport--

CH-47C Chinook	35
RH-53D	a few
(sub-total	35+)

medium transport--
AB-214A   55
AB-205   50
AB-212   10
NAS-330 Puma   3
SA-330/IAR-330 Puma   a few
                          (sub-total   118+)
light transport--
AB-206 JetRanger
IAR-316
IAR-317

                          (sub-total   50)
ASW--
SH-3D   a few
TOTAL (excluding not serviceable)   ca. 275
not serviceable: ca. 30 AH-1J, 10 CH-47C, a few
    RH-53D, 90 AB-214A, 20 AB-205, some Bell 206
on order: 30 CH-47D, 12 AS-61, 18 AB-212, A-109A
maritime surveillance aircraft:
P-3 Orion   2
miscellaneous aircraft:
AEW/AWACS aircraft--
    on order: two IL-A-50 (Mainstay) AEW/AWACS
        (negotiations in process)
advanced armament:
air-to-air missiles--
    AA-10 (Alamo, unconfirmed)
    AIM-54A Phoenix (a limited number serviceable)
    AIM-9 Sidewinder
    AIM-7 Sparrow
air-to-ground missiles--
    AGM-65 Maverick
    AS 10 (Karen)
    AS-12
    AS 14 (Kedge)
    on order: AS-1, AS-5, AS-6

anti-aircraft defenses:

    radars--

      AR-3D

	batteries
long-range missiles--	
HAWK/MIM-23B Improved HAWK	ca. 15
SA-2 (Guideline)	+
SA-5 (Gammon)	a few
HQ-2J	4
TOTAL	30-35

      on order: batteries of SA-10/SA-12; SA-5 (Gammon)

    aircraft shelters--

      in operational airfields

military airfields: 20+

    Bandar Abbas, Birjand, Bushehr, Ghaleh-Marghi, Isfahan, Kerman, Kharg Island, Mehrabad, Qeshm, Shiraz, Tabriz, Teheran, at least 8 additional

Navy:

combat vessels:	number
submarines--	
K class (Kilo)	1
MFPBs--	
Combattante II (Kaman) class	
(several without SSMs)	10
missile destroyers--(possibly not all in service)	
Battle class	1
Sumner class	2
Total	3
missile frigates--	
Vosper Mk.5	3
gun corvettes--	
PF-103 class	2
mine warfare vessels--	
MSC 292 & MSC 268 class minesweepers	2
Cape class minesweeper	1
Total	3

patrol craft--

PGM-71 (improved) class	3
Chaho class	3
Cape (US coastguard)	3
Peterson Mk.II 50 ft. (15 meter)	20
Sewart 40 ft. (12 meter)	6
Boghammar (13 meter; with IRGC)	35
Bertram Enforcer 30.4 ft. and 20 ft.	12
Total	82

on order: MFPBs from PRC, North Korea; 1-2 additional Kilo submarines from Russia, delivery uncertain (US pressuring Russia to abstain from further deliveries)

landing craft:

BH-7 (Wellington) class hovercraft	5
SRN-6 (Winchester) class hovercraft	8
Hengam class landing ship	2
750 ton LCT	3
LST (South Korean)	3
US LCU 1431	1
250 ton LCU	1
TOTAL	23

auxiliary vessels:

Amphion class repair ship	1
Cargo Vessel (765 DWT)	5
harbor tanker (1700 ton full load)	1
Luhring Yard 3,250 DWT supply ship	2
Mazagon Docks 9430 ton water tanker	2
Swan Hunter replenishment ship	1
YW-83 class 1250 ton water tanker	1
Jansen research vessel	1

on order: 2 1350 ton maintenance ships from Japan

advanced armament:

surface-to-surface missiles--	a few
RGM-84 Harpoon	
Seakiller	
C-801	
HY-2 (Silkworm) SSMs	50

surface-to-air missiles--
  Standard
  Seacat
on order: SSMs from France

coastal defense:	launchers
HY-2 (Silkworm) SSMs	100
C-801 SSM	100

special maritime forces:
frogmen and divers

Sea Horse midget submarine	1
Iranian midget submarines (unconfirmed)	2

on order: 5 400 ton midget submarines from Russia, negotiations not completed

naval bases: 9
Bandar Abbas, Bandar Anzelli, Bandar Khomeini, Bandar Lengeh, Bushehr, Chah Bahar, Farsi Island, Jask, Kharg Island

IRGC naval bases: 10
Abadan oil terminal, Abu Musa Island, al-Fayisiyah Island, Cyrus oilfield, Halul Island platform (unconfirmed), Larak Island, Qeshm Island, Rostam Island oilfield, Sir Abu Nuair, Sirri Island

ship maintenance and repair capability:
1 MAN Nordhaman 28,000 ton floating dock

5. IRAQ

BASIC DATA

Official Name of State: The Republic of Iraq

Head of State: President Saddam Hussein (also Supreme Commander of the Armed Forces)

Prime Minister: Muhammad Hamza al-Zubaidi

Defense Minister: General Ali Hasan al-Majid

Chief of the General Staff: General Iyad Futayih Khalifa al-Rawi

Commander of the Air Force: Lieutenant General Muzahim Sab Hassan

Commander of the Navy: Rear Admiral Abd Muhammad Abdallah

Area: 438,446 sq. km.

Population (not including Arab nationals working in Iraq): 18,920,000

ethnic subdivision:

Arabs	13,906,000	73.5%
Kurds	4,087,000	21.6%
Turkmens	454,000	2.4%
Others	473,000	2.5%

religious subdivision:

Shi'ite Muslims	10,406,000	55.0%
Sunni Muslims (incl. Kurds)	7,946,000	42.0%
Christians, Yazidis and others	568,000	3.0%

GDP:

1989--$66.19 billion

1990--$35.0 billion (estimate; no reliable figure available)

Balance of Payments (goods, services & unilateral transfer payments): not available

Defense Expenditure

1990--$13.3 billion (estimate; no reliable figure available)

Foreign Military Aid and Security Assistance Received:
military training:
foreign advisors/instructors/serving personnel from--PRC (unconfirmed); Russia (individual volunteers)
trainees abroad in--Yemen (during 1992, discontinued thereafter)
arms transfers from:
since the Gulf Crisis very few items have reached Iraq, via Jordan
use of facilities abroad:
Jordan (use of supply routes and harbor, refuge to Iraqi commercial a/c); Iran (refuge to a/c, fate unclear); Tunisia (refuge to Iraqi commercial a/c); Yemen (Iraqi pilots allowed to train and fly Yemeni aircraft during 1992, discontinued thereafter)
Foreign Military Aid and Security Assistance Extended:
military training:
advisors/instructors in--Sudan (technicians, unconfirmed)
foreign trainees from--Sudan (part of an exchange), Yemen
facilities provided to:
Palestinians (a camp for ALF, unconfirmed; PLO--headquarter facilities; PLA forces; Abu Nidal's FRC, offices); PKK personnel in northern Iraq; 15,000 pro-Iraqi Iranians of the Iranian National Liberation Army, organized and based in Iraq; PLF (HQ facilities)
Cooperation in Arms Production/Assembly with:
USSR until end of 1991 (small arms, artillery pieces, MRLs, ammunition, assembly of T-72 tank, upgrading other tanks)

INFRASTRUCTURE
Road Network:
length:	13,824 km
paved roads	8,290 km
improved earth roads	5,534 km

main routes:
Baghdad--Kirkuk--Mosul
Baghdad--Mosul--al-Qamishli (Syria)--Diyarbakir (Turkey)/Mosul--al-Hasakah (Syria)

Baghdad--al-Hadithah--Qusaybah--Dir e-Zor (Syria)/
Qusaybah--Palmyra (Syria)

Baghdad--al-Rutbah--Damascus (Syria)

Baghdad--H-3--Mafraq (Jordan)

Baghdad--al-Hillah--al-Najaf--al-Samawah--Basra

Baghdad--al-Kut--al-Nasiriyah--Basra/al-Kut--al-Amarah-
-Basra

Basra--Abadan (Iran, inoperative)

Basra--Kuwait

al-Najaf--Rafha (Saudi Arabia)

Railway Network (some inoperative due to Iran-Iraq War and the
1991 Gulf War):

length:	2,962 km
standard gauge	2,457 km
narrow gauge	505 km

main routes:

Baghdad--Mosul--al-Qamishli--Aleppo (Syria)/Mosul--
al-Qamishli--Ankara (Turkey)

Baghdad--Kirkuk--Arbil (Irbil)

Baghdad--al-Nasiriyah--Basra

Baghdad--al-Ramadi--al-Hadithah--al-Qaim (Syrian
border)

Kirkuk--al Hadithah

Baghdad--al-Musayyib--Karbala--Najaf--Kufah--
Samawah--Basra--Umm Qasr

Airfields:

airfields by runway type:	
permanent surface fields	73
unpaved fields and usable airstrips	29
airfields by runway length:	
over 3660 meters	9
2440--3659	52
1220--2439	15
under 1220	26
TOTAL	102

international airports: Baghdad, Basra

major domestic airfields: Arbil (Irbil), H-3, al-Hadithah, Kirkuk, Mosul

Airlines:

companies: Iraqi Airways (international and domestic)
aircraft (some in Tunisia and Jordan):

Antonov An-12	5
Antonov An-24	3
Boeing 747-200C	2
Boeing 747-SP	1
Boeing 737-200C	1
Boeing 727-200	6
Boeing 707-320C	1
Ilyushin IL-76	15
Lockheed Jetstar II	5
Mystere-Falcon 50	1
Piaggio P-166	4

on order: 5 A-310, pending end of international blockade

Iraqi civil aircraft plus a few aircraft captured in Kuwait flown to Iran during the Gulf War, 1991:

Boeing 747	4
Boeing 737-200	2
Boeing 727	2
Boeing 707	2
Ilyushin IL-76	15

Maritime Facilities (temporarily inoperative due to lack of peace settlement with Iran and the blockade resulting from the 1991 Gulf War):

harbors--Basra; Umm Qasr - part of harbor to be gradually transferred to Kuwait begining in early 1993

oil terminals--Khor al-Amaya, Faw, Mina al-Bakr

Merchant Marine (flag carrying, operating from non-Iraqi ports due to lack of peace settlement with Iran):

vessel type	number	DWT
barge	4	
ferry	1	
product tanker	2	
crude tanker	17	
general cargo/container/		

training	13	
refrigerated cargo	1	
ro/ro 2		
TOTAL	40	1,586,189

Nuclear Capability:

advanced clandestine efforts aimed at designing and producing nuclear weapons, with assistance from various commercial sources, despite NPT commitments and IAEA safeguards. Hundreds of Iraqi experts trained abroad. Iraqi efforts have centered on producing weapons-grade material by centrifuge, electromagnetic and chemical separation. Since the Gulf War, Iraqi efforts have been stalled by UN facility-destruction and monitoring regimes

Defense Production (efforts since Gulf Crisis strongly depend on outside assistance and supply of raw materials, which have slowed or stopped):

army equipment:

manufacture--small arms and artillery ammunition; electronics; chemical agents: mustard, tabun, sarin, soman; biological weapons (unconfirmed); SSMs under development; upgrading of Soviet-designed Scud B SSMs

production under license--ATRLs, rifles, artillery, MRLs (Brazilian and Yugoslav license); tank (Soviet model); artillery (South African license); artillery ammunition (Spanish and South African license)

optronics:

development of a spy satellite (with assistance from Brazilian, French and other foreign companies, suspended after 1991 Gulf War)

aircraft and air ammunition:

production under license--Chile-designed Cardoen aerial CBU and FAE bombs; aerial bombs; AEW aircraft (Soviet, with French electronics and Indian assistance)

naval craft and naval ammunition:

small patrol boats; rubber boats; copy of Soviet-designed naval mines

A R M E D   F O R C E S
Personnel:
military forces--

	regular
army	400,000
air force & AD	ca. 98,000
navy	1,600-2,000
TOTAL	ca. 500,000

reserves--mostly poorly trained; Iraq is capable of mobilizing several hundred thousand
para-military forces--
Popular Army--disbanded in April 1991

security troops

Army:
major units: (some units disorganized; all not fully manned; reserve units have regular cadres)

unit type	army corps HQ	divisions	independent brigades
all arms	7		
armored		6	-
mechanized		4	-
infantry/ special forces		18-20	14
TOTAL	7	28-30	14

small arms:
personal weapons--

7.62mm AK-47 (Kalashnikov)/Tabuk AR

7.62mm SKS (Simonov) SAR

5.45mm AK-74 (Kalashnikov) AR

machine guns--

14.5mm KPV HMG

14.5mm ZPU 14.5x4 HMG (in anti-aircraft role)

12.7mm D.Sh.K. 38/46 (Degtyarev) HMG

7.62mm SGM (Goryunov) MMG

7.62mm RPD (Degtyarev) LMG

7.62mm PK/PKS (Kalashnikov) LMG

light & medium mortars--
   82mm M-43
light ATRLs--
   RPG-7/al-Nasira

tanks:

model	number
high quality	
T-72/T-72M	sev. hundred
Assad Babil (Iraqi T-72)	a few
medium quality	
T-62	
T-55/Type 59/Type 69/M-77	
Chieftain	
TOTAL	ca.2500

APCs/ARVs: number

model	number
high quality	
BMP-1	
BMP-2	
YW-531	
Engesa EE-9/11	
others	
AML-90/60	
BRDM-2	
BTR-40/50/60	
FUG-70/PSZH-IV	
K-63	
M-60P	
M-3 (Panhard)	
OT-62/OT-64	
MT-LB (an artillery prime-mover, employed also as APC)	
TOTAL	3000-3500

artillery:

model	number
self-propelled guns and howitzers--	
155mm M-109 SP howitzer	
155mm GCT SP howitzer	

155mm Majnoon howitzer/gun (unconf.)
152mm M-1973 SP howitzer
122mm M-1974 SP howitzer
towed guns and howitzers--
    180mm S-23
    155mm G-5 howitzer/gun
    155mm GHN-45 howitzer/gun
    155mm M-114 A1 howitzer
    152mm D-20
    152mm M-1976 (2A36) howitzer
    152mm M-1943 (D-1) howitzer
    130mm M-46 gun/ 130mm Type 59 gun
    122mm D-30 howitzer/Saddam howitzer
    122mm M-1938 howitzer
    105mm M-56 Pack howitzer
    105mm M-102 howitzer
    85mm field/AT gun
mortars, heavy, over 160mm--
    160mm mortar
mortars, heavy, under 160mm--
    120mm x 4 SP
    120mm M-43 mortar
TOTAL   ca.1500
artillery/mortar locating radars--
    Thomson-CSF
    Cymbeline mortar locating radar
artillery ammunition carriers--
    MT-LB (some MT-LB used as artillery prime-
        movers, command post vehicles, mortar carriers,
        MRL carriers and other tasks)
MRLs--
    550mm Laith 90 (possibly still experimental)
    400mm Ababil-100 (unconfirmed)
    300mm SS-60 Astros II (also designated Sajeel-60)
    262mm Ababil-50
    180mm SS-40 Astros (also designated Sajeel-40)
    132mm BM-13
    130mm

128mm M-63
127mm SS-30 Astros II
122mm BM-21/BM-11
122mm Firos-25
107mm
on order (before the 1991 Gulf War, now suspended):
155mm GCT SP howitzers; 300mm SS-60

engineering equipment:
BLG-60
MTU-55 bridging tanks
GSP self-propelled ferries
mine-clearing rollers
minefield crossing system (similar to Viper)
PMP pontoon bridges
TPP pontoon bridges
Soviet-model tank-towed bridges

AFV transporters: 1500-2500
anti-tank weapons:
missiles--   launchers
AT-3 (Sagger)
AT-4 (Spigot)
AT-5 (Spandrel, carried on BMP-2 APCs)
BGM-71A TOW
BRDM-2 (carrying AT-3 Sagger) SP
M-3 (carrying HOT) SP
VCR/TH (carrying HOT) SP
MILAN
M-901 ITV (TOW under Armor)
Swingfire
TOTAL   1500
guns--
107mm B-11 recoilless rifle

surface-to-surface missiles and rockets:

model	launchers
FROG-7	+
SS-1 (Scud B)	+
al-Hussein mobile	up to 5

number of remaining missiles--
    estimated at 100-200 al-Hussein, concealed
    on order: All programs delayed by results of 1991 Gulf
        War, though not canceled; capability to fire SSMs
        depends on success or failure of UN arms control
        enforcement in Iraq

army anti-aircraft defenses:

missiles--	launchers
self-propelled/mobile	
SA-6 (Gainful)	
SA-8 (Gecko)	20
SA-9 (Gaskin) SP	
SA-13 (Gopher)	
Roland I/II	100
man-portable	
SA-7 (Grail)	
SA-14 (Gremlin)	
SA-16	

short-range guns--	number
57mm ZSU 57x2 SP	
57mm	
37mm M-1939	
23mm ZSU 23x4 SP (Gun Dish)	
23mm ZU 23x2	
TOTAL	

CW capabilities:

personal protective equipment
Soviet-type unit decontamination equipment
stockpile of chemical agents: mustard (sulphur mustard and
    purified mustard), sarin, tabun; soman, VX at
    experimental level; hydrogen cyanide (unconfirmed); a
    portion of chemical agents destroyed by UN missions
delivery systems (SSM warheads, thousands of artillery
    shells, mortar bombs, MRL rockets, aerial bombs and
    land mines)

biological warfare capabilities:
 toxins and other biological weapons, specifically anthrax
 and typhoid; BW capability largely unaffected by UN
 observer activity

Air Force:

	number
aircraft--general:	
combat aircraft	
(excluding a/c in Iran)	400
transport aircraft	a few
helicopters	ca. 400
combat aircraft:	number
interceptors--	
high quality	
MiG-25 (Foxbat)	20
MiG-29 (Fulcrum; multi-role	
aircraft employed	
in interceptor role)	25
(sub-total	ca. 45)
others	
MiG-21 MF/bis/U (Fishbed)/F-7	110
MiG-23 MF/ML	ca. 40
(sub-total	ca. 150)
Total	195
strike and multi-role aircraft--	
high quality	
Su-24 (Fencer C)	a few
medium quality	
MiG-23 B (Flogger)/MiG-27	40
Mirage F-1B/EQ5/EQ2/EQ4	40
Su-20/22 (Fitter C/H)	60
Su-25 (Frogfoot)	30
(sub-total	170)
others	
Su-7B (Fitter A, possibly not serviceable)	+
Total	ca. 195

bombers--

Tu-22 (Blinder)	ca. 4
Tu-16 (Badger)/H-6 (B-6D)	ca. 4
Total	8

TOTAL (all combat a/c,
excluding a/c in Iran)   ca. 400

Iraqi combat aircraft flown to Iran (not included in
the list of 400 combat a/c above)--

MiG-29 (Fulcrum)	4
Su-24 (Fencer, introduced into service by Iran)	24
MiG-23 (Flogger)	12
Mirage F-1	24
Su-20/22 (Fitter)	24
Su-25 (Frogfoot)	7
others	20
Total	115

Iraqi transport aircraft flown to Iran (partly
civilian, not including 6 Kuwaiti a/c)   15

transport aircraft (including tankers):

An-12 (Cub, some converted to refuelling a/c)	+
An-24 (Coke)	+
An-26 (Curl)	+
IL-76 (Candid, some tankers)	+
Mystere-Falcon 20/Falcon 50	+
Tu-124A/Tu-134 (Crusty)	+
TOTAL	a few

training and liaison aircraft:

with ground attack/close air support capability--

L-29 (Delfin)	20
L-39 (Albatross)	30
(sub-total	50)

others--

Embraer EMB-312 (Tucano)	+
MBB-223 Flamingo	+

Pilatus PC-7	+
Pilatus PC-9	+
(sub-total	ca. 150)
TOTAL	ca. 200
helicopters:	number
attack (part of Army Aviation)--	
Alouette III (armed)	30
Mi-24/Mi-25 (Hind)	30
SA-342 Gazelle	50
MBB BO-105	75
(sub-total	185)
heavy transport (mostly Army Aviation)--	
AS-61	5
SA-321 Super Frelon (also	
employed in maritime attack role)	10
Mi-6 (Hook)	15
(sub-total	30)
medium transport (mostly Army Aviation)--	
AS-332 Super Puma	a few
BK-117	20-25
Mi-8/Mi-17 (Hip)	100
SA-330 Puma	+
Bell 214	40
Mi-2 (Hoplite)	a few
light transport (part	
of Army Aviation)--	
Alouette III	
Hughes 500D	+
Hughes 300C	+
Hughes 530F	+
TOTAL	400
miscellaneous aircraft:	
AEW/AWACS aircraft--	
Adnan 1/Adnan 2 AEW	1-2
UAVs and mini UAVs--	
Mirach 100	
flown to Iran:	
2 Adnan 2 AEW	

advanced armament:
  air-to-air missiles--
    AA-2 (Atoll)
    AA-6 (Acrid)
    AA-7 (Apex)
    AA-8 (Aphid)
    AA-11 (Archer)
    R-530
    R-550 Magique
    Super 530D/F
  air-to-ground missiles--
    AM-39 Exocet
    Armat (anti-radar)
    AS-2 (Kipper, unconfirmed)
    AS-4 (Kitchen)
    AS-5 (Kelt)
    AS-6 (Kingfish)
    AS-7 (Kerry)
    AS-9 (Kyle)
    AS-10 (laser-guided)
    AS-12
    AS-14 (Kedge)
    AS-15TT anti-ship missile
    AS-20 (unconfirmed)
    AS-30L (laser-guided)
    AT-2 (Swatter)
    C-601
    HOT (unconfirmed)
    LX anti-ship missile (unconfirmed)
    X-23 anti-radiation missile (unconfirmed)
  bombs--
    Belouga CBU
    Cardoen CBU
    Fuel-air Explosive (FAE) bombs
anti-aircraft defenses:
  radars--
    P-35/37 Barlock
    P-15 Flat Face

P-15M Squat Eye
P-14 Tall King
P-12 Spoon Rest
TRS-2215
TRS-2230
long-range missiles--

model	batteries
SA-2 (Guideline)/ SA-3 (Goa)	60

aircraft shelters--
for all combat aircraft

military airfields (suffered damage during 1991 War): 38
Abu-Ajal (near Amara), al-Asad, Arbil, al Bakr, Balad, Basra, H-2, H-3 (al-Walid), Habbaniyah, Jalibah, Khalid (near Zakho), Kirkuk, Kut al-Amarah (Ubaydah bin al-Jarrah), Kut al-Amarah new field, Mosul, Mudaysis, Muthanah, al-Nasiriyah, al-Qadisiyah, al-Rashid (Baghdad), al-Rumaylah, Saddam, Salman, al-Shuaiba, al-Tallil, al-Taqaddum, al-Tuz, Wadi al-Khir, 10 additional

aircraft maintenance and repair capability:
repair of main models, until January 1991 with assistance from Soviet, Egyptian, and French technicians, discontinued thereafter; considerable indigenous repair capability

Navy:

combat vessels:	number
MFPBs--	
Ossa I	1
Ossa II (a second Ossa II fled to Iran and held there)	1
Total	2
gunboats/MTBs--	
Bogomol	2
patrol craft--	
PB-90	6
landing craft:	
Polnochny class LCT	2

on order: 3 3500 ton LSTs (ready for delivery, held in Denmark)

auxiliary vessels:
Stromboli class support ship
(held in Egypt)   1

advanced armament:
surface-to-surface missiles--
SS-N-2 Styx
on order: OTOMAT Mk.2, delivery only after UN embargo ends
naval mines--
Italian Manta mines
Soviet models

special maritime forces:
frogmen and divers

coastal defense:
HY-2 (Silkworm)   3-4 launchers

naval bases: 2
Basra, Umm Qasr, Faw (all damaged during the Iran-Iraq War and the 1991 Gulf War; Umm Qasr gradually ceded to Kuwait beginning in 1993)

ship maintenance and repair capability:
one 6,000 ton capacity floating dock (held in Egypt)

6. ISRAEL

BASIC DATA

Official Name of State: State of Israel

Head of State: President Haim Herzog (President Ezer Weizman after May 13, 1993)

Prime Minister: Itzhak Rabin (also Minister of Defense)

Chief of the General Staff: Lieutenant General Ehud Barak

Commander of the Air Force: Major General Hertzel Bodinger

Commander of Field Forces HQ: Major General Emanuel Sakel

Commander of the Navy: Rear Admiral Ami Ayalon

Area: 20,770 sq. km. including East Jerusalem and vicinity annexed in 1967 (not including Golan Heights, 1,176 sq. km., to which Israeli law was applied in 1981)

Population:		5,113,000
ethnic subdivision:		
Jews	4,177,000	81.9%
Arabs, Druze, and others (Armenian, Circassian, European)	936,000	18.1%
religious subdivision:		
Jews	4,177,000	81.9%
Muslims	715,000	14.0%
Christians	135,000	2.4%
Druze and others	86,000	1.7%

Administered Territories (data regarding the territories occupied by Israel in 1967; the Jewish population in the territories and the Golan Heights and the Druze in the Golan Heights are also included in Israeli population figures, above. East Jerusalem Jewish population listed as Israelis not in territories):

Territories	Area (sq. km.)	Arab population (thousands)		
		July 1967	1977	1992
Judea & Samaria	5,879	596	681	1005.6
Gaza Strip	378	390	441	676.1
Golan Heights (Druze populat.)	1,176	7		15.7

	Jewish population (thousands)			Jewish settlements		
	July 1967	1977	1992	1967	1977	1992
Judea & Samaria	0	4.4	90.6	0	39	119
Gaza Strip	0	0.1	3.0	0	4	14
Golan Heights	0	3.0	11.6	0	22	30

GDP:
  1990--$51.2 billion
  1991--$59.1 billion

Balance of Payments (goods, services & unilateral transfer payments):

year	income	expenditure	balance
1990	$22.38 bil.	$20.10 bil.	+$2.28 bil.
1991	$23.15 bil.	$22.70 bil.	+$450 mil.

Defense Expenditure (including US aid):
  1990--$5.5 billion
  1992--$6.3 billion (average rate of exchange 2.62 shekel
    per $1)

Foreign Military Aid and Security Assistance Received:
  financial aid from:
    USA--$1.8 billion grant (1992), a gift of surplus weapons
    from European drawdown arsenal worth approximately
    $700 million (spread over several years, i.e., possibly
    $100-150 million per annum); FRG--a commitment for
    ca.$140 million per year over five years, cost of a
    MIM-104 battery and current construction of 2 submarines
    in Germany
  military training:
    trainees abroad in--USA, Britain, France, FRG

arms transfers from:
USA (tanks, SP artillery, naval SSMs, combat aircraft, helicopters, tank transporters)
Belgium (LMGs)
Britain (spare parts)
France (spare parts, aircraft engines)
FRG (ABC detection vehicles; payment for US-made MIM-104 SAMs; submarines on order)
support forces from:
USA, Netherlands (MIM-104 Patriot batteries, January-March 1991)
Foreign Military Aid and Security Assistance Extended:
financial aid to:
South Lebanon militia--100 million
military training:
advisors/instructors/technicians in--Azerbaijan (unconfirmed), Colombia*, Ecuador*, Ethiopia* Liberia, Peru*, Singapore*, South Lebanon (SLA militia), Zaire
foreign trainees from--Azerbaijan (unconfirmed), Colombia*, Lebanon (SLA militia), Liberia, Papua New Guinea, Zaire
arms transfers to:
Argentina (aircraft sub-components, AAMs, aircraft radars, MRLs)
Australia (conversion of Boeing 707 aircraft to aerial tankers, electronics, conversion of executive jets to maritime patrol a/c)
Azerbaijan (Stinger SAMs, radio sets, unconfirmed)
Brazil* (naval SSMs)
Belgium* (naval tactical training center, ground forces radar)
Cameroon* (transport aircraft)
Cambodia (protective vests)
Canada (ammunition, mine clearing rollers)

---

* According to foreign and Israeli publications

Chile* (AAMs, AAGs, tanks, artillery, mortars, night vision devices, MFPBs, naval SSMs, radio transceivers, mini-UAVs)

Colombia* (combat aircraft, small arms, radio transceivers)

Ecuador* (AAMs, naval SSMs)

El Salvador* (transport aircraft)

Ethiopia* (rifles, T-55 tanks, CBUs during the Mengistu regime)

Fiji* (patrol boats on order)

France (protective vests)

FRG (ammunition, electronic equipment, ECMs, mini-UAVs jointly produced, protective vests)

Guatamala (rifles)

Haiti (Uzi SMGs, Galil rifles)

Honduras* (transport aircraft)

Ireland* (ballistic helmets, communications equipment, small arms ammunition)

Italy (tank ammunition)

Kenya (naval SSMs)

Lebanese militia - SLA (small arms, tanks, artillery pieces)

Liberia (transport aircraft)

Lithuania (sub-machine guns)

Netherlands (small arms)

Papua New Guinea (patrol craft, transport aircraft)

Paraguay (transport aircraft)

PRC* (AAMs; additional items)

Peru* (ARVs, helicopters, patrol boats)

Singapore* (electronic warfare systems, UAVs, aerial refuelling aircraft, electronic components for combat a/c, shipborne anti-missile missile on order, naval SSMs, AAMs, naval tactical training center)

South Africa* (refuelling aircraft, mini-UAVs; ATGMs)

Spain* (tank guns, tank fire control systems, optronics and range finders)

Swaziland* (transport aircraft)

---

* According to foreign and Israeli publications

Switzerland (jointly produced mini-UAVs, tank and artillery ammunition)

Sweden (protective vests)

Taiwan* (AAMs, naval SSMs; shipborne anti-missile missile on order)

Thailand (transport aircraft, mini-UAVs, AAMs, naval SSMs, upgrading avionics in trainer aircraft)

USA (parts, mini-UAVs jointly produced, light AT rockets, tactical air-launched decoys, mine ploughs for tanks, bridging equipment, AGMs jointly produced)

Venezuela (MRLs, aerial tanker a/c)

forces deployed in Lebanon:

Units on a small scale in the Southern Lebanese security zone (about 600 men, in case of clashes or tension reinforced by forces stationed in northern Israel)

Cooperation in Arms Production/Assembly/R&D with:

Argentina* (tank components, assistance in upgrading Argentinian ASW aircraft); Belgium (ground forces radar) ; Chile (assistance in upgrading combat aircraft in Chile; provision of AAGs and turrets for Chilean-made SP AAG vehicles); Colombia* (assistance in upgrading combat aircraft in Colombia); Czech Republic (upgrading electronics in trainer aircraft); FRG (joint production in FRG of mini-UAVs, joint development of an anti-radiation attack drone); Romania (jointly producing night vision for Romanian IAR-330 Puma helicopters, cooperation on ATGM production in Romania; upgrading 100 MiG-21s in Romania, negotiations not completed); South Africa* (joint production of a South African combat aircraft); Switzerland* (cooperation in production of mini-UAVs in Switzerland); USA (aircraft components, electronics, naval vessels, terminal guidance bombs, tactical air launched decoys, UAVs, AGMs; joint research on Arrow ATBM)

Joint Maneuvers with:

USA

---

* According to foreign and Israeli publications

INFRASTRUCTURE
Road Network:
length (paved):   4,760 km

    main routes:

        Tel Aviv--Jerusalem

        Tel Aviv--Hadera--Haifa

        Tel Aviv--Ashdod--Beer Sheva

        Hadera--Afula--Tiberias/ Afula--Amiad--Rosh-Pina

        Haifa--Tiberias

        Haifa--Nahariya--Naqura (Lebanon)

        Acco (Acre)--Safed--Rosh Pina/Acco--Amiad

        Rosh Pina--Kuneitra (Syria)

        Tiberias--Metula--Marj Ayoun (Lebanon)

        Beer Sheva--Eilat

        Rafah (Rafiah)--Nitsana--Eilat

        Eilat--Sharm al-Shaykh (Egypt)

        Beer Sheva--Nitzana--Ismailiya (Egypt)

        Tel Aviv--Gaza--Kantara (Egypt)

        Jerusalem--Hebron--Arad/Beer Sheva

        Jerusalem--Nablus--Afula

        Jerusalem--Allenby Bridge--Amman (Jordan)

        Jerusalem--Jericho--Beit Shean/Jericho--Eilat

Railway Network:
length (standard gauge):   594 km

    main routes:

        Tel Aviv--Haifa

        Haifa--Nahariya

        Tel Aviv--Jerusalem

        Tel Aviv--Beer Sheva--Oron

        Kiryat-Gat--Ashkelon--Ashdod

        Tel Aviv--Lod--Ashdod

        Lod--Haifa

Airfields:
airfields by runway type:

    permanent surface fields   26

    unpaved fields and usable airstrips   29

airfields by runway length:

2440--3659 meters	6
1220--2439	11
under 1220	38
TOTAL	55

international airports: Ben Gurion (Tel Aviv), Eilat; occasionally charter flights land at Uvda military airfield

major domestic airfields: Beer Sheva, Haifa, Jerusalem, Massada, Rosh Pina, Tel Aviv

Airlines:

companies: El Al (international); CAL (cargo); Arkia/Kanaf-Arkia (domestic and charter); Nesher (taxi and charter); Sun d'Or (charter); Shahaf (domestic and charter)

aircraft:

BN-2 Islander	1
Boeing 767/767ER	4
Boeing 757	5
Boeing 747-200B/200F/200B Combi/100F	8
Boeing 737-200	2
Boeing 707-320B/320C	3
Cessna 337	2
Commander 680FL	1
DHC-6 Twin Otter	1
DHC-7 Dash 7	5
Piper Navajo/Chieftain	5

on order: 2 additional Boeing 757; 1 DHC-6 Twin Otter; 2 Boeing 747-40

Maritime Facilities:

harbors--Ashdod, Eilat, Haifa

anchorages--Tel Aviv-Yaffo

oil terminals--Ashkelon, Eilat, Haifa

coal terminal--Hadera

Merchant Marine:

vessel type	number	DWT
general cargo	7	
container	21	
refrigerated cargo	2	
TOTAL	30	611,795

Nuclear Capability:

two nuclear research reactors

Defense Production:

army equipment:

manufacture--artillery pieces; small arms; ATGMs; ATRLs; heavy, medium and light mortars; MRLs; artillery, mortar and small arms ammunition; mines; mine-clearing rollers; tanks; tank guns; tread width mine ploughs for tanks (TWMP); SP AAGs (Soviet gun, USA carrier)

aircraft and air ammunition:

manufacture (some joint ventures with US companies)-- AAMs; AGMs; CBUs; TV and laser terminal guidance bombs; naval patrol aircraft; mini UAVs; operational flight trainer systems; radars; upgrading of combat aircraft; refuelling system for aircraft

production under license--helicopter parts; combat aircraft parts

naval craft and naval ammunition:

manufacture--LCTs; MFPBs; patrol boats; SSMs

production under license--patrol boats; torpedo components

electronics:

manufacture--radars; direction finders; ELINT equipment; EW jammers; radio transceivers; audio/video microwave transceivers; radio voice scramblers and encryption units; air launched decoys; AEW a/c conversion

optronics:

manufacture--night vision devices, laser rangefinders and target designators

space:

a satellite under development

ARMED FORCES
Personnel:
military forces--

	regular	reserve	total
army	134,000	365,000	499,000
air force	32,000	55,000	87,000
navy	10,000	10,000	20,000
TOTAL	176,000	430,000	606,000

para-military forces--
Nahal--7,500

border police--6,000

Army:
major units (including reserves):

unit type	divisions	independent brigades
armored	12	
mechanized/infantry/ territorial	4	8
airborne		5
TOTAL	16	13

anti-Intifada HQ: 2 divisional HQ for control of units engaged in anti-Intifada activities in Judea, Samaria and Gaza. Not counted as normal division HQs.

small arms:
personal weapons--

9mm Uzi SMG

7.62mm AK-47 (Kalashnikov)

7.62mm Galil sniper rifle

7.62mm M-14 SAR

5.56mm Galil AR

5.56mm M-16 A1 & A2 AR

machine guns--

12.7mm (0.5") Browning M2 HMG

7.62mm (0.3") Browning M-1919 A1 MMG

7.62mm MAG (FN) LMG

7.62mm RPD (Degtyarev) LMG

5.56mm Minimi (FN) LMG

5.56mm Negev LMG
automatic grenade launchers--
   40mm Mk.19
light and medium mortars--
   81mm Soltam
   60mm
   52mm IMI
light ATRLs--
   M-72 LAW
   RPG-7
   B-300

tanks:

model	number
high quality	
Merkava Mk.I/Mk.II/Mk.III	870
M-60 A3/upgraded M-60/Magach 7	750
(sub-total	1620)
medium quality	
Centurion/upgraded Centurion	1050
M-60/M-60 A1	650
M-48 A5	340
T-62	140
T-55	50
(sub-total	2230)
TOTAL	3850

on order: additional Merkava Mk.III

APCs/ARVs:

model	number
high quality	
Israeli APC	a few
M-113 (various marks)	
Nagmashot*	100
RBY	
(sub-total	5100)

---

* According to foreign and Israeli publications

others
    M-2 & M-3 halftrack
    BTR-50
    OT-62
    BRDM-2

	(sub-total	3000)

TOTAL   8100

artillery:
self-propelled guns and howitzers--
    203mm M-110 SP howitzer
    175mm M-107 SP gun
    155mm M-109 A1 & A2 SP howitzer
    155mm L-33 SP howitzer (possibly phased out)
    155mm M-50 SP howitzer (possibly phased out)
towed guns and howitzers--
    155mm M-71 howitzer
    130mm M-46 gun
    122mm D-30 howitzer
mortars, heavy, over 160mm--
    160mm SP mortar
mortars, heavy, under 160mm--
    120mm mortar   250
TOTAL   1300
artillery/mortar-locating radars--
    AN/TPQ-37
    AN/PPS-15
MRLs--
    290mm MAR 290
    240mm
    140mm
    122mm BM-21
    Keres anti-radar rocket
on order: 350mm MAR 350
engineering equipment:
Gilois motorized bridges
M-123 Viper minefield crossing system
M-60 AVLB
mine-clearing rollers

mine layers
Pomins II portable mine neutralization system[*]
tank-towed bridges
TLB (trailer launched bridge)
TWMP (tread width mine ploughs)

AFV transporters: +
anti-tank weapons:
  missiles--
    AT-3 (Sagger)
    BGM-71A TOW and BGM-71C Improved TOW
    M-47 Dragon
    Mapats SP
    Nimrod
    Israeli BGM-71C Improved TOW SP

surface-to-surface missiles and rockets:

model	launchers
MGM-52C (Lance)	12
Jericho Mk. I/II SSM[*]	

army anti-aircraft defenses:

missiles--	launchers
self-propelled/mobile	
MIM-72A Chaparral	ca. 50
man-portable	
FIM-92A Stinger	
MIM-43A Redeye	
SA-7 (Grail)	

short-range guns--	number
40mm Bofors L-70	
37mm M-1939 (possibly phased out)	
ZU 23x2	
20mm M-163 A1 Vulcan SP	
20mm TCM-20 Hispano Suiza SP	
20mm Hispano Suiza	
TOTAL	900

on order: ADAMS system

---

[*] According to foreign and Israeli publications

CW capabilities:
personal protective equipment
unit decontamination equipment
Fuchs (Fox) ABC detection vehicles   8
SPW-40 P2Ch ABC detection vehicles   50
ground forces radars:
AN/PPS-15

Air Force:

aircraft--general:	number
combat aircraft (including aircraft in storage)	694
transport aircraft	97
helicopters	224

combat aircraft:
interceptors--
    high quality
        F-15 Eagle   65
strike and multi-role aircraft--
    high quality
        F-16A/B/C/D (most F-16A/C may be
          employed as interceptors)   174
    others
        F-4E/RF-4E Phantom and Phantom 2000   140
        A-4 Skyhawk   165
        Kfir C-2/TC-2/C-7/TC-7   150
    Total   455
TOTAL   694
on order: 10 F-15A from USA drawdown in Europe, 30 F-16C/D (delivery in process, part of an order of 60 a/c), upgraded F-4 designated Phantom 2000; a few A-4 Skyhawk two seat a/c from US drawdown (unconfirmed)

transport aircraft (including tankers):
Arava   10
Beechcraft Queen Air   12
Boeing 707   10
Boeing 707 tanker (refuelling)   3
C-130H Hercules   22

DC-3 Dakota (C-47)	20
Dornier Do-28	17
KC-130 tanker (refuelling)	3
TOTAL	97

on order: Beechcraft Bonanza A-36 (light executive aircraft)

training and liaison aircraft:

with ground attack/close air support capability--

CM-170 Fouga Magister/Tzukit (some in storage)	80

others--

Cessna U-206 (Stationair-6)		21
Piper Cub		35
	(sub-total	56)
TOTAL		136

helicopters:

attack--

AH-64A Apache		18
AH-1G/1S Cobra		40
500MG Defender		33
	(sub-total	91)

naval attack/search & rescue--

HH-65A Dolphin	2

heavy transport--

CH-53	36

medium transport--

Bell-212	55

light transport--

AB-206 JetRanger/Bell-206L	40
TOTAL	224

on order: 6 additional CH-53, 10 UH-60 Black Hawk, 18-24 additional AH-64A Apache from US drawdown

maritime surveillance aircraft:

Seascan (Westwind 1124N)	3

miscellaneous aircraft:
  AEW/AWACS aircraft--
    E-2C Hawkeye AEW   4
    Boeing 707 AEW*
  ELINT and EW--
    Boeing 707 ELINT*
    Boeing 707 EW*
  target drones--
    Beech AQM-37A
    Beech BQM-107B
  UAVs and mini-UAVs--
    Mastiff mini-UAV
    Pioneer mini-UAV
    Scout mini-UAV
    Searcher mini-UAV
    MQM-74C Chuckar II UAV
    Teledyne Ryan 1241 UAV
    on order: Hunter mini UAV
advanced armament:
  air-to-air missiles--
    AIM-9 Sidewinder; AIM-9L
    AIM-7 Sparrow
    Python 3
    Shafrir
  air-to-ground missiles--
    AGM-78D Standard ARM
    AGM-65 Maverick
    AGM-62A Walleye
    AGM-45 A/B Shrike
    Popeye (equivalent to AGM-142)*
  bombs--
    CBU (including Tal-1, ATA-1000, ATA-500)
    runway-penetration bombs
    Pyramid TV terminal-guidance bombs
    Guillotine laser terminal-guidance bombs

---

* According to foreign and Israeli publications

Opher terminal-guidance bombs
on order: AIM-9M AAM
EW and CEW equipment:
chaff and flare dispensers for combat aircraft
Samson AN/ADM-141 TALD
on order: 20 AN/ALQ 131 electronic countermeasures
   systems
anti-aircraft defenses:
radars--
   Elta
   FPS-100
   AN/TPS-43
long-range missiles--
   model batteries
   HAWK
   MIM-23B Improved HAWK
   MIM-104 Patriot   3
   on order: 1 additional battery of MIM-104 Patriot
      SAMs, delivery 1993
aircraft shelters--
   in all operational airfields, for combat aircraft
military airfields: 11
   Haifa, Hatzerim, Hatzor, Lod, Nevatim, Palmachim,
   Ramat David, Ramon, Tel Aviv, Tel Nof, Uvda
aircraft maintenance and repair capability:
   maintenance on all models in service, partly in airfields,
   partly at Israel Aircraft Industries facilities

Navy:

combat vessels:	number
submarines--	
IKL/Vickers Type 206	3
MFPBs--	
Dvora	2
Sa'ar 2 and 3 class	6
Sa'ar 4 class (Reshef)	8
Sa'ar 4.5 class (Aliyah/Nirit)	5
Total	21

patrol craft--

Dabur class and Dvora/Super Dvora	40
PBR--Yatush	6
Total	46

on order: 3 Sa'ar 5 missile corvettes (delivery in 1994-95); additional Dvora patrol craft; 2 Dolphin submarines (delivery 1996-1997); upgrading of Sa'ar 4 class to improved Sa'ar 4.5 (Nirit) level

landing craft:

Ashdod class LCT	3
Bat-Sheva class LST	1
LSM 1 class	3
Sealand Mk III hovercraft	2
Shikmona class LCT	3
US type LCM	3
TOTAL	15

auxiliary vessels:

support ship	1

swimmer delivery vehicles

advanced armament:

surface-to-surface missiles--
Gabriel 2 & 3
RGM-84A Harpoon
sub-Harpoon (unconfirmed)

anti-missile guns--
20mm Vulcan-Phalanx radar-controlled anti-missile gun

advanced torpedoes--
Mk.37 anti-submarine torpedoe

on order: NT-37E anti-submarine torpedo, Barak anti-missile missile

special maritime forces:

frogmen and divers

naval bases: Ashdod, Eilat, Haifa   3

ship maintenance and repair capability:

repair and maintenance of all naval vessels at Haifa, partly in conjunction with Israel Wharves

Note: maritime surveillance aircraft and naval attack helicopters listed under Air Force

7. JORDAN

B A S I C   D A T A

Official Name of State: The Hashemite Kingdom of Jordan
Head of State: King Hussein Ibn Talal al-Hashimi
Prime Minister: Sharif Zaid Ben Shaker (also Defense Minister)
Chief of the Joint Staff of the Armed Forces: Field Marshal Fathi Abu Talib
Commander of the People's Army: Major General Hani al-Majaly
Commander of the Air Force: Major General Ihsan Shurdum
Commander of the Navy/Coast Guard: Hussein Hassuana
Area: 90,700 sq. km. (excluding West Bank; Jordan renounced all claims to this territory in July 1988)
Population (excluding West Bank Jordanian passport holders working abroad):
ethnic subdivision:

Arabs	3,004,500	98.0%
Circassians & Armenians	61,000	2.0%

religious subdivision:

Sunni Muslims	2,869,000	93.6%
Greek Orthodox & other Christians	169,000	5.5%
Others	27,000	0.9%

GDP:
1990--$3.95 billion
1991--$4.12 billion
Balance of Payments (goods, services & unilateral transfer payments):

year	income	expenditure	balance
1990	$3.67 bil.	$3.57 bil.	+$100 mil.
1991	$4.08 bil.	$3.34 bil.	+$740 mil.

Defense Expenditure:
1990--$570 million
1991--$500 million

Foreign Military Aid and Security Assistance Received:
    financial aid from:
        USA--$27 million grant (1992)
    military training:
        foreign advisors/instructors from--USA, USSR until 1991,
            Russia since (a few)
        trainees abroad in--Britain, Pakistan, Saudi Arabia, USA,
            USSR until 1991
    arms transfers from:
        Belgium (tank fire control systems)
        Brazil (APCs)
        Britain (bridging equipment, radars, ATRLs, patrol boats)
        France (helicopters, AAMs, AGMs, artillery fire control
            systems,ATRLs)
        Netherlands (night vision devices)
        Spain (transport aircraft, trainer aircraft)
        USA (tanks, SP artillery, terminally guided artillery shells,
            ATGMs, spare parts for US-made arms)
        USSR until end of 1991 (SAMs, AAGs, APCs)
    maintenance of equipment in:
        FRG (transport aircraft); Greece (combat aircraft)
Foreign Military Aid and Security Assistance Extended:
    military training:
        foreign trainees from--Algeria, Bahrain, Lebanon, Oman,
            Qatar, Saudi Arabia, UAE, Yemen
    arms transfers to:
        Iraq (ammunition, possibly discontinued in mid-1992)
        Badr unit of the PLA (small arms; controlled by Jordanian
            Army)
    facilities provided to:
        Iraq (use of harbor, airfields and supply route, refuge to
        Iraqi commercial a/c); PLA (camp for Badr unit); PLO and
        other organizations (offices)
Cooperation in Arms Production/Assembly with:
    Britain and USA (tank upgrading and electronics); Singapore
    (electronics)
Joint Maneuvers with:
    USA (Special Forces, Air Force); Egypt, Britain

INFRASTRUCTURE

Road Network:

length:	7,500 km
paved roads	5,500 km
gravel and stone roads	2,000 km

main routes:

Amman--Ramtha--Dara (Syria)

Amman--Mafaq--Baghdad (Iraq)

Amman--Maan--Tabuk (Saudi Arabia)/Maan-- Aqaba

Amman--Allenby Bridge--Jerusalem (Israel)

Amman--al-Salt--Damiah Bridge--Nablus (West Bank)

Railway Network:

length (narrow gauge):	619 km

main routes:

Amman--Ramtha--Dara (Syria)

Amman--Maan--Aqaba/Maan--Haret Ammar (Saudi Arabian border)

Airfields:

airfields by runway type:

permanent surface fields	14
unpaved fields and usable airstrips	2

airfields by runway length:

over 3660 meters	1
2440--3659	13
under 1220	2
TOTAL	16

international airports: Amman (Queen Alia), Aqaba

major domestic airfields: Amman (Marka), Mafraq, Zarqa, Maan, H-5

Airlines:

companies: Royal Jordanian Airline (international and domestic)

aircraft:

Airbus A-320	2
Airbus A-310-300	6
Boeing 727-200	3

Boeing 707-300C		3
L-1011-500 Tristar		4
on order: 1 additional A-320		

Maritime Facilities:
  harbors--Aqaba
  oil terminals--Aqaba

Merchant Marine:

vessel type	number	DWT
tanker	1	
cargo	1	
bulk carrier	1	
TOTAL	3	135,473

Defense Production:
  electronics:
    Assembly and production of computers (joint venture with companies from USA, Britain and Singapore); upgrading of avionics (joint venture)
  optronics:
    night vision devices (licenced production)

ARMED FORCES
Personnel:
  military forces (not all reserves are organized/operational)--

	regular	reserve	total
army	80,000-90,000	60,000	140,000-150,000
air force	9,700	-	9,700
navy	300	-	300
TOTAL	90,000-100,000	60,000	150,000-160,000

  para-military forces--
    one brigade of General Security Forces (gendarmerie)
    People's Army--200,000-250,000

Army:
  major units:

unit type	divisions	independent brigades
armored	2	
mechanized infantry	2	

infantry		2
airborne/		
special forces		1
TOTAL	4	3

small arms:
personal weapons--
  7.62mm AK-47 (Kalashnikov) AR
  7.62mm G-3 (Heckler & Koch) AR
  5.56mm M-16 A1/A2 AR
machine guns--
  12.7mm (0.5") Browning M2 HMG
  7.62mm (0.3") Browning M-1919 MMG
  7.62mm MAG (FN) LMG
  7.62mm M-60D GPMG/LMG
light and medium mortars--
  81mm M-29
light ATRLs--
  APILAS
  3.5" M-20 (being phased out)
  LAW-80

tanks (including about 300 in storage):

model	number
high quality	
Chieftain (Jordanian designation Khalid)	275
M-60 A3	100
(sub-total	375)
medium quality	
Centurion (improved, Jordanian designation	
Tariq)	290
M-60 A1	100
Chieftain (from Iran, captured by Iraq,	
in storage, not serviceable)	90
(sub-total	480)
low quality	
M-48 A1 (in storage, not operational)	212
TOTAL	1067

APCs/ARVs (including security service):

model	number
high quality	
BMP-2	25
M-113 A1/A2	1240
Engesa EE-11 (with Security Forces)	100
(sub-total	1365)
others	
Ferret (obsolete, probably in storage)	140
Saracen/Saladin (obsolete, in storage)	60
(sub-total	200)
TOTAL	1565

artillery:
self-propelled guns and howitzers--
203mm M-110 A2 SP howitzer
155mm M-109 A2 SP howitzer
155mm M-44 SP howitzer
105mm M-52 howitzer
towed guns and howitzers--
203mm (8") M-115 gun
155mm M-59 (Long Tom) gun
155mm M-114 howitzer
105mm M-102 A1 howitzer
mortars, heavy, under 160mm--
120mm mortar

TOTAL (including 200 in storage)	600

PGM--
100 155mm Copperhead projectiles (CLGP)

engineering equipment:
bridges (British model)
British mine-clearing ploughs and dozers
attached to Chieftain and Centurion tanks
UDK-1

AFV transporters (number unconfirmed):	200

anti-tank weapons:

missiles--	launchers
BGM-71A TOW/BGM-71C Improved TOW	
M-47 Dragon	

M-901 ITV SP (TOW under armor)	
TOTAL	550

army anti-aircraft defenses:

missiles--	launchers
self-propelled/mobile	
SA-8 (Gecko)	50
SA-13 (Gopher) SP	+
man-portable	
MIM-43A Redeye	300
SA-14 (Gremlin)	+
short-range guns--	number
40mm M-42 SP (to be phased out)	+
23mm ZSU 23x4 SP (Gun Dish)	+
20mm M-163 A1 Vulcan SP	100

CW capabilities:
personal protective and decontamination equipment

Air Force:

aircraft--general:	number
combat aircraft	103
transport aircraft	18
helicopters	54+

combat aircraft:

strike and multi-role aircraft--	
medium quality	
Mirage F-1 C/E	33
others	
F-5 E/F	70
TOTAL	103

transport aircraft:

Boeing 727	1
C-130 Hercules	6
CASA C-212	2
Dove	1
Gulfstream III	2

L-1011-500	1
Mystere-Falcon 50	3
Sabreliner 75A	2
TOTAL	18

training and liaison aircraft:
with ground attack/close air support capability--

CASA C-101	15

others--

AS-202 Bravo		20
Cessna 318 (T-37		10
BAe-SA-3-125 Bulldog		19
	(sub-total	49)
TOTAL		64

helicopters:
attack--

AH-1G/1S Cobra		24

medium transport--

S-76		5
UH-60A Black Hawk		3
AS-332 Super Puma		10
	(sub-total	18)

light transport--

Alouette III		1
500MG		8
MBB BO-105 (with Police)		3
BK-117		+
	(sub-total	12+)
TOTAL		54

miscellaneous aircraft:
target drones--
on order: 82 TTL BTT-3 Banshee target drones, 2
launchers

advanced armament:
air-to-air missiles--
AIM-9B/E/J/N/P Sidewinder
R-550 Magique

air-to-ground missiles--
 AS-30L
 AGM-65 Maverick
bombs--
 Belouga CBU
 Durandal anti-runway bombs
anti-aircraft defenses:
 radars--

model	units
AN/TPS-43	
AN/TPS-63	
S-711	5

 long-range missiles--

model	batteries
MIM-23B Improved HAWK	14

 aircraft shelters--
 for all combat aircraft

military airfields:	6

 Amman (Marka), Azrak, H-4, H-5, Jaafar, Mafraq
aircraft maintenance and repair capability:
 repair and maintenance of all models, possibly with
 French/American technical help

Navy:
 combat vessels:

	number
patrol craft--	
Bertram class (Enforcer)	4
VT Hawk	3
12 meter patrol boats (in Dead Sea)	3
Total	10

 special maritime forces:
 a few divers
 naval base:

Aqaba, Hingat al-Ramat	2

8. KUWAIT

BASIC DATA

Official Name of State: State of Kuwait

Head of State: Emir Jabir al-Ahmad al-Sabah

Prime Minister: Saad Abdallah al-Sabah (also Crown Prince)

Minister of Defense: Ali Sabah al-Salim al-Sabah

Chief of the General Staff: Major General Jaber al-Khalid al-Sabah

Commander of the Ground Forces: Colonel Abd al-Aziz al Barghash

Commander of the Air Force and Air Defense Forces: Major General Daud al-Ghanim

Commander of the Navy: Commodore Habib al-Hull

Area: 24,280 sq. km.

Population (August 1990; population figures after the Gulf War not available; many Palestinians, Europeans and Southeast Asians fled Kuwait): 2,050,000

ethnic subdivision:		
Arabs	1,644,000	80.2%
Persians	102,000	5.0%
Southeast Asians	43,000	2.1%
Europeans	185,000	9.0%
Others	76,000	3.7%
religious subdivision:		
Sunni Muslims	1,127,000	55.0%
Shi'ite Muslims	615,000	30.0%
Christians, Parsis, Hindus and others	308,000	15.0%

nationality subdivision:

Kuwaitis	800,000	39.0%
Aliens		
other Arabs	800,000	39.0%
Southeast Asians	184,000	9.0%
Iranians	82,000	4.0%
Others	184,000	9.0%

GDP:

1988--$20.02 billion

1989--$23.08 billion

Balance of Payments (goods, services & unilateral transfer payments):

year	income	expenditure	balance
1988	$ 8.87 bil.	$10.98 bil.	- $2.11 bil.
1989	$12.72 bil.	$11.22 bil.	+$1.50 bil.

Defense Expenditure:

1991--$1.55 billion (planned - actual expenditure higher)

1992--$9.00 billion (to replace arms losses)

Foreign Military Aid and Security Assistance Received:

military training received:

foreign advisors/instructors from--Britain, Egypt, France, Pakistan, USA, a defense agreement, including training, signed September 1991, USSR before end of 1991

trainees abroad in--Britain, Egypt, France, Pakistan, Saudi Arabia, UAE, USA, USSR before end of 1991

arms transfers from:

Austria (small arms)

Britain (APCs, trainer aircraft, naval patrol craft, landing craft)

Egypt (APCs, AA systems, gas masks, optronics)

France (radars, combat aircraft, helicopters, SP artillery, ATGMs, naval craft)

FRG (Fuchs/Fox ABC detection vehicles)

Norway (ATRLs)

USA (APCs, patrol boats, SAMs, combat aircraft, Command and Control systems, night vision equipment)

USSR (SAMs, AAGs, APCs until end of 1991)

Yugoslavia (tanks)

construction aid by:
USA (reconstruction of harbors and airfields); Britain
(naval base reconstruction)
maintenance of equipment in:
France (aircraft)
Foreign Military Aid and Security Assistance Extended:
financial aid to:
Grants to USA and other coalition members from August
1990 until the end of the Gulf War, exceeding $16 billion,
to cover part of the costs of the war; annual grant to US
($215 million in 1992) to pay for presence of US force in
Kuwait; Egypt--cancellation of debt, in framework of 17
country "Paris Club"
facilities provided to:
coalition troops until December 1991; USA (1300 soldiers
and 4 batteries of MIM-104 Patriot SAMs, in 1992-3);
prepositioning of US tanks (58), APCs (58) and artillery
pieces (equipment for one brigade)
forces deployed abroad in:
138 troops in UN forces in Somalia, 1993
Joint Maneuvers with:
cooperation with US-led coalition during the 1991 Gulf War
and participation of some army and air units in combat; USA
(amphibious exercise); USA, Britain (security agreement with
the USA and Britain; joint exercise with British Royal
Marines; France (unconfirmed)

INFRASTRUCTURE
Road Network:
length:	3,000 km
paved roads	2,500 km
gravel and improved earth roads	500 km

main routes:
Kuwait--al-Jahrah--Raudhatain--Basra (Iraq)
Kuwait--al-Jahrah--Hafr al-Batin (Saudi Arabia)
Kuwait--al-Ahmadi
Kuwait--Fahahil--Mina al-Ahmadi--Mina Saud--Ras Tanura
(Saudi Arabia)

Airfields:
    airfields by runway type:
        permanent surface fields   4
        unpaved fields and usable airstrips   3
    airfields by runway length:
        2440--3659 meters   4
        under 1220   3
    TOTAL   7
    international airport: Kuwait
    major domestic airfield: al-Ahmadi

Airlines:
    companies: Kuwait Airways (international)
    aircraft (excluding aircraft captured by Iraq):
        Airbus A-320   1
        Airbus A-310   5
        Boeing 767-200ER   3
        Boeing 747-200 combi   3
        Boeing 727-200   3
        Boeing 707   2
        DC-10   1
        L-100-30   3
    on order: 3 Boeing 747-400, 4 A-340-200, 2 A-320

Maritime Facilities:
    harbors--Shuwaikh (Kuwait City); Shuayba, Mina al-Ahmadi; Umm Qasr (ceded in part by Iraq to Kuwait beginning early 1993)
    anchorages--Khor al-Mufatta; al-Qulayah
    oil terminals--Mina al-Ahmadi/Sea Island; Mina Abdallah; Mina Saud (Zour)

Merchant Marine:

vessel type	number	DWT
tanker	5	
gas tanker (LPG)	4	
product tanker	21	
bulk	3	
livestock carrier	4	
TOTAL	37	2,519,518

ARMED FORCES

Personnel:

military forces--

army	18,000
air force	2,400
navy	600
TOTAL	21,000

reserves: under organization.

Army:

major units (some not fully manned):

unit type	brigades	batallions
armored	2	
mechanized	2	
border defense		1
Royal guard	1	
Commando		1
TOTAL	6	1

small arms:

personal weapons--
9mm Sterling Mk.4 SMG
7.62mm CAL/FAL (FN) SAR
7.62mm SSG-69 sniping rifle
machine guns--
7.62mm Browning M-1919 MMG
7.62mm MAG (FN) LMG
light and medium mortars--
81mm
light ATRLs--
M-72 LAW

tanks (after 1991 Gulf War):

model	number
high quality	
M-84	190

medium quality
    Chieftain   15
    Centurion   a few
    Vickers Mk.1   a few
                      (sub-total   45)
TOTAL   ca. 235
    on order: at least 236 M-1 A2, delivery 1994

APCs/ARVs:
model   number
    high quality
        BMP-2
        M-113
        TOTAL   a few
    on order: 60 additional Fahd; about 125 M-113 APCs,
        30 M-106 mortar carriers, 300-400 Desert Warrior
        APCs from Britain; some MOWAG Piranha

artillery:
self-propelled guns and howitzers--
    155mm M-109 A2 SP howitzer   24
    on order: 7 227mm MLRS (negotiations not completed);
        18 155mm GCT SP howitzers from France

AFV transporters: a few
anti-tank weapons:
missiles--
    AT-4 Spigot (unconfirmed)
    BGM-71A Improved TOW
    HOT
    M-901 ITV (TOW under Armor)
    M-47 Dragon
    on order: additional HOT

army anti-aircraft defenses:
missiles--   launchers
    self-propelled/mobile
        Skyguard AA system (Amoun, missiles, radars
            and guns)   +
    man-portable
        FIM-92A Stinger
        SA-7 (Grail)

short-range guns (most lost during the Iraqi invasion)--
40mm Bofors L-70/L-60
35mm Oerlikon-Buhrle 35x2 GDF-002
23mm ZSU 23x4 SP (Gun Dish)
20mm Oerlikon GAI
on order: Crotale SAMs (unconfirmed); additional Skyguard (Amoun) air defense systems (total order 3 batteries, partly delivered); additional ZSU 23x4, SA-14, SA-8, Mistral SAMs

CW capabilities:
personal protective equipment
decontamination units

Air Force:

aircraft--general:	number
combat aircraft	59
transport aircraft	3
helicopters	24

combat aircraft:

	number
strike and multi-role--	
high quality	
F/A-18C/D	20
medium quality	
Mirage F-1B/C	15
others	
A-4 KU/TA-4 KU Skyhawk II	24
TOTAL	59

on order: 20 additional F/A-18C/D (the first F/A-18D delivered from January 1992 through 1993)

transport aircraft:

Boeing 737-200	1
C-130-30 Hercules/L-100-30	2
DC-9	1
TOTAL	4

training and liaison aircraft:

with ground attack/close air support capability--

BAC-167 Strikemaster Mk.83	8
Hawk	6
TOTAL	14

on order: 16 S-312 Tucano from Britain (delivery probable in 1993)

helicopters:

attack--

SA-342K Gazelle	13

maritime attack--

AS-332 Super Puma	5

medium transport--

SA-330 Puma	6
TOTAL	24

on order: SA-365N maritime attack; 24 AH-64A, negotiations not concluded; 20 UH-60A Blackhawk, negotiations not concluded

advanced armament:

air-to-air missiles--

AIM-9M Sidewinder

R-550 Magique

Super R-530D/F

air-to-ground missiles--

AS-11

AS-12

HOT (unconfirmed)

bombs--

Paveway II laser-guided

on order: AM-39 Exocet air-to-ship missiles, 300 AGM-65G Maverick AGMs, 200 AIM-7 Sparrow AAMs, 120 AIM-9 Sidewinder AAMs

anti-aircraft defenses:

radars--

on order: AN/TPS-63

long-range missiles--

on order: batteries of MIM-23B and 6 batteries of MIM-104 Patriot, negotiations in process

aircraft shelters:
>in airfields, for combat aircraft; some damaged in 1991 Gulf War

military airfields: 3
>al-Ahmadi, al-Jahra (Ali al-Salam AFB), Kuwait international Airport; al-Ahmadi and al-Jahra undergoing reconstruction

Navy:

combat vessels: number

MFPBs--

Lurssen FPB-57	1
Lurssen TNC-45	1
Total	2

patrol craft--

Cougar 1300	4
Cougar 1200	4
Cougar 1000	3
Predator	3
CAT-900	3
Total	17

>on order: 20 Magnum Sedan patrol boats; 5 Seagull PBs; 2 ASI-315 or OPV-310 (Jervoise Bay, Australia) PBs; 12 Simonneau patrol craft; 4 Combattante-4 MFPBs, negotiations not completed

advanced armament:
>surface-to-surface missiles--
>MM-40 Exocet
>on order: additional MM-40 Exocet

special maritime forces:
>frogmen and divers

naval bases:
>Kuwait City, al-Qulayah   2

ship maintenance and repair capability
>Kuwait City (Shuwaikh harbor)--190 meter floating dock, repair capacity 35,000 DWT, damaged during 1991 Gulf War

9. LEBANON

BASIC DATA

Official Name of State: Republic of Lebanon
Head of State: President Elias al-Herawi
Prime Minister: Rafiq al-Kharari
Defense Minister: Mukhsen Dalloul
Commander-in-Chief of the Armed Forces: Lieutenant General Emile Lahoud
Chief of General Staff: Brigadier General Riad Hamed Taki al-Din
Commander of the Air Force: Brigadier General Mahmoud Mater
Commander of the Navy: Rear Admiral Albert al-Gharib
Area: 10,452 sq. km.
Population (estimate; all data uncertain): 3,500,000

ethnic subdivision:		
Arabs	3,167,500	90.5%
Armenians	157,500	4.5%
Kurds	52,500	1.5%
Others	122,500	3.5%
religious subdivision:		
Shi'ite Muslims	1,120,000	32.0%
Sunni Muslims	735,000	21.0%
Druze	210,000	6.0%
Alawis	35,000	1.0%
Christians		
Maronites	735,000	21.0%
Greek Orthodox	280,000	8.0%
Greek Catholic	175,000	5.0%
Armenians (Orthodox and Catholic)	140,000	4.0%
Others	70,000	2.0%

nationality subdivision:

Lebanese	3,052,000	87.2%
Palestinians	395,500	11.3%
Others	52,500	1.5%

GDP:

1977--$3.34 billion (latest year available)

1991-$3-3.5 billion (estimate)

Defense Expenditure:

1991--$168 million

1992--$230 million (actual; plan was for $430 million)

Foreign Military Aid and Security Assistance Received:

financial aid from:

France--$1.16 million grant for trainees in France; FRG--grant (unconfirmed); Qatar--$1 million grant; Saudi Arabia--$60 million grant (1991); USA ($400,000 for training)

military training:

foreign instructors/advisors from--France; Syria

trainees abroad in--Egypt, France, Italy, Syria, Jordan; USA (unconfirmed)

arms transfers from:

Britain (patrol craft)

Syria (tanks, artillery, MRLs to al-Amal and other militias until May 1991, later ceded to the Lebanese Army, various items to the Lebanese Army)

USA (jeeps, trucks)

maintenance of equipment in:

France (helicopters)

Support and Foreign Forces from:

Syria (30,000 in Biqa, Tripoli area and Beirut); UNIFIL (5,800 in South Lebanon); Palestinian organizations (see Part III/Chapter 13); Israeli observation units (600 men in the security zone in South Lebanon permanently; during periods of clashes or tension Israeli forces are increased by units stationed in Northern Israel); several hundred Iranian Islamic Revolution Guards Corps (IRGC) troops in the Syrian-held Biqa' with Hizb Allah non-government militia; a few PKK (Kurds) training in Biqa' (Syrian controlled) until mid-1992

INFRASTRUCTURE
Road Network:
length:	7,370 km
paved roads	6,270 km
gravel and stone roads	450 km
improved earth tracks	650 km

main routes:
Beirut--Sidon--Tyre--Naqurah--Haifa (Israel)
Beirut--Tripoli--Tartus (Syria)/Homs (Syria)
Beirut--Zahlah--Baalbek--Homs
Beirut--Shtaurah--Damascus (Syria)
Tyre--Bint J'bail
Zahlah--Shtaurah--Marj Ayoun--Metulla (Israel)
Marj Ayoun--Jezzin--Sidon
Baalbek--Tripoli

Railway Network:
length (partly not in use):	378 km
standard gauge	296 km
narrow gauge	82 km

main routes:
Beirut--Sidon
Beirut--Tripoli--Homs
Beirut--Zahlah--Rayaq--Homs/Rayaq--Damascus (narrow gauge)

Airfields:
airfields by runway type:
permanent surface fields	6
unpaved fields and usable airstrips	2

airfields by runway length:
2440--3659 meters	3
1220-2439	2
under 1220	3
TOTAL	8

international airports: Beirut
major domestic airfields: Rayaq, Kleiat

Airlines:
companies: Middle East Airlines (international); Trans Mediterranean Airways (cargo)

aircraft:

Airbus A-310-200	2
Boeing 747/747-200B Combi	3
Boeing 737-200/300/400	6
Boeing 720B	4
Boeing 707-320C	11

Maritime Facilities:

harbors--Beirut, Juniah, Sidon, Tripoli, Tyre

anchorages--al-Abde, Chekka (Shikka), Salata (Silata), al-Minya, al-Jiya, Naqura, Khalde, Sill al-Ouzai, 5 others

oil terminals--Sidon, Tripoli

Merchant Marine:

vessel type	number	DWT
general cargo	21	
refrigerated cargo	1	
vehicle carrier	1	
bulk carrier	4	
livestock carrier	8	
ro/ro	1	
container	1	
tanker	1	
TOTAL	38	274,490

ARMED FORCES

Personnel:

military forces--

army	ca. 41,000-43,000
air force	1,600
navy	500
TOTAL	ca. 43,100-45,100

para-military forces--

gendarmerie	7,000

Army:

major units (partly skeleton, undermanned or disorganized):

unit type	brigades	battalions (called regiments)
infantry/ mechanized	11	
Presidential Guard	1	
Special Forces/ Airborne		5
TOTAL	12	5

note: infantry/mechanised brigades include some tanks and APCs

small arms:

personal weapons--
7.62mm AK-47 (Kalashnikov)
7.62mm FAL (FN) SAR
5.56mm CAL (FN) AR (unconfirmed)
5.56mm HK-33 (Heckler & Koch) AR
5.56mm M-16 A1 AR
5.56mm SG-540 AR

machine guns--
12.7mm (0.5") Browning M2 HMG
7.62mm (0.3") Browning M-1919 MMG
7.62mm MAG (FN) LMG
7.62mm M-60D GPMG
7.62mm RPD (Degtyarev)
7.5mm AA-52 MMG (possibly no longer in service)
7.5mm Chatellerault M-24/29 LMG
   (possibly no longer in service)

light and medium mortars--
81mm Hotchkiss-Brandt
81mm M-29
60mm Hotchkiss-Brandt

light ATRLs--
RPG-7
89mm M-65

tanks (partly not serviceable):

model	number
medium quality	
AMX-13/105mm gun	20
M-48 A1/M-48 A5	
(not all serviceable)	130
T-55/upgraded T-54	180
(sub-total	330)
low quality	
AMX-13/75mm gun	20
TOTAL	350

APCs/ARVs (some not serviceable):

model	number
high quality	
AML-90	45
AMX-VCI	
M-3 (Panhard VIT)	
M-113 A1/A2	300
VAB	50
V-150 Commando	+
(sub-total	ca. 400)
others	
Saracen/Saladin (probably not serviceable)	100
TOTAL	ca. 500

artillery:

towed guns and howitzers--	
155mm M-198 howitzer	36
155mm M-114 howitzer	18
155mm M-50 howitzer	12
130mm D-46 gun	ca. 20
122mm D-30 howitzer	18
122mm M-1938	36
mortars, heavy, under 160mm--	
120mm Brandt M-50 & M-60 mortars	+
TOTAL	150
MLRs--	
122mm BM-21/BM-11	ca. 30

anti-tank weapons:
  missiles--   launchers

BGM-71A TOW	
MILAN	
TOTAL	ca. 80
guns--	
106mm M-40 A2 recoilless rifle	
85mm M-1945/D-44	a few
others	a few

army anti-aircraft defenses:
  short-range guns--

40mm M-42 SP (probably in storage)	a few
23mm ZU 23x2	
20mm	
TOTAL	ca. 30

Air Force:

aircraft--general: number

combat aircraft (mostly grounded)	14
transport aircraft	1
helicopters	22

combat aircraft:
  interceptors--
    medium quality

Mirage III BL/EL (grounded)	10

  strike and multi-role aircraft--
    low quality

Hawker Hunter F-70/T-66	4
TOTAL	14

transport aircraft:

Hawker Siddeley Dove	1

training and liaison aircraft:
  with ground attack/close air support capability--

CM-170 Fouga Magister (not serviceably)	4

  others--

BAe SA-3-120 Bulldog	4
TOTAL	8

helicopters (some grounded):
  attack--
    SA-342 Gazelle   5
  medium transport--
    AB-212   5
    SA-330 Puma/possibly IAR-330   5
           (sub-total   10)
  light transport--
    Alouette II
    Alouette III
           (sub-total   7)
  TOTAL   22

advanced armament:
  air-to-air missiles--
    Matra R-530 (not serviceable)

military airfields: 3
  Rayaq, Kleiat, Beirut

aircraft maintenance and repair capability:
  routine repairs for existing models

Navy:
  combat vessels: number
    patrol craft--
      Tracker II class   2
      Attacker   5
      TOTAL   7
    note: 20 additional small patrol craft up to 10 meters in service

landing craft:
  EDIC class LCT   2

naval bases: 5
  Beirut, Junieh, Sidon, Tripoli, Tyre

ship maintenance and repair capability:
  a 55-meter slipway for light craft repairs

Non-Government Military Forces

military force/organization	armed personnel[*]
Lebanese Forces: alliance of various Christian militias (led by Samir Geagea, regulars + reserves)	10,000
Lebanese Forces splinter group (led by Eli Hobeiqa, under Syrian patronage)	a few hundred
Druze Community Forces, under Walid Jumblatt, and non-Druze followers (regulars + reserves)	14,000
Al-Amal (Shi'ites)	7,000-8,000
Tripoli-based pro-Syrian militias (Arab Democratic Party Militia, also known as Farsan al-Arab, or Arab Cavalry)	a few hundred
Army of South Lebanon (pro-Israel, commanded by Major General Antoine Lahd)	2,500
Communist Labor Organization	a few hundred
"Giants" (Franjieh)	1,000
Islamic Unification Movement and Islamic Resistance (Tripoli)	a few hundred
Lebanese Communist Party	500

---

[*]All figures are estimates, with wide margins of error. In May 1991 all militias except Hizb Allah, Army of South Lebanon, Popular Nasserite Organization and the Palestinian organizations surrendered to the Herawi government almost all their heavy arms and part of their small arms. Some joined the Lebanese Army. All numbers represent the situation before May 1991. Throughout 1992 all organizations, except Hizb Allah and SLA, concentrated on political activity, though they still possessed small arms and men capable of using arms. Some terror activity by SSNP and other small organizations took place during 1991-92.

Socialist Arab Ba'ath Party (pro-Iraqi)	a few hundred
Socialist Arab Ba'ath Party (pro-Syrian)	a few hundred
Syrian Social Nationalist Party (SSNP; pro-Syrian terror and suicide squads)	1,000
Independent Nasserites (Murabitun)	a few hundred
Popular Nasserite Organization (in Sidon, led by Mustapha Saad)	
Hizb Allah (pro-Iran Shi'ites)	5,000

Palestinian Organizations: see Part III/Ch.13, "Palestinian Military and Para-Military Forces"

Note: several hundred Iranian IRGC personnel in Lebanon--listed above under Support and Foreign Forces

Tanks, APCs and Artillery in Non-Government Militia

militia	tanks	APCs	artillery pieces
Army of South Lebanon	45 Sherman & T-54	a few M-113	30 including 155mm
Hizb Allah		several M-113	several, mainly MRLs, 107mm and 122mm BM-21

note: Hizb Allah units have AT-3 (Sagger) ATGMs supplied by Iran via Syria and some SA-7 man portable SAMs

10. LIBYA

BASIC DATA

Official Name of State: The Great Socialist People's Libyan Arab Jamahiriya (Jamahiriya is an Arabic term meaning "public" or "polity of the masses")

Head of State: Colonel Muammar al-Qaddafi (leader, does not hold any other title; in practice also in charge of the Defense Ministry and Commander-in-Chief of the Armed Forces)

Deputy Head of State (second in the hierarchy): Major Abd al-Sallam Jallud

Prime Minister: Abu Zayd Oumar Durda

Commander-in-Chief of the Armed Forces: Colonel Abu-Bakr Yunis Jaber

Inspector General of the Armed Forces: Colonel Mustapha al-Kharrubi

Commander of the Air Force and Air Defense Forces: Colonel Ali al-Sharif Al-Riffi

Commander of the Navy: Captain Abdallah al-Latif al-Shakshuki

Area: 1,759,540 sq. km.

Population:		4,540,000
ethnic subdivision:		
Arabs	4,190,000	92.3%
Berbers	182,000	4.0%
Africans	114,000	2.5%
Europeans and others	54,000	1.2%
religious subdivision:		
Sunni Muslims	4,403,000	97.0%
Christians	137,000	3.0%
nationality subdivision:		
Libyans	3,963,000	87.3%
Egyptians	377,000	8.3%
Tunisians	109,000	2.4%
Others	91,000	2.0%

Balance of Payments (goods, services & unilateral transfer payments):

year	income	expenditure	balance
1989	$7.40 bil.	$8.49 bil.	-$1.09 bil.
1990	$11.48 bil.	$9.45 bil.	+$2.03 bil.

Defense Expenditure:

1990--$2.0 billion

1991--$1.4 billion

Foreign Military Aid and Security Assistance Received:

military training:

> foreign advisors/instructors/serving personnel from-- following the embargo on Libya, most foreign advisors left Libya. 300-500 are still serving under individual contracts.

trainees abroad in--Syria (a few, unconfirmed)

arms transfers from (before the April 1992 embargo):

> Brazil (APCs, ARVs; and MRLs, unconfirmed)
>
> Czech Republic (trainer and transport aircraft, spare parts for tanks and tank upgrading)
>
> France (spare parts for French-made systems)
>
> FRG (floating dock); company from FRG (aerial refuelling systems)
>
> Italy (electronics, spares for aircraft)
>
> North Korea (SSMs on order)
>
> USSR/Russia (combat aircraft, tanks, SAMs, SSMs, missile corvettes, naval mines)

use of facilities abroad:

> Sudan (combat aircraft from Libya flown to Sudan to avoid attack by the USA, April 1992)

maintenance of equipment in (before the embargo):

> Malta (corvettes); France (SAMs, combat aircraft); Italy (aircraft, helicopter engines); Belgium (aircraft, at least until January 1991); Morocco (aircraft); Russia (submarine, at a Russian base in Latvia)

Foreign Military Aid and Security Assistance Extended:

financial aid to:

> Palestinian organizations (small amounts of money to PFLP-GC and Abu Musa faction of Fatah; as of October

1990--also to mainstream PLO); Sudan--grant (money and oil); Syria--grant

military training:

advisors/instructors/serving personnel in--Uganda; Nicaragua (unconfirmed)

foreign trainees from--Abu Musa faction of Fatah and PFLP-GC groups; Syria (a few pilots)

arms transfers to:

Egypt (Czech-made trainer aircraft, a gift)

Iran (APCs, ARVs, other Soviet weapons)

Palestinian military organizations

Somalia (small arms)

Sudan (small arms)

Syria (Soviet AAMs, unconfirmed)

facilities provided to:

Palestinian organizations (FRC); USSR until end of 1991 (use of naval bases at Bardiyah & Tobruk), discontinued by Russia

forces deployed abroad in:

Sudan (3-4 aircraft supporting Sudanese forces in Southern Sudan)

Joint Maneuvers with: USSR (naval maneuvers until 1991)

Cooperation in Arms Production/Assembly with (before the embargo):

Czech Republic (tank upgrading facility); company from Italy (assembly of light aircraft, unconfirmed); upgrading SSMs, possibly development of SSMs with individual experts hired mainly from FRG (unconfirmed)

INFRASTRUCTURE
Road Network:

length:	32,500 km
paved roads	24,000 km
gravel, stone & improved earth roads	8,500 km

main routes:

Tripoli--Benghazi--Tobruk--Bardiyah

Tripoli--Misratah (Misurata)--Waddan--Sabha (Sebha)--Marzuq (Murzuq)

Tripoli--Tunis (Tunisia)
Tripoli--Ghadams (Ghadames)--Ghat
Tobruk--Alexandria (Egypt)
Benghazi--Zighan--Kufra
Tripoli--Nalut--Sabha
Sabha--Ghat
Tobruk--Jaghbud
Bardiyah--Jaghbud

Airfields:

airfields by runway type:

permanent surface fields	53
unpaved fields and usable airstrips	70

airfields by runway length:

over 3660 meters	7
2440--3659	31
1220--2439	44
under 1220	41
TOTAL	123

international airports: Tripoli, Benghazi (Baninah)

major domestic airfields: Ghadams (Ghadames), Ghat, Kufra, Marsa al-Brega, Misratah, Sabha, Surt (Sidra, Sirt), Tobruk

Airlines:

companies: Jamahiriya Libyan Arab Airlines (international, domestic, cargo and charter)

aircraft:

Airbus A-300	2
Airbus A-310-200	2
Boeing 727-200	9
Boeing 707-320C/320B	5
DHC-6 Twin Otter	5
Fokker F-27-600/500/400	14
Fokker F-28-4000 (including a/c on lease)	3
Ilyushin IL-76T/76TD/76M	18
L-100-30	3
Mystere-Falcon 20	1
Mystere-Falcon 50	1

on order: 3 Tu-154M (unconfirmed)

Maritime Facilities:

harbors--Benghazi, Derna, Misratah, Tobruk, Tripoli
anchorages--Kasr Ahmed
oil terminals--Surt (Sidra), Marsa al-Brega, Marsa al-Hairqa
(Tobruk), Ras Lanuf, Zawiyah, Zueitinah

Merchant Marine:

vessel type	number	DWT
product tanker	2	
gas tanker	1	
short sea passenger	3	
tanker/crude	8	
general cargo/cargo container	11	
ro/ro	5	
chemical tanker	1	
TOTAL	31	1,213,429

Nuclear Capability:

basic R&D, declared ambition to acquire nuclear weapons; a
5 MW Soviet-made research reactor at Tadjoura

Defense Production:

army equipment:

toxic chemical agent; plans to upgrade SSMs, with
assistance by foreign experts, and effort to produce an
indigenous SSM, al-Fatih, not yet operational; cooperation
in rocket development with German commercial support
(OTRAG); tank upgrading facility, with assistance of Czech
Republic

aircraft and air ammunition:

assembly of a light aircraft (assisted by foreign experts
hired individually)

A R M E D   F O R C E S

Personnel:

military forces (reduction of forces planned)--

	regular
army	85,000
air force & AD	9,000
navy	6,500
TOTAL	100,500

para-military forces--
20,000

Army:

major units (not all with full strength, not all trained; following Qaddafi statement claiming to abolish the army, no divisions exist):

unit type	brigades
armored/tank	6
mechanized/infantry/paratroop	9
Republican Guard	2
TOTAL	17

small arms:

personal weapons--
9mm Model 12 Beretta SMG
7.62mm AK-47 (Kalashnikov) AR
7.62mm SKS (Simonov) SAR
7.62mm FAL (FN) SAR
5.45mm AK-74 (Kalashnikov) AR
machine guns--
12.7mm D.Sh.K. 38/46 (Degtyarev) HMG
7.62mm MAG (FN) LMG
7.62mm PK/PKS (Kalashnikov) LMG
7.62mm RPD (Degtyarev) LMG
7.62mm SGM (Goryunov) MMG
light and medium mortars--
82mm M-43
light ATRLs--
RPG-7

tanks:

model	number
high quality	
T-72/T-72M	360
medium quality	
T-62	700-800
T-55	1600
(sub-total	2300-2400)
TOTAL (about half in storage)	2660-2760

APCs/ARVs:

model		number
high quality		
BMP-1/BMP-2		1050
Engesa EE-9/11		300
Fiat Type 6614/6616		400
M-113 A1		50-100
	(sub-total	1800-1850)
others		
BTR-50/60		750
BRDM-2		220
OT-62		100
OT-64		130
	(sub-total	1200)
TOTAL (about half in storage)		ca.3000

on order: EE-9/11

artillery (partly in storage):

self-propelled guns and howitzers--		
155mm M-109 SP howitzer		20
155mm Palmaria SP howitzer		160
152mm M-1973 SP howitzer		60
122mm M-1974 SP howitzer		130
	(sub-total	370)

towed guns and howitzers--	
155mm GHN-45 howitzer (possibly transferred to Iran, unconfirmed)	
130mm M-46 gun	330
122mm D-30 howitzer	270
105mm M-101 howitzer (possibly phased out)	60
other models	+
mortars, heavy, over 160mm--	
240mm mortar	+
160mm mortar	+
mortars, heavy, under 160mm--	
120mm mortar	+
TOTAL	2000-2400
MRLs--	
140mm	+

130mm M-51	+
122mm BM-21/RM-70	600
107mm Type 63	+
on order: 180mm SS-40 Astros II MRLs	

AFV transporters: 1000

anti-tank weapons:

missiles--	launchers
AT-3 (Sagger)	620
AT-4 (Spigot)	+
AT-5 (Spandrel)	+
BRDM-2 carrying AT-3 (Sagger) SP	40
TOTAL	1000-2000

guns--
106mm recoilless rifle

surface-to-surface missiles and rockets (some in storage, not all serviceable):

model	launchers
FROG-7	30
SS-1 (Scud B)	80
TOTAL	110

on order: Nodong from North Korea

army anti-aircraft defenses:

missiles--	launchers
self-propelled/mobile	
Crotale	30
SA-6 (Gainful)	100
SA-8 (Gecko)	20
SA-9 (Gaskin)	60
SA-13 (Gopher)	ca.20
man-portable	
SA-7 (Grail)	+
SA-14 (Gremlin)	+

short-range guns--	number
57mm	
40mm Bofors L-70	
30mm 30x2 M-53/59 SP (in storage)	
23mm ZSU 23x4 SP (Gun Dish)	
23mm ZU 23x2	

TOTAL 450

on order: SAMs from Russia; AD weapons from PRC

CW capabilities:

personal protective equipment

Soviet type decontamination units

ABC protection of SSM sites

stockpile of chemical agents (mustard)

biological warfare capabilities:

toxins and other biological weapons (unconfirmed)

Air Force:

	number
aircraft--general:	
combat aircraft (ca. 280 in storage, or not serviceable)	528-533
transport aircraft	138
helicopters	204
combat aircraft:	
interceptors--	
high quality	
MiG-25 and MiG-25R (Foxbat)	65-70
medium quality	
Mig-23 (Flogger G)	ca.40
MiG-21 bis (Fishbed)	70
(sub-total	110)
Total	175-180
strike and multi-role aircraft--	
high quality	
Su-24 (Fencer C)	6
medium quality	
MiG-23/27 (Flogger, incl. MiG-23G)	140
Su-20/22 (Fitter C)	90
Mirage F-1	30
Mirage 5	80
(sub-total	340)
Total (including a/c in storage)	346
bombers--	
Tu-22 (Blinder)	7
TOTAL	528-533

transport aircraft (including tankers):

An-26 (Curl)	36
Boeing 707	1
C-130H Hercules/L-100-20/L-100-30	8
C-140 Jetstar	1
DHC-6 Twin Otter	10
Fokker F-27-600	8
G-222L	19
IL-76 (Candid)	28
KC-130H/L-100-20/L-100-30 tanker (refuelling)	2
L-410 UVP	19
Mystere-Falcon 20	6
TOTAL (some in storage)	138

on order: 25 EMB-121

training and liaison aircraft (some in storage):

with ground attack/close air support capability--

G-2AE Galeb	80
J-1E Jastreb	30
L-39 Albatross	180
(sub-total	290)

others--

SIAI--Marchetti SF-260 M/L	55
TOTAL (some in storage)	345

helicopters: number

attack--

Mi-24/Mi-25/Mi-35 (Hind, number unconfirmed)	70

heavy transport--

CH-47C Chinook	15
SA-321 Super Frelon (also employed in ASW role)	8
(sub-total	23)

medium transport--

A-109A	2
AB-212	3
Mi-2 (Hoplite)	35
Mi-8/Mi-17 (Hip)	25
(sub-total	65)

light transport--
   Alouette III   14
   AB-206 JetRanger   3
                 (sub-total   17)
ASW--
   Mi-14 (Haze)   29
   TOTAL (some not serviceable)   204

advanced armament:
  air-to-air missiles--
    AA-2 (Atoll)
    AA-6 (Acrid)
    AA-7 (Apex)
    AA-8 (Aphid)
    R-530
    R-550 Magique
    Super 530D/F
  air-to-ground missiles--
    AS-9
    AS-10 (Karen)
    AS-14 (Kedge)
    AT-2 (Swatter)
    AT-6 (Spiral, unconfirmed)

anti-aircraft defenses:
  long-range missiles (some in storage)--

model	batteries
SA-2 (Guideline) & SA-3 (Goa)	93
SA-5 (Gammon)	6
TOTAL	99

    on order: additional SA-5 (possibly delivered); other
       SAMs from Russia
  aircraft shelters--
    for combat aircraft

military airfields: 16
al-Adem (Tobruk), Benghazi (Baninah), Beni Walid, al-Bumbah, Ghurdabiyah (Surt), Jufra, Kufra, Maatan al-Sarra, Misratha, Ouqba ben Nafi (Al-Watiya), Ouzu, Sabhah, Tripoli International (Idriss), Umm al-Tika, 2 additional

aircraft maintenance and repair capability:
foreign technicians employed for all models

Navy:
  combat vessels: number

	number
submarines--	
F class (Foxtrot)	6
MFPBs--	
Combattante II	9
Ossa II	12
Total	21
missile frigates--	
Vosper Thornycroft Mk.7	1
Koni (with SS-N-2C SSMs; usually in ASW role)	2
Total	3
missile corvettes--	
Assad class (formerly Wadi class)	4
Nanuchka class	3
Total	7
gun corvettes--	
Vosper Thornycroft Mk.1B (Tobruk)	1
mine warfare vessels--	
Natya class minesweepers	8
patrol craft--	
Garian class	4
Poluchat	1
Thornycroft 100 ft. (30.5 meter)	3
Thornycroft 78 ft. (23.5 meter)	1
Total	9
on order: 4 Rade Koncar MFPBs	

landing craft:

C-107 LCT	2
PS-700 class LST	2
Polnochny class LCT	3
TOTAL	7

auxiliary vessels:
maintenance & repair craft, ex-British
Yelva diving-support ship   1

advanced armament:
    surface-to-surface missiles--
        OTOMAT Mk.2
        SS-N-2 Styx/SS-N-2C
        SS-12
    surface-to-air missiles--
        Seacat
        Aspide
        SA-N-4
    mines--
        Soviet-made acoustic mines; magnetic mines (unconfirmed)

special maritime forces:
    R-2 Mala midget submarine   2-3
    remotely controlled explosive
    motor craft   50-125

naval bases: 6
    al-Khums, Benghazi, Misratah, Ras Hillal, Tobruk, Tripoli

ship maintenance and repair capability:
    facilities at Tripoli with foreign technicians for repair of vessels up to 6000 DWT; a 3200 ton lift floating dock; floating docks at Benghazi and Tobruk

11. MOROCCO

BASIC DATA

Official Name of State: Kingdom of Morocco

Head of State: King Hassan II (also Minister of Defense, Commander-in-Chief of the Armed Forces and Chief of the General Staff)

Prime Minister: Muhammad Karim Lamrani

Inspector General of the Armed Forces: General Idriss Bin-Issa

Commander of the Air Force: Abd al-Aziz Marani

Commander of the Navy: Captain Muhammad al-Tariqi

Area: 622,012 sq. km., including the former Spanish Sahara (409,200 sq. km. excluding this territory)

Population: 26,320,000

ethnic subdivision:

Arabs	15,687,000	59.6%
Berbers	10,396,000	39.5%
Europeans and others	237,000	0.9%

religious subdivision:

Sunni Muslims	25,978,000	98.7%
Christians	290,000	1.1%
Jews	52,000	0.2%

GDP:

1988--$21.99 billion

1989--$22.39 billion

Balance of Payments (goods, services & unilateral transfer payments):

year	income	expenditure	balance
1990	$5.20 bil.	$7.72 bil.	- $2.52 bil.
1991	$8.34 bil.	$7.57 bil.	+$770 mil.

Defense Expenditure:

1987--$850 million

1991--$1.4 billion

Foreign Military Aid and Security Assistance Received:
    financial aid from:

Saudi Arabia, Kuwait, Qatar, UAE--grants, finance of purchase of various arms from France and Spain, as compensation for Morocco's participation in the Gulf War (unconfirmed, estimated to be $2.8 billion); USA--$100 million grant (1991, unconfirmed); some arms from US drawdown in Europe

    military training:

foreign advisors/instructors from--USA, France; Egypt (unconfirmed)

trainees abroad in--USA, Spain

    arms transfers from:

Austria (recovery vehicles, tanks)

Brazil (APCs)

Canada (jeeps)

Denmark (patrol craft)

Egypt (mortars; APCs on order, unconfirmed)

France (ATGMs, combat aircraft, naval SSMs, naval vessels, tank transporters)

Italy (helicopters, vehicles and mines, shipborne SAMs)

Spain (AFVs, mortars, MRLs, naval vessels, electronic equipment, night vision devices, communications equipment)

USA (ATGMs, SAMs, tanks, spare parts for aircraft and helicopters, Naval radio equipment)

    maintenance of equipment in:

France (aircraft)

    construction aid by:

USA (upgrading airfields)

Foreign Military Aid and Security Assistance Extended:
    military training:

advisors/instructors/serving personnel in--UAE

    facilities provided to:

USA (use of Sidi Slimane, Marrakech and Casablanca airfields in emergencies; permission for space shuttle to land at Marrakech AFB; use of communications center at Kenitra; storage and use of naval facilities at Mohammedia) forces deployed abroad in:

> 1,284 troops in UN forces in Somalia, 1993; 1,200 in Saudi Arabia (from August 1990 through the Gulf War)

Joint Maneuvers with:

Belgium (joint training of pilots in both countries), France, Spain, USA

Cooperation in Arms Production/Assembly with:

Portugal (aircraft industry, overhauls and production of a light trainer aircraft)

INFRASTRUCTURE

Road Network:

length:	59,198 km
paved roads	27,740 km
gravel, crushed stone roads and earth tracks	31,458 km

main routes:

Rabat--Tangier

Tangier--Tetouan--Nador--Oran (Algeria)

Ceuta--Tetouan--Kenitra--Rabat

Rabat--Meknes--Fez--Oujda--Oran

Oujda--Bouarfa--Bechar (Algeria)

Rabat--Casablanca--Marrakech

Casablanca--Safi--Agadir--Tarfaya--L'Ayoun--Bir Moghreim (Mauritania)

Railway Network:

length (standard gauge):   1,893 km

main routes:

Rabat--Casablanca--Marrakech

Rabat--Sidi Kacem--Tangier

Rabat--Sidi Kacem--Meknes--Fez--Oujda--Sidi-bel-Abbes (Algeria)

Airfields:

airfields by runway type:

permanent surface fields	26
unpaved fields and usable airstrips	41

airfields by runway length:

over 3660 meters	2
2440--3659	13
1220--2439	27
under 1220	25
TOTAL	67

international airports: Agadir, Casablanca (Nouasseur), Fez, Marrakech, Oujda, Rabat (Sale), Tangier

major domestic airfields: L'Ayoun, Casablanca (Arfa), Ouarzazate, Sidi Ifni, Smara-Ferduja, Tantan, Tarfaya

Airlines:

companies: Royal Air Maroc (international & domestic)

aircraft:

ATR-42	3
Boeing 757-200	2
Boeing 747-200 Combi/747SP	2
Boeing 737-200/737-200C	7
Boeing 737-400/737-500	6
Boeing 727-200	8
Boeing 707-320C	2

on order: 1 Boeing 737-400, 1 737-500, 2 737-TBD

Maritime Facilities:

harbors--Agadir, L'Ayoun (Fousbucra Port), Casablanca, El Jedida/Jorf al-Asfar, Kenitra, Mohammedia, Nador, Safi, Tangier

anchorages--Essaouira (Mogador), Larache, Martil (Tetouan)

oil terminals--Agadir, Kenitra, Mohammedia, Safi

Merchant Marine:

vessel type	number	DWT
tanker	3	
chemical tanker	11	
cargo	10	
bulk carrier	4	
refrigerated cargo	12	
short sea passenger	3	
ro/ro	6	
container	2	
TOTAL	51	487,490

Defense Production:
army equipment:
small arms ammunition; assembly of trucks
aircraft and air ammunition:
trainer aircraft, with foreign aid

ARMED FORCES
Personnel:
military forces--

army	170,000
air force	8,000
navy and marines	6,000
Total	184,000

para-military forces--
gendarmerie--8,000; internal security forces--3,000

Army:
major units:

unit type	brigades/ regiments	indep. battalions
armored	2	3
mechanized	4	5
infantry	2	2
motorized infantry	1	4
camel corps		4
paratroops	2	
commando		3
TOTAL	11	21

small arms:
personal weapons--
9mm MAT 49/56 SMG
9mm Model 38/49 Beretta SMG
7.62mm AK-47 (Kalashnikov) AR
7.62mm G-3 AR
7.5mm MAS 49/56 SAR
machine guns--
14.5mm ZPU 14.5x4 HMG (in anti-aircraft role)
14.5mm ZPU 14.5x2 HMG (in anti-aircraft role)

12.7mm (0.5") Browning M2 HMG
7.62mm M-60 D GPMG
7.62mm MAG (FN) LMG
7.62mm RPD (Degtyarev) LMG
7.5mm AA-52 MMG
7.5mm Chatellerault M-24/29 LMG
light and medium mortars--
    82mm M-43
    81mm ECIA
    81mm M-29
    60mm M-2
light ATRLs--
    RPG-7
    89mm Strim-89
    3.5" M-20 (Bazooka)
    M-72 A1 LAW

tanks:

model		number
high quality		
M-60 A3		60
medium quality		
M-48 A5		150
SK-105 (Kurassier)		80
	(sub-total	230)
low quality		
AMX-13		50
T-54		60
	(sub-total	110)
TOTAL		400

on order: 50 M-60 A3 (out of an order of 110); SK-105 (Kurassier); 200 additional M-60 A3 from US drawdown

APCs/ARVs:

model	number
high quality	
AMX-10RCM	50
Engesa EE-9/EE-11 (unconfirmed)	+
M-113 A1/A2	460

M-3 (Panhard, unconfirmed)	+
Ratel 20/90	60
Steyr 4K 7FA (unconfirmed)	+
VAB	+
(sub-total	950-1000)
others	
AML-90/AML-60	200
EBR-75	25
M-3 half-track	50
OT-62	60
UR-416	30
other models	+
(sub-total	500-550)
TOTAL	1450-1550

on order: 140 M-113, additional AMX-10RCM; Fahd (unconfirmed)

artillery:	number
self-propelled guns and howitzers--	
155mm M-109 A1 SP howitzer	56
155mm Mk. F-3 (AMX) SP howitzer	90
105mm Mk. 61 SP howitzer	+
towed guns and howitzers--	
155mm M-114 howitzer	70
152mm howitzer	
130mm M-46 gun	
105mm Light Gun	36
105mm M-101 howitzer	10
85mm M-1945/D-44 field/AT gun (possibly phased out)	
mortars, heavy, under 160mm	
120mm mortar	
TOTAL	300-400
MRLs--	
122mm BM-21	36

on order: additional 155 mm M-109 SP from US drawdown

anti-tank weapons:	
missiles--	
BGM-71A TOW	330
HOT/HOT Commando	+

M-47 Dragon	480
MILAN	80
TOTAL	ca. 950

guns--
106mm M-40 A2 recoilless rifle
90mm recoilless rifle

army anti-aircraft defenses:

missiles	launchers
self-propelled/mobile	
MIM-72A Chaparral	36
man-portable	
SA-7 (Grail)	+

short-range guns--	number
57mm M-1950 (S-60, not serviceable)	+
37mm M-1939	20
23mm ZU 23x2	150
20mm M-163 Vulcan SP	55
20mm	+
TOTAL	225+

Air Force:

aircraft--general:	number
combat aircraft	71
transport aircraft	54
helicopters	142

combat aircraft:

strike and multi-role aircraft--	
medium quality	
Mirage F-1/F-2B	40
others	
F-5E/F-5F	20
F-5A/B	10
RF-5E	1
(sub-total	31)
TOTAL	71

transport aircraft (including tankers):

Beechcraft King Air	9
Boeing 707 tanker (refuelling)	2
C-130H Hercules (including C-130H with SLAR, employed for electronic surveillance)	17
CN-235	7
DC-3 Dakota (C-47)	8
Dornier DO-28 D-2	3
Gulfstream II/III	2
KC-130 tanker (refuelling)	3
Mystere-Falcon 50	1
Mystere-Falcon 20	2
TOTAL	54

on order: 4 BN Islander (possibly civilian)

training and liaison aircraft:

with ground attack/close air support capability--

Alpha Jet	22
CM-170 Fouga Magister	22
(sub-total	44)

others--

AS-202/18A Bravo	10
Beechcraft T-34C	12
Broussard (possibly phased out)	9
(sub-total	31)
TOTAL	75

helicopters:

attack--

SA-342 Gazelle	30

heavy transport--

CH-47C Chinook	8

medium transport--

AB-212	11
AB-205	30
SA-330 Puma	37
(sub-total	78)

```
light transport--
    Alouette III                                    8
    AB-206 JetRanger                               16
    SA-315B Lama                                    2
                                (sub-total        26)
TOTAL                                             142
on order: 24 500MG or 530MG
```

miscellaneous aircraft:
```
counter insurgency--
    OV-10 Bronco                                    4
UAVs and mini-UAVs--
    Skyeye R4E-50 mini-UAV
```
advanced armament:
```
air-to-air missiles--
    AIM-9J Sidewinder                             320
    R-530
    R-550 Magique
    Super 530D
air-to-ground missiles--
    AGM-65 Maverick                               380
    HOT
```
anti-aircraft defenses:
```
radars--
    AN/TPS-43                                       8
    AN/TPS-63                                       8
```
military airfields: 10

Agadir, Casablanca (Nouasseur), Fez, Kenitra, Larache,
L'Ayoun, Marrakech, Meknes, Rabat, Sidi Slimane

aircraft maintenance and repair capability:
for all existing models

Navy:

combat vessels: number
```
    MFPBs--
        Lazaga                                      4
    missile frigates--
        Descubierta                                 1
```

mine warfare vessels--
Sirius class	1

gunboats/MTBs--
PR-72 class	2
P-200D Vigilance (Cormoran)	6
Total	8

patrol craft--
P-32	6
VC large patrol craft	1
CMN 40.6 meter	1
Osprey-55	2
Total	10

on order: an additional Descubierta missile frigate; 2 additional Osprey 55; 2-4 Assad class missile corvettes, vessels ordered in 1981 by Iraq and held by Italy, negotiations in progress between Italy and Morocco

landing craft:
Batral LSL	3
EDIC LCT	1
TOTAL	4

auxiliary vessels:
cargo ship, 1500 GRT	2

advanced armament:
surface-to-surface missiles--
MM-40 Exocet
MM-38 Exocet

naval bases: 6
Agadir, Casablanca, Kenitra, Dakhla, Safi, Tangier

ship maintenance and repair capability:
at Casablanca--156 meter dry-dock, repairs up to 10,000 DWT; at Agadir--minor repairs

12. OMAN

BASIC DATA

Official Name of State: Sultanate of Oman

Head of State: Sultan Qabus bin Said (also Prime Minister and Minister of Defense)

Deputy Prime Minister for Security and Defense: Fahr ibn Taymur al-Said

Chief of the General Staff: General Khamis Ibn Humaid al-Kalabani

Commander of the Ground Forces: Major General Ali Ibn Rashad al-Kalabani

Commander of the Air Force: Major General Mohammad Mahfoud

Commander of the Navy: Rear Admiral Shihab Bin Tariq Taymur al-Said

Area: 212,200 sq. km.

Population: 1,500,000

ethnic subdivision:		
Arabs	1,359,000	90.6%
Others (Africans, Persians, Southeast Asians)	141,000	9.4%
religious subdivision:		
Ibadi Muslims (Kharadjites)	1,125,000	75.0%
Sunni Muslims	282,000	18.8%
Shi'ite Muslims, Hindus	93,000	6.2%

GDP:

1990--$10.62 billion

1991--$10.20 billion

Balance of Payments (goods, services, & unilateral transfer payments):

year	income	expenditure	balance
1989	$4.07 bil.	$3.48 bil.	+$590 mil.
1990	$5.50 bil.	$4.13 bil.	+$1.37 bil.

Defense Expenditure:
  1991--$1.49 billion
  1992--$1.73 billion
Foreign Military Aid and Security Assistance Received:
  military training:
    foreign advisors/instructors/serving personnel from--
      Britain (officers and NCOs, some of whom are seconded from the British forces, the balance hired on a personal basis); Egypt; Jordan; Pakistan; USA
    trainees abroad in--Britain, Egypt, France, FRG, Jordan, Saudi Arabia
  arms transfers from:
    Austria (small arms)
    Britain (tanks, artillery pieces, combat aircraft, training aircraft, aircraft radars and navigation systems, MFPBs, radars, target drones)
    Egypt (jeeps, APCs, optronics)
    France (ATGMs, AAMs, naval SSMs)
    Switzerland (trainer aircraft)
    USA (AAMs, tanks, SP artillery)
  construction aid by:
    USA (air force bases)
Foreign Military Aid and Security Assistance Extended:
  facilities provided to:
    USA (airfields at Masirah, Seeb, al-Khasb, Thamarit; storage facilities and prepositioning of army equipment; naval facilities at Masirah and Ghanam; communications center); Britain (use of airfields, a squadron of combat aircraft from August 1990 through the Gulf War)
Joint Maneuvers with:
  Britain, Egypt, USA; participation of some units in the Gulf War, 1991; security agreement with the USA

INFRASTRUCTURE
Road Network:

length:	22,800 km
paved roads	3,800 km
gravel, improved earth roads and tracks	19,000 km

main routes:
  Muscat--Ras al-Khaimah/Dubai--Abu Dhabi (UAE)
  Muscat--Izki--Fuhud/Izki--Salalah
  Muscat--Sur
  Muscat--Fujairah (UAE)
  Izki--Sur
  Hajma--Ras al-Daqm
  Salalah--al-Mukalla (Yemen)
  Muscat--al-Khasb (Musandam Peninsula)

Airfields:
  airfields by runway type:
permanent surface fields	6
unpaved fields and usable airstrips	108

  airfields by runway length:
over 3660 meters	1
2440--3659	8
1220--2439	64
under 1220	41
TOTAL	114

  international airport: Muscat (Seeb)
  major domestic airfield: Salalah

Airlines:
  companies: Gulf Air (international)--jointly owned by Bahrain, Qatar, UAE and Oman (aircraft listed under Bahrain); Oman Aviation Service (domestic)
  aircraft (excluding Gulf Air):
BAe-146-200	3
Boeing 727 (Sultan's personal aircraft)	1
Cessna Citation II	1
DHC-6 Twin Otter	2
Fokker F-27-500	3

Maritime Facilities:
  harbors--Mina Qabus, Mina Raysut (Salalah)
  oil terminals--Mina Fahal

Merchant Marine:
vessel type	number	DWT
passenger	1	1320

ARMED FORCES
Personnel:
military forces--
army	18,700
air force	5,000
navy	3,400
TOTAL	27,100

para-military forces--
tribal force--5,000

police/border police--7,000 (operating aircraft, helicopters and patrol boats)

Army:
major units:

unit type	brigades	independent battalions
royal guard	1	
armored		2
armored reconnaissance		1
infantry (partly mechanized)	2	2
paratroop/special forces		1
TOTAL	3	6

small arms:
personal weapons--
9mm Sterling Mk.4 SMG
7.62mm FAL (FN) SAR
5.56mm M-16 A1 AR
5.56mm AUG Steyr AR
machine guns--
7.62mm (0.3") Browning M-1919 MMG
7.62mm MAG (FN) LMG
light and medium mortars--
81mm L-16 A1
60mm Hotchkiss-Brandt
light ATRLs--
on order: LAW-80

tanks:

model	number
high quality	
Chieftain	34
M-60 A3	27
(sub-total	61)
medium quality	
M-60 A1	6
low quality	
Scorpion	30
TOTAL	97

on order: 18 Challenger 2

APCs/ARVs:

model	number
high quality	
V-150 Commando	20
VAB (number unconfirmed)	14
VBC-90	6
(sub-total	40)
others	
AT-105 Saxon	15
Fahd	7
(sub-total	22)
TOTAL	62

on order: AFVs from US drawdown in Europe, including 119 V-300 Commando Scout; negotiations--BTR-80

artillery:

	number
self-propelled guns and howitzers--	
155mm M-109 A2 SP howitzer	12
towed guns and howitzers--	
155mm FH-70	12
130mm Type 59 gun	12
105mm Light Gun	36
105mm M-102 howitzer	36
25 lb. (87mm) howitzer (possibly phased out)	18
(sub-total	114)

mortars, heavy, under 160mm--
120mm mortar	12
107mm (4.2") M-30 SP mortar	12
(sub-total	24)
TOTAL	150

anti-tank weapons:
missiles--
BGM-71A Improved TOW
MILAN

army anti-aircraft defenses:
missiles--	launchers
self-propelled/mobile	
Rapier	24
Tigercat (unconfirmed)	
man-portable	
Blowpipe	
Javelin	28
short-range guns--	
40mm Bofors L-60 (unconfirmed)	12
23mm ZU 23x2	
20mm VDAA SP	9

on order: upgrading of Rapier including Rapier Mk.2 missiles and Blindfire radar; Javelin (unconfirmed)

Air Force:
aircraft--general:	number
combat aircraft	38
transport aircraft	41
helicopters	37

combat aircraft:
strike and multi-role aircraft--	
medium quality	
SEPECAT Jaguar S(O) Mk.1/Mk.2/T2	22
others	
Hawker Hunter FGA-6/FR-10/T-67	16
TOTAL	38

transport aircraft:

BAe-111	3
Britten-Norman BN-2 Defender/Islander	6
C-130H Hercules	3
DC-8	1
DC-10	1
DHC-5D Buffalo	4
Dornier Do-228-100 (used by police air wing for maritime surveillance & border patrol)	2
Gulfstream	1
Learjet (in police service)	1
Mystere-Falcon 20	1
Mystere-Falcon 10	1
Mystere-Falcon 900	2
Short Skyvan Srs 3M (some employed in maritime patrol role)	15
TOTAL	41

training and liaison aircraft:

with ground attack/close air support capability--

BAC-167 Strikemaster Mk.82	12
Hawk	8
(sub-total	20)

others--

AS-202 Bravo	4
TOTAL	24

on order: 4 Hawk 100/103, 12 Hawk 200/203

helicopters: number

medium transport--

AB-205	19
AB-212B/Bell 212	3
AB-214	10
AS-332 Super Puma/SA-330 Puma	2+
(sub-total	34)

light transport--

AB-206 JetRanger	3
TOTAL	37

miscellaneous aircraft:
    target drones--
        TTL BTT-3 Banshee (original number supplied)   53
advanced armament:
    air-to-air missiles--
        R-550 Magique
        AIM-9P/AIM-9J Sidewinder
    bombs--
        BL-755 CBU
anti-aircraft defenses:
    radars--
        AR-15
        S-713 Martello 3D   2
        S-600
        Watchman
    aircraft shelters--
        for all combat aircraft, at Masirah and Thamarit
military airfields: 6
    Bureimi, Dukha, Masirah, Muscat (Seeb), Salalah, Thamarit

Navy:
    combat vessels: number
        MFPBs--
            Province class   4
        gunboats/MTBs--
            Brooke Marine 123 ft. (37.5 meter)   4
        patrol craft (some in police service)--
            CG-29 (28.9 meter, with police)   3
            CG-27 87.6 ft. (26.7 meter)   1
            Vosper Thornycroft 25 meter   5
            P-2000   1
            P-1903   1
            Vosper 25 meter   4
            Cheverton 27 ft. (8.2 meter)   8
            Total   23
    on order: 2 Vosper Thornycroft Type 83 missile corvettes (1400 ton)

landing craft:

Brooke Marine 2000 ton landing ship-logistics/tank	1
Brooke Marine 2500 ton landing ship-logistics/tank	1
Lewis Offshore 85 DWT LCU	1
Cheverton 45 DWT LCU	2
Vosper 230 ton LCM	3
TOTAL	8

on order: Skima 12 hovercraft (unconfirmed)

auxiliary vessels: number

troop carrier	1
Brooke Marine 900 ton royal yacht	1
Conoship Groningen 1380 DWT coastal freighter	1
survey craft, 23.6 ton	1

advanced armament:

surface-to-surface missiles--
MM-38 Exocet SSM
MM-40 Exocet SSM
on order: Crotale NG SAMs

naval bases: 4

Mina Raysut (Salalah), al-Khasb (Musandam Peninsula), Muscat, Wuddam

ship maintenance and repair capability:
Muscat

13. PALESTINIAN MILITARY AND PARA-MILITARY UNITS

The Palestinian forces remain as diverse and devoid of central authority as ever. The chairman of the PLO Executive Committee and designated president of the state of Palestine is Yasir Arafat, who also heads Fatah, the largest constituent organization. Seven major organisations are members of PLO institutions: Fatah, PLF, ALF, PFLP, DFLP, PPSF and PCP. Palestinian military and para-military forces not belonging to the PLO are FRC (Abu Nidal), Fatah rebels (Abu Musa), PFLP-GC and al Saiqa. They are not controlled by the PLO executive organizations mentioned under Armed Forces. Ten Palestinian organizations, some formally belonging to the PLO, others not, convened in September 1992 in Syria and declared themselves an "opposition front," opposed to the peace negotiations now in process. The ten are PFLP, Hamas-Islamic Resistance, PPSF, the Palestinian Islamic Jihad, the Revolutionary Communist Party, DFLP, PFLP-GC, PLF, al-Saiqa and the Abu Musa Fatah Rebels (called also "Fatah-Intifada").

The anti-Arafat Palestine National Salvation Front comprises four members: al-Saiqa, Fatah Rebels, PFLP-GC and PPSF. PPSF is the only organization that belongs to the PLO and to the Palestine National Salvation Front.

In early 1990 several of Abu Nidal's close associates seceded from the FRC, and formed "Fatah Revolutionary Command--Emergency Command." Their posture is closer to that of Fatah (Arafat).

Although the PLO attempts to coordinate the activities of its member organizations, it lacks operational control. In practice, the military forces of all organizations are responsible only to their own leadership.

Palestinian forces may be divided into four categories: a) quasi-regular units of the various organizations; b) terror squads; c) the regular Palestinian Liberation Army (PLA); and d) militias which occasionally supplement the quasi-regular units.

We count the members of the various organizations as single entities regardless of their presumed location. Movement back to Lebanon from Tunisia, Algeria, Iraq, and Yemen proceeded apace after 1990. The quasi-regular forces of Fatah were scattered among a number of Arab countries, mainly Lebanon, Tunisia, Algeria, Iraq and Yemen. All organizations (except for Fatah, the Abu Abbas faction of the PLF and the ALF) were deployed in Syria and Lebanon. The PLF (Abu al-Abbas faction) were in Iraq and Tunisia. The PLF (Talat Yaqub faction) were in the Biqa' area of Lebanon controlled by Syria. The ALF were in Iraq. Militiamen remained concentrated mainly in Lebanon. Terror squads continued their operations mainly from Lebanon, directed against Israeli forces in the "security zone" in South Lebanon and against Israel, and occasionally against targets elsewhere in the world. They also operated from Algeria, Iraq, Libya, and Syria.

During the 1990-1991 Gulf Crisis the PLO expressed sympathy with Iraq. In early 1993 Arafat visited Saddam Hussein in Iraq. This attitude, and the occupation of Kuwait, led to cuts in financial aid to the PLO from Arab states and from wealthy Palestinians in Kuwait.

In June-July 1991, Palestinian forces in South Lebanon surrendered their heavy weapons to the government of Lebanon. Arafat also stated in January 1992 that the Fatah-PLO military units in Lebanon would be disbanded, though "defensive" militias would remain. In 1992 the PLO military units concluded an agreement with the Lebanese government not to carry arms outside the Palestinian camps in Lebanon. The "Palestinian Islamic Jihad" factions led by Fathi Shkaki and Ibrahim Odeh were active in South Lebanon. During 1992 they raided Israel and Israeli forces, both on their own and in cooperation with the Lebanese Hizb Allah militia.

ARMED FORCES
Personnel:
quasi-regular forces--

organization	commander	armed personnel (estimate)
PLO		
Arafat Loyalist:		
Al-Fatah	Yasir Arafat	5,000
Palestine Liberation Front (PLF)	Mahmud al-Zaidan, alias Abu al-Abbas	300+
Palestine Liberation Front (PLF, faction led by the now deceased Talat Yaqub)	not known	ca.100
Arab Liberation Front (ALF)	Abd al-Rahim Ahmad	300
Democratic Front for the Liberation of Palestine (DFLP)	Naif Hawatmeh	500
Popular Front for the Liberation of Palestine (PFLP)	Dr. George Habash	300
Palestine Popular Struggle Front (PPSF)	Dr. Samir Ghusha	600
Palestine National Salvation Front (pro-Syrian, anti-Arafat):		
Fatah Rebels (also called "Fatah Intifada")	Muhammad Said Musa, alias Abu Musa	400
Popular Front for the Liberation of Palestine-- General Command (PFLP--GC)	Ahmad Jibril	700
Al-Sa'iqa	Dr. Issam al-Qadi	100

Secessionist organizations belonging neither to the Arafat Loyalists nor to the Palestine National Salvation Front:

al-Fatah Revolutionary	Sabri al-Bana,	

Council (FRC)	alias Abu Nidal	400-600
FRC-Emergency Command (Secessionists from Abu Nidal)		100-150
Popular Front for the Liberation of Palestine-- Special Command (PFLP-SC)	Salim Abu Salem, alias Abu Muhammad	100
Palestinian Islamic Jihad	Shaykh Asad Bayud al-Tamimi, Fathi Shkaki, Ibrahim Odeh, Ahmad Muhana and others	+

TOTAL, all organizations
9,000-10,000

Approximate Deployment, mid-1992
(all organizations):

country	number
Lebanon:	
Biqa'	800
Mount Lebanon Area	250
Tripoli & Northern Lebanon	450
Beirut & vicinity	350
South Lebanon (Tyre, Sidon & vicinity)	1,800
(sub-total	ca. 3,650)
Syria (excluding PLA)	1,100
Other countries:	
Algeria	300
Iraq	600
Libya	900
Sudan	300
Tunisia (administrative personnel)	700
Yemen	600
Jordan (not counting PLA)	a few
(sub-total	3,400)
TOTAL	9,000-10,000
terror squads	about 200
militias	10,000+

Ground Forces:
    major units--   brigades
        PLA

	brigades
in Syria & Syrian-occupied Lebanon	2
in Jordan	1
in Iraq	1
TOTAL	4

quasi-regular forces of the major organizations

	brigades	battalions	companies
Al-Fatah	3		
PFLP		6	
PFLP-GC			5-6
Al-Sa'iqa		5	
DFLP		8	
PLF (estimate)			2
TOTAL, all organizations	3	19	7-8

small arms:
    personal weapons--
        9mm P.P.Sh.41 SMG
        7.62mm AK-47 (Kalashnikov) AR
        7.62mm AKM AR
        7.62mm Type 56 AR
        7.62mm SSG-69 sniping rifle
        5.56mm HK-33 AR
        5.56mm M-16 A1 AR

machine guns--
    14.5mm ZPU 14.5x4 HMG (in anti-aircraft role)
    14.5mm ZPU 14.5x2 HMG (in anti-aircraft role)
    12.7mm D.Sh.K. 38/46 (Degtyarev) HMG
    7.62mm SGM (Goryunov) MMG
    7.62mm RPD (Degtyarev) LMG
    7.62mm RPK LMG
    7.62mm PK/PKS (Kalashnikov) LMG
light and medium mortars--
    82mm M-43
light ATRLs--
    M-72 LAW
    RPG-7

tanks (a few; most surrendered to Lebanese Army; a few with PFLP-GC in Biqa', Syrian controlled part of Lebanon):
model
    medium quality
        T-55/improved T-54

APCs/ARVs (a few, unconfirmed; most surrendered to Lebanese Army):

model	number
high quality	
M-113	
medium and low quality	
BTR-152	
BRDM-2 (also an SP ATGM carrying AT-3 Sagger)	
UR-416	
TOTAL	a few

artillery (part surrendered to Lebanese Army; a few, possibly held in camps):
towed guns and howitzers--
    155mm M-1950 howitzer
    130mm M-46 gun
    122mm D-30 howitzer
    122mm M-1938 howitzer
    105mm M-102 howitzer
    100mm M-1955 field/AT gun
    85mm M-1945/D-44 field/AT gun

mortars, heavy, over 160mm--
   160mm mortar
mortars, heavy, under 160mm--
   120mm mortar
TOTAL   a few dozen
MRLs--
   122mm BM-21
   122mm BM-11
   107mm
   improvised MRLs on light vehicles
   TOTAL   a few dozen

anti-tank weapons:
  guns--
     107mm B-11 recoilless rifle
     106mm M-40 A2 recoilless rifle
     82mm B-10 recoilless rifle
     57mm gun

army anti-aircraft defenses:
  missiles--
    man-portable
      SA-7 (Grail)
  short-range guns--
     23mm ZSU 23x4 SP (Gun Dish, some surrendered to
      Lebanese Army)
     23mm ZU 23x2
     20mm 20x3 M-55 A4

Air Units:

The PLO-affiliated organizations have no air force. The so-called "Fatah Air Force" is designated Force 14. About 200 Palestinians have reportedly undergone training as fighter and helicopter pilots in Libya, Yemen, Romania, Pakistan, Cuba, North Korea and the USSR (until 1991). Other PLO members have learned to fly commercial aircraft in civilian flight schools in Romania, Yugoslavia and several western countries. Some are now flying diverse aircraft, including MiG-23 and MiG-21 fighters, in Libya. Some pilots belong to Jibril's PFLP-GC. Helicopters flown include the Mi-24, Mi-8, CH-47 and AS-321. Transport aircraft flown include the Fokker F-27. Palestinian terrorists have trained with hot air balloons and hang-gliders equipped with auxiliary motors. Hang-gliders have been used twice in action, in 1981 and in 1987. It is estimated that the PFLP-GC and Abu al-Abbas faction of the PLF have purchased a few ultra-light aircraft.

In recent years a concentration of Palestinian pilots and affiliated personnel was reportedly located in Yemen. The PLO has de facto control of an airline company registered in Guinea Bissau, where Palestinians fly commercial aircraft. One Fokker F-27 crashed in Guinea Bissau in August 1991, with 3 Palestinian crew members killed.

Naval Forces:

swimmer-delivery vehicles	
underwater demolition squads	a few
small boat units	200 men
	(concentrated in Yemen,
	in Libya, in Annaba,
	Algeria; some in Lebanon)

Foreign Military Aid and Security Assistance Received:

financial aid from:

Iran (to Fatah Rebels--Abu Musa, and since late 1989 also to PFLP-GC), Iraq (to al-Fatah, Abu al-Abbas faction of PLF, ALF, 15th May organization); Libya (to PFLP, PFLP-GC, PLF, Fatah Rebels, Palestine Islamic Jihad; after October 1990 also to mainstream PLO); Saudi Arabia ($86 million annually to al-Fatah suspended during the 1990-1991 Gulf Crisis but recently renewed on a smaller scale); Syria (to al-Sa'iqa, PFLP-GC, Fatah Rebels, FRC, PLF [Abd al-Fateh al-Ghanem and Tal'at Ya'qub factions only], PPSF); UAE (grant, suspended during the 1990-91 Gulf Crisis, renewed in 1993 on a smaller scale)

military training:

trainees abroad in--Algeria, Libya, North Korea, Pakistan, Sudan, Yemen arms transfers from:

Iraq (small arms)

Libya (small arms)

Yemen (PDRY before the unification of Yemen, Soviet arms)

Syria (small arms,to the Palestine Salvation Front organizations)

Foreign Military Aid and Security Assistance Extended:

military training, sabotage instruction, and cooperation extended by the PLO and affiliated organizations to the following non-Palestinian organizations:

Hizb Allah in Lebanon (cooperation)

14. QATAR

BASIC DATA

Official Name of State: State of Qatar

Head of State: Shaykh Khalifa ibn Hamad al-Thani (also Prime Minister)

Minister of Defense: Major General Shaykh Hamad ibn Khalifa al-Thani (also Heir Apparent and Commander in Chief of the Armed Forces)

Chief of the General Staff: Brigadier General Shaykh Hamid ibn Abdallah al-Thani

Commander of the Ground Forces: Colonel Muhammad Rashid Sharaan

Commander of the Air Force: Colonel Ahmad Abdallah al-Kuawari

Commander of the Navy: Captain Said al-Suwaydi

Area: 10,360 sq. km.

Population:		420,000
ethnic subdivision:		
Arabs	168,000	40.0%
Pakistanis	76,000	18.0%
Indians	76,000	18.0%
Persians	42,000	10.0%
Others		
(mostly Southeast Asians)	58,000	14.0%
religious subdivision:		
Sunni Muslims	295,000	70.3%
Shi'ite Muslims	102,000	24.3%
Others	23,000	5.4%
nationality subdivision:		
Qataris	105,000	25.0%
Alien Arabs	84,000	20.0%

Alien Non-Arabs
   Southeast Asians (Indians,
   Pakistanis, Chinese, Thais,
   Filipinos, others)   143,000   34.0%
   Iranians   67,000   16.0%
   Others   21,000   5.0%

GDP:
  1990--$7.36 billion
  1991--$6.67 billion

Defense Expenditure:
  1990--$200 million (estimate)
  1991--$500 million

Foreign Military Aid and Security Assistance Received:
  military training:
    foreign advisors/instructors/serving personnel from--Britain, Egypt, France, Pakistan
    trainees abroad in--Britain, Egypt, France, Pakistan, Saudi Arabia, Jordan
  arms transfers from:
    Britain (helicopters, SAMs, target drones)
    Egypt (APCs, MRLs, gas masks, optronics)
    France (tanks, APCs, MFPBs, naval SSMs, combat aircraft, artillery pieces, anti-ship AGMs)
    USA (upgrading of air defense)

Foreign Military Aid and Security Assistance Extended:
  financial aid to:
  Syria, Lebanon--$1 million grant
  facilities provided to:
    USA, Canadian, French fighter aircraft squadron, following the August 1990 Iraqi annexation of Kuwait and during the 1991 Gulf War

Joint Maneuvers with:
  participation in fighting during the 1991 Gulf War, with US-led coalition

INFRASTRUCTURE
Road Network:
length: 1,500 km
    paved roads   1,000 km
    gravel roads   500 km
main routes:
    Doha--Umm Said
    Doha--Salwa--al-Hufuf (Saudi Arabia)
    Doha--Dukhan--Umm Bab (oil fields)
    Doha--al-Ruwais--Zubara
    Doha--UAE

Airfields:
airfields by runway type:
    permanent surface fields   1
    unpaved fields and usable airstrips   3
airfields by runway length:
    over 3660 meters   1
    1220--2439   2
    under 1220   1
TOTAL   4
international airport: Doha

Airlines:
companies: Gulf Air--jointly owned by Oman, Qatar, Bahrain
    and UAE (aircraft listed under Bahrain)

Maritime Facilities:
harbor--Doha
oil terminals--Halul Island, Umm Said

Merchant Marine:

vessel type	number	DWT
tanker	3	
general cargo	12	
container	5	
TOTAL	20	707,089

ARMED FORCES
Personnel:
military forces--

army	6,000
air force	1,500
navy, including marine police	700
TOTAL	8,200

Army:
major units:

unit type	regiments	battalions
armored/tank		1
guard infantry	1	
infantry (partly mechanized)	5	
TOTAL	6	1

small arms:
personal weapons--
7.62mm G-3 AR
7.62mm L-1 A1 SAR
machine guns--
7.62mm MAG (FN) LMG
light and medium mortars--
81mm

tanks:

model	number
medium quality	
AMX-30	24

APCs/ARVs:

model	
high quality	
AMX-10P	30
VAB	158
VPM 81 mortar carrier	4
V-150 Commando	8
(sub-total	200)

others

Fahd		6-10
Ferret		10
Saracen		25
	(sub-total	45)
TOTAL		245

on order: Engesa APCs, ARVs (unconfirmed); 6 French armored vehicles (command post, medical evacuation vehicles); additional VAB

artillery:

self-propelled guns and howitzer--

155mm Mk. F-3 (AMX) SP howitzer	6

towed guns and howitzers--

155mm G-5 Howitzer/gun	12
25 lb. (87mm) howitzer (possibly phased out)	8
(sub-total	20)
TOTAL	26

on order: additional 155mm Mk. F-3 SP howitzers undergoing upgrading

MRLs--

122mm BM-21

anti-tank weapons:

missiles--

MILAN

guns--

84mm Carl Gustav light recoilless rifle

army anti-aircraft defenses:

missiles--	launchers
self-propelled/mobile	
Rapier	18
Roland 2	9
Tigercat	5
man-portable	
Blowpipe	6
FIM-92A Stinger	12

on order: Crotale SAMs (possibly delivered); Mistral SAMs

Air Force:
  aircraft--general: number

	number
aircraft--general:	
combat aircraft	17
transport aircraft	7
helicopters	45
combat aircraft:	
strike and multi-role aircraft--	
medium quality	
Mirage F-1E/B	14
others	
Hawker Hunter FGA-78/T-79	
(possibly phased out)	3
TOTAL	17
transport aircraft:	
Boeing 707	2
Boeing 727	1
Britten-Norman BN-2 Islander	1
Mystere-Falcon 900	3
TOTAL	7
training and liaison aircraft:	
with ground attack/close air support capability--	
Alpha Jet	6
helicopters:	
attack--	
SA-342 Gazelle (employed as light helicopter, incl. 2 with police)	14
heavy transport--	
Westland Commando Mk.2/3	12
medium transport--	
AS-332 Super Puma	6
Westland Lynx	3
Westland Whirlwind Series 3	2
(sub-total	11)
maritime attack--	
Westland Sea King (in attack role)	8
TOTAL	45

miscellaneous aircraft:
    target drones--
        TTL BTT-3 Banshee target drone (unconfirmed)
advanced armament:
    air-to-ground missiles--
        AM-39 Exocet
anti-aircraft defenses:
    long-range missiles--
        on order: MIM-23B Improved HAWK (possibly
           delivered); 4 Thomson CSF (TRS-2100) radars

military airfield:	1

    Doha

Navy:

combat vessels:	number
MFPBs--	
Combattante III	3
patrol craft--	
Vosper Thornycroft 110 ft. (33.5 meter)	6
Damen Polycat 1450	6
Keith Nelson type 44 ft. (13.5 meter)	2
Fairey Marine Interceptor class	2
MV-45	4
Fairey Marine Spear class	25
P-1200	5
Total	50

on order: 4 Vita Vosper Thornycroft 56m class MFPBs,
    delivery 1996

landing craft:	
48.8 meter LCT	1

advanced armament:
    MM-40 Exocet SSM

coastal defense:	launchers
MM-40 Exocet coastal defense missiles	3x4
naval bases:	2

    Doha, Halul Island

15. SAUDI ARABIA

BASIC DATA

Official Name of State: The Kingdom of Saudi Arabia

Head of State: King Fahd ibn Abd al-Aziz al-Saud (also Prime Minister)

First Deputy Prime Minister and Heir Apparent: Crown Prince Abdallah ibn Abd al-Aziz al-Saud (also Commander of the National Guard)

Defense and Aviation Minister: Prince Sultan ibn Abd al-Aziz al-Saud (also Second Deputy Prime Minister)

Chief of the General Staff: General Muhammad bin Saleh al-Hammad

Commander of the Ground Forces: Lieutenant General Salih Ibn Ali al-Muhaya (also Deputy Chief of Staff of the Armed Forces)

Commander of the Air Force: Lieutenant General Ahmad bin Ibrahim al-Buheiri

Commander of the Air Defense Forces: Lieutenant General Majid Ibn Talhab al-Qutaibi

Commander of the Navy: Vice Admiral Talal Ibn Salem al-Mufadhi

Area: 2,331,000 sq. km. (approximation; some borders undefined or undemarcated)

Population (census held in 1992)		16,929,000
ethnic subdivision:		
Arabs	15,473,000	91.4%
Afro-Arabs	846,000	5.0%
Others	610,000	3.6%
religious subdivision:		
Sunni Muslims	15,592,000	92.1%
Shi'ite Muslims	846,000	5.0%
Others (mainly Christians)	491,000	2.9%

nationality subdivision:

Saudis	12,305,000	72.7%
Foreigners	4,624,000	27.3%

      (includes Yemenis, Palestinians, Americans, Thais, Filipinos, Chinese, Indians, Pakistanis and others)

GDP:

1988--$76 billion

1989--$83 billion

Balance of Payments (goods, services & unilateral transfer payments):

year	income	expenditure	balance
1990	$47.30 bil.	$59.91 bil.	-$12.61 bil.
1991	$51.17 bil.	$84.94 bil.	-$33.77 bil.

Defense Expenditure:

1991--$14.0 billion

1992--$14.4 billion

Foreign Military Aid and Security Assistance Received:

military training:

      foreign advisors/instructors/serving personnel from--Britain (3,500 men, mostly BAe personnel related to the Tornado and Hawk aircraft sales), Egypt (on individual basis), France, FRG, India, Italy (technicians), Japan, Pakistan, PRC, USA (partly civilians, related to sales, upgrading and construction)

      trainees abroad in--Britain, France, Jordan, Pakistan, Switzerland, Turkey, USA

arms transfers from:

      Austria (small arms; artillery, unconfirmed)

      Britain (combat aircraft, trainer aircraft, hovercraft, SSB radio transceivers, helicopters, minesweepers, electronics for air defense system, AAMs)

      Canada (LAV APCs/ARVs)

      Egypt (engineering equipment)

      France (APCs, radars, SAMs, SP artillery, anti-ship AGMs, gas masks)

      FRG (small arms, electronics, EW equipment, patrol boats)

      Italy (helicopters)

      Japan (electronics, radio transceivers)

Spain (transport aircraft, small arms)
Sweden (ABC personal protective equipment, unconfirmed)
Switzerland (trainer aircraft co-produced with Britain)
USA (AAMs, AGMs, ATGMs, artillery pieces, AWACS aircraft, combat aircraft, aircraft engines, SAMs, tanks, transport aircraft, aircraft simulators, integration of air defense system)
USSR before end of 1991 (gas masks)
support forces from:
USA
construction aid by:
firms from South Korea, USA, Britain, Netherlands, other
maintenance of equipment in:
France (naval vessels)
Foreign Military Aid and Security Assistance Extended:
financial aid to:
Bosnia--grant; Egypt--grant, coverage of Egyptian participation in Gulf War, and forgiveness of a $6.7 billion Egyptian debt (with other GCC countries); Lebanon--grant ($60 million in 1991 and additional grant in 1992); Morocco; Syria--grants for participation in Gulf War, estimated at $1.5-$2 billion (with other GCC countries); Pakistan--grant; Turkey--$1 billion, grant in oil; USA, Britain and other coalition members, from August 1990, grants to cover costs of war; Saudi pledge to USA was ca. $16 billion dollars, plus (with other GCC countries) coverage of food and fuel of US forces in Saudi Arabia; grant to USSR, in return for Soviet support for anti-Iraq coalition, 1990-91; Palestinian organizations (all aid suspended during Gulf Crisis, but renewed in 1993 on a smaller scale)
military training:
foreign trainees from--Bahrain, Djibouti, Kuwait, Mauritania, Oman, Qatar, Somalia, Tunisia, UAE, Palestinians
arms transfer to:
SPLA in Sudan (small arms, artillery, AT guns)

facilities provided to:

USA (pre-positioned equipment, facilities to USA and other coalition forces from August 1990 until the end of the Gulf War on a large scale; in 1992-93 some air force units and prepositioning of air force equipment)

forces deployed abroad in:

678 troops in UN forces in Somalia, 1993

Cooperation in Arms Production/Assembly with:

Britain (electronics, AAMs); France (electronics); FRG (small arms and ammunition, ATGMs; unconfirmed reports--Germans on an individual basis working on development or upgrading of SSMs); USA (electronics)

Joint Maneuvers with:

France; Pakistan; cooperation with US-led coalition before and during the 1991 Gulf War and participation of several army and air force units in combat; USA

INFRASTRUCTURE

Road Network:

length:	74,000 km
paved roads	35,000 km
gravel and improved earth roads	39,000 km

main routes:

Jiddah--al-Qunfudhah--Jizan--Hodeida (Yemen)

Jiddah--Medina--Tabuk--Maan   (Jordan)/Yanbu--Wajh--Haql--Aqaba (Jordan)

Tabuk--Sakhakh--Badanah (on TAPline road)

Tabuk--Tayma--Hail

Jiddah--Mecca

Mecca--Taif--Qalat   Bishah--Khamis   Mushayt/Qalat Bishah--Najran

Mecca--Taif--Abha--Khamis Mushayt

Riyadh--Buraydah--Hail/Buraydah--Medina

Riyadh--al-Hufuf--Dhahran/al-Hufuf--Doha   (Qatar) /al-Hufuf--Abu Dhabi (UAE)

Dhahran--al-Dammam--Qatif--Ras   Tanura--Jubayl--al-Qaysumah--H-5 (Jordan, TAPline)

Dhahran--al-Manamah (Bahrain): 25 km bridge causeway

Riyadh--al-Kharj--al-Sulayyil--Najran
al-Sulayyil--Sharawrah
Najran--Sana (Yemen)
Rafha (on TAPline road)--al-Najaf (Iraq)

Railway Network:

length (standard gauge): 886 km

main routes:

Riyadh--al-Hufuf--Abqaiq--Dhahran--al-Dammam

Airfields:

airfields by runway type:

permanent surface fields	69
unpaved fields and usable airstrips	119

airfields by runway length:

over 3660 meters	13
2440--3659	38
1220--2439	103
under 1220	34
TOTAL	188

international airports: Dhahran, Jiddah, Medina, Riyadh

major domestic airfields: Abha/Khamis Mushayt, al-Dammam, Arrar, Bishah, Gassim, Qurayat, Hail, al-Hufuf, Jawf, Jizan, Mecca, Najran, al-Qaysumah, Rafha, Sharawra, Tabuk, Taif, Turayf, Wajh, Wadi al-Dawasir, Yanbu

Airlines:

companies: Saudia (international and domestic), Saudi Arabian Airlines (domestic)

aircraft:

Airbus A-300-600	11
Beechcraft King Air A-100	2
Boeing 747-100/747-300/747-SP/747-200F	23
Boeing 737-200/737-200C	20
Boeing 707-200C	2
Cessna Citation II	2
DHC-6 Twin Otter	1
DC-8/DC-8-63F	1
Gulfstream II	4
Gulfstream III	3
Gulfstream IV	4

L-100-30	6
Lockheed L-1011 Tristar 300/500	17
Mystere-Falcon 900	1

Maritime Facilities:

harbors--al-Dammam (King Abdul Aziz Port), Jizan, Jiddah (Jiddah Islamic Port), Jubayl, Ras al-Mishab, Ras Tanura, Yanbu Commercial-Yanbu Industrial Port (King Fahd Port); al-Duba (under construction)

oil terminals--Halul Island, Juaymah (offshore oil terminal), Ras Tanura, Yanbu

Merchant Marine:

vessel type	number	DWT
cargo/cargo container	10	
bunkering tanker	21	
bulk carrier	2	
ro-ro	11	
livestock carrier	5	
container	3	
passenger	1	
refrigerated cargo	6	
producted tanker	2	
methanol tanker	2	
tanker/crude carrier	10	
TOTAL	73	1,292,719

Defense Production:

army equipment:

production under license--G-3 ARs

manufacture--small arms ammunition, electronic components

planned: tank guns, under FRG license; electronic equipment, under British, French and US license and cooperation; APCs; artillery and AAMs in cooperation with Britain; ATGMs, in cooperation with FRG

electronics: assembly--radio transceivers

ARMED FORCES
Personnel:
military forces--(Saudi Army is in the midst of a reorganization which may involve considerable growth)

army	40,000
air force	17,000
navy (including a marine unit)	11,000
national guard (regular, about 25,000 in combat units, 30,000-35,000 in internal security units)	55,000-60,000
royal guards	2,000
TOTAL	125,000-130,000

para-military forces--

Mujahidun (affiliated with national guard)	29,000+
coast guard and border guard	10,000-15,000

Army and National Guard:
major units:

unit type	brigades/ regiments	independent battalions
armored	3	
mechanized	6	
royal guard infantry	1	
infantry	4	19+
marines		1
airborne/special force	1	
TOTAL	15	20+

note: Saudi Army comprises 8 brigades, plus one royal guard brigade; the national guard has 6 brigades

small arms:
personal weapons--
- 9mm Model 12 Beretta SMG
- 7.62mm FAL (FN) SAR
- 7.62mm G-3 AR
- 7.62mm SSG-69 sniping rifle
- 5.56mm AUG Steyr AR
- 5.56mm HK-33 AR
- 5.56mm M-16 A1 AR

machine guns--
7.62mm (0.3") Browning M-1919 A1 MMG
automatic grenade launchers--
40mm Mk.19
light and medium mortars--
81mm
light ATRLs--
APILAS
M-72 LAW

tanks:

model	number
high quality	
M-60 A3	400
medium and low quality	
AMX-30	300
TOTAL	700

on order: 465 M-1 A2, terms of payment and date of delivery being negotiated; delivery of first 315 tanks to begin 1993, remaining 150 not clear

APCs/ARVs (some of the older models in internal security duty):

model	number
high quality	
AMX-10/AMX-10P	500
LAV-25 & other models of LAV/Piranha	+
M-2/M-3 Bradley	100
M-113 A1/A2	1000
V-150 Commando (number unconfirmed)	450
Engesa EE-11 Urutu (unconfirmed)	+
(sub-total	ca.2050)
others	
AML-60/90	200
BMR-600 (with marines)	140
Fox/Ferret (possibly phased out)	200
M-3 (Panhard)	150
UR-416	+
(sub-total	950)
TOTAL	ca.3000

on order: 300 additional M-2/M-3 Bradley with BGM-71D TOW II (delivery 1993-1994); ca. 700 additional LAV-25 and other LAV (total order including 73 armed with 120mm armored mortar); negotiations regarding 550 additional M-2/M-3 Bradleys

artillery:

self-propelled guns and howitzers--

155mm M-109 A2 SP howitzer	220
155mm GCT SP howitzer	50

towed guns and howitzers--

155mm FH-70 howitzer	72
155mm M-198 howitzer	50
105mm M-56 Pack howitzer	+
105mm M-101 howitzer	+

mortars, heavy, under 160mm

107mm (4.2") M-30 mortar	+
TOTAL	700

artillery/mortar locating radars--
AN/TPQ-37

MRLs--	launchers
180mm SS-40 Astros II	
127mm SS-30 Astros II	
Total	ca.70

on order: 93 M-992 ammunition carriers from the USA; 300mm SS-60 ASTROS II, 180mm SS-40 ASTROS II, and 127mm SS-30 Astros II; 9 227mm MLRS

engineering equipment:

M-123 Viper minefield crossing system
M-69 A1 bridging tanks
bridging equipment

AFV transporters:	600

anti-tank weapons:

missiles--	launchers
AMX-10P SP (carrying HOT)	
BGM-71C Improved TOW	
M-47 Dragon	
TOTAL	700

guns--
106mm M-40 recoilless rifle
84mm Carl Gustav light recoilless rifle
on order: 2000 BGM-71D (TOW II, possibly BGM-71F
TOW IIA)

surface-to-surface missiles and rockets:

model	launchers
CSS-2 SSM (DF-3, East Wind, IRBM, number unconfirmed)	8-12
number of missiles: 30-50	

army anti-aircraft defenses:

missiles--	launchers
self-propelled/mobile	
Crotale	
Shahine I/II	
(sub-total	48)
man-portable	
FIM-92A Stinger	400
MIM-43A Redeye	
Mistral	700
short-range guns--	number
35mm Skyguard AD system (guns, radars and SAMs)	60
35mm Oerlikon-Buhrle 35x2 GDF-002	
30mm AMX DCA 30 (twin 30 mm) SP	
20mm M-163 Vulcan SP	72

on order: 50 additional FIM-92A Stinger SAMs; 100
Gepard 35mm SP AAGs; 60 30mm 30x2 Wildcat SP
AAGs; additional Crotale/Shahine II batteries; 800-1500
Mistral SAMs

CW capabilities:

personal protective equipment	
decontamination units	
US-made CAM chemical detection systems	
Fuchs (Fox) ABC detection vehicles	10

Air Force:
  aircraft--general: number

combat aircraft	273
transport aircraft	108
helicopters	145

  combat aircraft:
    interceptors--
      high quality

F-15 C/D Eagle	93
Tornado ADV (F Mk.3)	24
Total	117

    strike and multi-role aircraft--
      high quality

Tornado IDS (GR Mk.1/GR-1A reconn. a/c)	48
medium or low quality	
F-5E/F	ca. 83
F-5A/B (mostly employed as trainer a/c)	15
RF-5E	10
(sub-total	108)
Total	156
TOTAL	273

    on order: additional 48 Tornado IDS, part of the Yamama II agreement, negotiations on terms of payment not completed; 24 F-15 H/F-15XF and 48 F-15E/F-15XF, delivery 1995-98; existing Tornado ADVs may be converted to IDS

  transport aircraft (including tankers):

C-130E/H Hercules	46
C-212	30
CN-235	4
KC-130H tanker (refuelling)	8
KE-3/Boeing 707 tanker (refuelling)	8
Gates Learjet 35 (employed in target-towing role)	3
Gulfstream III	1
Mystere-Falcon 20	2
VC-140 JetStar (equivalent to C-140 JetStar)	2

HS-125	4
TOTAL	108

on order: Super King Air 200; 5 additional KE-3 tanker aircraft

training and liaison aircraft:

with ground attack/close air support capability--

BAC-167 Strikemaster	36
Hawk	30
(sub-total	66)

others--

BAe Jetstream 31 (employed as cockpit training a/c for Tornado pilots)	1
Cessna 172 G/H/L	13
Pilatus PC-9	30
(sub-total	44)
TOTAL	110

on order: 60 additional Hawk 100/200/205 aircraft and 30 additional PC-9 aircraft, part of Yamama II (undergoing renewed negotiations)

helicopters:

attack--(part of Army Aviation)

OH-58D (Combat Scout, AHIP)	15

maritime attack--

SA-365 Dauphin 2	6
AS-332 Super Puma	12
(sub-total	18)

heavy transport--

SH-3 (AS-61A)	3
KV-107/KV-107 IIA-17	17
(sub-total	20)

medium transport--

AB-212 (number unconfirmed)	35
SA-365N Dauphin 2 (employed in medical evacuation role)	+
UH-60A Black Hawk/Desert Hawk/Medevac (part of Army Aviation)	+
(sub-total	ca. 62)

light transport--
AB-206 JetRanger   30
TOTAL   145
on order: additional 40-50 British helicopters, reportedly
    UH-60A (WS-70) and other models; 12 AH-64A
    Apache; 4 CH-47D Chinook; 8 additional UH-60A for
    Medevac

miscellaneous aircraft:
AEW/AWACS aircraft--
E-3A AWACS   5
target drones--
TTL BTT-3 Banshee
UAVs and mini-UAVs--
MQM-74C Chukar II UAV
on order: negotiations in process regarding purchase of 4
    additional E-3A AWACS, or new Boeing 767 AWACS,
    or conversion of KC-135 to AWACS

advanced armament:
air-to-air missiles--   number
AIM-7F Sparrow   850
AIM-9J/P Sidewinder
AIM-9L Sidewinder
Red Top
Sky Flash
Firestreak
air-to-ground missiles--
AGM-65A Maverick   2400
AS-15TT anti-ship missile
Sea Eagle anti-ship missile
bombs--
laser-guided bombs   3000
CBU   1000
BL-755 CBU
JP-233 anti-runway bombs
Paveway II laser guided
on order: AS-15TT air-to-sea missile, 100 AGM-84
    Harpoon air-to-sea missile, AIM-7M AAMs, AIM-9M
    and AIM-9S AAMs, AIM-9L AAMs, AIM-9P-4

AAMS, ALARM anti-radiation missiles, AM-39 Exocet air-to-sea missiles, AGM-65 AGMs (partly AGM-65D/G), CBU-87, GBU-10/12, connected with the acquisition of new F-15/E/F/XF

anti-aircraft defenses:

radars--

AN/FPS-117 (Seek Igloo)	17
AN/TPS-43G	
AN/TPS-59	

long-range missiles--

model	batteries
MIM-23B Improved HAWK	17

on order: some MIM-104 Patriot SAMs, delivery 1993; additional batteries of MIM-104, delivery 1995-96; AN/TPS-70(V)X2 radars

aircraft shelters--

for combat aircraft

military airfields: 20-24

Abqaiq, al-Ahsa, al-Sulayyil, Dhahran (King Abd al-Aziz), al-Hufuf, Jiddah (Amir Abdallah), Jubail, Khamis Mushayt (King Khalid), al-Kharj, Medina, Riyadh, Sharawrah, Tabuk (King Faisal), Taif (King Fahd), 6-10 additional

aircraft maintenance and repair capability:

for all models, dependent on foreign technicians

Navy:

combat vessels:	number
MFPBs--	
PGG-1 class (Peterson Builders)	9
missile frigates--	
F-2000	4
missile corvettes--	
PCG-1 class (Tacoma Boatbuilding)	4
mine warfare vessels--	
MSC-322 class minesweeper	4
gunboats/MTBs--	
Jaguar class MTB	3

patrol craft (some serving with coast guard)--

Blohm & Voss 38.6 meter (with coast guard)	4
Skorpion class (with coast guard)	15
Rapier class 50 ft. (with coast guard)	12
Simonneau Type	20
Total	51

note: coast guard has 110 additional small patrol craft

on order: 6 Sandown minehunters (1 launched August 1989, undergoing refit and trials in Britain, to become operational in 1993, a second Sandown undergoing sea trials, a third launched); 3 La Fayette class air defense missile frigates; 10 additional Simonneau Type patrol boats

landing craft:

LCM-6 class	8
SRN-6 class hovercraft (with coast guards)	24
US LCU 1610 class LCU	4
26 ton LCM	4
TOTAL	40

auxiliary vessels:

training ship, 350 ton	1
royal yacht, 1450 DWT	1
royal yacht, 650 ton	1
Durance class tanker, 10,500 ton	2

advanced armament:

surface-to-surface missiles--

OTOMAT Mk.2	
RGM-84A Harpoon	120

surface-to-air missile--

Crotale Navale

anti-missile guns--

20mm Vulcan-Phalanx radar-controlled anti-missile gun

advanced torpedoes--

F-17P

coastal defense:

OTOMAT coastal defense missile

special maritime forces:

frogmen and divers

naval bases (including Coast Guard):   12
    al-Dammam, al-Haql (coast guard), Jiddah, Jizan, Jubayl, Makna (coast guard), al-Qatif, Ras al-Mishab, Ras Tanurah, al-Sharma, al-Wajh, Yanbu

ship maintenance and repair capability:
    repair of vessels, dependent on foreign experts; 22,000 ton and 62,000 ton floating docks at Dammam; 45,000 ton and 16,000 ton floating docks at Jiddah

16. SUDAN

BASIC DATA
Official Name of State: The Republic of Sudan
Chairman of the National Salvation Revolutionary Command Council: Lieutenant General Omar Hassan Ahmad al-Bashir (also Defense Minister)
State Minister at the Ministry of Defense: Major General Uthman Muhammad al-Hassan
Chief of the General Staff: Lieutenant General Hassan Abd al-Rahman Ali
Commander of the Air Force: Major General Ali Mahjoub Mardi
Commander of the Air Defense Force: Major General Muhammad al-Radi Nasr-al Din Mahjoub
Commander of the Navy: Commodore Hussein Abd al-Karim
Area: 2,504,530 sq. km.
Population: 27,210,000
    ethnic subdivision (exact
      percentages not known):
      Arabs
      Nilotics, Negroes and others
    religious subdivision:
      Sunni Muslims
      Animists
      Christians (Coptic,
        Greek Orthodox,
        Catholic, Protestant)

Refugees: (excluded from total)	1,200,000
Ethiopians	800,000
Chadians	150,000
Ugandans	250,000

GDP:
    1987--$11.08 billion
    1990--$8.97 billion

Balance of Payments (goods, services & unilateral transfer payments):

year	income	expenditure	balance
1990	$993 mil.	$2.20 bil.	-$1.21 bil.
1991	$522 mil.	$2.20 bil.	-$1.68 bil.

Defense Expenditure:
1991--$610 million

Foreign Military Aid and Security Assistance Received:
financial aid from:
> Libya--grant, oil shipments; PRC--$30 million loan (possibly civilian); Iran--grant and loan ($300 million)

military training:
> foreign advisors/instructors from--Iran (technicians and IRGC), Iraq (technicians), PRC (pilot training), USA (including aircraft maintenance personnel, suspended in 1991), Yugoslavia (unconfirmed)

> trainees abroad in--Iran, Iraq, Yugoslavia (before the 1991 civil war in Yugoslavia)

arms transfers from:
> France (artillery pieces)

> Iran (small arms, ammunition, EW equipment, vehicles, spare parts for Soviet and Chinese arms)

> Libya (small arms)

> PRC (tanks, artillery, APCs, combat aircraft)

> Romania (helicopters)

support forces from:
> Libya (two or more aircraft flying close air support missions)

maintenance of equipment in:
> USA (aircraft, now suspended); Jordan (civil aircraft)

Foreign Military Aid and Security Assistance Extended:
military training:
> foreign trainees from--Islamic fundamentalists from several countries (Egypt, Tunisia, Algeria, Mauritania) trained to engage in anti-governmental activity

facilities provided to:
> facilities for Libyan combat a/c in an AFB, after April 1992; Palestinian organizations (al-Fatah forces evacuated

from Lebanon, camps); Iranian IRGC and facilities to
Iranian ships at Port Sudan
Joint Maneuvers with:
Iran (naval maneuvers)

INFRASTRUCTURE
Road Network:
length:	20,000 km
paved roads	1,600 km
gravel and crushed stone roads	3,700 km
earth tracks	14,700 km

main routes:
   Khartoum--Shendi--Atbara--Suakin--Port Sudan
   Atbara--Wadi Halfa (Egyptian border)
   Atbara--Merowe--Wadi Halfa
   Khartoum--Kassala--Asmara (Ethiopia)
   Khartoum--Wad Medani--Gedaref--Gondar (Ethiopia)
   Kosti--Malakal--Juba--Kampala (Uganda)/Juba--Niangara
     (Zaire)
   Khartoum--al-Dueim--Rabak/Kosti
   Kosti--Gedaref--Kassala--Port Sudan
   Kosti--al-Obeid--al-Fasher--al-Geneina--Abeche (Chad)
   Port Sudan--Hurghada (Egypt)

Railway Network:
length:	5,441 km
narrow gauge (1.067 meter)	4,725 km
1.6096 meter gauge (plantation line)	716 km

main routes:
   Khartoum--Wadi Halfa
   Khartoum--Atbara--Port Sudan
   Khartoum--Sennar--Kosti--El Obeid
   Khartoum--WadMedani--Sennar--Damazin/Sennar--Kosti--
     Babanusa
   Babanusa--Nyala
   Babanusa--Wau

Airfields:
    airfields by runway type:

permanent surface fields	8
unpaved fields and usable airstrips	58

    airfields by runway length:

2440--3659 meters	4
1220--2439	30
under 1220	32
TOTAL	66

    international airport: Khartoum
    major domestic airfields: Atbara, Dongola, al-Fasher, al-Geneina, Juba, Kassala, Malakal, Merowe, Myala, al-Obeida, Port Sudan, Wadi Halfa, Wau

Airlines:
    companies: Sudan Airways (international, charter, domestic), Nile Safari Cargo (cargo charter), Trans Arabian Air Transport (cargo)
    aircraft:

Airbus A-310-300	1
Boeing 737-200C	2
Boeing 707-320C	7
Fokker F-27-200	1
Fokker F-50	2

    on order: 2 additional F-50, delivery uncertain due to lack of funds

Maritime Facilities:
    harbors--Port Sudan, Osman Digna

Merchant Marine:

vessel type	number	DWT
general cargo	3	
general cargo/container	5	
ro/ro	2	
TOTAL	10	122,991

ARMED FORCES
Personnel:
military forces--

army	70,000
air force (including air defense)	6,000
navy	500
TOTAL	76,500

para-military forces--

People's Defense Forces	15,000
border guards	2,500
Sudan People's Liberation Army (SPLA), anti-government rebels in control of parts of Southern Sudan (estimate, total SPLA)	29,000-30,000

SPLA factions:

Garang faction (led by John Garang)	ca. 14,000
Nasser faction (led by Ric Mashar & Lam Akoul)	ca. 10,000
Niyon faction (led by William Bani Niyon)	ca. 5,000
Anya Nya 2 faction	a few

Army:
major units (not all fully organized nor fully manned):

unit type	divisions	brigades
armored	1	10
infantry	6	18
airborne	1	1
corps of engineers	1	1
united patrimony div.	1	
TOTAL	10	30

small arms:
personal weapons--
9mm Sterling SMG
7.62mm AK-47 (Kalashnikov) AR
7.62mm G-3 AR
7.62mm SKS (Simonov) SAR

machine guns--
    12.7mm D.Sh.K. 38/46 (Degtyarev) HMG
    7.62mm MG-3 LMG
    7.62mm RPD (Degtyarev) LMG
    7.62mm SGM (Goryunov) MMG
light and medium mortars--
    82mm M-43
light ATRLs--
    RPG-7

tanks:

model	number
high quality	
M-60 A3	20
medium quality	
T-55/Type 59 (number unconfirmed)	200-250
low quality	
T-54	70
M-47	15
M-41	55
Type 62	70
(sub-total	210)
TOTAL	430-480

APCs/ARVs:

model	number
high quality	
M-113	80
V-150 Commando	55
AMX-VCI	a few
(sub-total	135+)
others	
al-Walid	150
AML-90	5
BTR-50	20
BTR-152	80
Ferret	60
M-3 (Panhard, unconfirmed)	+
OT-64	55

OT-62	+
Saladin	50
(sub-total	815)
TOTAL	950

artillery:
self-propelled guns and howitzers--

155mm Mk. F-3 (AMX) SP howitzer	10

towed guns and howitzers--

155mm M-114 howitzer	12
130mm Type 59 gun	10
122mm M-1938 howitzer	+
105mm M-101 howitzer	+
100mm M-1955 field/AT gun	+
25 lb. (87mm) howitzer	+
85mm M-1945/D-44 field/AT gun	+

mortars, heavy, under 160mm--

120mm mortar	+
TOTAL	200-250

MRLs--

122mm Saqr (unconfirmed)	+

anti-tank weapons:
missiles--

BGM-71C Improved TOW (unconfirmed)	+
Swingfire	+
AT-3 (Sagger, unconfirmed)	+

army anti-aircraft defenses (low serviceability):
missiles--
man-portable

SA-7 (Grail)	+
MIM-43A Redeye	+

short-range guns-- number

37mm M-1939	+
23mm ZU 23x2	+
20mm M-163 A-1 Vulcan SP	+
20mm M-167 Vulcan (number unconfirmed)	+

CW capabilities:
personal protective equipment
unit decontamination equipment

Air Force:

aircraft--general (low serviceability):	number
combat aircraft	59
transport aircraft	24
helicopters	59

combat aircraft:

interceptors--

medium and low quality

F-6 Shenyang	27
MiG-21 (Fishbed)/F-7	12
Total	39

strike and multi-role aircraft--

medium and low quality

MiG-17 (Fresco)/Shenyang F-5	
(many not serviceable)	20
TOTAL	59

on order: ca. 18 additional F-7

transport aircraft:

An-24 (Coke)/An-26	5
C-130H Hercules (some being	
overhauled in USA)	4
DHC-5D Buffalo	4
Fokker F-27	4
Mystere-Falcon 50	1
Mystere-Falcon 20	1
others	5
TOTAL	24

training and liaison aircraft:

with ground attack/close air support capability--

BAC-145 Jet Provost	5
BAC-167 Strikemaster	3
TOTAL	8

helicopters:	number
medium transport--	
Mi-4 (Hound, possibly phased out)	3
Mi-8 (Hip)	14

SA-330 Puma/IAR-330 Puma	14
Bell 212/AB-212	5
(sub-total	34)
light transport--	
MBB BO-105 (some serving police)	22
Bell 206	3
(sub-total	25)
TOTAL	59

advanced armament:
air-to-air missiles--
AIM-9M Sidewinder
AA-2 (Atoll)
anti-aircraft defenses:
long range missiles--

model	batteries
SA-2 (Guideline)	5

military airfields (some not in service): 13

Atbara, al-Fasher, al-Geneina, Juba, Khartoum, Malakal, Merowe, al-Obeid, Port Sudan, Port Sudan (new), Wad Medani, Wadi Sayidina, Wau, one additional

Navy:

combat vessels:	number
patrol craft--	
Abeking and Rasmussen 75.2 ft. (22.9 meter)	2
Sewart class	4
Yugoslav type 15	4
TOTAL	

landing craft:

DTM-221 LCT	2

naval base:

Port Sudan	1

17. SYRIA

BASIC DATA
   Official Name of State: The Arab Republic of Syria
   Head of State: President Hafez al-Assad
   Prime Minister: Mahmoud al-Zuebi
   Defense Minister: Lieutenant General Mustafa al-Tlass
   Chief of the General Staff: General Hikmat Shihabi
   Commander of the Air Force: Major-General Ali Malakhafji
   Commander of the Navy: Rear Admiral Mustafa Tayara
   Area: 185,680 sq. km.

Population:		12,900,000
ethnic subdivision:		
Arabs	11,649,000	90.3%
Kurds, Armenians and others	1,251,000	9.7%
religious subdivision:		
Sunni Muslims	9,546,000	74.0%
Alawis, Druzes and Shi'ite Muslims	2,064,000	16.0%
Christians (Greek Orthodox, Gregorian Armenian, Catholics, Syrian Orthodox, Greek Catholics)	1,290,000	10.0%
Jews	a few thousand	

GDP (figures unreliable; calculated according to the official rate
   of exchange of 11.225 Syrian Pounds per US dollar in 1988
   and thereafter):
   1990--$23.9 billion
   1991--$27.22 billion (estimate)

Balance of Payments (goods, services & unilateral transfer payments):

year	income	expenditure	balance
1989	$4.35 bil.	$3.35 bil.	+$1.00 bil.
1990	$5.46 bil.	$3.78 bil.	+$1.68 bil.

Defense Expenditure:

1990--$1.46 billion, unreliable, probably excluding foreign grant

1991--$2.5 billion

Foreign Military Aid and Security Assistance Received:

financial aid from:

Saudi Arabia and other GCC countries, about $1.5-$2 billion--grant; with civilian grant, the Gulf countries' grant figures reach $2-$3 billion between mid-1990 and late 1991

military training:

foreign advisors/instructors from--CIS, mainly Russia; a few scores from Bulgaria, Hungary, PRC

trainees abroad in--Russia, France, Libya, North Korea, PRC (unconfirmed)

arms transfers from:

Bulgaria (SP artillery)

Czech Republic (tanks)

France (ATGMs)

India (CW chemical components)

North Korea (SSMs)

USSR/Russia (SP artillery, combat aircraft, helicopters, SAMs, SSMs, tanks, radars)

Foreign Military Aid and Security Assistance Extended:

financial aid to:

Palestinian organizations (Fatah Rebels, al-Saiqa, PPSF, PLF and PFLP-GC)--grants

military training:

advisors/instructors/serving personnel in--Libya (pilots), Lebanese army

foreign trainees from--Yemen, Libya, Lebanon

arms transfers to:

Palestinian military forces (small arms)

Lebanese army (artillery, tanks)

facilities provided to:
> USSR until end of 1991 (use of Latakia and Tartus harbors); Fatah Rebels, PPSF, PFLP-GC, PFLP, DFLP, al-Saiqa (camps); PKK in Syrian-controlled Biqa', Lebanon until September 1992 and until mid-1992 some facilities also in Syria; Palestinian Islamic Jihad (camps, officers in Biqa', Syrian-controlled)

forces deployed abroad in:
> Lebanon--30,000 in Biqa', northern Lebanon (Tripoli area) and Beirut;

Cooperation in Arms Production/Assembly with:
North Korea (planned production of SSMs)

INFRASTRUCTURE
Road Network:

length:	27,000 km
paved roads	21,000 km
gravel and crushed stone roads	3,000 km
improved earth tracks	3,000 km

main routes:
> Damascus--Homs--Hama--Aleppo
> Tartus--Banias--Latakia
> Latakia--Aleppo--Dir e-Zor--Qusaybah (Iraq)
> Tartus--Homs--Palmyra--Qusaybah
> Banias--Hama
> Damascus--Beirut (Lebanon)
> Damascus--Palmyra--Dir e-Zor--al-Hasakah--al-Qamishli
> Damascus--al-Rutbah (Iraq)
> Damascus--Dara--Ramtha (Jordan)
> Damascus--Kuneitra--Rosh Pina (Israel)
> Tartus--Tripoli (Lebanon)

Railway Network:

length:	2,241 km
standard gauge	1,930 km
narrow gauge	311 km

main routes:
   Aleppo--Adana (Turkey)
   Aleppo--Latakia
   Aleppo--Hama--Homs--Tripoli   (Lebanon)/Homs--Zahlah
      (Lebanon)/Homs--Damascus
   Aleppo--al-Qamishli--Mosul (Iraq)
   Aleppo--Dir e-Zor--al-Qamishli
   Damascus--Dara--Ramtha (Jordan)
   Damascus--Beirut (Lebanon)
   Latakia--Tartus
   Latakia--Aleppo
   Tartus--Homs
   Dir e-Zor--Abu Kemal

Airfields:
   airfields by runway type:
      permanent surface fields   24
      unpaved fields and usable airstrips   72
   airfields by runway length:
      2440--3659 meters   21
      1220--2439   4
      under 1220   71
   TOTAL   96
   international airports: Aleppo, Damascus, Latakia
   major domestic airfields: Dir e-Zor, Palmyra, al-Qamishli,
      al-Hasakah

Airlines:
   companies: Syrian Arab Airlines (international and domestic)
   aircraft:
      Boeing 747 SP   2
      Boeing 727-200   3
      Caravelle 10B (Super Caravelle)   2
      Tupolev Tu-154   3

Maritime Facilities:
   harbors--Latakia, Tartus
   anchorages--Arwad, Jablah, Banias
   oil terminals--Banias, Latakia, Tartus

Merchant Marine:

vessel type	number	DWT
general cargo	22	
ro-ro	1	
bulk carrier	1	
TOTAL	24	119,078

Nuclear Capability:

basic R&D; contract for purchase of a 30 KW research reactor from PRC; Syria is a signatory to NPT

Defense Production:

army equipment:

ammunition; toxic gases; chemical warheads for SSMs (unconfirmed); upgrading of tanks; upgrading of SSMs (with assistance from North Korea, unconfirmed); planned production of SSMs (in cooperation with North Korea)

ARMED FORCES

Personnel:

military forces--

	regular	reserves	total
army	306,000	100,000	406,000
air force & air defense	80,000	40,000	120,000
navy	4,000	2,500	6,500
TOTAL	390,000	142,500	532,500

Beyond 142,500 trained reserves, Syria can mobilize another 750,000 reserves, not organized in units

para-military forces--

Workers' Militia	400,000

Army:

major units:

unit type	army corps HQ	divisions	independent brigades/groups
all arms	2		
armored		7	1
mechanized		3	1
infantry/			
special forces		1	2

airborne/
  special forces   7

TOTAL	2	11	11

note: one additional new division being organized

small arms:
  personal weapons--
    9mm Model 23/25 SMG
    7.62mm AK-47 (Kalashnikov) AR
    7.62mm AKM AR
    7.62mm SKS (Simonov) SAR
  machine guns--
    12.7mm D.Sh.K. 38/46 (Degtyarev) HMG
    7.62mm PK/PKS (Kalashnikov) LMG
    7.62mm RPD (Degtyarev) LMG
    7.62mm SG-43 (Goryunov) MMG
    7.62mm SGM (Goryunov) MMG
  automatic grenade launchers--
    30mm AGS-17 (unconfirmed)
  light and medium mortars--
    82mm M-43
  light ATRLs--
    RPG-7
    RPG-18 (unconfirmed)

tanks (some in storage):

model	number
high quality	
T-72/T-72M	1500
medium quality	
T-62	1000
T-55/T-54 (some upgraded)	2300
(sub-total	3300)
TOTAL	4800

APCs/ARVs (some in storage):

model	number
high quality	
BMP-1	2450
BMP-2	ca.70
(sub-total	2520)

others

BTR-152		560
BTR-40/50/60		1000
BRDM-2		900
	(sub-total	2460)
TOTAL		4980

artillery (some in storage):

self-propelled guns and howitzers--		number
152mm M-1973 SP howitzer		55
122mm M-1974 SP howitzer		290
122mm (Syrian)		55
	(sub-total	400)
towed guns and howitzers--		
180mm S-23 gun		10
152mm M-1943 howitzer		155
152mm D-20 howitzer/gun		35
130mm M-46 gun		730
122mm D-30 howitzer		475
122mm D-74 gun		110
122mm M-1938 howitzer		385
	(sub-total	1900)
mortars, heavy, over 160mm--		
240mm mortar		10
160mm mortar		80
	(sub-total	90)
mortars, heavy, under 160mm--		
120mm mortar		+
TOTAL		2400
MRLs--		
122mm BM-21		ca.100
107mm		

engineering equipment:

MTU-67 bridging tank/MT-55 bridging tanks	ca. 90
tank-towed bridges	
mine-clearing rollers	
AFV transporters:	800

anti-tank weapons:

missiles--	launchers
AT-3 (Sagger)	1050
AT-4 (Spigot)	
AT-5 (Spandrel) mounted on BMP-2	
BRDM-2 carrying AT-3 (Sagger) SP	
MILAN	
TOTAL	2000

surface-to-surface missiles and rockets:

model	launchers
FROG-7	18
SS-1 (Scud B)	18
SS-1 (Scud C variant from North Korea)	very few
SS-21 (Scarab)	18
TOTAL	ca.60

on order: additional SSMs: Scud C from North Korea; M-9 from PRC; Nodong

army anti-aircraft defenses:

missiles--	batteries
self-propelled/mobile	
SA-6 (Gainful) and SA-8 (Gecko)	ca.70
SA-9 (Gaskin)	
SA-13 (Gopher)	+
man-portable	
SA-7 (Grail)	
SA-14 (Gremlin)	
SA-16	

short range guns (some in storage)--	number
57mm M-1950 (S-60)	
37mm M-1939 (possibly phased out)	
23mm ZSU 23x4 SP (Gun Dish)	
23mm ZU 23x2	
TOTAL	ca.1500

CW capabilities:

personal protective equipment
Soviet type unit decontamination equipment
stockpiles of nerve gas, including sarin
mustard gas

VX nerve gas (unconfirmed)
chemical warheads for SSMs
biological warfare capabilities:
biological weapons and toxins (unconfirmed)

Air Force:

	number
aircraft--general:	
combat aircraft	530
transport aircraft	23
helicopters	285
combat aircraft:	
interceptors--	
high quality	
MiG-25 and MiG-25R (Foxbat)	40
MiG-29 (Fulcrum, multi-role,	
employed as interceptor)	20
(sub-total	60)
others	
MiG-21 MF/bis/U (Fishbed)	220
MiG-23 ML/MF/MS	80
MiG-17 (possibly phased out)	a few
(sub-total	300)
Total	360
strike and multi-role aircraft--	
high quality	
Su-24 (Fencer)	20
medium quality	
MiG-23 U/BN (Flogger)	50
Su-20/22 (Fitter C)	100
(sub-total	150)
Total	170
TOTAL	530

on order: 24 additional Su-24 (Fencer); additional MiG-29 (Fulcrum), negotiations not completed; Su-27, negotiations in process

transport aircraft:		number
An-24/26 (Coke/Curl)		6
IL-76 (Candid)		4
Mystere-Falcon 20/900		5
Piper Navajo		2
Yak-40 (Codling)		6
TOTAL		23

training and liaison aircraft:
with ground attack/close air support capability--

L-39 Albatross		90
others--		
MBB 223 Flamingo		40
TOTAL		130

helicopters:
attack--

Mi-25 (Hind)		55
SA-342 Gazelle		45
	(sub-total	100)

medium transport--

Mi-8 (Hip)/Mi-17 (Hip H)		150
Mi-2 (Hoplite, limited serviceability)		10
	(sub-total	160)

ASW--

Ka-28 (Helix)		5
Mi-14 (Haze)		20
	(sub-total	25)
TOTAL		285

miscellaneous aircraft:
UAVs and mini-UAVs--

Soviet-made UAVs	+

on order: Malachit/Pchela-1/Shmel-1 UAV system, for reconnaissance and EW

advanced armament:
air-to-air missiles--
AA-2 (Atoll)
AA-6 (Acrid)
AA-7 (Apex)
AA-8 (Aphid)

AA-10 (Alamo)
AA-11 (Archer, unconfirmed)
air-to-ground missiles--
AS-7 (Kerry)
AS-9 (Kyle)
AS-10 (Karen)
AS-11 (Kegler)
AS-12
AS-14 (Kedge)
AT-2 (Swatter)
HOT

anti-aircraft defenses:
radars--
Long Track
P-15 Flat Face
P-12 Spoon Rest
long-range missiles--

model	batteries
SA-2 (Guideline) & SA-3 (Goa)	100
SA-5 (Gammon)	8
TOTAL	108

on order: SA-10 (Grumble), negotiations not completed
aircraft shelters--
in all airfields, for combat aircraft

military airfields: 21
Abu Duhur, Afis North, Aleppo, Blay, Damascus (international), Damascus (Meze), Dir e-Zor, Dumayr, Hama, Jarah, Khalkhala, Latakia, Nassiriyah, Palmyra, al-Qusayr, Rasm al-Aboud, Sayqal, Shayarat, al-Suweida, T-4, Tabaka

aircraft maintenance and repair capability:
for all models in service

Navy:

combat vessels:	number
submarines--	
R class (Romeo)	3

MFPBs--
Komar	5
Ossa I	6
Ossa II	8
Total	19

note: possibly some phased out
ASW vessels--
Petya II submarine chaser frigate	2

mine warfare vessels--
T-43 class minesweeper	1
Vanya class minesweeper	2
Yevgenia class minesweeper	5
Total	8

patrol craft--
Zhuk class	8
Natya (formerly a minesweeper)	1
Total	9

landing craft:
Polnochny B class LCT	3

auxiliary vessels:
training ship (al-Assad)	1
Poluchat torpedo recovery vessel	1

advanced armament:
surface-to-surface missiles--
SS-N-2 Styx/SS-N-2C SSM
coastal defense:
SSC-1B Sepal coastal defense missile
SSC-3 coastal defense missile
naval bases: 3
Latakia, Minat al-Baida, Tartus
ship maintenance and repair capability:
repairs at Latakia
note: ASW helicopters have been listed under Air Force

18. TUNISIA

BASIC DATA

Official Name of State: The Republic of Tunisia
Head of State: President General Zine al-Abedine Bin Ali (also Defense Minister)
Prime Minister: Hamid al-Karoui
Minister of Defense: Abd al-Aziz Bin Diya
Chief of the General Staff: General Muhammad Said al-Katib
Commander of the Ground Forces: Major General Muhammad Hadi Bin Hassin
Commander of the Air Force: Major General Rida Hamuda Atar
Commander of the Navy: Vice Admiral al-Shadli Sharif
Area: 164,206 sq. km.

Population: 8,466,000

ethnic subdivision:		
Arabs/Berbers	8,297,000	98.0%
Europeans	67,000	0.8%
Others	102,000	1.2%
religious subdivision:		
Sunni Muslims	8,297,000	98.0%
Christians	84,500	1.0%
Others	84,500	1.0%

GDP:
1989--$9.08 billion
1990--$9.58 billion

Balance of Payments (goods, services & unilateral transfer payments):

year	income	expenditure	balance
1988	$4.91 bil.	$4.20 bil.	+$710 mil.
1989	$5.18 bil.	$4.86 bil.	+$320 mil.

Defense Expenditure:
1990--$331 million (unconfirmed)

Foreign Military Aid and Security Assistance Received:
financial aid from:
Saudi Arabia--grant; USA--$30 million grant; Japan--$80 million loan, for civilian and military infrastructure; Qatar--$7 million grant
military training:
foreign advisors/instructors from--USA; France (unconfirmed)
trainees abroad in--Egypt, France, Saudi Arabia, USA
arms transfers from:
Austria (light tanks, small arms)
Belgium (small arms)
Brazil (APCs, ARVs)
Britain (patrol craft, target drones)
France (helicopters, naval SSMs)
Germany (patrol vessels of former GDR)
Italy (trainer aircraft, APCs)
USA (artillery pieces, SAMs, tanks, transport aircraft, spare parts)
Foreign Military Aid and Security Assistance Extended:
facilities provided to:
France (radar station); PLO/Fatah (camps); Iraq (refuge for commercial a/c)
forces deployed abroad in: 133 troops in UN forces in Somalia, 1993
Cooperation in Arms Production/Assembly with:
Algeria and Italy (diesel engines); South Korea (patrol craft)
Joint Maneuvers with:
France, USA; Spain (unconfirmed)

INFRASTRUCTURE
Road Network:

length:	17,700 km
paved roads	9,100 km
gravel roads and improved earth tracks	8,600 km

main routes:
Tunis--Bizerta
Tunis--Annaba (Algeria)

Tunis--Kairouan--Gafsa--Tozeur--Touggourt (Algeria)
Tunis--Sousse--Sfax--Gabes--Tripoli (Libya)
Sousse--Kasserine
Gabes--Gafsa

Railway Network:

length:	2,154 km
standard gauge	465 km
narrow gauge (1.0 meter)	1,689 km

main routes:
Tunis--Bizerta
Tunis--Annaba (Algeria)
Tunis--Kasserine--Gafsa--Tozeur
Tunis--Sousse--Sfax--Gabes
Sfax--Gafsa--Tozeur

Airfields:

airfields by runway type:

permanent surface fields	14
unpaved fields and usable airstrips	14

airfields by runway length:

2440--3659 meters	7
1220--2439	7
under 1220	14
TOTAL	28

international airports: Jerba, Monastir, Sfax, Tabarka, Tozeur, Tunis (Carthage)

major domestic airfields: Gafsa, Gabes

Airlines:

companies: Tunis Air (international and domestic), Tunisavia (domestic charter and air taxi), Tuninter (domestic)

aircraft:

Airbus A-320-200	3
Airbus A-300 B4-200	1
Beechcraft King Air	1
Boeing 737-200C/737-200/737-500	5
Boeing 727-200	8
DHC-6 Twin Otter	2
MD-83	2

on order: 4 additional A-320, 2 additional Boeing 737-500,
1 MD-83, 1 ATR-42, 2 ATR-72

helicopters:

SA-318 Alouette II	3
SA-365N/365C Dauphin 2	2

Maritime Facilities:

harbors--Bizerta, Gabes, La Goulette (Tunis), Sfax, Sousse,
Zarzis

oil terminals--Ashtart, Bizerta (Menzel Bourguiba), Gabes, La
Goulette (Tunis), Sekhira

Merchant Marine:

vessel type	number	DWT
general cargo	5	
passenger ferry	1	
chemical tanker	6	
tanker and crude carrier	2	
bulk carrier	3	
gas tanker (LPG)	1	
ro/ro cargo	2	
TOTAL	20	222,423

Defense Production:

army equipment:

production under license--diesel engines (with Italy and
Algeria)

naval craft:

production--20 meter patrol craft, with assistance from
South Korea

ARMED FORCES

Personnel:

military forces--

army	42,000
air force	4,000
navy	4,500
TOTAL	50,500

reserves: some (unconfirmed)

para-military forces--
gendarmerie	2,000
national guard	5,000

Army:

major units:

unit type	regiments/brigades
armored reconnaissance	1
infantry/mechanized	1
commando/paratroops	3
Sahara Brigade	1
TOTAL	6

small arms:

personal weapons--
9mm Model 38/49 Beretta SMG
9mm Sterling SMG
7.62mm FAC (FN) SAR
5.56mm AUG Steyr AR

machine guns--
7.62mm (0.3") Browning M-1919 MMG
7.62mm MAG (FN) LMG

light and medium mortars--
81mm	100
60mm	

tanks:

model		number
high quality		
M-60 A3		50
medium quality		
M-48 A3		15
SK-105 (Kurassier)		55
	(sub-total	70)
low quality		
AMX-13		50
M-41		20
	(sub-total	70)
TOTAL		190

APCs/ARVs:
    model   number

model	number
high quality	
Engesa EE-9/EE-11	+
Fiat Type 6614	110
M-113 A1/A2/M-125/M-577	120
(sub-total	+230)
others	
AML-60/AML-90	35
EBR-75	+
Saladin	20
(sub-total	+55)
TOTAL	330

  on order: Fahd

artillery:
  self-propelled guns and howitzers--
    155mm M-109 howitzer (unconfirmed)
    105mm M-108 howitzer (possibly phased out)
  towed guns and howitzers--

155mm M-114 howitzer (unconfirmed)	18
105mm M-101 howitzer	
TOTAL	200+

  on order: 57 155mm M-198 howitzers

AFV transporters:
  on order: US-made transporters

anti-tank weapons:
  missiles--   launchers

missiles--	launchers
BGM-71A TOW	100
M-901 ITV SP (TOW under armor)	35
MILAN (number unconfirmed)	500

army anti-aircraft defenses:
  missiles--
    self-propelled/mobile
      MIM-72A Chaparral
    man-portable
      RBS-70
      SA-7 (Grail)

short-range guns--   number
   40mm
   37mm
   on order: 26 20mm M-163 Vulcan SP AAG; Egyptian
     AD systems (unconfirmed)

Air Force:
  aircraft--general: number
    combat aircraft   11
    transport aircraft   8
    helicopters   42
  combat aircraft:
    strike and multi-role aircraft--
      medium and low quality
      F-5E/F-5F   11
    on order: additional F-5E/F-5F, negotiations in process
  transport aircraft:
    C-130H Hercules (not all serviceable)   4
    other   4
    TOTAL   8
  training and liaison aircraft:
    with ground attack/close air support capability--
      Aermacchi MB-326 B/KT/LT   10
    others--
      Rockwell T-6 (not serviceable)   12
      SIAI-Marchetti SF-260WT/C   18
      Piper Cub   10
               (sub-total   40)
    TOTAL   50
  helicopters:
    attack--
      SA-342 Gazelle   6
    medium transport--
      AB-205/Bell-205   18

light transport--
   Alouette III   6
   AS-350 Ecureuil   12
                (sub-total   18)
TOTAL   42

advanced armament:
air-to-air missiles--
   AIM-9J Sidewinder

anti-aircraft defenses:
radars--
   TRS-2100 Tiger S

military airfields: 4
Bizerta (Sidi Ahmad), Gabes, Sfax, one additional

aircraft maintenance and repair capability:
routine maintenance and repairs

Navy:

combat vessels:	number
MFPBs--	
Combattante III	3
P-48	3
Total	6
gun frigates--	
Savage class	1
ASW vessels--	
Le Fougeux class corvette	1
mine warfare vessels--	
Adjutant class minesweeper	2
Kondor II minesweeper	4
Total	6
gunboats/MTBs--	
Shanghai II gunboat	2
patrol craft--	
Vosper Thornycroft 103 ft. (31 meter)	2
Ch. Navals de l'Esterel 83 ft. (25 meter)	6
Total	8

auxiliary vessels:
tug   3

advanced armament:
MM-40 Exocet
SS-12
naval bases: 5
Bizerta, Kelibia, Sfax, Sousse, Tunis
ship maintenance and repair capability:
4 drydocks and 1 slipway at Bizerta; 2 pontoons and 1 floating dock at Sfax. Capability to maintain and repair existing vessels.

19. UNITED ARAB EMIRATES (UAE)

BASIC DATA

Official Name of State: United Arab Emirates[*]

Head of State: President Shaykh Zayid ibn Sultan al-Nuhayan, Emir of Abu Dhabi (also Supreme Commander of the Armed Forces)

Prime Minister: Shaykh Maktum ibn Rashid al-Maktum, Emir of Dubai (also Vice President)

Minister of Defense: Shaykh Muhammad ibn Rashid al-Maktum

Chief of the General Staff: Lieutenant General Muhammad Said al-Badi

Commander of the Ground Forces: Major General Abid Ali al-Qatabi

Commander of the Air Force and Air Defense Forces: Brigadier General Rashid Mubarak al-Riami

Commander of the Navy: Commodore Haza Sultan al-Darmaki

Area: approximately 82,900 sq. km. (borders with Oman, Saudi Arabia and Qatar partly undemarcated and/or disputed)

Population:		1,630,000
ethnic subdivision:		
Arabs	815,000	50.0%
Southeast Asians	714,000	43.8%
Others (Europeans, Persians)	101,000	6.2%
religious subdivision:		
Sunni Muslims	1,019,000	62.5%
Shi'ite Muslims	244,000	15.0%
Others	367,000	22.5%

---

[*] The UAE consists of seven principalities: Abu Dhabi, Dubai, Ras al-Khaimah, Sharjah, Umm al-Qaiwain, Fujairah and Ajman.

nationality subdivision:

UAE nationals	310,000	19.0%
Alien Arabs	375,000	23.0%
Southeast Asians (Indians, Pakistanis, Thais, Filipinos)	815,000	50.0%
Others (Europeans, Iranians)	130,000	8.0%

GDP:

1990--$33.98 billion

1991--$33.67 billion

Defense Expenditure:

1989--$1.59 billion

1990--$2.50 billion

Foreign Military Aid and Security Assistance Received:

military training:

foreign advisors/instructors/serving personnel from-- Britain, Egypt, France, Pakistan, USA (some civilians); Indians and Taiwanese (on an individual basis)

trainees abroad in--Britain, Egypt, France, Pakistan, Saudi Arabia, USA

arms transfers from:

Brazil (APCs)

Britain (APCs, artillery pieces, mobile workshops, SAMs, trainer aircraft, AFV transporters)

Egypt (APCs)

France (combat aircraft, AGMs, AAMs; Leclerc tanks on order)

FRG (tank transporters)

Italy (trainer aircraft, transport aircraft)

Russia (BMP-3 APCs)

Spain (transport aircraft)

South Africa (artillery pieces)

Switzerland (trainer aircraft)

USA (aircraft training simulator, transport aircraft, SAMs, light reconnaissance vehicles, radio systems; Appache helicopters and A/F-18 aircraft on order) support forces from:

Egypt and Syria (during 1991 Gulf War); Pakistan (1000); coalition forces during the Gulf Crisis and War, August 1990 through April 1991

construction aid by:

Britain (naval base)

maintenance of equipment in:

Indonesia (helicopters)

Foreign Military Aid and Security Assistance Extended:

financial aid to:

Syria; Britain, USA--grant, coverage of coalition costs of the Gulf War jointly granted with other GCC countries, mainly Saudi Arabia; grant extended to USA exceeding $1 billion, plus a commitment for an additional $1 billion; grant to the USSR, in return for Soviet support for the anti-Iraq coalition, 1990-91 (unconfirmed); Palestinian organizations--grants before the Gulf Crisis 1990-91, suspended during the Crisis, recently renewed on a smaller scale

military training:

foreign trainees from--Bahrain, Kuwait, Qatar

facilities provided to: USA (storage facilities); Britain (logistical facilities); facilities to coalition ground, air and naval forces during the 1991 Gulf War; Russia (services to Russian naval vessels in the Gulf)

Forces Deployed Abroad in:

Saudi Arabia (part of GCC Rapid Deployment Force); 639 troops in UN forces in Somalia, 1993

Joint Maneuvers with:

France; cooperation with the US-led coalition during the Gulf Crisis and War; a unit from the UAE participated in combat, including the battle at Khafji

INFRASTRUCTURE

Road Network:

length:	2,000 km
paved roads	1,800 km
gravel and improved earth tracks	200 km

main routes:
    Abu Dhabi--Jebel Dhanna--Sila--al-Hufuf (Saudi Arabia)
    Abu Dhabi--Bu Hasa
    Abu Dhabi--Muscat (Oman)
    Abu Dhabi--Dubai--Sharjah--Ajman--Ras al-Khaimah
    Dubai--Muscat
    Ajman--Fujairah--Muscat
    Ajman--Daba al-Bayah (Oman)

Airfields:
    airfields by runway type:
        permanent surface fields   20
        unpaved fields and usable airstrips   15
    airfields by runway length:
        over 3660 meters   7
        2440--3659   5
        1220--2439   5
        under 1220   18
    TOTAL   35
    international airports: Abu Dhabi, Dubai, Fujairah, Ras
        al-Khaimah, Sharjah
    major domestic airfields: Jebel Dhanna, Mina Khor Fakkan

Airlines:
    companies: Gulf Air (international)--jointly owned by UAE,
        Oman, Qatar and Bahrain (aircraft listed under Bahrain);
        Emirates Air Services (domestic and international);
        Emirates Airline (international); Emirates Express
        (domestic, subsidiary of Emirates Air Services)
    aircraft (excluding Gulf Air):
        Airbus A-310-300   6
        Airbus A-300-600R   4
        BAe 748   2
        BN-2 Islander   1
        Boeing 727-200   3
        DHC-6 Twin Otter   3
        DHC-7 Dash-7   1
        on order: 1 Airbus A-300-600R, 2 additional Airbus
            A-310-300, 7 Boeing 777

Maritime Facilities:

harbors--Fujairah, Mina Jebel Ali (Dubai), Mina Khalid (Sharjah), Mina Khor Fakkan (Sharjah), Mina Rashid (Dubai), Mina Sakr (Ras al-Khaimah), Mina Zayid (Abu Dhabi)

anchorages--Abu Bukhush (Abu Dhabi), Ras al-Khaimah

oil terminals--Dasa Island (Abu Dhabi), Halat al-Mubarras (Abu Dhabi), Jebel Dhanna (Abu Dhabi), Mina Rashid (Dubai), Fatih Oil Storage Terminal (Dubai), Mubarak Oil Terminal (Sharjah)

Merchant Marine:

vessel type	number	DWT
general cargo/container	11	
bulk container	2	
cement carrier	2	
container	7	
tanker/crude carrier	6	
bunkering tanker	7	
product tanker	7	
LP (gas) tanker	1	
TOTAL	43	1,333,384

Defense Production:

naval craft:

construction of patrol boats at Ajman (with British cooperation)

space:

a spy satellite to be acquired from the USA, negotiations in process

ARMED FORCES

Personnel:

military forces--

army	42,000
air force	4,500
navy	1,900
TOTAL	48,400

Army:
  major units:

unit type	brigades
armored	2
mechanized	2
infantry	1
royal guard	1
TOTAL	6

small arms:
  personal weapons--
    9mm Sterling Mk.4 SMG
    7.62mm AK-47 (Kalashnikov) AR
    7.62mm FAL (FN) SAR
  machine guns--
    7.62mm (0.3") Browning M-1919 MMG
    7.62mm MAG (FN) LMG
  light and medium mortars--
    81mm L-16 A1

tanks:

model	number
medium quality	
AMX-30	100
OF-40 Lion MK.2	36
(sub-total	136)
low quality	
Scorpion	80
TOTAL	216

on order: 390 Leclerc tanks, deliveries 1994-99

APCs/ARVs:

model	number
high quality	
AMX-VCI	
AMX-10P	
BMP-3	50
Engesa EE-11 Urutu	30
M-3 (Panhard)	

VAB	20
VBC-90	
(sub-total	430)
others	
AML-60/AML-90	
AT-105 Saxon	8
Fahd	50
Ferret	
Saladin	
Saracen	
Saxon (possibly with police)	
(sub-total	235)
TOTAL	665

on order: M-113 A2; EE-11; 200 M-2/M-3 Bradley; 450 BMP-3

artillery:

self-propelled guns and howitzers--	
155mm Mk. F3 (AMX) SP howitzer	20
155mm G-6 (unconfirmed)	78
(sub-total	98)
towed guns and howitzers--	
105mm Light Gun	50
105mm M-102 howitzer	50
105mm M-56 Pack howitzer	12
(sub-total	112)
mortars, heavy, under 160mm--	
120mm mortar	12
TOTAL	222
MRLs--	
122mm Firos-25	a few

on order: 227mm MLRS

anti-tank weapons:

missiles--	launchers
BGM-71B Improved TOW	24
Vigilant	
guns--	
120mm BAT L-4 recoilless rifle	
84mm Carl Gustav M-2 light recoilless rifle	

army anti-aircraft defenses:
  missiles--   launchers
    self-propelled/mobile
      Crotale   9
      Rapier
      Skyguard AA system
      Tigercat
    man-portable
      Blowpipe
      FIM-92A Stinger
      Javelin (unconfirmed)
      RBS-70
      SA-7 (Grail)
  short-range guns--
    2x30mm M-3 VDA SP
    2x20mm GCF-BM2 SP
  on order: additional Crotale SAMs; Mistral SAMs
CW capabilities:
  personal protective equipment
  unit decontamination equipment

Air Force:
  aircraft--general: number
    combat aircraft   76
    transport aircraft   33
    helicopters   59
  combat aircraft:
    strike and multi-role aircraft--
      high quality
        Mirage 2000   35
      medium quality
        Mirage V--AD/RAD/DAD 18
        Mirage III   12
              (sub-total 30)
      others
        Hawker Hunter   11
    TOTAL   76
    on order: 24 F/A-18

transport aircraft:

BAe 125	1
Boeing 707	3
Boeing 737	1
Britten-Norman BN-2 Islander	2
C-130H Hercules/L-100-30	8
CASA C-212 (employed in EW role)	4
DHC-4 Caribou (possibly not serviceable)	3
DHC-5D Buffalo	5
G-222 (number unconfirmed)	5
Mystere-Falcon 20	1
TOTAL	33

training and liaison aircraft:

with ground attack/close air support capability--

Aermacchi MB-326 KD/LD	8
Aermacchi MB-339	5
Hawk	16
(sub-total	29)

others--

Cessna 182 Skylane	1
Pilatus PC-7	23
SIAI-Marchetti SF-260 WD	7
(sub-total	31)
TOTAL	60

on order: additional Hawk (Hawk 100/102)

helicopters: number

attack--

SA-342K Gazelle	13
Alouette III	7
(sub-total	20)

maritime attack--

AS-332/532 Super Puma	4

medium transport--

AB-205/Bell 205	8
AB-212	3

AB-214	4
AS-332/532 Super Puma	3
SA-330 Puma	8
(sub-total	26)

light transport--

AB-206 JetRanger/Bell 206L	6
BO-105 (employed in liaison role, number unconfirmed)	3
(sub-total	9)
TOTAL	59

on order: 20 AH-64A Apache, delivery 1993-1994; A-109 (negotiations)

miscellaneous aircraft:

ELINT and EW--

on order: C-130 EW (unconfirmed)

target drones--

TTL BTT-3 Banshee

UAVs and mini-UAVs--

Beech MQM-107A UAV	20

advanced armament:

air-to-air missiles--

AIM-9L Sidewinder

R-550 Magique

air-to-ground missiles--

AS-11

AS-12

AS-30L

AM-39 Exocet

on order: al-Hakim (PGM-1, British-made)

anti-aircraft defenses:

radars--

AN/TPS-70	3
Watchman	
long-range missiles--	batteries
MIM-23B Improved HAWK	7

on order: MIM-104 Patriot (negotiations in process)

aircraft shelters--

for combat aircraft at Abu Dhabi and Jebel Ali AF bases

military airfields: 7

Abu Dhabi (international), al-Dhafra (Sharja), Batin (Abu Dhabi), Dubai (international), Fujairah, Sharjah, one additional

Navy:
combat vessels:

MFPBs--	number
Lurssen TNC-45	6
missile corvettes--	
Lurssen 62 meter type	2
patrol craft-- (some with coast guard)	
Vosper Thornycroft type 110 ft. (33.5 meter)	6
Camcraft 77 ft.	5
Camcraft 65 ft.	16
Watercraft 45 ft.	10
Cantieri Posillipo 68 ft.	1
Keith Nelson type 57 ft. (17.4 meter)	3
Keith Nelson (Dhafeer) class 40.3 ft. (12.3 meter)	6
Fairey Marine Spear	6
Boghammar (13 meter, police boat)	3
P-1200 (coast guard)	10
Baglietto GC-23 (serving coast guard)	4
Total	70

landing craft:

Siong Huat 40 meter landing craft logistics 1

on order: 2 54 meter LCTs from Vosper QAF, Singapore

auxiliary vessels:

Cheverton Type tenders 2

on order: 2 Crestitalia 30-meter diver support vessels

advanced armament:

surface-to-surface missiles--

MM-40 Exocet SSMs

on order: 30 mm Vulcan-Goalkeeper anti-missile guns

coastal defense:

MM-40 Exocet (unconfirmed)

special maritime forces:
a unit of frogmen, divers

naval bases: 10
Ajman, Dalma (Abu Dhabi), Fujairah, Mina Jebel Ali (Dubai), Mina Khalid (Sharjah), Mina Khor Fakkan (Sharjah), Mina Rashid (Dubai), Mina Sakr (Ras al-Khaimah), Mina Sultan (Sharja), Mina Zayd (Abu Dhabi)

ship maintenance and repair capability:
Dubai wharf capable of maintenance and repairs of merchant marine and naval vessels; two dry docks available

20. YEMEN

BASIC DATA

Official Name of State: Republic of Yemen. On May 22, 1990, YAR and PDRY proclaimed their formal unification as one state. "Unity day" was Nov. 30, 1990. Unification is taking place over a two-and-a-half year transition period. Merger of the armed forces is in process.

Head of State: President Lieutenant General Ali Abdallah Salih

Prime Minister: Haydar Abu Bakr al-Attas

Deputy Prime Minister for Security and Defense: Salih Ubaid Ahmad

Minister of Defense: Brigadier General Haytham Qasim Tahir

Chief of the General Staff: Major General Abdallah Hussayn al-Bashari

Commander of the Air Force: Colonel Muhammad Salih al-Ahmad

Commander of the Navy: Captain Ali Qasim Talib

Area: 481,750 sq. km. (borders with Saudi Arabia partly undemarcated and/or disputed)

Population: 10,040,000

ethnic subdivision:

Arabs	9,207,000	91.7%
Afro-Arabs	637,000	6.3%
Others	196,000	2.0%

religious subdivision:

Sunni Muslims	6,225,000	62.0%
Shi'ite Zaydi Muslims	3,614,000	36.0%
Shi'ite Ismaili Muslims	53,000	0.5%
Others	148,000	1.5%

GDP (only former YAR):

1986--$3.98 billion (unreliable, due to several rates of exchange)

1987--$4.21 billion (unreliable, due to several rates of exchange)

Balance of Payments (goods, services & unilateral transfer payments; only former YAR):

year	income	expenditure	balance
1986	$ 893 mil.	$1.02 bil.	-$127 mil.
1987	$1.07 bil.	$1.52 bil.	-$450 mil.

Defense Expenditure (unreliable, due to several rates of exchange):

1991--$1.41 billion

1992--$1.04 billion

Foreign Military Aid and Security Assistance Received:

military training:

> foreign advisors/instructors from--USSR before end of 1991 (500, unconfirmed), Russia (a few)

> trainees abroad in--Jordan, USSR before end of 1991, Russia (a few); Egypt (1992), Iraq

arms transfers from:

> USSR before the end of 1991 (tanks, combat aircraft, SAMs, SSMs)

maintenance of equipment in:

> USSR before end of 1991 (aircraft), later Russia, (unconfirmed)

Foreign Military Aid and Security Assistance Extended:

military training:

> foreign trainees from--PLO organizations; Iraqi pilots trained on Yemeni aircraft in 1992, discontinued by 1993

facilities provided to:

> al-Fatah (Palestinian): camps, use of airfield and naval facilities; refuge to a few Iraqi aircraft (unconfirmed)

INFRASTRUCTURE

Road Network:

length:	15,500 km
paved roads	4,000 km
gravel and stone roads	500 km
earth and light gravel tracks	11,000 km

main routes:

    Sana--al-Hudaydah (Hodeida)
    Sana--Taizz--al-Mukha (Mocha)
    al-Hudaydah--Zabid--al-Mukha/Zabid--Taizz
    Taizz--Aden
    Sana--Sadah--Abha (Saudi Arabia)
    al-Hudaydah--al Salif--Jizan (Saudi Arabia)
    Aden--Shuqra--Lawdar/Shuqra--al-Mukalla
    al-Mukalla--al-Qatn--Tarim
    al-Mukalla--al-Riyan--Salalah (Oman)

Airfields:

airfields by runway type:

permanent surface fields	10
unpaved fields and usable airstrips	30

airfields by runway length:

2440--3659 meters	20
1220--2439	12
under 1220	8
TOTAL	40

international airports: Aden (Khormaksar), al-Hudaydah, Sana

major domestic airfields: Ataq, Bayhan, al-Ghaydah, Kamaran Island, al-Mukalla/al-Riyan, Mukayris, al-Qatn, Qishin, Sadah, Saywun/Tarim, Taizz

Airlines:

companies: Yemenia--Yemen Airway Corporation (international and domestic); Alyemda (international and domestic); the two companies are in the process of merging

aircraft:

An-24	1
An-26	1
Boeing 737-200/200C	3
Boeing 727-200	4
Boeing 707-320C	2
DHC-7 Dash 7	4
Tupolev Tu-154	1

Maritime Facilities:

harbors--Aden, al-Hudaydah, al-Khalf, Nishtun, al-Salif
anchorages--al-Mukha (harbor planned)

oil terminals--al-Hudaydah

Merchant Marine:

vessel type	number	DWT
tanker	1	
cargo	1	
storage tanker	1	
TOTAL	3	411,547

A R M E D   F O R C E S

Personnel:

military forces (combination of personnel of former YAR and PDRY; no information regarding reorganization)--

army	55,000-59,000
air force	5,000
navy	2,500
TOTAL	62,500-66,500

Army:

major units (not all fully operational/fully organized):

unit type	brigades
armored	7
mechanized	6
infantry (mostly skeleton or undermanned)	17
commando/paratroops	1
special forces	1
central guards	1
TOTAL	33.

small arms:

personal weapons--
7.62mm AK-47 (Kalashnikov) AR
7.62mm SKS (Simonov) SAR

machine guns--
12.7mm D.Sh.K. 38/46 (Degtyarev) HMG
7.62mm PK/PKS (Kalashnikov) LMG
7.62mm RPD (Degtyarev) LMG
7.62mm SG-43 (Goryunov) MMG

light and medium mortars--
82mm M-43

```
light ATRLs--
  RPG-7
  M-72 LAW
```

tanks:

model		number
medium quality		
T-62		250
M-60 A1		60
T-55		690
	(sub-total	1000)
low quality		
T-54		200
T-34 (unconfirmed)		100
	(sub-total	300)
TOTAL		1300

APCs/ARVs:

model	number
high quality	
BMP-1	
M-113 A1 and its derivatives	100
others	
AML-90	
BTR-40/50/60	
BTR-152	
al-Walid	
Ferret (possibly phased out)	
Saladin (possibly phased out)	
TOTAL	950

artillery: number

```
self-propelled guns and howitzers--
  100mm SU-100 gun
towed guns and howitzers--
  155mm M-114 howitzer
  130mm M-46 gun
  122mm D-30 howitzer
  122mm M-1938 howitzer
  105mm M-102 howitzer
  100mm M-1955 field/AT gun
```

```
85mm M-1945/D-44 field/AT gun
76mm M-1942 divisional gun
mortars, heavy, over 160mm--
    160mm mortar
mortars, heavy, under 160mm--
    120mm mortar
TOTAL                                   ca.1000
MRLs--
    122mm BM-21
```
anti-tank weapons:
```
missiles--
    AT-3 (Sagger)
    BGM-71A Improved TOW
    M-47 Dragon
    Vigilant
guns--
    107mm B-11 recoilless rifle
    85mm M-1945/D-44 field/AT gun
    82mm recoilless rifle
    75mm recoilless rifle
    57mm gun
surface-to-surface missiles--            launchers
    FROG-7                                   12
    SS-1 (Scud B)                             6
    SS-21 (Scarab)                            4
    TOTAL                                    22
```
army anti-aircraft defenses:
```
missiles--
    self-propelled/mobile
        SA-9 (Gaskin)
    man-portable
        SA-7 (Grail)
short-range guns--                       number
    57mm ZSU 57X2 SP                          +
    57mm S-60                                 +
    37mm M-1939                               +
    23mm ZSU 23x4 SP (Gun Dish)              +
    23mm ZU 23x2                              +
```

20mm M-163 Vulcan SP	+
20mm M-167 Vulcan	+

Air Force:

aircraft--general:	number
combat aircraft (some in storage)	175
transport aircraft	23
helicopters	97
combat aircraft:	
interceptors--	
medium quality	
MiG-21 (Fishbed)	85
strike and multi-role aircraft--	
medium quality	
MiG-23/27 (Flogger B/D)	15
Su-20/22 (Fitter C)	40
(sub-total	55)
others	
F-5E/B	15
MiG-17 (Fresco)/MiG-15 (Faggot/Midget, in training role)	20
(sub-total	35)
Total	90
TOTAL	175
transport aircraft:	
An-24/An-26 (Coke/Curl)	13
C-130H Hercules	4
IL-14 (Crate, possibly phased out)	4
Short Skyvan Srs. 3	2
TOTAL	23
training and liaison aircraft:	
others--	
model not known	+
helicopters:	
attack--	
Mi-24 (Hind)	15

medium transport--	
AB-212	5
AB-204	2
AB-205	2
Mi-8/Mi-17 (Hip)	60
Mi-4 (Hound, possibly phased out)	5
(sub-total	74)
light transport--	
AB-206 JetRanger	6
Alouette III	2
(sub-total	8)
TOTAL	97

advanced armament:
air-to-air missiles--
AIM-9M Sidewinder
AA-2 (Atoll)
air-to-ground missiles--
AT-2 (Swatter)

anti-aircraft defenses:

	batteries
long-range missiles--	
SA-2 (Guideline)	+
SA-3	+
TOTAL	21
military airfields:	18

Aden (Khormaksar), al-Anad, al-Ansab (Nisab), Ataq,
Bayhan, al-Qasab, al-Dali, Ghor Ubyad, al-Hudaydah,
Ir-Fadhl, Kamaran Island, Lawdar, al-Mukalla, Mukayris,
Perim Island, Sana (Martyr Dilmy AFB), Socotra, Zamakh

Navy:

combat vessels:	number
MFBs--	
Ossa II	6
missile corvettes--	
Tarantul	2

mine warfare vessels--

Yevgenia class	6
Natya class	2
Total	8

gunboats/MTBs--

P-6 MTB	2

patrol craft--

Broadsword class (unconfirmed)	3
Fairey Marine Interceptor	1
Fairey Marine Spear	1
Fairey Marine Tracker 2	1
Poluchat class (unconfirmed)	4
Zhuk class	7
Total	17

landing craft:

Ondatra LCU	2
Polnochny class LCT	2
Ropucha class LST	1
T-4 LCM	5
Total	10

advanced armament:
SS-N-2 Styx SSM

coastal defense:
land based SS-N-2 Styx

naval bases: 6

Aden, al-Hudaydah; anchorage at Kamaran Island (unconfirmed); al-Mukalla, Perim Island, Socotra

ship maintenance and repair capability:
National Dockyards, Aden (4,500-ton floating dock and 1,500-ton slipway)

PART IV

COMPARATIVE TABLES
GLOSSARY OF WEAPONS SYSTEMS
LIST OF ABBREVIATIONS
CHRONOLOGY
MAPS

Table 1. Major Armies of the Middle East

Country	Year	Personnel (thousands)			Divisions			Indep. Brigades		
		Reg.	Res.	Total	Armor	Mec.	Inf.	Armor	Mec.	Inf./ Para./ Com./ Terr.
Egypt	91-92	320	600	920	4	7	1	3	2	9
	90-91	320	600	920	4	7	1	3	-	14
Iran*	91-92	385	+	385	6	2	32	1	-	6
	90-91	550	1145	1695	6	1	20	-	-	5
Iraq**	91-92	400	+	400+	6	4	28-30	-	-	14
	90-91	355	680	1035	8	4	30	1	-	14
Israel	91-92	134	365	499	12	-	4	-	-	13
	90-91	134	365	499	12	-	4	-	-	13
Jordan	91-92	80-90	60	145	2	2	-	-	-	3
	90-91	80	90	170	2	2	-	-	-	3
Libya	91-92	85	-	85	-	-	-	6	9	2
	90-91	85	30	115	2	3	-	2	2	1
Saudi Arabia#	91-92	100	-	100	-	-	-	3	6	6
	90-91	70	-	70	-	-	-	2	6	6
Syria	91-92	306	100	406	7	3	1	1	1	9
	90-91	306	100	406	7	3	1	1	1	7

Note:
+   indicates precise number unknown
-   indicates no entry
*   Army and IRGC excluding Baseej reserves
**   excluding Popular Army
#   Army and National Guard
For classification of tanks according to quality see introductory note, Part III.
All figures include equipment in storage

Indep. Battalions			Tanks			APCs & ARVs	Guns & Mortars	ATGM Launchers	SSM Launchers
Armor	Mec.	Inf./ Para./ Com./ Terr.	High Quality	Others	Total				
-	-	-	875	2350	3225	4400	2200	1600-1800	24
-	-	-	850	2250	3100	4100	2200	1600-1800	24
-	-	-	+	+	750	700	1750	+	10+
-	-	-	+	+	700	800	1400	+	+
-	-	-	+	+	2500	3250	1500	+	5+
-	-	-	700	2300	3000	3500	2000	+	20
-	-	-	1620	2230	3850	8100	1300	+	12
-	-	-	1450	2400	3850	8100	1300	+	12
-	-	-	375	692	1067	1565	600	550	-
-	-	-	375	692	1067	1565	600	550	-
3	8	13	360	2350	2710	3000	2200	1500	110
3	8	13	300	2250	2550	2000	2100	2000	100
-	-	20+	400	300	700	3000	700	700	8-12
-	-	19	100	450	550	3140	700	700	8-12
-	-	-	1500	3300	4800	4980	2400	2000	60
-	-	-	1100	3100	4200	3800	2400	2000	60

Figure 1
Tanks in Major Middle East Armies

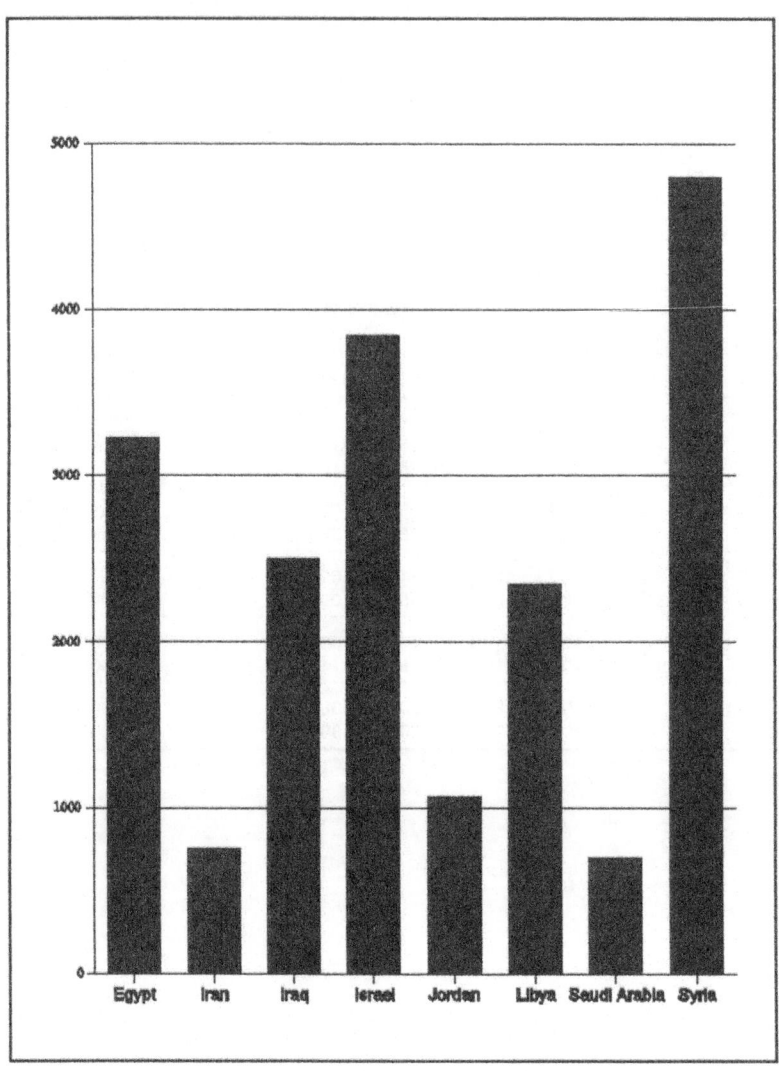

Figure 2
Surface-to-Surface Missiles & Rockets in Service in Middle East Armies*

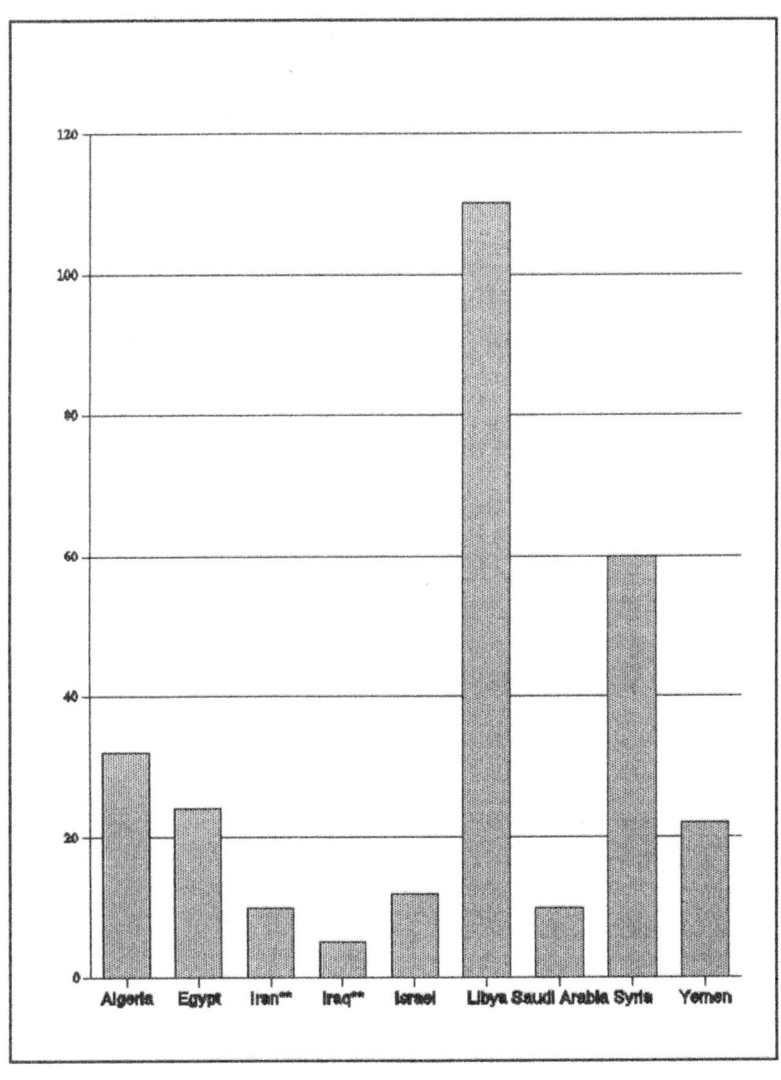

*   by number of launchers
**   number not certain

Table 2. Major Air Forces of the Middle East
(including Air Defense Forces)

Country	Year	Personnel (thousands)			Interceptors		Strike & Multi-role Aircraft	
		Reg.	Res.	Total	High Quality	Others	High Quality	Others
Egypt****	91-92	95	80	175	128	240-250	-	139
	90-91	95	80	175	97	310	-	140
Iran***	91-92	35	-	35	50	25	35	85
	90-91	35	-	35	90	20	12	145
Iraq	91-92	98	+	98	45	150	+	195
	90-91	40	20	60	+	+	+	+
Israel****	91-92	32	55	87	65	-	174	455
	90-91	32	55	87	47	-	144	455
Jordan	91-92	9.7	-	9.7	-	-	-	103
	90-91	9.7	-	9.7	-	-	-	103
Libya****	91-92	9	-	9	65-70	110	6	340
	90-91	9	-	9	80	50	6	395
Saudi Arabia	91-92	17	-	17	117	-	48	108
	90-91	17	-	17	104	-	48	108
Syria	91-92	80	40	120	60	300	20	150
	90-91	80	37.5	117.5	65	245	20	200

Note:

+   indicates precise number unknown

-      indicates no entry

For classification of combat aircraft according to quality see introductory note, Part III. All F-16s in Israel listed in 1991 as multi-role a/c.

*   including 24 maritime attack

**   classification of long-range SAMs, see introductory note, Part III.

***   in 1990-1991 number of a/c includes about 40% not serviceable; in 1991-92 all aircraft listed are serviceable, with another 95 combat a/c and 150 helicopters not serviceable, beyond the figures listed here.

****   including a/c in storage

Bombers	Total Combat A/C	Transport Aircraft	Helicopters Attack	Helicopters Transport +ASW	Helicopters Total	Military Airfields	Long-Range SAM Batteries
8	515-525	45	80	117	197	28	122
12	559	44	80	117	197	29	132
-	195	120	70	205	275	20+	30-35
-	267	120	105	320	425	20+	20
8	400	+	185	215	400	38	60
16	400	+	140	340	480	38	60
-	694	97	91	133	224	11	+
-	646	97	91	142	233	11	+
-	103	18	24	30+	54+	6	14
-	103	14	24	35	59	6	14
7	528-533	138	70	134	204	16	99
7	543	139+	40	134	174	16	99
-	273	108	33*	117	145	22	16
-	260	118	45*	96	141	22	16
-	530	23	100	185	285	21	108
-	530	28	105	165	270	21	108

Figure 3
Combat Aircraft in the Middle East

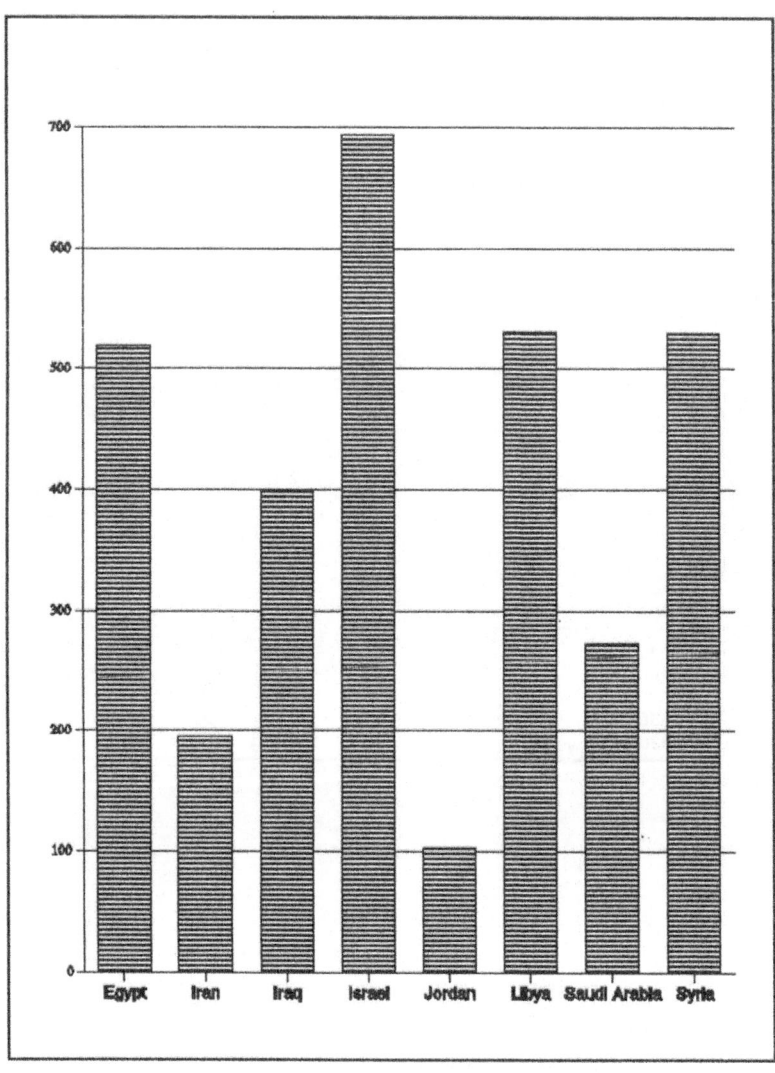

Figure 4
Missile Craft in Major Middle East Navies

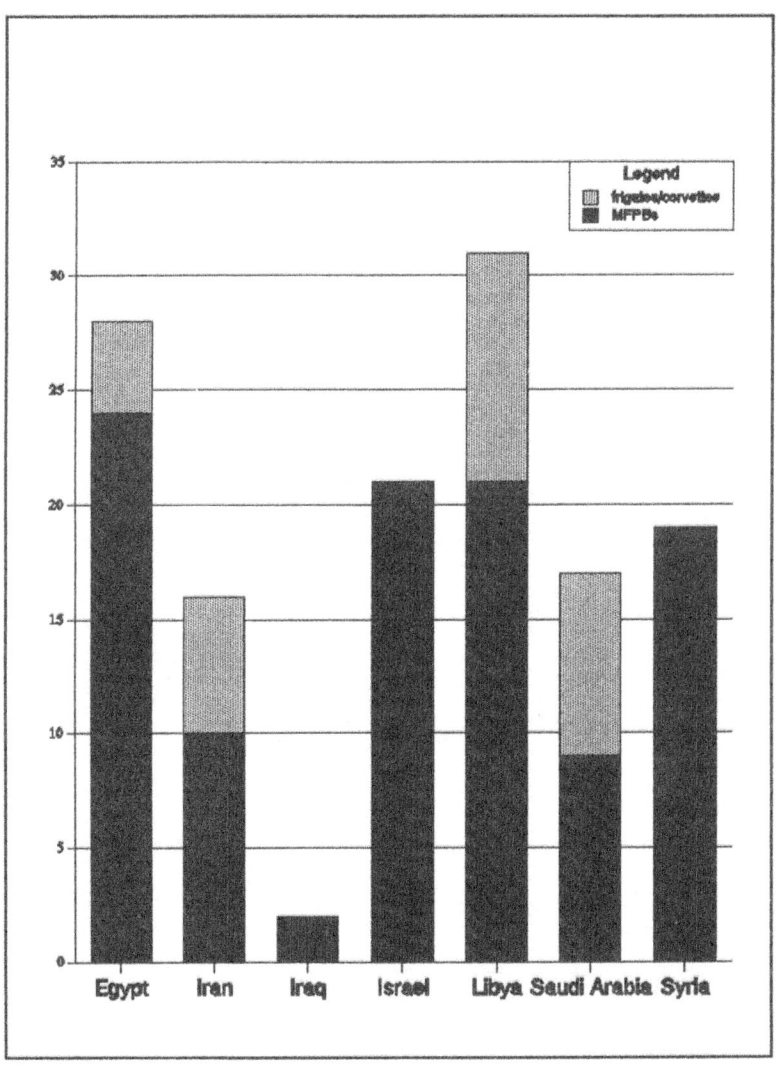

Table 3. Major Navies of the Middle East

Country	Year	Personnel (thousands)			Sub-Marines	MFPBs	Missile Destrcyers, Frigates & Corvettes	SSMs
		Reg.	Res.	Total				
Egypt	91-92	20	15	35	8	24	4	Harpoon, Otomat, Styx
	90-91	20	11	31	8	24	4	Harpoon, Otomat, Styx
Iran*	91-92	20	-	20	1	10	6	Harpoon, Sea Killer C-801
	90-91	20	-	20	-	10	6	Harpoon, Sea Killer C-801
Iraq	91-92	1.6-2	-	1.6-2	-	2	-	Styx
	90-91	5	-	5	-	1	-	Styx
Israel	91-92	10	10	20	3	21	-	Gabriel, Harpoon
	90-91	10	10	20	3	23+2 hydrofoils	-	Gabriel, Harpoon
Libya	91-92	6.5	-	6.5	6	21	10	Otomat, SS-12, Styx
	90-91	8	-	8	6	21	10	Otomat, SS-12, Styx
Saudi Arabia	91-92	11	-	11	-	9	8	Harpoon, Otomat 2
	90-91	7.8	-	7.8	-	9	8	Harpoon, Otomat 2
Syria	91-92	4	2.5	6.5	3	19	-	Styx
	90-91	4	2.5	6.5	3	21	-	Styx

Note:
-   indicates no entry
*   including IRGC

Gun Destroyers, Frigates & Corvettes	ASW Vessels	Mine Warfare	MTBs & Gunboats	Patrol Craft	Landing Craft	Hover-Craft	Naval Bases
1	-	9	18	36	19	3	8
1	-	9	18	36	19	3	8
2	-	3	-	82	10	13	19
2	-	5	-	132	12	14	18
-	-	-	2	6	2	-	2
-	-	-	1	-	1	-	3
-	-	-	-	46	13	2	3
-	-	-	-	46	13	2	3
1	-	8	-	9	7	-	6
1	-	8	-	23	7	-	6
-	-	4	3	51	16	24	12
-	-	4	3	50	16	24	12
-	2	9	-	9	3	-	3
-	2	7	-	7	3	-	3

Table 4. The Israel-Syria Military Balance

Army

Country	Personnel (thousands)			Divisions			Indep. Brigades		
	Reg.	Res.	Total	Armor	Mec.	Inf.	Armor	Mec.	Inf./Para./Com./Terr.
Israel	134	365	499	12	-	4	-	-	13
Syria	306	100	406	7	3	1	1	1	9

Air Force and Air Defense

Country	Personnel (thousands)			Interceptors		Strike & Multi-role Aircraft	
	Reg.	Res.	Total	High Quality	Others	High Quality	Others
Israel	32	55	87	65	-	174	455
Syria	80	40	120	60	300	20	150

Navy

Country	Personnel (thousands)			Sub-Marines	MFPBs	Missile Destroyers, Frigates & Corvettes	SSMs
	Reg.	Res.	Total				
Israel	10	10	20	3	21	-	Gabriel, Harpoon
Syria	4	2.5	6.5	3	19	-	Styx

Note:
+   indicates precise number unknown
-     indicates no entry
For classification of tanks, long-range SAMs and combat aircraft according to quality see introductory note, Part III.

Tanks	APCs & ARVs	Guns & Mortars	ATGM Launchers	SSM Launchers
3850	8100	1300	+	12
4800	4980	2400	2000	60

Total Combat	Transport Aircraft	Helicopters			Military Airfields	Long-Range SAM Batteries
		Attack	Transport +ASW	Total		
694	97	91	133	224	11	+
530	23	100	185	285	21	108

ASW Vessels	Mine Warfare Vessels	Patrol Craft	Landing Craft	Hover-Craft	Naval Bases
-	-	46	13	2	3
2	8	9	3	-	3

Table 5. Eastern Front-Israel Military Balance

Full participants: Israel, Syria, Jordan, Palestinian Forces.

Army

	Personnel (thousands)			Divisions			
	Reg.	Res.	Total	Armor	Mec.	Inf.	Total
Eastern Front	526	174	700	11	7	3	21
Israel	134	365	499	12	-	4	16
Ratio, 91-92	3.9:1	0.5:1	1.4:1	0.9:1	*	0.8:1	1.3:1
Ratio, 90-91	4.4:1	0.5:1	1.6:1	0.9:1	*	1:1	1.4:1

Air Force and Air Defense

	Personnel (thousands)			Interceptors		Strike & Multi-role Aircraft	
	Reg.	Res.	Total	High Quality	Others	High Quality	Others
Eastern Front	151	40	191	140	330	60	253
Israel	32	55	87	65	-	174	455
Ratio, 91-92	4.7:1	0.7:1	2.2:1	2.2:1	*	0.3:1	0.6:1
Ratio, 90-91	3.3:1	0.7:1	1.7:1	2.9:1	*	0.5:1	0.9:1

Navy

	Personnel (thousands)			Sub-Marines	MFPBs	Missile Destr., Frig. Corvettes	SSMs
	Reg.	Res.	Total				
Eastern Front	13.5	2.5	16	9	40	10	Styx, Otomat
Israel	10	10	20	3	21	-	Gabriel, Harpoon
Ratio, 91-92	1.4:1	0.3:1	0.8:1	3.1	2:1	*	*
Ratio, 90-91	1.4:1	0.3:1	0.8:1	3.1	2:1	*	*

Note: the constellation of full and partial participants presented here is only one of several reasonable possibilities; it reflects neither an absolute certainty nor the maximum force which all countries involved are thought to be capable of deploying

+ indicates precise number unknown   - indicates no entry

Partial participants: Saudi Army (three brigades) and Air Force (three combat a/c squadrons and one transport squadron); Kuwaiti Air Force (one squadron); Iraq (five divisions, 5 SSM launchers, 100 combat aircraft, 100 helicopters); Libyan Army (three armored brigades, three mechanized brigades, 20 SSM launchers), Libyan Air Force (two combat a/c squadrons, one squadron attack helicopters), and the entire Libyan Navy.

Indep. Brigades				Tanks	APCs & ARVs	Guns & Mortars	ATGM Launchers	SSM Launchers
Armor	Mec.	Inf./Para./ Com./Terr.	Total					
6	5	16	27	7400	8550	3750	3400	95
-	-	13	13	3850	8100	1300	+	+
*	*	1.2:1	2.1:1	1.9:1	1.1:1	2.9:1	*	*
*	*	1.2:1	2.2:1	1.7:1	1:1	2.8:1	*	*

Bombers	Total Combat	Transport Aircraft	Helicopters			Military Airfields	Long-Range SAM Batteries
			Attack	Transport + ASW	Total		
4	840	75	190	315	505	37	122
-	694	97	91	133	224	11	+
*	1.2:1	0.8:1	2.1:1	2.4:1	2.3:1	3.4:1	*
*	1.6:1	0.7:1	2.0:1	2.0:1	2.0:1	3.3:1	*

Gun Destr., Frig. & Corvettes	ASW Vessels	Mine Warfare Vessels	MTBs & Gunboats	Patrol Craft	Landing Craft	Hover-Craft	Naval Bases
1	2	17	-	21	10	-	10
-	-	-	-	46	13	2	3
*	*	*	*	0.5:1	0.8:1	*	3.3:1
*	*	*	*	1.0:1	1.1:1	2.0:1	4.0:1

For classification of tanks, long-range SAMs and combat aircraft according to quality see introductory note, Part III.
* indicates no basis for calculation

Table 6.   Arab-Israel Military Balance

Full participants: Israel, Syria, Jordan, Palestinian Forces, Egypt, Libyan Navy.
Partial participants: Saudi Army (three brigades) and Air Force (three squadrons); Iraq (five divisions, 10 SSM launchers, 100 combat aircraft, 100 helicopters); Kuwaiti Air Force (one squadron); Algerian Army (two brigades)

Army

| | Personnel (thousands) | | | Divisions | | | |
	Reg.	Res.	Total	Armor	Mec.	Inf.	Total
Arab Coalition	860	780	1640	15	12	4	31
Israel	134	365	499	12	-	4	16
Ratio, 91-92	6.4:1	2.1:1	3.3:1	1.3:1	*	1:1	2:1
Ratio, 90-91	6.8:1	2.2:1	3.4:1	1.3:1	*	1.3:1	2.1:1

Air Force and Air Defense

| | Personnel (thousands) | | | Interceptors | | Strike & Multi-role Aircraft | |
	Reg.	Res.	Total	High Quality	Others	High Quality	Others
Arab Coalition	202	120	322	295	490	75	392
Israel	32	55	87	65	-	174	455
Ratio, 91-92	6.3:1	2.2:1	3.7:1	4.5:1	*	0.4:1	0.9:1
Ratio, 90-91	6.3:1	2.2:1	3.7:1	5.2:1	*	0.6:1	1.2:1

Navy

| | Personnel (thousands) | | | Sub-Marines | MFPBs | Missiles, Destr., Frig. & Corvettes | SSMs |
	Reg.	Res.	Total				
Arab Coalition	33.5	17.5	51	17	64	14	Styx, Otomat, Harpoon
Israel	10	10	20	3	21	-	Gabriel, Harpoon
Ratio, 91-92	3.4:1	1.8:1	2.5:1	5.7:1	3.0:1	*	*
Ratio, 90-91	3.5:1	1.4:1	2.4:1	5.7:1	3.0:1	*	*

Note: the constellation of full and partial participants presented here is only one of several reasonable possibilities; it reflects neither an absolute certainty nor the maximum force which all countries involved are thought to be capable of deploying

(Israel vs. Arab Coalition, including Egypt and Iraq)

and Air Force (2 combat a/c squadrons, 3 vessels), Moroccan Army (one brigade) and Air Force (one squadron); Libyan Army (three armored brigades, three mechanized brigades, 20 SSM launchers), and Air Force (two combat a/c squadrons and one squadron attack helicopters).

Indep. Brigades				Tanks	APCs & ARVs	Guns & Mortars	ATGM Launchers	SSM Launchers
Armor	Mec.	Inf./Para./ Com./Terr.	Total					
10	9	25	44	10830	13250	6000	5200	119
-	-	13	13	3850	8100	1300	+	+
*	*	1.9:1	3.4:1	2.8:1	1.6:1	4.6:1	*	*
*	*	1.9:1	3.4:1	2.6:1	1.5:1	4.6:1	*	*

Bombers	Total Combat A/C	Transport Aircraft	Helicopters			Military Airfields	Long-Range SAM Batteries
			Attack	Transport +ASW	Total		
12	1264	123	270	437	707	65	244
-	694	97	91	133	224	11	+
*	1.8:1	1.3:1	3:1	3.3:1	3.2:1	5.9:1	*
*	2.2:1	1.2:1	2.9:1	2.8:1	2.9:1	5.9:1	*

Gun Destr., Frig. & Corvettes	ASW Vessels	Mine Warfare Vessels	MTBs & Gunboats	Patrol Craft	Landing Craft	Hover-Craft	Naval Bases
2	2	26	18	57	29	3	18
-	-	-	-	46	13	2	3
*	*	*	*	1.2:1	2.2:1	1.5:1	6:1
*	*	*	*	1.8:1	2.5:1	1.5:1	7:1

+   indicates precise number unknown   - indicates no entry
*   indicates no basis for calculation

Table 7. Arab-Israel Military Balance 1984-1992

Participants: See Table 6

Army

	Divisions							
	Armor		Mechanized		Infantry		Total	
	84	92	84	92	84	92	84	92
Arab Coalition	10	15	10	12	3	4	23	31
Israel	11	12	-	-	-	4	11	16
Ratio	0.9:1	1.3:1	*	*	*	1:1	2.1:1	2:1

Air Force and Air Defense

	Interceptors				Strike & Multi-role Aircraft			
	High Quality		Others		High Quality		Others	
	84	92	84	92	84	92	84	92
Arab Coalition	130	295	620	490	496	75	354	392
Israel	40	65	-	-	445	174	185	455
Ratio	3.3:1	4.5:1	*	*	1.1:1	0.4:1	1.9:1	0.9:1

Navy

	Submarines		MFPBs		Missile Destroyers, Frigates & Corvettes	
	84	92	84	92	84	92
Arab Coalition	18	17	67	64	8	14
Israel	3	3	24	21	-	-
Ratio	6:1	5.7:1	2.8:1	3:1	*	*

Note:
+   indicates precise number unknown
-   indicates no entry
*   indicates no basis for calculation

Independent Brigades		Tanks		APCs & ARVs		Guns & Mortars		ATGM Launchers		SSM Launchers	
84	92	84	92	84	92	84	92	84	92	84	92
51	44	8065	10830	8470	13250	6050	6000	5150	5200	54	119
20	13	3650	3850	8000	8100	1000	1300	+	+	+	+
2.5:1	3.4:1	2.2:1	2.8:1	1.1:1	1.6:1	6:1	4.6:1	*	*	*	*

Total Combat A/C		Helicopters						Military Airfields		Long-Range SAM Batteries	
		Attack		Transport + ASW		Total					
84	92	84	92	84	92	84	92	84	92	84	92
1635	1264	161	270	324	437	485	707	48	65	304	244
670	694	55	91	133	133	188	224	11	11	+	+
2.4:1	1.8:1	2.9:1	3:1	2.4:1	3.3:1	2.6:1	3.2:1	4.4:1	5.9:1	*	*

Gun Destroyers, Frigates & Corvettes		Landing Craft		Naval Bases	
84	92	84	92	84	92
8	2	36	29	17	18
-	-	13	13	3	3
*	*	2.8:1	2.2:1	5.7:1	6:1

Table 8. The Iran-Iraq Military Balance

Army

Country	Personnel (thousands)			Divisions			Indep. Brigades		
	Reg.	Res.	Total	Armor	Mec.	Inf.	Armor	Mec.	Inf./Para./Com./Terr.
Iran*	385	+	385	6	2	32	1	-	6
Iraq**	400	+	400	6	4	28-30	-	-	14

Air Force and Air Defense

Country	Personnel (thousands)			Interceptors		Strike & Multi-role Aircraft	
	Reg.	Res.	Total	High Quality	Others	High Quality	Others
Iran*	35	-	35	50	25	35	85
Iraq	98	+	98	45	150	+	195

Navy

Country	Personnel (thousands)			Sub-Marines	MFPBs	Missile Destroyers, Frigates & Corvettes	SSMs
	Reg.	Res.	Total				
Iran	20	-	20	1	10	6	Harpoon, Sea Killer, C-801
Iraq	1.6-2	-	1.6-2	-	2	-	Styx

Note:
+ indicates precise number unknown   * Army and IRGC; only serviceable aircraft incl. in total
- indicates no entry   ** excluding Popular Army
For classification of tanks, long-range SAMs and combat aircraft according to quality see introductory note, Part III.

446

Tanks	APCs & ARVs	Guns & Mortars	ATGM Launchers	SSM Launchers
700-800	700	1500-2000	+	10
2500	3500	2000	+	5

Bombers	Total Combat	Transport Aircraft	Helicopters			Military Airfields	Long-Range SAM Batteries
			Attack	Transport + ASW	Total		
-	195	120	70	205	275	20+	30-35
8+	400	+	185	215	400	38	60

Gun Destroyers, Frigates & Corvettes	ASW Vessels	Mine Warfare Vessels	MTBs & Gunboats	Patrol Craft	Landing Craft	Hover-Craft	Naval Bases
2	-	3	-	82	12	14	18
-	-	-	2	6	2	-	2

Table 9. The USA in the Middle East: Financial Aid (Military), Arms Sales, Advisors, Trainees and Facilities

Country	Financial Aid ($millions)			Arms (major items) Granted or Sold
	Grants	Loans	Total	
Algeria	.15	-	-	-
Bahrain	-	-	-	ATGMs, combat aircraft, helicopters, tanks, APCs, SAMs, landing craft
Egypt	1,300+	-	1,300+	tanks, APCs, artillery, UAVs, helicopters, combat aircraft, SAMs, naval SSMs, early warning aircraft, radars, fire control for submarines, sonars, ATGMs
Israel	1,800+	-	1,800+	tanks, APCs, artillery, combat aircraft, SAMs, naval SSMs, tank transporters, attack helicopters
Jordan	27	-	27	tanks, ATGMs, artillery, SAMs, AAGs, terminally guided artillery shells, spares
Kuwait	-	-	-	SAMs, APCs, patrol boats, combat a/c, night vision equipment; tanks on order
Lebanon	-	-	-	Jeeps, trucks
Morocco	100	-	100	tanks, ATGMs, SAMs, spares, naval radio equipment
Oman	-	-	-	SP artillery, AAMs, tanks
Qatar	-	-	-	upgrading air defense
Saudi Arabia	-	-	-	tanks, APCs, artillery, ATGMs, combat aircraft, transport aircraft, SAMs, AGMs, AWACS, AD systems
Tunisia	30	-	30	tanks, SAMs, transport aircraft, artillery, spares
UAE	-	-	-	transport aircraft, SAMs, aircraft training simulator, light reconnaissance vehicles, radio systems; combat a/c and helicopters on order

Advisors Present	Trainees in US	Facilities Provided to US	Joint Maneuvers
-	-	-	-
+	+	naval, storage and intelligence facilities	-
+	+	use of airfields	+
-	+	-	+
+	+	-	+
+	+	naval and ground forces	+
-	+	-	-
+	+	use of airfields, naval communications, storage	+
+	-	use of airfields, naval communications, storage	+
-	-	same as Saudi Arabia, below	+
+	+	air, ground, naval forces and logistical facilities, including prepositioned equipment	-
+	+	-	+
+	+	storage facilities	-

449

Table 10. The USSR/Russia in the Middle East: Arms Sales, Advisors, Trainees, and Facilities

Country	Arms (major items) Granted or sold	Advisors Present	Trainees in USSR/Russia	Facilities Provided to
Algeria	tanks, combat aircraft, SAMs	+	+	-
Egypt	spare parts for Soviet weapons, APC turrets	-	-	-
Iran	APCs, SAMs, combat a/c, tanks, submarine	+	-	-
Jordan*	SAMs, AAGs, APCs	+	+	-
Kuwait	SAMs, AAGs, APCs	+	+	-
Libya**	tanks, artillery, SSMs, combat aircraft, SAMs, naval vessels, naval mines	+	+	use of naval facilities (unconfirmed)
Syria*	tanks, artillery, SSMs, combat aircraft, helicopters, SAMs, naval vessels, radars	+	+	use of naval facilities
Yemen*	SSMs, tanks, SAMs, combat aircraft	+	+	?

*   until end of 1991 at least
**   before the April 1992 UN embargo

Table 11. France in the Middle East:
Arms Sales, Advisors and Trainees

Country	Arms (major items) Granted or sold	Advisors Present	Trainees in France
Algeria	ARVs, ATGMs	-	-
Bahrain	ARVs, helicopters, AGMs	+	+
Egypt	ATGMs, combat aircraft, helicopters, SAMs, AAMs, radars for AAGs	+	+
Iran	artillery ammunition, spare parts for MFPBs, rubber boats, helicopters via Indonesia	-	+
Israel	spares (via intermediaries), a/c engines	-	+
Jordan	AAMs, AGMs, helicopters, ATRL, artillery fire control system	-	-
Kuwait	SP artillery, ATGMs, combat aircraft, helicopters, radars, naval craft	+	+
Lebanon	-	+	+
Libya*	spare parts	-	+
Morocco	tank transporters, ATGMs, combat aircraft, helicopters, AAMs, naval vessels, naval SSMs	+	-
Oman	ATGMs, naval SSMs, AAMs	-	+
Qatar	tanks, APCs, artillery, combat aircraft, MFPBs, naval SSMs, anti-ship AGMs	+	+
Saudi Arabia	APCs, SP artillery, ATGMs, radars, SAMs, anti-ship AGMs, frigates on order, gas masks	+	+
Sudan	artillery pieces	-	-
Syria	ATGMs	-	+
Tunisia	helicopters, naval SSMs	+	+
UAE	combat aircraft, AAMs, AGMs; Leclerc tanks on order	+	+

* before the April 1992 UN embargo

Table 12. Britain in the Middle East: Arms Sales, Advisors, Trainees, and Cooperation in Arms Production.

Country	Arms (major items) Granted or sold	Advisors Present	Trainees in Britain	Cooperation in Arms Production
Algeria	radars, target drones, naval vessels	-	-	naval vessels
Bahrain	patrol craft, electronics	+	+	
Egypt	ATGMs, helicopter spares, radio transceivers, electronics, tank guns, torpedoes, naval radars	-	+	ATGMs, radio transceivers, tank guns, electronics
Iran	workshops, spare parts for tanks & ARVs, radars, landrovers	-	-	-
Israel	spare parts		+	-
Jordan	bridging equipment, radars, ATRLs, patrol boats	-	+	upgrading of tanks
Kuwait	APCs, trainer aircraft, patrol craft, landing craft	+	+	
Libya	-	non gvt. personnel on individual basis*	-	-
Oman	tanks, artillery pieces, combat and training aircraft, ground and a/c radars, MFPBs, target drones	seconded & hired personnel	+	-
Qatar	helicopters, SAMs, drones	+	+	-
Saudi Arabia	combat and trainer aircraft, hovercraft, radio transceivers, helicopters, AAMs, minesweepers, electronics for air defense	+	+	assembly of electronics and AAMs
Tunisia	naval patrol craft, target drones	-	-	-
UAE	APCs, artillery pieces, SAMs, workshops, trainer aircraft, tank transporters	+	+	-

* most advisors left after the April 1992 UN embargo on Libya

Table 13. Surface-to-Surface Missiles and Rockets in Service in Middle Eastern Armies (by Number of Launchers)

Country	Model								total number
	FROG 7/4	SS-1 Scud B	al-Hussein	Scud C	SS-21 Scarab	CSS-2	CSS-8	Other	
Algeria	30-35	-	-	-	-	-	-	-	30-35
Egypt	+	+	-	-	-	-	-	-	24
Iran	-	+	-	+	-	-	+	?	10+
Iraq	+	+	5	-	-	-	-	-	5+
Israel	-	-	-	-	-	-	-	MGM-52C Lance, Jericho I, II*	12
Libya	30	80	-	-	-	-	-	-	110
Saudi Arabia	-	-	-	-	-	8-12	-	-	8-12
Syria	18	18	-	+	18	-	-	-	ca.60
Yemen	12	6	-	-	4	-	-	-	22

* according to foreign sources

GLOSSARY OF

WEAPONS SYSTEMS

ARMY

AA Guns, Short Range
(caliber, designation, NATO codename if relevant, SP when relevant, tracked or wheeled when relevant, country of origin)
57mm ZSU 57x2 SP, tracked, USSR
57mm M-1950 (S-60), USSR
40mm M-42 (twin 40mm) SP, tracked, USA
40mm Bofors L-70, Sweden
40mm Bofors L-60, Sweden
37mm M-1939, USSR
35mm Contraves Skyguard, see below, Air Defense Systems
35mm Gepard SP, FRG
35mm Oerlikon-Buhrle 35x2 GDF-002, Switzerland; may be part of 35mm Skyguard system 30mm AMX DCA 30 (twin 30mm) SP, tracked, France
30mm Artemis (twin 30mm), Greece, based on 30mm Mauser AAG, FRG
30mm 30x2 M-53/59 SP, wheeled, Czechoslovakia
30mm Oerlikon, Switzerland
30mm 30x2 Wildcat SP, wheeled, FRG
23mm ZSU 23x4 (Gun Dish) SP, tracked, USSR (Soviet designation Shilka)
23mm ZU 23x2, USSR
20mm TCM-20x2 SP (on M-3 halftrack), France (gun)/Israeli mounting of gun on US-made halftrack
20mm Oerlikon GAI, Switzerland 20mm Hispano-Suiza, France
20mm M-163 A1 Vulcan SP, USA
20mm M-167 Vulcan, USA
20mm 20x2mm SP (mounted on Panhard VCR 6x6), France
20mm 20x3 M-55 A4, Yugoslavia
20mm VDAA SP (mounted on VAB 6x6), France

Air Def. Sys., short-range
(caliber of gun, designation, missiles, SP when relevant, country of origin)
ADAMS, based on naval Barak missile, Israel; not yet operational
35mm Skyguard (Contraves Skyguard) 2x35, Aspide or RIM-7M Sparrow SAM, SP, Italy (gun--Switzerland, SAM--Italy or USA,

chassis and radar--Italy or Austria); Egyptian designation Amoun
23mm Nile 23, 2x23, 4xSA-7, SP, Egypt (gun + SAM--USSR or
   Egypt, chassis--USA, radar--France)
23mm Sinai 23, see 23mm Nile 23

Anti-Tank Guns
(caliber, designation, recoilless if relevant, country of origin)
120mm BAT L-4 recoilless rifle, Britain
107mm B-11 recoilless rifle, USSR
106mm M-40 A1C/A2 recoilless rifle, USA/Israel
100mm M-1955 gun (field/AT gun), USSR; see guns and howitzers
90mm light gun, low recoil gun, Belgium; used on AFVs
85mm M-1945/D-44 field/AT gun, USSR; see guns and howitzers
84mm Carl Gustav light recoilless rifle, Sweden
82mm B-10 recoilless rifle, USSR
76mm M-1942 divisional gun (ZIS-3), USSR; (field/AT gun, see
   guns and howitzers)
75mm M-20 recoilless rifle, USA
57mm AT gun, Czechoslovakia

APCs/ARVs
(designation, tracked or wheeled, APC or ARV, amphibious if
   relevant, ATGM equipped if relevant, country of origin)
al-Walid, wheeled APC, Egypt
AML-60, wheeled ARV, France
AML-90, wheeled ARV, France
AMX-10 R/S/P, tracked, amphibious APC, France
AMX-VCI, tracked APC, France
AT-105 Saxon, wheeled APC, Britain
BMP-1, tracked, amphibious, ATGM-equipped APC (usually AT-3
   Sagger), with 73mm gun, USSR
BMP-2, tracked, amphibious, ATGM equipped APC (usually AT-5
   Spandrel), with 30mm cannon, USSR
BMR-600, wheeled, amphibious APC, Spain
BRDM-2, wheeled, amphibious, ATGM-equipped ARV, USSR
BTR-40, wheeled, amphibious ARV, USSR
BTR-50, tracked, amphibious APC, USSR
BTR-60, wheeled, amphibious APC, USSR
BTR-152, wheeled APC, USSR
Cadillac Gage Commando Scout, ARV (occasionally
   ATGM-equipped), USA

EBR-75, wheeled ARV, France

Eland, wheeled ARV, South Africa/licensed production of French AML-90/AML-60

Engesa EE-3 Jararaca, wheeled ARV, Brazil

Engesa EE-9 Cascavel, wheeled ARV, Brazil

Engesa EE-11 Urutu, wheeled, amphibious APC, Brazil

Engesa EE-17 Sucuri, wheeled, amphibious tank destroyer, Brazil

Fahd, wheeled APC, Egypt (FRG collaboration)

Ferret, wheeled ARV, Britain

Fiat Type 6614, wheeled, amphibious APC, Italy

Fiat Type 6616, wheeled, amphibious ATGM-equipped ARV, Italy

Fox, wheeled, amphibious ARV, Britain

FUG-70/PSZH-IV, see above, BRDM-2, usually without ATGM, Hungary (licensed production of Soviet BRDM-2)

Israeli APC, Israel (with foreign components); new, no details available

K-63, tracked, amphibious, APC, PRC

LAV-25, wheeled, amphibious APC, Canada; licensed production of Swiss MOWAG Piranha 8x8; produced by GM of Canada, subsidiary of US GMC

M-2, half-tracked APC, USA

M-3, half-tracked APC--see M-2

M-3 (Panhard, VTT), wheeled, amphibious APC (occasionally 4xHOT are added, see Anti-Tank Missiles), France

M-60P, APC, Yugoslavia

M-125, derivative of M-113, 81mm mortar carrier, USA

M-901 ITV (TOW under armor), tracked, amphibious ATGM-equipped ARV (tank destroyer) (based on M-113 APC), USA; see also under ATGM

M-113 A1/A2, tracked, amphibious APC, USA/Italy (licensed production)

M-125, derivative of M-113, 81mm mortar carrier, USA

M-577/M-577 A1, tracked artillery command post vehicle (based on M-113 APC), USA

MOWAG Piranha 8x8, wheeled, amphibious APC, Switzerland

MT-LB, USSR; see under Artillery Ammunition Carriers

OT-62, APC, Czechoslovakia, see BTR-50

OT-64, wheeled APC, Czechoslovakia

PSZH-IV, wheeled, amphibious APC, Hungary; derived from FUG-70/BRDM-2

RAM, wheeled ARV, Israel; improvement of RBY-2
Ratel 20, wheeled APC, South Africa
Ratel 90, same as Ratel 20 with a 90mm gun and turret, South Africa
RBY/RBY-2, wheeled ARV, Israel
Saladin, wheeled ARV, Britain
Saracen, wheeled APC, Britain
Steyr 4K 7FA tracked APC, Austria
Type 77, PRC copy of Soviet BTR-50, PRC; see BTR-50
UR-416, wheeled APC, FRG
V-150 Commando, wheeled, amphibious ATGM-equipped ARV/APC, USA
V-300, wheeled APC, USA
VAB, wheeled, amphibious APC, France
VBC-90, wheeled ARV, France; derivative of VAB, with a 90mm gun
VCR/TH, wheeled, amphibious ATGM-equipped APC/tank destroyer (see anti-tank missiles), France
VPM 81 mortar carrier, wheeled amphibious derivative of VAB, France
YW-531, tracked, amphibious APC, PRC

Army AA Defense--missiles
(designation, NATO codename if relevant, SP when relevant, man-portable if relevant, range, country of origin)
Ain al-Saqr (Egyptian-improved version of Soviet SA-7), man-portable, 4.4 km, Egypt
Blowpipe, man-portable, Britain
Crotale SP, 9 km, France; see also Shahine 2
FIM-92A Stinger, man-portable, 5.4 km, USA
HN-5, man-portable, 4 km, PRC; improved version of Soviet SA-7
MIM-43A Redeye, man-portable, 3 km, USA
MIM-72A Chaparral SP, 8 km, USA
Mistral (Matra Mistral), man-portable, 6 km, France
Rapier, 6 km, Britain
RBS-70, 5 km, Sweden
Roland, I/II 6.3 km, France and FRG
SA-6 Gainful, SP, 3-21 km, USSR
SA-7 Grail, man-portable, 3.5 km (Soviet designation Strella), USSR
SA-8 Gecko, SP, 1.4-9.9 km, USSR
SA-9 Gaskin SP, 0.6-8 km, USSR

SA-11 Gadfly, SP, 3-28 km, USSR/Russia

SA-13 Gopher SP, 0.5-5 km (Soviet designation Strella 10), USSR

SA-14 Gremlin, man-portable, 0.6-6 km (unconfirmed), USSR

SA-16, man-portable, 0.6-5 km, USSR; improvement of SA-7

Shahine 2/Crotale Shahine 2, SP, 13km, France; improvement of Crotale listed above

Shahine 2 ATTS (Air Transportable Towed System); a towed version of Shahine 2

Tigercat, Britain

Artillery Ammunition Carriers

(designation, tracked or wheeled, armored, country of origin)

M-992, tracked USA

MT-LB, tracked, armored, USSR; also serves as prime mover for towed artillery and APC

Artillery/mortar locating radars

(designation, country of origin)

AN/TPQ-37, USA

AN/PPS-15, USA

ATGMs

(anti-tank guided missiles, designation, NATO codename if relevant, SP if relevant, range, country of origin)

AT-1 Snapper, 500-2300m., USSR

AT-2 Swatter, 600-2500m., USSR

AT-3 Sagger, 500-3000m. (Soviet designation Malyutka), USSR

AT-4 Spigot, 2000m., USSR

AT-5 Spandrel, 3600m., USSR

AT-6 Spiral, USSR

BGM-71A TOW/BGM-71C Improved TOW, 65-3750m. (range of Improved TOW), USA

BGM-71D TOW II, USA; improvement of BGM-71C

BRDM-2 carrying AT-3 (Sagger) SP, 500-3000m., USSR

Dragon III, 1500m.,USA; improved M-47A

HOT, 75-4000m., France/FRG

HOT Commando, HOT mounted on a Peugeot P-4 4x4 jeep-like vehicle, France

Israeli BGM-71C Improved TOW SP, 65-3750m.; derivative of M-113 APC, USA; missile and APC, USA; mounting and hydraulics--Israel

460

M-3 (Panhard) carrying HOT SP, 75-4000m., France; see also APC

M-47A Dragon, 1000m., USA

M-901 ITV SP (TOW under armor), BGM-71A TOW, 65-3750m., derivative of M-113 APC, USA; see also APC/ARV

Mapats, 5000m., Israel; laser-beam riding Israeli improvement of US-made BGM-71A TOW

MILAN, 25-2000m., France/FRG

Nimrod, land based variant of Nimrod AGM, Israel

SS-11, 500-3000m., France

SS-12, 6000m., France (can be employed as ATGM or as anti-ship missile launched from ground, helicopter or ship)

Swingfire 300-4000m., Britain/Egypt

T-1/T-16 SP, ATGM system/tank destroyer (unconfirmed), USSR

Vigilant, 200-1375m., Britain

VCR/TH carrying HOT SP, 75-4000m., France; see also APC

Automatic grenade launchers
(caliber, designation, country of origin)
40mm Mk.19, USA

Engineering equipment
(designation, type, country of origin)
Bar mine-laying system, Britain
EWK pontoon bridge (Faltschwimmbrucke), FRG
Gilois motorized bridge, France
GSP self-propelled ferry, USSR
M-69 A1 bridging tank, USA
M-123 Viper minefield-crossing system, USA
MT-55 bridging tank, USSR
MTU-55 bridging tank, USSR
PMP pontoon bridge, USSR
Pomins II, portable (infantry) mine neutralization system, Israel
PRP motorized bridge, USSR
TLB, trailer launched bridge, Israel
TWMP, tread width mine ploughs, Israel

Guns & Howitzers, SP
(caliber, designation, gun or howitzer, range, country of origin)
210mm al-Faw, 57 km (with base bleed and RAP ammunition), Iraq (with assistance of companies from Belgium and Britain)
203mm/8" M-110 A1 SP howitzer, 16.8 km, USA

175mm M-107 SP gun, 32.7 km, USA

155mm Mk. F-3 (AMX) SP howitzer, 18 km, France

155mm G-6 SP howitzer, 30.8 km (39 km with base bleed ammunition), South Africa

155mm GCT SP howitzer, 23.5 km, France

155mm L-33 (Sherman/Soltam) SP howitzer, 21 km, Israel

155mm M-44 SP howitzer, 14.6 km, USA

155mm M-50 (Sherman) SP howitzer, 17.5 km, Israel (gun-France; chassis-USA, improved in Israel)

155mm M-109 A1/A2 SP howitzer, 21 km, USA

155mm Majnoon SP howitzer, Iraq, with assistance from a company in Belgium

155mm Palmaria SP howitzer, 24 km, Italy

152mm M-1973 SP howitzer, 18 km, USSR

122mm M-1974 SP howitzer, 15.3 km, USSR

122mm D-30 SP howitzer, 16 km, USSR (gun)/Egypt (conversion to SP with British/US aid)

122mm ISU SP gun, 16 km, USSR

105mm M-108 SP howitzer, 11.5 km, USA

105mm M-52 SP howitzer, 11.3 km, USA

105mm Mk.61 SP howitzer, 15 km, France

100mm SU-100 SP gun, USSR

Guns & Howitzers, Towed

(caliber, designation, gun or howitzer, range, country of origin)

203mm/8" M-115 howitzer, 16.8 km, USA

180mm S-23 gun, 32 km, USSR

155mm M-41 gun, 30 km, Iraq/Austria; a combination of the 130mm gun and Austrian 155mm tubes

155mm FH-70 howitzer, 24 km, FRG

155mm G-5 gun/howitzer, 30 km, South Africa

155mm GHN-45 howitzer/gun, 17.8 km, Austria

155mm M-198 A1 howitzer, 18.1 km, USA

155mm M-114 A2 howitzer, 14.6 km, USA

155mm M-1950 howitzer, 17.5 km, France

155mm M-71 gun/howitzer, 24 km, Israel

155mm M-59 (Long Tom) gun, 22 km, USA

152mm D-20 howitzer/gun, 18 km, USSR

152mm M-1943 (D-1) howitzer, USSR

130mm M-46 gun, 27.1 km, USSR

130mm Type 59 gun, 27.4 km, PRC; copy of Soviet 130mm M-46
122mm M-1938 howitzer, 11.8 km, USSR
122mm D-30 howitzer, 16 km, USSR
122mm Saddam, Iraq/USSR (Soviet 122mm D-30 produced in Iraq, with assistance from Yugoslavia)
105mm Gun, 17.2 km, Britain
105mm M-102 A1 howitzer, 11.5 km, USA
105mm M-101 A1 howitzer, 11.3 km, USA
105mm M-56 Pack howitzer, 10.6 km, Italy
100mm M-1955 gun, 21 km (field/AT gun), USSR
25 lb. (87mm) howitzer, 12.2 km, Britain
85mm M-1945/D-44 gun, 15.8 km (field/AT gun), USSR
76mm M-1942 divisional gun (ZIS-3), 13.3 km, USSR

Light ATRLs
(designation, effective range, country of origin)
al-Nassira, Iraq; copy of Soviet RPG-7
APILAS (APILAS Manurhin), 330m., France
LAW-80, 500m., Britain
M-72 A1/A2 LAW, 300m., USA
RPG-2, 150m., USSR
RPG-7, 500m., USSR
89mm M-65, Spain
89mm Strim-89, 360m., France
3.5" M-20 (Bazooka), 110m., USA

Machine Guns
(caliber, designation, type, country of origin)
14.5mm KPV HMG, USSR
14.5mm ZPU 14.5x4 HMG, USSR; employed in anti-aircraft role
14.5mm ZPU 14.5x2 HMG, USSR; employed in anti-aircraft role
12.7mm D.Sh.K. 38/46 (Degtyarev) HMG, USSR
12.7mm (0.5") Browning M2 HMG, USA
7.62mm Aswan MMG, Egypt; a copy of Soviet 7.62mm SG-43
7.62mm MAG (FN) LMG, Belgium
7.62mm PK/PKS (Kalashnikov) LMG, USSR
7.62mm PKT (Kalashnikov) LMG, USSR
7.62mm RPD (Degtyarev) LMG, USSR
7.62mm RPK LMG, USSR
7.62mm Suez, Egypt; copy of Soviet 7.62mm RPD
7.62mm (0.3") Browning M-1919 MMG, USA

7.62mm (0.3") BAR (Browning) LMG, USA

7.62mm MG 1A1/1A3 LMG, Iran (licensed production of FRG's MG-3)

7.62mm MG-3, LMG, FRG

7.62mm M-60 D GPMG/LMG, USA

7.62mm SG-43 (Goryunov) MMG, USSR

7.62mm SGM (Goryunov) MMG, USSR

7.5mm AA-52/M2 MMG, France

7.5mm Chatellerault M-24/29 LMG, France

5.56mm Minimi (FN) LMG, Belgium

5.56mm Negev LMG, Israel

Mortars, heavy, 160mm and over
(caliber, designation, SP if relevant, range, country of origin)
240mm M-240, 9.7 km, USSR

160mm M-43/53, 5.1 km, USSR

160mm M-66 SP, 9.3 km, Israel

Mortars, heavy, under 160mm
(caliber, designation, SP if relevant, range, country of origin)
120mm M-43, 5.7 km, USSR

120mm Brandt M-50/M-60, 6.6 km (unconfirmed), France

120mm M-65, 6.3 km, Israel; also available as SP, mounted on US-made M-2 halftrack

120mm x 4 SP, 11.5 km, Iraq; mounted on Soviet made MT-LB carrier

107mm (4.2") M-30 SP/towed (SP on M-106 A2 carrier, a derivative of M-113 APC), 5.6 km, USA

Mortars, Light and Medium
(caliber, designation, range, country of origin)
82mm M-41/43, 2550 m., USSR

81mm Hotchkiss Brandt, 4550 m. (unconfirmed), France

81mm M-29, 4590 m., USA

81mm Soltam, 4100 m. (short barrel), 4900 m. (long barrel), Israel

81mm ECIA, Spain

81mm L-16 A1, 5660 m., Britain

60mm Hotchkiss-Brandt, 2050 m., France

60mm M-2, 2550 m., Israel

60mm M-19, 1810 m., USA

52mm IMI, 420 m., Israel

MRLs

(caliber, designation, number of launchers, range, country of origin)

550mm Laith 90, 90 km, Iraq (possibly experimental, copy of soviet FROG-7 rocket, with alleged improvement of range to 90 km; see below SSMs)

400mm Ababil-100, 4, 100 km, Iraq; improved version of Yugoslavia's 262mm LRSV M-87

355mm Nazeat, 90 km, Iran

333mm Shahin 2, 20 km, Iran

300mm SS-60, 4, 68 km, Brazil

300mm Sajeel 60, Iraq; copy of Brazilian 300mm SS-60

290mm (MAR 290), 4, 25 km (unconfirmed), Israel

262mm Ababil-50, 12, 50 km, Iraq; copy of Yugoslavia's 262mm LRSV M-87

240mm BM-24, 12, 10.2 km, USSR

240mm Fajr 3, Iran

230mm Oghab, 3, 80 km (unconfirmed), Iran; improved version of PRC's Type 83 273mm rocket

227mm MLRS, 12, 30km, USA

180mm SS-40 Astros II, 16, 35 km, Brazil

180mm Sajeel 40, Iraq; copy of Brazilian 180mm SS-40

140mm BM-14-16, 16, 9.8 km, USSR

140mm RPU-14, 16, 9.8 km, USSR

140mm Teruel, 40, 18.2 km, Spain

132mm BM-13-16, 16, 9 km, USSR

130mm M-51 (=130mm RM-130), 32, 8.2 km, Romania/USSR

130mm M-51, 32, 8.2 km, Czechoslovakia

130mm Type 63, 19, 10.4 km, PRC

128mm M-63, 32, 8.5 km, Yugoslavia

127mm SS-30 Astros II, 32, 30 km, Brazil

127mm Sajeel 30, Iraq; copy of Brazilian 127mm SS-30

122mm BM-11, 30, North Korea; a variant of Soviet BM-21

122mm BM-21, 40, 20.8 km, USSR

122mm Firos-25, 40, 25 km, Italy

122mm RM-70, 40, 20.4 km, Czechoslovakia; similar to Soviet BM-21

122mm Saqr 36, similar to Saqr 30, with 36 launchers, Egypt

122mm Saqr 30, 22.5 km, Egypt

122mm Saqr 10 and Saqr 18, short range versions of Saqr 30, Egypt

107mm RM-11, 8.1 km, North Korea

107mm, Iraq; copy of 107mm from PRC or RM-11 from North Korea

Personal Weapons
(caliber, designation, type, country of origin)
9mm Aqaba SMG, Egypt (improved Port Said)
9mm Carl Gustav Model 45 SMG, Sweden
9mm L-34 A1 SMG, Britain
9mm MAT 49/56 SMG, France
9mm Mini Uzi SMG, Israel
9mm Model 12 Beretta SMG, Italy
9mm Model 23/25 SMG, Czechoslovakia
9mm Model 38/49 Beretta SMG, Italy
9mm Port Said SMG, Egypt (copy of Swedish Carl Gustav)
9mm P.P.Sh. 41/42/43 SMG, USSR (also available in 7.62mm caliber)
9mm Sterling Mk.4 SMG, Britain
9mm Uzi SMG, Israel; produced under licence in Belgium
9mm Vigneron M2 SMG, Belgium
7.62mm AK-47/AKM (Kalashnikov) AR, USSR
7.62mm FAL (FN) SAR, Belgium
7.62mm L-1 A1 SAR, Britain
7.62mm FAC (FN) SAR, Belgium; similar to 7.62mm CAL/FAL, above
7.62mm FAL (FN) SAR, Belgium; same as 7.62mm CAL/FAL, above
7.62mm Galil sniper rifle, Israel
7.62mm G-3 (Heckler & Koch) AR, FRG/Iran (licensed production)
7.62mm M-1 Garand SAR, USA
7.62mm M-14 SAR, USA
7.62mm Rashid SAR, Egypt
7.62mm SKS (Simonov) SAR, USSR
7.62mm SSG-69 sniper rifle (Steyr), Austria
7.62mm SVD (Dragunov) sniper rifle, USSR
7.62mm Tabuk AR, Iraq; copy of Soviet AK-47/AKM
7.62mm Type 56 AR, PRC; PRC copy of Soviet AK-47
7.5mm MAS 49/56 SAR, France
5.56mm AR-180 SAR, USA
5.56mm AUG Steyr AR, Austria
5.56mm CAL (FN) AR, Belgium

5.56mm Galil AR, Israel
5.56mm HK-33 (Heckler & Koch) AR, FRG
5.56mm M-16 A1/A2 AR, USA
5.56mm SG-540 AR, Switzerland
5.45mm AK-74 (Kalashnikov) AR, USSR

Recovery Vehicles
(designation, APC/tank chassis, country of origin)
M-578 A1 APC, USA
M-88 A1 Recovery Tank, USA
T-55 Recovery Tank, USSR
T-62 Recovery Tank, USSR

SS Missiles & Rockets
(designation, NATO codename if relevant, range, circular error
    probability (CEP), payload, country of origin)
al-Hussein (Iraqi modified SS-1), 590-640 km, 300kg, USSR/Iraq
CSS-2 (East Wind) IRBM, 1500 km, 2045 kg (with conventional
    warhead), PRC
FROG-4, 45 km, USSR
FROG-7 (Soviet designation Luna), 60 km, 450 kg, 500m, USSR
Jericho I, 450 km, 500 kg (according to foreign publications), Israel
Jericho II, 800 km, 500 kg (according to foreign publications), Israel
MGM-52C Lance, 75 km (with conventional warhead), 225 kg, USA
M-9, 600 km (unconfirmed), PRC
Nodong, 960-1000 km, North Korea (still under development, on
    order by countries in the Middle East)
Saqr 80, 80 km, 200 kg, Egypt; launched from FROG-7 launcher
SS-1 Scud B, 280 km, 800-1000 kg, 1000m, USSR
SS-21 Scarab, 80 km, 100m, USSR
SS-1 Scud C, 500 km, 700 kg., 2000-3000m, North Korea (similar
    to Scud C made in USSR)
Tamuz 1, 2000 km, Iraq (with assistance from German, Italian and
    French experts)

Tanks
(designation, caliber of gun, weight, country of origin)
AMX-13 LT, 75mm/105mm, 14.5 ton, France
AMX-30 MBT, 105mm, 36 ton, France
Assad Babil, Iraqi designation for locally assembled T-72
Centurion MBT, 105mm, 52 ton, Britain

Challenger 2 MBT, 120mm, 62 ton, Britain
Chieftain Mk.3/Mk.5 MBT, 120mm, 52.3 ton, Britain
Khalid--Jordanian designation for Chieftain; see above
Leclerc MBT, 120mm, 53 ton, France
M-1 A1 MBT, 120mm, 57 ton, USA/Egypt (assembly)
M-1 A2, same as M-1 A1 with improved fire control, USA
M-41 LT, 76.2mm, 24 ton, USA
M-47 A1/2/5 MBT, 90mm, 44 ton, USA
M-48 A1/5 Patton MBT, 90mm/105mm, 46.6 ton, USA
M-60/M-60 A1/A2/A3 MBT, 105mm, 49 ton, USA
M-77 MBT (improved Soviet T-55), Romania
M-84 MBT, Yugoslavia; licensed production of Soviet T-72
Merkava Mk.1/Mk.2 MBT, 105mm, 56 ton, Israel
Merkava Mk.3 MBT, 120mm, 59 ton, Israel
OF-40 Lion MBT, 105mm, 43 ton, Italy; heavily reliant on FRG's
    Leopard 1 in design and components
Osorio (EE-T1) MBT, 105mm/120mm, Brazil
PT-76 amphibious LT, 76mm, 14 ton, USSR
Ramses II MBT, 105mm, 36 ton (unconfirmed), Egypt; Soviet
    T-54/T-55 upgraded with USA model gun and USA stabilizer,
    laser range finder, fire control and night vision
Scorpion LT, 76mm, 7.8 ton, Britain
SK-105 (Kurassier) LT/tank destroyer, 105mm, 18 ton, Austria
T-34 Medium Tank, 85mm, 32 ton, USSR
T-54 B/C MBT, 100mm, 36 ton, USSR
T-55 B/C/D MBT, 100mm, 36 ton, USSR
T-62 MBT, 115mm, 37.5 ton, USSR
T-72 MBT, 125mm, 41 ton, USSR
T-72M MBT, same as T-72 with upgraded fire control and jammer,
    USSR
Type-59 (=T-55), PRC
Type-62 Medium Tank, 85mm, 21 ton, PRC
Type-69, improved Type-59, above, PRC
Vickers Mk.1 MBT, 105mm, 38.1 ton, Britain

AIR FORCE

AA Guns, Long Range
(caliber, designation, country of origin)
100mm M-49, USSR
85mm M-44, USSR

AEW/AWACS Aircraft
(designation, NATO codename if relevant, derivation if relevant,
function, speed, range, radar range, country of origin)
E-3A Sentry, AWACS, Boeing 707, 853 km/h., 6 hrs. endurance,
radar range 370 km, USA
E-2C Hawkeye, AEW, 602 km/h., 6 hrs. 6 min. endurance, radar
range 250 km, USA
TU-126 Moss, AWACS, TU-114, 850 km/h., 12,550 km, USSR

Air-to-Air Missiles (AAMs)
(designation, NATO codename if relevant, guidance systems,
effective range, country of origin)
AA-1 Alkali, semi-active radar guidance, 6-8 km, USSR
AA-2 Atoll, infra-red homing, 5-6.5 km, USSR
AA-2 Advanced Atoll, active radar homing, 5-6.5 km, USSR
AA-6 Acrid, infra-red guidance, 37 km, USSR
AA-7 Apex, infra-red or semi-active guidance, 27 km, USSR
AA-8 Aphid, 5-7.4 km, USSR
AA-10 Alamo, radar homing, 20-34 km, USSR/Russia
AA-11 Archer, active terminal radar, 39-68 km, USSR/Russia
AIM-7/AIM-7E/F Sparrow III, semi-active radar guidance, 44 km,
USA
AIM-9B Sidewinder, infra-red homing, now obsolete, USA
AIM-9E/F Sidewinder, infra-red guidance, USA; improved AIM-9B
AIM-9J Sidewinder, USA; advanced version of AIM-9E with
enhanced dogfight capability
AIM-9L Sidewinder, infra-red guidance and active laser fuse, 18 km,
USA
AIM-9M Sidewinder, similar to AIM-9L, with improved target
acquisition and lock-on capabilities, USA
AIM-9P/P4 Sidewinder, improved AIM-9B, USA
AIM-54A Phoenix, semi-active radar guidance and fully active radar

during terminal guidance, 44 km, USA

Firestreak, infra-red homing, 1.8 km, Britain

Python 3, infra-red guidance, 15 km, Israel

Red Top, infra-red homing, 12 km, Britain

R-530 (Matra R-530), infra-red guidance version/semi-active radar version, 18 km, France

R-550 Magique, infra-red guidance, 10 km, France

Shafrir, infra-red guidance, 5 km, Israel

Sky Flash, semi-active radar, 40 km, Britain

Super 530D/F (improved R-530), semi-active homing radar, 25 km, France

Air-to-Ground Missiles (AGMs)

(designation, NATO codename if relevant, function, guidance, range, country of origin)

AGM-45A/B Shrike, anti-radar/SAM sites, radar-guidance, 12-16 km, USA

AGM-62A Walleye, anti-ship/airbase/bridge, TV-guided, USA

AGM-65A/B Maverick, anti-tank/hard target, TV-guided, USA

AGM-65C Maverick (=65A/B guided by Laser designator), USA

AGM-78D Standard ARM anti-radar/SAM site, passive radar homing, USA

AGM-84, anti-ship missile, air-launched variant of RGM-84A Harpoon SSM, USA; see Navy

AGM-114 Hellfire, helicopter-borne, ATGM, guidance by Laser designator, USA

ALARM, air-launched anti-radar missile, Britain

AM-39, anti-ship, radio and radar guided, 50-70 km, France; air-launched derivative of the MM-38 & MM-40 Exocet SSMs

Armat, air launched anti-radar missile, homing on radar emission, France; enhanced successor version of French-British AS-37

AS-1 Kennel, anti-ship/hard target, radar guidance, 90 km, USSR

AS-2 Kipper, autopilot command override, active terminal homing, 160 km, USSR

AS-4 Kitchen, inertial guidance with radar terminal homing, 400 km, USSR

AS-5 Kelt, anti-ship and hard target, radar guidance, 160 km, USSR

AS-6 Kingfish, inertial guidance, 240 km, USSR

AS-7 Kerry, 9.6 km, USSR/Russia

AS-9 Kyle, passive radar, 90km, USSR; designated Nisan in Iraq

AS-10 Karen, semi-active laser guidance, 9.6 km, USSR/Russia

AS-11, anti-ship, wire-guided (optical/tracked navigation), 3 km, France, helicopter-launched anti-ship & anti-tank version of SS-11 ATGM

AS-11 Kegler/Kilter, 30 km, USSR/Russia

AS-12, anti-ship, wire-guided (optical/tracked navigation), 6 km, France; helicopter-launched anti-ship version of the SS-12 ATGM

AS-14 Kedge, anti tank/hard target, mid-course guidance and electro-optical homing, 30km (unconfirmed), USSR

AS-15TT, anti-ship, radar and radio-guided, 14.4 km, France; helicopter-launched

AS-30, radio-guided, 11.2 km, France

AS-30L, laser-guided, France

C-601, anti-ship, semi-active radar, active radar terminal guidance, 80km, PRC; similar to Hai Ying-2 (HY-2, Silkworm) shipborne SSM

LX, anti-ship missile (unconfirmed), USSR

Nimrod, anti-tank missile, semi-active laser, 25 km, Israel

Popeye (also designated Have Nap, AGM-142), inertial and TV, 80km, Israel/Israel in cooperation with USA

Sea Eagle, anti-ship missile, inertial navigation and radar homing, 100 km, Britain

X-23, anti-radiation missile (unconfirmed), USSR

Aircraft, Bombers

(designation, NATO codename, maximum speed, range, armament, country of origin)

H-6 (B-6D), copy of Soviet Tu-16, can carry C-601 anti-ship missile, PRC

IL-28 Beagle, 900 km/h., 2260 km, 2040 kg. bombs, 4x23mm gun, USSR

Tu-16 Badger, 945 km/h., 4800 km, Kelt AGM/9000 kg. bombs, 2x2x23mm gun, USSR

Tu-22 Blinder, Mach 1.4, 2250 km, Kitchen AGM and bombs, 1x23mm gun, USSR

Aircraft, Counter-insurgency

OV-10 Bronco (also Rockwell OV-10 Bronco), counter-insurgency/surveillance aircraft, FLIR sensor, laser designator, 272 kg. weapon pods/20mm guns/bombs, 463 km/h., 367 km (combat radius with weapon load), USA

Aircraft, Interceptors

(designation, NATO codename if relevant, maximum speed, combat radius, armament, country of origin)

F-6 Shenyang (=MiG-19), PRC; see also aircraft, strike & multi-role, & MiG-19, below

F-7 Shenyang (=MiG-21), PRC; see MiG-21, below

F-14A Tomcat, Mach 2.4, 4xAIM-7 or 4xAIM-54A Phoenix + 4xAIM-9, 1x20mm gun, USA

F-15A/B/C/D Eagle, Mach 2.5+, 1000 km, 4xAIM-7/4xAIM-9, 1x20mm gun, USA

FT-6, PRC; two-seater training version of F-6; also JJ-6, copy of Soviet MiG-19 UTI

MiG-19 PF/PFM Farmer C/D, 1452 km/h., 685 km, 2xAA-2 Atoll AAM, 2 or 3x30mm gun, USSR

MiG-21 MF/S/U Fishbed, Mach 2.1, 1100 km, 2xAA-2 Atoll AAM/Advanced Atoll, 1x23mm gun, USSR

MiG-23 ML/MF/MS Flogger B/E, Mach 2.3, 1200 km, 5xAA-7 Apex/AA-8 Aphid AAM, 1x23mm gun, USSR

MiG-25 Foxbat A/B/E/U, Mach 2.8, 1450 km, 4xAA-8 Aphid/AA-6 Acrid AAM, USSR

MiG-25R, reconnaissance version of MiG-25

Mirage III C/E/BL/EL, Mach 2.2, 1200 km, 1xR530/2xAIM-9, 2x30mm gun, France

Su-27 Flanker A, Mach 2.3, 1500 km, 6-8xAA-10 AAM, 23mm gun, USSR/Russia

Tornado (Panavia Tornado) ADV, (F Mk.3) Mach 2.2, radius 620 km, AIM-9L, Sky Flash AAM, 1x27mm Mauser cannon, Britain, FRG and Italy (joint production); see also Aircraft, Strike and Multi-Role

Xian J-7, copy of MiG-21, PRC; export version designated F-7 Shenyang, see above

Aircraft, Maritime Surveillance

(designation, jet/turboprop, speed, endurance, range, sonar, radar, country of origin)

EMB-111N Bandeirante, based on EMB-110 transport aircraft, turboprop, 360 km/h., 2940 km, sea patrol radar, Brazil

P-3 Orion, turboprop, 608 km/h., 3 hours on station, 3835 km, sonar (ARR-72), APS-115 radar, USA; may carry depth bombs

Westwind I/Sea Scan/1124 Sea Scan, based on Westwind 1124, maritime reconnaissance aircraft, 872 km/h., 6 hrs. 30 min.

endurance, equipped with search radar, Israel

Beechcraft 1900C, derivative of commuter/light transport aircraft employed in Egypt in ELINT and/or maritime surveillance role, USA; see Aircraft, Transport and Executive

Aircraft, Strike & Multi-Role

(designation, NATO codename if relevant, maximum speed, combat radius/range, armament, country of origin)

A-4 A/B/D/E/J/KU Skyhawk, 1085 km/h., 3200 km, 2x20mm gun, 4,500 kg. bombs, USA (A-4E data)

F-4 D/E Phantom, Mach 2+, 1145 km, 4xAIM-7 + 4xAIM-9, 1x20mm gun, 7250 kg. bombs, USA

F-4 Shenyang (=MiG-17), PRC, see MiG-17

F-5 A/B/E/F (Tiger II), Mach 1.64, 890 km, 2xAIM-9, 2x20mm gun, 3.17 ton bombs, USA (F-5E data)

F-6 Shenyang, PRC (copy of Soviet MiG-19 interceptor); see MiG-19, Aircraft, Interceptors

F-16 A/B/C/D Fighting Falcon, Mach 1.95, 925 km, 2xAIM-9, 1x20mm gun, 6.8 ton bombs, USA

F/A-18C/D Hornet, Mach 1.7+, 2xAIM-9, AIM-120, AGM-84, AGM-65F, various bombs; various combinations of armament to a maximum of ca. 7 ton, USA

Hawker Hunter FGA-6/F-70/FR-10/T-66/T-67, Mach 0.8, 4x30mm gun, 0.5 ton bombs, Britain

J-1 Jastreb, light attack version of SOKO G-2 Galeb; see Aircraft, Training

Kfir C-2/TC-2/C-7/TC-7, Mach 2.3, 768 km, 2xShafrir AAM, 2x30mm gun, 3150 kg. bombs, Israel

MiG-15 Faggot, 1070 km/h., 1400 km, 1x37mm gun, 2x23mm gun, USSR; also employed as advanced trainer

Mig-17 Fresco, 1145 km/h., 1400 km, 1x37mm gun, 2x23mm gun, 500 kg. bombs, USSR

MiG-23 S/BN/U Flogger A/F/C/S/G, Mach 2.3, 1200 km, AA-7 Apex & AA-8 Aphid AAMs, 1x23mm twin barrel gun, USSR; see also Aircraft, Interceptors

MiG-27 Flogger D, Mach 1.6, ca. 500 km, AA-7 Apex & AA-8 Aphid AAMs, 1x23mm twin barrel gun, USSR

MiG-29 Fulcrum, Mach 2.8 (unconfirmed), USSR/Russia

Mirage 5/50, Mach 2.2, 1300 km, 2xAIM-9 AAM/2xR-530, 2x30mm gun, up to 4000 kg. bombs, France

Mirage F-1 B/C/D/E, Mach 2.2, AIM-9/R-530 and R-550 Magique, AS-30 AGM, 2x30mm gun, 3600 kg. bombs, France

Mirage F-1 EQ5 = F-1 E equipped to fire AM-39 Exocet ASM, France

Mirage 2000, Mach 2.2+, 1480 km with external tanks and bombs, 2xSuper R-530 AAM and 2xR-550 Magique AAM, 2x30mm gun, up to 5000 kg. bombs, France

Phantom 2000, an Israeli upgrade of F-4E, above

RF-4E Phantom, reconnaissance version of F-4E

RF-5E Northrop Tiger II, reconnaissance/photography version of F-5E (unarmed), USA

SEPECAT Jaguar S/E-01, Mach 1.6, 1408 km, 2xR-550 Magique or 2xAIM-9 AAM or AS-37 AGM, 1-2x30mm gun, 3600 kg. bombs, Britain and France

Su-7 BM/U Fitter A/B, Mach 1.6, 480 km, 2x30mm gun, 1 ton bombs, USSR

Su-20/22 Fitter C, Mach 2.17, 630 km, AA-2 Atoll AAMs, 2x30mm gun, 4000 kg. bombs, USSR

Su-24 Fencer C, Mach 2.18, 1800 km, 11,000 kg. bombs/AGMs including AS-7 Kerry AGM, one gun, USSR

Su-25 Frogfoot, 880 km/h., 556 km, AA-2 Atoll/AA-8 Aphid AAMs, 30mm guns, maximum armament and bomb load 4 tons, USSR

TA-4 KU, USA--see A-4; designation of advanced two-seater training aircraft for Kuwait

Tornado (Panavia Tornado) IDS, (GR Mk.1) Mach 2.2, 1390 km with heavy weapons load, AIM-9, AGM-65/AS-30 AGM/CBU-15, 2x27mm gun, maximum armament and bomb load 8.1 tons, Britain, FRG and Italy (joint production); see also Aircraft, Interceptors

Aircraft, Tanker

(aerial refuelling) (designation, derivation, fuel load, country of origin)

Boeing 707 Tanker, USA--see KC-135; also a Boeing 707 made in USA, converted to aerial refuelling role in Israel

KC-135A Stratotanker, Boeing 707, USA

KC-130H, C-130H Hercules, 23,923 liter, USA

KE-3A, similar to KC-135A, USA; designation of aircraft for Saudi Arabia

Aircraft, Training and Liaison

(designation, jet, turboprop or piston engine, ground attack capability
if relevant, country of origin)

Aermacchi MB-326 B/KT/LT, jet, ground attack capability, Italy

Aermacchi MB-339, jet, ground attack capability, Italy

al-Gumhuriya, piston, Egypt (German/Spanish model)

Alpha Jet, jet, ground attack capability, France & West
Germany/Egypt-assembly

Alpha Jet MS-2, same as Alpha Jet, licensed production in Egypt
with improved ground attack and naval attack capabilities

AS-202/18A Bravo and AS-202/26A, piston, Switzerland

BAC-145 Jet Provost, jet, ground attack capability, Britain

BAC-167 Strikemaster Mk.82/Mk.83, jet, ground attack capability,
Britain; development of BAC-145

BAe Jetstream 31, turboprop, Britain; a transport aircraft employed
for cockpit training for Tornado aircrews

BAe-SA-3-120 Bulldog series 125/126, piston, Britain (formerly
Scottish Aviation B-125 Bulldog and Beagle B-125 Bulldog)

Beechcraft Bonanza F-33A and V-35B, piston, USA

Beechcraft T-34C Turbo Mentor, turboprop, USA

Broussard, piston, France

Cessna 172 G/H/L, piston, USA

Cessna 182 Skylane, piston, USA

Cessna 185 Skywagon, piston, USA; same as Cessna U-206

Cessna 318 (T-37), jet, USA

Cessna U-206 Skywagon, piston, USA

CM-170 Fouga Magister, jet, ground attack capability, France/Israel
(assembly)

Embraer EMB-312 (T-27), turboprop, Brazil; produced under license
by Egypt and Britain; also designated Tucano T-27

FT-6, trainer, two-seat version of F-6 (interceptor), PRC; see
interceptors

Galeb--see SOKO

Gepal IV (AMIN Gepal IV), turboprop, Morocco

Grob G-109B, ultra-light, FRG

Hawk, jet, ground attack capability, Britain

L-29 Delfin, jet, ground attack capability, Czechoslovakia

L-39 Albatross, jet, ground attack capability, Czechoslovakia

L-59, advanced variant of L-39, above, Czech Republic

MBB-223 Flamingo/MBB-Flamingo, piston, FRG/Spain; produced

in FRG by MBB or SIAT, and in Spain by CASA

MiG-15 UTI--see Aircraft, Strike and Multi-Role

Mushshak (Saab Safari Supporter, Saab MF-17, also designated PAC Mushshak), piston, Pakistan; produced under license from Sweden (Saab)

Pilatus PC-6 Turbo-Porter, turboprop, Switzerland

Pilatus PC-7 Turbo-Trainer, turboprop, Switzerland

Pilatus PC-9, turboprop, Switzerland

Piper Cub/Piper/PA-18 Super Cub, piston, USA

Piper PA-44, USA

PZL-104 Wilga 35/80, piston, Poland

Rockwell T-6 (Texan, Harvard), piston, USA

SIAI-Marchetti SF-260M/WT/C/L Warrior, piston, Italy

SIAI-Marchetti S-208A, piston, Italy

SOKO G-2A/G-2AE Galeb, jet, ground attack capability, Yugoslavia; J-1 Jastreb derived from G-2A for light attack roles and advanced training

Strikemaster--see BAC-167 Strikemaster

T-33, jet, ground attack capability, USA

Tzukit, (French) CM-170 Fouga Magister upgraded by Israel (strengthened frame and new avionics)

YAK-11 Moose, piston, USSR

YAK-18 Max, piston, USSR

Aircraft, Transport & Executive

(designation, NATO codename if relevant, piston, turboprop or jet engine, maximum cruising speed, range, load, accommodation, paratroop dropping capability if relevant, country of origin)

An-2 Colt, piston, 200 km/h., 905 km, 1240 kg./14 paratroopers, USSR

An-12 Cub, turboprop, 670 km/h., 3600 km, 20 ton/100 paratroopers, USSR

An-24 Coke, turboprop, 450 km/h., 640 km, 5700 kg./ 38 passengers or 30 paratroopers, USSR

An-26 Curl, turboprop, 440 km/h., 1100 km, 5500 kg./ 38-40 passengers, USSR

Arava (IAI 101/201/202 Arava), turboprop, 319 km/h., 630 km, 2351 kg./24 passengers/16 paratroopers, Israel (IAI 202 data)

BAe-111 (BAC-111), jet, 870 km/h., 3013 km, 10,733 kg./119 passengers, Britain

BAe-125 (also known as HS-125), jet, 845 km/h., 5318 km, 1088kg./2 pilots + 14 passengers, Britain

Beechcraft Bonanza A-36, piston, 326 km/h, pilot + 4-6 passengers, USA; an executive aircraft

Beechcraft 1900C, turboprop, 435 km/h., 1469 km, 19 passengers/EW/CEW equipment, USA; a commuter aircraft employed in EW/CEW and/or maritime surveillance role in Egypt

Beechcraft King Air B-100, turboprop, 486 km/h., 2232 km, 13 passengers, USA

Beechcraft Queen Air, turboprop, 370 km/h., 2520 km, 1599 kg./9 passengers, USA; an executive aircraft

Beechcraft Super King Air, turboprop, 536 km/h., 3,658 km, 14 passengers, USA

Boeing 707/707-200/707-320, jet, 973 km/h., 7700 km, 43 ton/180 passengers, USA

Boeing 720/720B/720B-023B, jet, 897 km/h., 6690 km, 112 passengers, USA

Boeing 727, jet, 960 km/h., 14,740 kg./131 passengers, USA

Boeing KC-135--see Boeing 707, aerial refuelling aircraft

Boeing 737/737-200, jet, 943 km/h., 3521 km, 15 ton/115 passengers, USA

Boeing 747/747-200B/747-200C, jet, 967 km/h., 10,562 km, 160 ton/450 passengers, USA

Britten-Norman BN-2A Islander/Pilatus BN-2B Islander II, piston, 251 km/h., 1530 km, 10 passengers, Britain/ Switzerland

C-47--see DC-3 Dakota

C-119, piston, 315 km/h. 725 km, 10 ton/67 troops, fewer paratroopers, USA

C-130H-30, stretched version of C-130H, see L-100-30

C-130 E/H Hercules, turboprop, 621 km/h., 3791 km (maximum payload), 19,685 kg./92 paratroopers, USA

C-140 Jetstar, jet, 885 km/h., 3185 km, 1360 kg./10 passengers, USA

C-212--see CASA C-212 Aviocar

Caravelle Super B, 835 km/h., 2,725 km, 9,265 kg./104 passengers, France

CASA C-212-5 series 100/C-212 series 200 Aviocar, turboprop, 365 km/h., 408 km, 2770 kg./24 passengers/23 paratroopers, Spain/Indonesia (licensed production)

CASA/Nurtanio CN-235 (also Airtech CN-235), turboprop, 454

km/h., 796 km, 3,575 kg./39 passengers/30 paratroopers, Spain/Indonesia; Airtech is company jointly owned by CASA (Spain) and Nurtanio (Indonesia)

Cessna 310, piston, 361 km/h., 2842 km, 6 passengers, USA

CN-235--see CASA/Nurtanio CN-235

DC-3 Dakota (C-47), piston, 220 km/h., 500 km, 2.5 ton/24 paratroopers, USA

DC-8, jet, Mach 0.8, 11,410 km, 30,240 kg./ 189 passengers, USA

DC-9, jet, 907 km/h., 3095 km, 14,118 kg./119 passengers, USA

DC-10, jet, 925 km/h.. 7,400 km, 43.3 ton/380 passengers, USA

DHC-4/DHC-4A Caribou, piston, 293 km/h., 2,103 km, 3965 kg./32 passengers/26 paratroopers, Canada

DHC-5/DHC-5D Buffalo, turboprop, 467 km/h., 1112 km, 8,164 kg./41 passengers, Canada

DHC-6 Twin Otter, turboprop, 338 km/., 1297 km, 1940 kg./20 passengers, Canada

Dornier Do-28 D/Do-28 D2 Skyservant, piston, 286 km/h., 2875 km, 1000 kg./13 passengers, FRG

Dornier Do-228-100, turboprop, 428 km/h., 600-1,740 km, 2.2 ton/15-20 passengers, FRG

EMB-110/EMB-110 P2 Bandeirante, turboprop, 417 km/h., 1900 km, 1681 kg./21 passengers, Brazil

EMB-121 Xingu, turboprop, 450 km/h., 2,352 km, 1,477 kg./9 passengers, Brazil; an executive aircraft

Falcon 20--see Mystere-Falcon 20

Fokker F-27 Mk.400/F-27 Mk.600, turboprop, 480 km/h., 1926/1935 km, 5727/5696 kg/40/44 passengers, Netherlands

Fokker F-27 Mk.400M, military version of F-27 Mk.400, 46 paratroopers, Netherlands

Fokker F-28, jet, 843 km/h., 1900 km, 10,478 kg./85 passengers, Netherlands

G-222L, turboprop, 439 km/h., 2409 km, 9000 kg./53 passengers/42 paratroopers, Italy

Gates Learjet 35, jet, 872 km/h., 4200 km, 8 passengers, USA

Gulfstream II, jet, 0.85 Mach, 6,579 km, 8 passengers, USA; an executive jet

Hawker Siddeley Dove, piston, 338 km/h., 620 km, 670 kg./11 passengers, Britain

IL-14 Crate, piston, 358 km/h., 2600 km, 5.3 ton/18 passengers/paratroopers, USSR

IL-18 Coot, turboprop, 675 km/h., 4,700 km, 13,500 kg./122 passengers, USSR

IL-76 Candid, jet, 800 km/h., 6700 km, 40 ton/over 100 passengers, USSR

L-100-20, turboprop, 581 km/h., 3889 km (maximum payload), 21,130 kg./92 paratroopers (optional), USA; civilian or military stretched Hercules

L-100-30, turboprop, 583 km/h., 3326 km (maximum payload), 23,014 kg./passengers--not less than L-100-20, USA; civilian or military stretched Hercules

L-410 UVP, turboprop, 360 km/h., 540km, 1300 kg./2 crew + 19 passengers, Czechoslovakia

MD-315 Flamant, piston, 147 km/h., 10 passengers, France

Merlin IV (corporate version of Metro III), turboprop, 524 km/h., 1805 km, 13-16 passengers, USA

Mystere-Falcon 10, jet, 900 km/h., 3,370 km, 7 passengers, France; an executive jet

Mystere-Falcon 20, jet, 855 km/h., 4170 km, 1180 kg./7 passengers, France; an executive jet

Mystere-Falcon 50, jet, 800 km/h., 6480 km, 8 passengers, France; an executive jet

Mystere-Falcon 900, jet, 927 km/h., 6412 km, 1,045 kg./15-18 passengers, France; an executive jet

Piper Navajo, turboprop, 386 km/h., 1742 km, 6-8 passengers, USA; an executive aircraft

Sabreliner 75A, jet, Mach. 0.80, 3,173 km, 10 passengers, USA; an executive jet

Short SC-7 Skyvan Srs. 3M, turboprop, 327 km/h., 1075 km, 2358 kg./22 passengers/16 paratroopers, Britain

Tu-124/Tu-134 Crusty, jet, 885 km/h., 3020 km, 8,200 kg./84 passengers, USSR

Turbo-Commander 690B, turboprop, 532 km/h., 11 passengers, USA

Westwind I/Westwind 1124, jet, 872 km/h., 4490 km, 10 passengers, Israel; an executive jet

Yak-40 Codling, jet, 550 km/h., 2,000 km, 2,720 kg./ 32 passengers, USSR

Bombs, Advanced

(designation, function, weight, country of origin)

ATA-1000, Cluster Bomb Unit (CBU), anti-personnel and AFV, 450 kg., Israel

ATA-500, CBU, 225 kg., Israel

Belouga Dispenser Weapon (BLG-66) Cluster Bomb Unit (CBU), anti-personnel & AFV, 290 kg., France

BL-755 Cluster Bomb, France

Cardoen CBU, cluster bomb, Chile

CBU-7A Cluster Bomb, USA

CBU-55 Cluster Bomb, anti-personnel, USA

Durandal Penetration Bomb, anti-runway bomb, 195 kg., France

Guillotine, laser guided bomb, Israel

JP-233 anti-runway bomb, Britain

Opher terminal guidance bomb, a kit added to US Mk.82 241 kg. bomb, Israel

Pyramid, anti-personnel, with terminal TV guidance, Israel

Rockeye Cluster Bomb Mk.20, anti-tank CBU, USA

Tal, cluster bomb unit (CBU), 220 kg., Israel

Helicopters, ASW

A-109/AS-109--see Helicopters, Attack

AB-212/Bell 212--see Helicopters, Medium Transport

Kamov Ka-25 Hormone--see Helicopters, Medium Transport

Mi-14 Haze, USSR

SH-3D (=Westland S-61), USA--see Helicopters, Heavy Transport

Westland Sea King HAS Mk.1/S-61A/AS-61A--see Helicopters, Heavy Transport

Westland Sea King Mk.47--nearly identical to Westland Sea King HAS Mk.1

Helicopters, Attack

(designation, NATO codename if relevant, max. speed, range, armament, country of origin)

Agusta A-109A, 311 km/h., 583 km, 4-8 BGM-71C Improved TOW, 2-3x7.62mm MG., 1x12.7mm HMG, 12x68mm rockets, Italy; a variant employed in ASW and/or naval attack role

AH-1S/AH-1G/AH-1J/AH-1Q Huey Cobra, 333 km/h., 577 km, 8xBGM-71C Improved TOW, 2x20mm mini-gun pod/68mm rockets/grenade dispensers, USA

AH-64A Apache, 300 km/h., 689 km, 8xAGM-114 Hellfire, 30mm gun, 68mm rockets, USA

Alouette III--see Helicopters, Light Transport; armed with AS-12 AGMs

500MG Defender/ TOW Defender/ Advanced Scout Defender, 244 km/h., 589 km range, 4xBGM-71C Improved TOW, 30mm chain gun, USA (derivative of Hughes 500D light transport helicopter, renamed McDonnell Douglas 500MD)

530MG, armament equivalent to Hughes 500MD, USA (military derivative of Hughes 530F, renamed McDonnell Douglas 530MG); see above and Helicopters, Light Transport

MBB BO-105, 6xHOT--see Helicopters, Light Transport

Mi-24 Hind D/E 330 km/h., 4xAT-2 Swatter ATGM, 1x12.7mm MG, 4x32 57mm rockets, 8 troops, USSR

Mi-25 Hind, improved version of Mi-24, USSR

Mi-35, export version of Mi-24, USSR

OH-58D, Combat Scout (AHIP), 22 km/h., 556 km, BGM-71C Improved TOW, LGM/or 2 AAMS, USA; derived from Bell 206 light helicopter, also designated Bell 406

SA-342/SA-342K/L/M Gazelle, 310 km/h., 360 km, 4xHOT/6xHOT/4xAS-11/2xAS-12, 2x7.62 mm. MG, France

Westland Lynx, 259 km/h., 630 km, 8xBGM-71C Improved TOW/8xHOT/6xAS-11 AGM, 2x20mm gun/7.62mm MG, 18x68mm rockets, 10 troops, Britain; also employed as medium transport

Helicopters, Heavy Transport

(designation, NATO codename if relevant, speed, range, accommodation, load, country of origin)

AS-61A/A4, Italy (licensed production of US-made S-61A); see S-61A

CH-47C Chinook, 304 km/h., 185 km radius (ferry range 2142 km), 44 troops/9843 kg., USA/Italy (licensed production)

CH-53/CH-53D, 315 km/h., 413 km, ca. 50 troops/5.9 ton/9 ton external payload, USA

KV-107/KV-107 IIA-17, 270 km/h., 1097 km, 25 passengers/12 passengers and 2268 kg, Japan (licensed production of USA-Boeing Vertol 107, Model II)

Mi-6 Hook, 300 km/h., 1450 km ferry range, 65 passengers/12,000 kg. internal payload/ 9000 kg. external payload, USSR

S-61 A/S-61 A4 (Sikorsky SH-3 Sea King), 267 km/h., 1005 km, 25 passengers/3630 kg., USA; employed mainly in ASW role, and in search and rescue with sonar, navigation Doppler radar

SA-321 Super Frelon (SA-3200--earlier aircraft), 275 km/h., 1020 km, 27-30 troops/5000 kg. external/internal load, France; can carry AM-39 Exocet AGM

SH-3 (AS-61A) VIP version of S-61 or AS-61, Italy; licensed production of S-61

Westland Commando Mk.2 (=S-61A & Westland Sea King transport version), 28 troops, Britain

Westland Sea King HAS Mk.1, 211 km/h., 1110 km, 22 passengers/2720 kg. internal load/3630 kg. external load, Britain; employed mostly in ASW role or in search and rescue role; equipped with Plessey dipping sonar, navigation Doppler radar system and search radar (licensed production of S-61A)

Helicopters, Light Transport

(designation, NATO codename if relevant, speed, range, accommodation, country of origin)

AB-47G/3B-1, 196 km/h., 367 km, pilot + 3 passengers, USA/Italy; licensed production of Bell 47

AB-206 (=Bell 206), Italy

Alouette II (early versions designated Sud-Aviation SE 313/3130; later version designated Aerospatiale SA-318), 205 km/h., 720 km, pilot + 4 passengers/600 kg., France

Alouette III (early version designated Sud-Aviation SE-316/3160; later version designated Aerospatiale SA-316/319), 210 km/h., 540 km, pilot + 6 passengers/750 kg., France

AS-350 Ecureuil, 230 km/h., 700 km, pilot + 5 passengers, France

Bell 206/206B JetRanger II/III, 225 km/h., 608 km, 2 pilots + 4 passengers, USA

Bell 206L LongRanger, improved Bell 206, 2 pilots + 5 passengers, USA

BK-117 (MBB/Kawasaki BK-117), 248 km/h., 493 km, pilot + 6 passengers, FRG/Japan

Hiller UH-12E, 154 km/h., 565 km, pilot + 3 passengers, USA

Hughes 500D, 282 km/h., 531 km, pilot + 4 passengers, USA (=Hughes 500MD attack helicopter for civilian or observation tasks); renamed 500D (McDonnell Douglas)

Hughes 530F, improvement of 500D, renamed 530F (McDonnell

Douglas), USA

Hughes 300C, 169 km/h., 370 km, pilot + 2 passengers, USA

IAR-316, Romania; license produced French SA-316 Alouette III, above

MBB B0-105, 270 km/h., 1112 km, pilot + 4 passengers /ca. 300 kg., FRG (=Nurtanio MBB NBO 105, Indonesia); can be fitted with HOT ATGM and used as attack helicopter; licensed production in Spain and Indonesia

Helicopters, Maritime Attack

(designation, maximum cruising speed, range, armament, country of origin)

AS-365 Dauphin=SA-365

HH-65A Dolphin, 257 km/h., USA (licensed production of French Aerospatiale SA-366 Dauphin 2)

SA-365N/365F Dauphin 2, 252 km/h., 4xAS-15TT air-to-ship missiles, France

SA-366--improved SA-365

Helicopters, Medium Transport

(designation, NATO codename if relevant, speed, range, accommodation, load, country of origin)

AB-205 (=Bell 205), Italy; production under USA license

AB-212 (=Bell 212), Italy; production under USA license

AB-214/214A (Bell 214), 250 km/h., 654 km, 16 passengers, Italy; production under USA license

AB-412 (=Bell 412), 226 km/h., 461 km, 14 troops, Italy; production under USA license

AS-332 Super Puma, 296 km/h, 644 km, 20 passengers, France

AS-532, also AS-532 Cougar, improved version of AS-332, above, France

Bell 205, 204 km/h., 511 km, 14 troops/1759 kg., USA (AB-205 in Italy)

Bell 212/212B, 259 km/h., 420 km, 10 troops/2268 kg. external load/1814 kg. internal load, USA (AB-212 in Italy)

Bell 222, 259 km/h., 532 km, 8-10 passengers/3,810 kg. external load/3,742 kg. internal load, USA

Bell 412, 259 km/h., 695 km, 14 troops/2268 kg. external load/1814 kg. internal load, USA; a four blade derivative of the Bell 212

HH-34F (S-58), 158 km/h., 450 km, 16 troops, USA

IAR-330 Puma, Rumania; licensed production of French SA-330 Puma (see below) Kaman HH-43F Huskie (also Kaman model 600-3/5/43B), 193km/h., 445 km, 10 passengers/1760 kg., USA; employed as maritime rescue or VIP helicopter

Kamov Ka-25 Hormone, 209 km/h., 650 km, in ASW role--search radar and dipping sonar, 12 passengers in search and rescue role, USSR; see Helicopters, ASW

Mi-2 Hoplite (also PZL Swidnik), 210 km/h., 580 km, 8 troops/2372 kg., Poland (designed in USSR)

Mi-4 Hound, 210 km/h., 400 km, 14 troops/1740 kg., USSR

Mi-8 Hip, 250 km/h., 425 km, 24 troops/4000 kg. internal/3000 kg. external load, USSR

S-76, 269 km/h., 1112 km, 12 troops/1814 kg. external payload, USA

SA-330 Puma, 263 km/h., 550 km, 16 equipped troops/3,200 kg., France

UH-60A Black Hawk (also designated S-70), 268 km/h., 600 km, 14 troops/3630 kg. external load, USA

Westland Lynx--see Helicopters, Attack

Westland Whirlwind Series 3, 159 km/h., 480 km (ferry range--834 km), 10 troops/ca. 1000 kg., Britain

Radars

(designation, effective range, country of origin)

AN/FPS-110, USA

AN/FPS-117, 350 km, USA

AN/TPS-32, 556 km, USA

AN/TPS-43, 408 km, USA

AN/TPS-59, 370 km, USA

AN/TPS-63, 296 km, USA

AN/TPS-70, 350 km, USA

AR-3 D, 24 km, Britain

AR-15, Britain

Cossor SSR, also Cossor monopulse secondary surveillance system, Britain

ELTA-2220/2206 148 km, Israel

Long Track, 150 km, USSR; associated with SA-6 & SA-8

P-12 Spoon Rest, 275 km, USSR

P-14 Tall King, 500-600 km, USSR

P-15 Flat Face, 210-250 km, USSR

P-15M Squat Eye, 200 km, USSR
P-35/37 Barlock, 390 km, USSR
S-713 Martello 3-D, 500 km, Britain
S-711, Britain
Square Pair, USSR
S-600, Britain
TRS-2100 (Tiger S), 110 km, France
TRS-2215, France
TRS-2230, France
Watchman, Britain

SAMs, Long Range
(designation, NATO codename if relevant, SP if relevant, range,
    country of origin)
HAWK, 35 km, USA
HQ-2J (CSA-1), PRC; copy of SA-2
MIM-23B Improved HAWK, 40 km, USA
SA-2 Guideline, 34.8 km, USSR
SA-3 Goa, 2.4-18.2 km, USSR
SA-5 Gammon, 250 km, USSR
SA-7, SA-9, Crotale, Crotale/Shahine, Rapier, Redeye, Stinger--see
    Army AA Defense--Missiles
SA-10 Grumble 70 km, USSR/Russia, a SAM with alleged ATBM
    capability
SA-12 Gladiator, 150 km, SAM, ATBM, USSR/Russia

Target Drones
(designation,type, country of origin)
Aerospatiale CT-20, target drone, France
Beech AQM-37A, target drone, USA
Beech MQM-107B, target drone, USA
MQM-74C Chukar II (also Northrop MQM-74C), target drone, USA
TTL BTT-3 Banshee, target drone, Britain

UAVs and Mini-UAVs
(designation, type, country of origin)
DRC-30, USSR
Hunter, mini-UAV, Israel
Mastiff, mini-UAV, Israel
Mirach-100, mini-UAV, Italy; can serve as target drone, or tactical
    cruise missile

MQM-74C Chukar II, UAV, USA
Pioneer, mini-UAV, Israel
R4E-50, Skyeye, mini-UAV, USA
Scout, mini-UAV, Israel
SD-3 UAV, USSR
Searcher, mini-UAV, Israel
Teledyne Ryan model 124 Firebee, mini-UAV, USA
Teledyne Ryan model 324 Scarab, UAV, USA

NAVY

Advanced AA & Anti-Missile Guns
(caliber, designation, guidance and task, country of origin)

30mm Vulcan-goalkeeper, radar-controlled AAG and anti-missile gun, Netherlands (system and radar) and USA (gun)

20mm Vulcan-Phalanx, radar-controlled AAG and anti-missile gun, USA

Air-to-Surf./anti-Ship Missiles
(designation, guidance system, range, launching aircraft, country of origin)

AM-39 Exocet, inertial + active homing, 70 km, Super Etendard and Mirage F-1 EQ5 fighters, SA-330, SA-321 helicopters, France; a derivative of MM-38 Exocet SSM

AS-15TT, radar, 14.8 km, AS-365 helicopter, France

Gabriel 3 AGM, active, 52.9 km, F-4E, Kfir, A-4, Seascan, Israel; a derivative of Gabriel 3 SSM

See also Air Force AGMs; the following can be employed against naval targets: AGM-62A Walleye; AGM-65A/B/C Maverick; AS-11; AS-12; AS-1 (Kennel); AS-5 (Kelt)

Armament, Advanced (excluding missiles)
(designation, type of weapon, guidance system, country of origin)

Mk.37, anti-submarine torpedo, acoustic homing, USA

NT-37E, anti-submarine torpedo, acoustic homing, USA; improvement of Mk.37

Stingray, anti-submarine torpedo, acoustic homing, Britain

ASW Vessels
(designation, standard displacement, full load displacement, speed, AS weapons, guns, missiles, country of origin)

Chinese ASW vessel, PRC

Koni class ASW frigate, 1700 ton, 2000 ton, 32 knots, 2x12 barrelled RBU 6000, 4x3", 4x30mm, SA-N4 SAM (in Algeria)/SS-N-2C SSM (in Libya), USSR

Le Fougeux class, 325 ton, 400 ton, 18.5 knots, 2x anti-submarine mortar, 1x76mm, 2x40mm, France

Petya II class, 950 ton, 1160 ton, 32 knots, 4x16 barrelled RBU, 2 depth charge racks, 4x3", USSR

Shanghai III, 120 ton, 155 ton, 30 knots, 8 depth charges and variable depth sonar, 2x5mm, 1x25mm, PRC; similar to Shanghai II, see Gunboats/MTBs

Sirius class--see patrol craft

SO-1 class, 170 ton, 215 ton, 28 knots, 4x5 barrelled RBU, 4x25mm, USSR

Auxiliary Vessels

(designation, function, displacement, speed, country of origin)

Amphion class, repair ship, 14,490 ton full load, 16.5 knots, USA

Armed fishing vessel, coast guard & fishery protection, Algeria

Brooke Marine 900 ton, royal yacht, 900 ton, 12 knots, Britain

Cargo vessel (765 DWT), Pakistan

Cargo ship, 1500 GRT, 11 knots, Norway

Cheverton type tender, 3.3 ton, 8 knots, Britain

Conoship Groningen coastal freighter, 1380 DWT, 11 knots, Netherlands

Durance class, tanker/supply ship, 10,500 ton full load, 19 knots, France

Harbor craft, 746 ton, 14 knots (former royal Iraqi yacht)

Harbor tanker, 1700 ton full load, Italy

Jansen research vessel (named Ekteshaf), 1,250 ton, FRG

LSD-1 type, logistic support ship, 2470 ton full load, 15 knots, Britain

Luhring Yard, supply ship, 3250 DWT, 16 knots, FRG

Maintenance and repair craft, ex-British LCT, 900 ton full load, 9 knots, Britain

Mala midget submarine (2-man vessel, 7.6 meter), Yugoslavia

Mazagon Docks, water tanker, 9430 ton, 15 knots, India

Niryat diving tender--see Patrol Craft

Okhtensky tugs, USSR (assembled in Egypt)

P-6, employed as training vessel--see Gunboats/MTBs

PN-17 support tanker, 650 ton full load, Yugoslavia

Poluchat I class, employed as torpedo recovery vessel--see Patrol Craft

Ro-ro transport ship, 3100 ton full load, Italy

Royal Yacht, 1450 DWT, 22.5 knots, Denmark; carries a helicopter

Royal yacht, 650 ton, 26 knots, Netherlands

Spasilac, salvage ship, 1300 ton, 15 knots, Yugoslavia

Sekstan survey ship (also training ship), 345 ton full load, 10 knots, USSR

Stromboli class, support ship, 8706 ton full load, 20 knots, Italy

Survey craft, 23.6 ton, 13.5 knots, Britain

Survey ship, 240 ton, Yugoslavia

Swan Hunter replenishment ship, 33,014 ton full load, 21.5 knots, Britain

Swimmer delivery vehicles

Training craft, 109 ton full load, 22 knots, FRG

Training frigate, 1850 ton full load, 27 knots, can carry 4 Exocet SSM launchers, 1x57mm gun, 2x20mm gun, Yugoslavia

Training ship, 350 ton, FRG

Training ship (former royal yacht), 4650 ton, 16 knots, Britain

Water carrier boat, 125 DWT, Yugoslavia

Water tanker, 9430 ton, 15 knots, India--see Mazagon Docks water tanker

Yelva class, diving support ship, 295 ton, 12.5 knots, USSR

YW-83 water tanker, 1250 ton, 10 knots, similar to Italian harbor tanker, USA

"108" class, target craft, 60 ton full load, 26 knots, Yugoslavia

Gunboats/MTBs

(designation, gunboat or MTB, length, speed, torpedo tubes if relevant, guns, country of origin)

Brooke Marine gunboat, 123 ft., 25 knots, 1x76mm, 1x20mm (=Brooke Marine 123 ft. MFPB), Britain

Fredrikshavn Vaerft gunboat, 45.8 meter, 20 Knots, 1x40mm, Denmark

Hainan class gunboat, 59 meter, 30.5 knots, 2x2x57mm, 2x2x25mm, 4xRBU 1200 ASW and depth charges, PRC

Jaguar class MTB, 139.4 ft., 42 knots, 4x21" torpedo tubes, 2x40mm, FRG

Kebir, see Brooke Marine 123 ft; same vessel, licensed production in Algeria, 2x23mm gun instead of 1x20mm

Lurssen FPB 38 type gunboat, 38.5 meter, 32 knots, 2x40mm, 1x57mm rocket launcher, FRG

P-4 class MTB, 62.3 ft., 55 knots, 2x21" torpedo tubes, 2x14.5mm, 8x122mm MRL, USSR

P-6 class MTB, 84.2 ft., 43 knots, 2x21" torpedo tubes, 4x25mm, USSR

PR-72 class gunboat, 57.5 meter, 28 knots, 1x76mm, 1x40mm, France

Shanghai II class gunboat, 128 ft., 30 knots, 4x37mm, 4x25mm, PRC

Shershen class MTB/gunboat, 118.1 ft., 40 knots, 4x21" torpedo tubes, 4x30mm, USSR

Gun Corvettes

(designation, standard displacement, full load displacement, speed, guns, country of origin)

C-58, 560 ton, 36 knots, 1x76mm, 2x40mm, Algeria; with assistance from Bulgaria

PF-103 class, 900 ton, 1135 ton, 20 knots, 2x3", 2x40mm, 2x23mm, USA

Vosper Thornycroft Mk.1B (Tobruk), 440 ton, 500 ton, 18 knots, 1x4", 2x40mm, Britain

Gun Frigates

(designation, standard displacement, full load displacement, speed, guns, country of origin)

Savage class, 1200 ton, 1490 ton, 19 knots, 2x3", 2x20mm, USA

Hovercraft

(designation, gross weight, disposable weight, speed, guns, country of origin)

BH-7 (Wellington) class, 50 ton, 14 ton, 60 knots, 2 Browning MG or 4xRGM-84A Harpoon SSM, Britain

Sealand Mk.2/Mk.3 class, 3 ton, 1 ton, 42 knots, Britain

Skima 12 class, Britain

SRN-6 (Winchester) class, 10 ton, 3.6 ton, 52 knots, 1x7.62mm MG, Britain

Tropmire Ltd., 6.4 ton, 4.2 ton, 45 knots, Britain

Landing Craft, Logistics (LCL)

(designation, full load displacement, speed, country of origin)

Siong Huat 40 meter, Singapore

Vosper 320 ton, 9.5 knots, Singapore

Landing Craft, Mechanized (LCM)

(designation, full load displacement, speed, country of origin)

150 ton Fairy Marine, 150 ton, 8 knots, Britain

Loadmaster, 350 ton (max. load 150 ton), 10.5 knots, Britain (also
   designated as LCT)
LCM-6, 62 ton, 9 knots, USA
T-4, 94 ton, 9 knots (unconfirmed--10 knots), USSR
US type LCM, 60 ton, 11 knots, USA
26 ton LCM, FRG

Landing Craft, Tank (LCT)
(designation, full load displacement, speed, guns, country of origin)
Ashdod class, 730 ton, 10.5 knots, 2x20mm, Israel
C-107 class, 600 ton, 8.5 knots, 2x20mm, Turkey
DTM-221 class, 410 ton, 9 knots, 1x20mm, 2x12.7mm HMG,
   Yugoslavia
EDIC class, 670 ton, 8 knots, 2x20mm, 1x120mm mortar, France
Loadmaster, 150 ton, 10.5 knots, Britain
Polnochny class, 1150 ton, 18 knots, 4x30mm, 2x140mm rocket
   launchers, USSR
Shikmona class, 230 ton, 10 knots, 2x20mm, Israel (occasionally
   designated Kishon class)
750 ton LCT, 750 ton, 9 knots, Netherlands
48.8 meter LCT, no details

Landing Craft, Utility (LCU)
(designation, full load displacement, speed, guns, country of origin)
250 ton LCU, Iran
Cheverton 45 ton, 7 knots, Britain
Cheverton 30 ton, 6 knots, Britain
Impala Marine 75 ton, 9 knots, Britain
Lewis Offshore, 85 ton, 8 knots, Britain
Ondatra class, 93 ton, 10 knots, USSR
SMB-1 class, 360 ton, 10 knots, USSR
Swiftships, 390 ton, USA
US LCU 1431 class (similar to LCU 510 class), 320 ton, 10 knots,
   2x20mm, USA
US LCU 1466 class, 360 ton, 10 knots, 2x20mm, USA
US LCU 1610 class, 375 ton, 11 knots, 2x12.7mm HMG, USA
Vosper Thornycroft 170 ton, 10 knots, Britain
Vydra class, 600 ton, 11 knots, USSR

Landing Ship, Logistics (LSL)

(designation, full load displacement, speed, guns, country of origin)

Batral class, 1409 ton, 16 knots, 2x40mm, 2x81mm mortars, France

Brooke Marine, 2000 ton class, 12 knots, 1x76mm, 2x20mm, Britain (also LST)

Brooke Marine, 2500 ton, 15.5 knots, 2x2x40mm, Britain (also LST)

Hengam class, 2540 ton, 14.5 knots, 4x40mm, Britain (also LST)

Landing Ship, Mechanized (LSM)

(designation, full load displacement, speed, guns, country of origin)

LSM-1, 1095 ton, 12.5 knots, 2x40mm, 4x20mm, USA

Landing Ship, Tank (LST)

(designation, full load displacement, speed, guns, country of origin)

3500 ton, 15.5 knots, Denmark

Bat Sheva class, 1150 ton, 10 knots, 2x20mm, Netherlands

LST (South Korean), South Korea

PS-700 class, 2800 ton, 15.4 knots, 6x40mm, 1x81mm mortar, France

Ropucha class, 4400 ton, 17 knots, 4x57mm, USSR

MFPBs

(designation, standard displacement, full load displacement, speed, missiles, guns, country of origin)

"400" Type, Yugoslavia

Aliya--see Sa'ar 4.5, below

Combattante II, 234 ton, 255 ton, 34.5 knots, 4xRGM-84A Harpoon or 4xOTOMAT 2, 1x76mm or 1x40mm, France

Combattante III, 395 ton, 425 ton, 38.5 knots, 8xMM-40 Exocet, 1x76mm, 2x40mm, 2x30mm, France

Combattante IV, MM-40 Exocet, France; advanced version of Combattante III, above

Dvora, 47 ton, 36 knots, 2xGabriel 2/3 SSM, 2x20mm, Israel; see also Patrol Craft

Hegu, 68 ton, 81 ton, 40 knots, 2 HY-2 SSM (Chinese SS-N2 Styx), 2x25mm, PRC; copy of Soviet Komar

Komar, 68 ton, 81 ton, 40 knots, 2xSS-N-2 (Styx), 2x25mm, USSR

Lazaga (formerly Cormoran/Lazaga), 355 ton (full load), 36 knots, 4xExocet, 1x76mm, 1x40mm, Spain (licensed production of FRG's Lurssen Type-143); boats for Sudan to be armed with RGM-84 Harpoon SSM

Lurssen FPB-57, 353 ton, 398 ton, 38 knots, 4xMM-40 Exocet, 1x76mm, 2x40mm, FRG

Lurssen TNC-45, 228 ton (half load), 38 knots, 4xExocet, or 4xOTOMAT 2, 1x76mm, 1x40mm, FRG

October, 71 ton, 82 ton, 40 knots, 2xOTOMAT, 2x30mm, Egypt (electronics installed in Britain)

Ossa I, 160 ton, 210 ton, 36 knots, 2xSS-N-2 (Styx), 2x2x30mm, USSR

Ossa II--see Ossa I, stronger engine

P-48, 250 ton full load, 22 knots, 8xSS-12, 2x40mm, France/Belgium

PGG-1 class (Peterson), 384 ton full load, 38 knots, 4xRGM-84A Harpoon, 1x76mm, 2x20mm, 2x20mm Vulcan-Phalanx, USA

Province class, 311 ton, 363 ton, 40 knots, 6xMM-40 Exocet, 1x76mm, 2x40mm, Britain

Rade Koncar, 240 ton (full load), 40 knots, 4xSSN-2 (Styx), 1x76mm, 1x40mm, 2x30mm, Yugoslavia

Ramadan, 262 ton, 312 ton, 37 knots, 4xOTOMAT 2, 1x76mm, Britain

Reshef--see Sa'ar 4

Sa'ar 2 & 3, 220 ton, 250 ton, 40 knots, Gabriel 2/3 SSM, 1x76mm or 2x40mm, France

Sa'ar 4, 415 ton, 450 ton, 32 knots, 4xRGM-84A Harpoon, 5xGabriel 2/3, 2x76mm, 2x20mm, Israel

Sa'ar 4.5, 488 ton, 31 knots, 4xGabriel, 4xRGM-84A Harpoon, 1x76mm, Israel; carries a helicopter

Mine Warfare Vessels

(designation, standard displacement, full load displacement, guns, mines if relevant, country of origin)

Adjutant class minesweeper, 320 ton, 375 ton, 1x20mm, USA

Cape class minesweeper, 180 ton, 235 ton, 1x12.7mm HMG, USA

Kondor II minesweeper, 635 ton full load, 3x2x25mm, FRG (former GDR)

MSC 292/MSC 268 class, 320 ton, 378 ton, 2x20mm, USA

MSC 322 class, 320 ton, 407 ton, 2x20mm, USA

Natya class minesweeper, 650 ton, 950 ton, 4x30mm, 4x25mm, 10 mines, USSR

Nestin minesweeper, 65 ton (standard), 3x20mm, Yugoslavia

Sirius class minesweeper/patrol craft, 400 ton, 440 ton, 1x40mm, 1x20mm, France

Sonya class, 450 ton (full load), 2x30mm, 2x25mm, 5 mines, USSR

SRN-6--see Hovercraft; may serve as mine-laying vessel

T-43 class minesweeper, 500 ton, 580 ton, 4x37mm, 8x14.5mm, 20 mines, USSR

T-58 minesweeper corvette, 900 ton (full load), 4x57mm, 4x25mm, USSR

T-301 class, 159 ton, 180 ton, 2x37mm, 2xMMG, USSR

Tripartite type minesweeper, 510 ton, 588 ton, 1x20mm, Netherlands, Belgium and France

Vanya class minesweeper, 200 ton, 245 ton, 2x30mm, 5 mines, USSR

Yevgenia class minesweeper, 70 ton, 80 ton, 2x14.5mm HMG, USSR

Yurka class minesweeper, 400 ton, 460 ton, 4x30mm, 10 mines, USSR

Missile Corvettes

(designation, standard displacement, full load displacement, speed, missiles, guns, country of origin)

Assad class, 670 ton full load, 33 knots, 4xOTOMAT, 1x76mm, 2x35mm, Italy; formerly designated Wadi class

Lurssen 62 meter type, 630 ton, 32 knots, 4xMM-40 Exocet/RGM-84A Harpoon, Aspide/Albatros SAMs (in Bahrain) or Sadral SAMs (in UAE), FRG

Nanuchka II class, 780 ton, 900 ton, 30 knots, 4xSS-N-2 SSM, 2xSA-N4, 2x57mm, USSR; in Syria--4xSS-N-9 SSM (unconfirmed)

PCG-1 class (Tacoma Boatbuilding 245 ft.), 732 ton, 815 ton, 30 knots, 8xRGM-84A Harpoon, 1x76mm, 1x20mm Vulcan-Phalanx, 2x20mm, USA

Sa'ar 5 (Lahav) 1075 ton, 1200 ton full load, 33 knots, 8xHarpoon, 8xGabriel, Barak, 1x76mm, 25mm Sea Vulcan, USA/Israeli components; operational 1994-95

Tarantul class, 580 ton full load, 36 knots, 4xSSN-2C, 1x76mm 2x30mm 6 barrels, USSR

Wadi class--see Assad class

Missile Destroyers

(designation, standard displacement, full load displacement, speed, missiles, guns, country of origin)

Battle class, 2325 ton, 3360 ton, 31 knots, 4xStandard, 4x4.5", 2x40mm, Britain

Sumner class, 2200 ton, 3320 ton, 34 knots, 4x2xStandard, 4x5", USA

Missile Frigates

(designation, standard displacement, full load displacement, speed, missiles, guns, country of origin)

Descubierta, 1233 ton, 1479 ton, 26 knots, MM-38 Exocet or MM-40 Exocet, Aspide SAMs, 1x76mm, 2x40mm, Spain; in Morocco carrying MM-38/MM-40, in Egypt carrying RGM-84A Harpoon SSM

F-2000, 2610 ton full load, 30 knots, 8xOTOMAT 2, 1x100mm, 4x40mm, France; carries a helicopter

Jianghu, 1568 ton, 1900 ton, 26.5 knots, 4xHY-2 (Hai Ying 2), 2x100mm, 4x2x37mm, 2xRBU 1200 ASW rocket launcher, 2 depth charge racks, PRC; planned: RGM-84A Harpoon SSMs

Koni, see ASW Vessels

La Fayette, 3,500 ton, 25 knots, 8xMM-40 Exocet, Crotale Navale, 1x100mm, France

Lupo class, 2208 ton, 2500 ton, 35 knots, 8xOTOMAT 2, 1x5", 4x40mm, Italy; carries a helicopter

Vosper Mk.5 class, 1220 ton, 1540 ton, 34 knots, 5xSea Killer SSM, 3x Seacat SAM, 1x4.5", 2x35mm, Britain

Vosper Thornycroft Mk.7, 1325 ton, 1625 ton, 37.5 knots, 4x OTOMAT, 1x4.5", 2x40mm, 2x35mm, Britain, refitted and modernized in Italy

Patrol Craft

(designation, length in feet or meters, speed, guns, country of origin)

Abeking & Rasmussen, 75.2 ft., 27 knots, 3x20mm, FRG

Abeking & Rasmussen, 26.2 meters, 40 knots, FRG

Acror 46, 14.5 meters, 32 knots, 2x12.7mm HMG, France

Attacker, Britain

Aztec (Crestitalia), 9 meters, Italy

Baglietto type Mangusta, 98.4 ft., 32.5 knots, 1x40mm, 1x20mm, Italy

Baglietto type 20 GC, 66.9 ft., 36 knots, 1x20mm, Italy

Baglietto GC-23, 23 meters, 38 knots, 1x20mm, 2x12.7mm HMG, Italy

Bertram class (Egypt), 28 ft., 3x12.7mm, 4x122mm MRL, USA

Bertram class Enforcer (Jordan), 38 ft., USA

Bertram 20 ft., USA

Bertram (Jordan), 30.4 ft., 1x12.7mm HMG, 1x7.62mm MG, USA

Blohm & Voss 38.9 meters, 38 knots, 2x20mm, FRG

Boghammar, 13 meters, Sweden

Bogomol, 39 meters, 37 knots, 1x76mm, USSR

Broadsword class, 105 ft., 32 knots, 1x75mm recoilless rifle, 1x12.7mm, USA

Byblos class, 66 ft., 18.5 knots, 1x20mm, 2xMG, France

Camcraft 77 ft., 25 knots, 2x20mm, USA

Camcraft 65 ft., 25 knots, 1x20mm, USA

Cantieri Posillipo, 65 ft., 24 knots, 1x20mm, Italy

Cape class (US Coast Guard)--see Mine Warfare Vessels

CG-27, 87.6 ft., 25 knots, Sweden

CH class, 130.8 ft., 16 knots, 2x20mm, France

Ch. Navals de l'Esterel, 124.7 ft., 27 knots, 2x40mm, 2x12.7mm HMG, France

Ch. Navals de l'Esterel, 104 ft., 30 knots, 1x20mm, France

Ch. Navals de l'Esterel, 83 ft., 23 knots, 1x20mm, France

Chaho, 26 meters, 40 knots, 2x23mm, 2x14.5mm, 1 BM-21 MRL, North Korea

Cheverton, 27 ft., 8 knots, Britain

Chinese 25 meter patrol boat, 25 meters, PRC

CMN, 40.6 meters, 25 knots, 2x40mm, 2xMG, France

Crestitalia, 70 ft., 35 knots, 1x30mm, 1x20mm, Italy

Dabur, 64.9 ft., 21.8 knots, 2x20mm, 2xMG, USA/Israel (licensed production)

Damen Polycat 1450, 14.5 meters, 26 knots, 1x20mm, Netherlands

de Castro (Nisr class), 1x20mm, Egypt

Dvora=Dvora MFPB without missiles, Israel

Fairey Marine Interceptor class, 25 ft., 35 knots, Britain

Fairey Marine Spear class, 29.8 ft., 26 knots, 3x7.62mm MG, Britain

Fairey Marine Sword class, 44.9 ft., 28 knots, 1x7.62mm MG, Britain

Fateh, 18 meters, 35 knots, Iran

Garian class, 106 ft., 24 knots, 1x40mm, 1x20mm, Britain

Hyundai, South Korea

Kedma class, 67 ft., 25 knots, 2 MG, Japan

Keith Nelson, 57 ft., 19 knots, 2x20mm, Britain

Keith Nelson, 44 ft., 26 knots, 1x12.7mm HMG, 2x7.62mm MG, Britain

Keith Nelson (Dhafeer) class, 40.3 ft., 19 knots, 2x7.62mm MG, Britain

Le Fougeux (modified)--see ASW vessels

Lurssen, 23 meters, FRG/Spain (under license)

Magnum Sedan, 27.3 ft., 60 knots, USA

Niryat II, 95.1 ft., 12 knots, USSR

Osprey, 55 meters, 20 knots (unconfirmed), Denmark

P-6--see Gunboats/MTBs (same craft with torpedo tubes removed)

P-32, 32 meters, 29 knots, 2x20mm, France

P-200D Vigilance, 60 meters, similar to Lazaga MFPB, Spain; armed with guns only

P-802 (Watercraft P-802), 30 knots, Britain/Algeria (assembly)

P-1200, 39 ft., 21 knots, Britain

P-1903, 19.2 meters, 30 knots, 2x12.7mm, HMG, Netherlands

P-2000, 20 meters, 22.5 knots (unconfirmed), 1x20mm, Britain

PBR (Yatush), 32 ft., 25 knots, 2x12.7mm HMG, USA/Israel

Peterson Mk. II, 50 ft., 28 knots, 4x12.7mm, HMG, USA

PGM-71 (Improved PGM), 100 ft., 1x40mm, 2x20mm, 2x12.7mm HMG, USA

PO-2, 82 ft., 30 knots, 2x25mm or 2x12.7mm HMG, USSR

Police boat, 20 ft.

Poluchat I, 97.1 ft., 20 knots, 2x14.5mm, USSR

Rapier class, 50 ft., 28 knots, 2xMG, USA

Seagull, 24 meters (aluminum boat), 30 knots, South Korea

Sewart class, 40 ft., 30 knots, 1x12.7mm HMG, USA

Simmoneau Type, 15.8 meters, 33 knots, 1x20mm, 2x7.62mm MG, France

Sirius class, 152 ft., 10 knots, 1x40mm, 1x20mm, France

Skorpion class, 55.8 ft., 30 knots, 2x7.62mm MG, FRG SO-1--see ASW vessels

Super Dvora (Improved Dvora), 21.6 meters, 40 knots, 2x20mm Oerlikon, 2x7.62mm MAG LMG, Israel

Swift FPB-20, 65 ft., USA

Swiftships, 32 meters, USA/Egypt

Thornycroft 100 ft., 12/18 knots, 1x3.7" howitzer, 2x3" mortar, 4xMG or 1x20mm, Britain (Libyan boats--18 knots, Iraqi boats--12 knots; Iraqi boats built under license in Yugoslavia)

Thornycroft 78 ft., 22.5 knots, 1xMG, Britain

Thornycroft 50 ft., Singapore

Thornycroft 45.5 ft., 23 knots, Singapore (similar to Vosper Thornycroft 46 ft.)

Thornycroft 36 ft., 27 knots, Britain

Thornycroft 21 ft., Britain

Timsah class, 31 meters, 25 knots, 2x20mm Oerlikon, Egypt

Tracker/Tracker II, 64 ft., 29 knots, 1x20mm, Britain

USCG type 95 ft.--see above, Cape class, and Mine Warfare Vessels

VC large patrol craft, 31.5 meters, 30 knots, 2x20mm (can carry SS-12 SSMs), France

Vosper 56 ft., 29 knots, Singapore, similar to Vosper Thornycroft 56 ft.

Vosper 25 meters, 25.8 knots, 1x20mm, 2x7.62mm MG, Singapore

Vosper 36 ft., Singapore; similar to British Thornycroft 36 ft.

Vosper Thornycroft 110 ft., 27 knots, 2x20mm, Britain

Vosper Thornycroft 103 ft., 27 knots, 2x20mm, Britain

Vosper Thornycroft 78 ft.--see Thornycroft 78 ft.

Vosper Thornycroft 75 ft., 24.5 knots, 2x20mm, Britain

Vosper Thornycroft 56 ft., 30 knots, 2xMG, Britain

Vosper Thornycroft 50 ft., Britain/Singapore (identical to Thornycroft 50 ft.)

Vosper Thornycroft 36.4 ft.--see Thornycroft 36 ft.

VT HAWK (Vosper Thornycroft), 30 meters, 32 knots, 2x30mm, 1x20mm, 2x12.7mm, Britain

Wasp 30 meters, 22 knots, 1x25mm chain gun, 2x7.62mm MG, Britain

Wasp 20 meters (65.8 ft.), 37 knots, 2xMG, Britain

Wasp 11 meters, 24 knots, Britain

Watercraft & Shoreham 45.6 ft., 22 knots, 1xMG, Britain; in UAE--25 knots, 2x7.62mm MG

Whittingham & Mitchell 75 ft., 2x20mm, Britain

Yugoslav type 15, 16.9 meters, 16 knots, 1x20mm, 2x7.62mm MG, Yugoslavia

Zhuk class, 80.7 ft., 34 knots, 2x14.5mm, 1x12.7mm HMG, USSR

SAMs (Shipborne)

(designation, guidance system, range, country of origin)

Aspide (Albatross/Aspide), semi-active radar, 18 km, Italy

Barak--see SSMs (Shipborne)

Crotale Navale, radar or IR guidance, 13 km, France; derived from Crotale SAM

SA-N-4, radar-guided, 9.6 km, USSR; derived from SA-8B (see Army AA Defense--missiles)

Sadral, infra-red homing, 6km, France; maritime version of short range Mistral SAM

Standard, semi-active radar homing, 18.5 km, USA

Seacat, radio-command, radar/TV or visual, 6 km, Britain; can be employed as SSM or as shipborne SAM

Special Maritime Forces

(partial list; designation, crew, displacement in tons, country of origin)

R-2 Mala midget submarine, 2, 1.5 ton, Yugoslavia

Sea Horse midget submarine, 2+6-7 divers, 17 ton (surfaced), 25 ton (dived), North Korea

SSMs (Shipborne)

(designation, NATO codename if relevant, guidance system, effective range, country of origin)

Barak (employed as SAM, SSM and anti-missile missile), 10 km, Israel

C-801, SSM, PRC; copy of French MM-38 or MM-40 Exocet

Gabriel 2, semiactive, 20.4 km, Israel

Gabriel 3, active, 36 km, Israel

HY-2 (Hai Ying-2, Silkworm), PRC; copy of Soviet SS-N-2

MM-38 Exocet, inertial and active homing, 42.6 km, France

MM-40 Exocet, inertial, 70.4 km, France

OTOMAT Mk.1/OTOMAT Mk.2, active homing radar, 183.3 km, joint French-Italian manufacture

RGM-84A Harpoon, active radar guidance, 111.2 km, USA

Seacat--see SAMs (Shipborne)

Seakiller, radio command, 25 km, Italy

SS-12, ATGM, France; employed on naval craft as anti-ship missile; see Army, ATGMs and Air Force, AGMs

SS-N-2/SS-N-2B (Improved Styx), autopilot, active radar homing, 40 km, USSR

SSMs (coastal defense)

(designation, guidance system, range, country of origin)

SSC-1B Sepal, radio command and active radar guidance, 250 km, USSR

SSC-2B Samlet, radar homing, 80 km, USSR

SSC-3, inertial and terminal homing, 80-90 km, USSR; coastal defense version of SSN-2 improved Styx shipborne SSM

HY-2 (Hai Ying-2, Silkworm), PRC; identical to Hai Ying-2 SSM shipborne

C-801, 70km (unconfirmed), PRC

Submarines

(designation/NATO codename if relevant, surfaced displacement, dived displacement, main armament, country of origin)

F class Foxtrot, 1950 ton, 2400 ton, 10x21" torpedo tubes, USSR

IKL type 209, 1260 ton, 1440 ton, 8x21", FRG

IKL/Vickers type 206, 420 ton, 600 ton, 8x21" torpedo tubes, Britain, FRG design

K class Kilo, 2500 ton, 3200 ton, 8x21" torpedo tubes, USSR/Russia

R class Romeo, 1400 ton, 1800 ton, 8x21" torpedo tubes, USSR

W class Whiskey, 1080 ton, 1350 ton, 6x21" torpedo tubes, USSR

CHRONOLOGY

Chronology: Key Strategic Events, 1992-93

1992

January 11 Shadli Ben Jedid resigns from the presidency of Algeria. Army suspends national elections (won by the Muslim fundamentalist Islamic Salvation Front) and deploys military units in main cities of Algeria. Muhammad Boudiaf, returning from exile in Morocco, is sworn in as Head of Higher State Council (the ruling junta).

January 13-16 Third session of bilateral peace negotiations in Washington DC.

January 17 IAEA reports that Iraq has destroyed German-made equipment for the production of enriched uranium.

January 17 Moledet and Tehiya parties withdraw from the Shamir government in Israel, leaving it with the support of 59 out of 120 Knesset members. Labor and Likud parties subsequently agree to hold elections on June 23, 1992.

January 21 US intelligence claims Libya might be building a second chemical weapons plant.

January 28 Multilateral Middle East peace conference opens in Moscow, under US-Russian auspices. Palestinian, Lebanese and Syrian delegations abstain from participation.

January 30 German naval vessel apprehends German freighter carrying 16 Czech T-72 tanks, part of a sale of 300 to Syria.

January 31-February 1 George Habash, leader of PFLP, hospitalized in Paris for medical treatment; expelled from France after 14 hours.

February 9 Military junta declares state of emergency for a year in Algeria.

February 12 IAEA inspectors visit Iran, declare that all nuclear programs there are for peaceful purposes.

February 14-15 Three Israeli Arab Muslim activists infiltrate military camp in Israel, killing three soldiers.

February 16 Israeli helicopters attack a Hizballah convoy in South Lebanon, killing Shaykh Abas Mussawi, his wife and son. Mussawi was the secretary general of the Hizballah party and terror group.

February 19 Israeli Labor Party primaries; Yitzhak Rabin selected as party's candidate for the premiership.

February 24 US Secretary of State James Baker testifies before US House Appropriations Committee's Subcommittee on Foreign Operations regarding Israel's request to receive $10 billion in loan guarantees over five years. Baker argues that Israel should either agree to a settlement freeze in the Territories or accept a much smaller one-year loan guarantee.

February 24-March 4 Fourth round of Israeli-Arab peace talks held in Washington.

February 26-29 Iraq refuses to allow UN team to dismantle a Scud-related production plant and to destroy missile production equipment.

March 7 Israeli embassy staffer in Ankara dies in Hizballah car bomb attack.

March 9 A North Korean ship allegedly carrying Scud missiles for Iran anchors at Bandar Abbas, despite US attempts to intercept it. A second ship arrives in Iran on March 13.

March 11 Iraqi Deputy Prime Minister Tariq Aziz states to the UN Security Council that Iraq has destroyed all its weapons of mass destruction.

March 12 King Hussein of Jordan meets in Washington with President George Bush. First meeting since the 1991 Gulf War.

March 17 A Palestinian Arab fanatic stabs to death two Israelis (one of them a girl of 14) and wounds about 19 children before being shot to death in Tel Aviv.

March 17 Israeli embassy in Argentina blown up, 8 persons dead, 260 wounded. Islamic Jihad takes credit for the attack.

March 18 Presidents Mubarak of Egypt and Asad of Syria meet in Cairo, state opposition to renewed military action against Iraq.

March 19 Iraq discloses that it has concealed 89 Scuds and other ballistic missiles from UN inspectors.

March 20-25 Fighting in Northern Iraq between Turkish troops and planes and Kurdish PKK. Allegedly 75 killed.

March 22 IAEA officials allege that Iraq is withholding information on its nuclear programs.

March 22 A team of US Army inspectors visits Israel to investigate charges that Israel has exported Patriot technology to PRC. On April 2 the US Department of State announces that its investigators found no such evidence.

March 24 A UN team leaves Iraq after destroying 463 leaky chemical rockets during a 32-day stay.

March 30 UN inspection team in Iraq reports that Iraq destroyed 80-100 Scud missiles in 1991, but that many more missiles remained.

April 5 Iranian F-4 fighter aircraft attack a camp of pro-Iraqi Mujahidin i-Halq in Iraq. One F-4 shot down, its pilots captured by Iraq.

April 6 An attack on a convoy of Israeli army vehicles in South Lebanon claims two Israeli soldiers killed and five wounded.

April 7 PLO Chairman Yasir Arafat disappears briefly over the Libyan desert during a flight from Sudan to Tunisia. The aircraft performs an emergency landing; Arafat slightly injured.

April 9 Iraq has reportedly moved SAMs (SA-2 & SA-3) to Mosul, north of the 36th parallel, allegedly as a defense against Iranian air attacks. On April 10, allied forces in northern Iraq issue a warning that this could lead to confrontation.

April 15 UN sanctions against Libya go into effect. The sanctions halt air flights to and from Libya and sales of arms to Libya. US freezes US-held assets of Libyan companies. The sanctions are imposed following Libya's refusal to surrender persons accused of blowing up Pan Am flight 103 over Scotland in 1988 and a UTA flight over Niger in 1989.

April 16 UN committee for the demarcation of the border between Iraq and Kuwait resolves to move the border in Kuwait's favor in Umm Qasr harbor and near the Rumaylah oil field.

April 27 Fifth round of bilateral Israeli-Arab peace talks opens in Washington.

May 6-16 Lebanese Prime Minister Oumar Karame resigns (May 6). Rashid al-Solh forms a new government (May 16).

May 11 Multilateral Arab-Israeli working groups meet in Brussels and Washington.

May 19-28 Escalation of hostilities in the Israeli Security Zone in South Lebanon.

May 20 US House Judiciary Committee announces inquiry into the US government's relations with Iraq prior to the Iraqi invasion of Kuwait. Allegedly the US administration pressed for continued aid programs to Iraq despite information that Iraq was diverting funds to buy weapons, and despite the $5 billion bank fraud involving the Atlanta branch of Italian BNL.

May 25 An Arab from Gaza stabs to death an Israeli girl in Bat Yam, near Tel Aviv. Israel forbids the entry of workers from Gaza into Israel until June 8, than imposes new limitations on number and age of laborers permitted to work in Israel.

May 29 World's five major arms suppliers, the US, Russia, China, France and Britain, meet in Washington to discuss limitations on the sale of conventional arms to the Middle East. Two days' discussions lead to no results.

May 30 Two Arab terrorists, one a Palestinian, swim from Aqaba to Eilat and kill an Israeli guard. Jordan denies that the perpetrators came from Jordan.

June 3 A joint US-Jordanian military exercise postponed due to alleged continued flow of goods via Jordan to Iraq, in violation of the UN embargo on Iraq.

June 5 UN observers remove a stock of enriched uranium, claimed to be "Iraq's last stock," from Iraq. Earlier (June 1) UN experts demolished a central building at the Atheer nuclear facility.

June 17 Two German hostages held by the Lebanese Shi'ites for three years are freed in Beirut.

June 23 Israeli general elections result in a small majority (62 seats out of 120) for a coalition led by the Labor Party, under Yitzhak Rabin.

June 29 President Muhammad Boudiaf of Algeria assassinated in Annaba. On July 2 Ali Kafi appointed president by Higher State Council.

July 5 Jordanian parliament lifts a ban (in effect since 1957) on the formation of political parties.

July 5 UN observers denied permission to inspect Iraq's Ministry of Agriculture, which allegedly holds documents on production of weapons of mass destruction.

July 19-23 US Secretary of State James Baker on a Middle East tour to promote the peace process following Israel's elections. Visits Israel, Jordan, Syria, Lebanon, and Egypt; meets Prime Minister Yitzhak Rabin of Israel, King Hussein of Jordan, President Herawi of Lebanon, President Asad of Syria, President Mubarak of Egypt, and Faysal al-Husseini, Palestinian leader.

July 20-21 Israel's new Prime Minister Yitzhak Rabin visits Egypt, confers with Egyptian President Muhammad Hosni Mubarak.

July 23 The Israeli government announces a freeze on construction of some 6,880 new houses in the Territories. It allows the completion of 8,700 houses already under construction.

July 26 After a 21-day standoff, UN observers are allowed to inspect the Iraqi Ministry of Agriculture. Suspect documents have apparently been removed.

August 3-4 2,000 US troops, mainly marines, land in Kuwait for a two-week joint exercise with Kuwaiti forces.

August 9-12 Israeli Prime Minister Yitzhak Rabin visits US, meets President George Bush and presidential candidate Bill Clinton. Bush approves the $10 billion loan guarantee to Israel over five years for the absorption of immigrants. Rabin states that two weeks earlier, Syria had test-fired two Scud C missiles acquired from North Korea.

August 18-26 Britain and France agree to participate in a US-sponsored plan to impose a no-fly zone south of the 32nd parallel in Iraq, to protect Shi'ite dissidents from Iraqi air attacks.

August 20 King Hussein of Jordan undergoes surgery for cancer in the US.

August 23 Israeli Prime Minister's Office announces "goodwill gestures" toward the Palestinians, including the release of 800 prisoners, the opening of streets and homes sealed for political reasons, and the loosening of restrictions on Palestinians entering Israel provided they are over 50 years of age.

August 24 Israeli Prime Minister Yitzhak Rabin cancels an order issued by the Shamir government late in 1991 regarding the expulsion of 11 Palestinians from the Territories.

August 24-September 3 Sixth round of peace talks between Israel and the Arabs opens in Washington. Israel's new government appoints Prof. Itamar Rabinovich to head talks with Syria, declares it is ready to return part of the Golan Heights as part of a peace agreement.

September 6 Final round of parliamentary elections in Lebanon (they began on August 23). Many Maronites boycott the elections.

September 10 Iran declares sovereignty over the three islands Abu Musa, Greater Tunb and Lesser Tunb. Since 1971, the islands were jointly governed by Iran and the UAE.

September 10 Iranian President Rafsanjani visits PRC, announces that PRC has consented to sell and construct in Iran a 300 MW nuclear power reactor, subject to IAEA inspection.

September 13 US President George Bush states the administration will sell 72 F-15 fighters--the export version of the F-15E/F--to Saudi Arabia. Israeli Knesset issues a statement of protest.

September 14-24 Sixth round of Israel-Arab peace talks resumes in Washington. Syria states for the first time it is willing to negotiate a peace treaty with Israel.

October 5 Kuwait holds first National Assembly elections in six years; results give critics of government control over Assembly.

October 5 US Congress passes foreign aid bill containing $10 billion loan guarantees for Israel.

October 8 Israel states that it will no longer object to the participation of Palestinian delegates from outside the Territories in discussions on regional economic and security issues.

October 12 An earthquake of 5.9 on the Richter scale in Cairo, Egypt. Over 500 persons killed, thousands wounded. Government rescue and recovery efforts criticized heavily.

October 15 Lebanese government led by Rashid al-Sulh resigns. Rafiq al-Kharari forms a new government on October 22.

October 21-29 Seventh round of Middle East peace talks produces Israeli-Jordanian tentative agreement on agenda for further negotiations; disperses temporarily for US elections.

November 3 Bill Clinton wins US presidential elections.

November 8-11 Israel masses troops along the Lebanese border, following heightened activity by both sides. Ultimately Israel refrains from launching a major operation against Hizballah.

November 9-19 Seventh round of Arab-Israel bilateral peace talks continues in Washington.

October-December Escalation in activity of Palestinian terrorists in Israel and Territories, including kidnapping and murder of border policeman in Lod.

December 8 Large scale Egyptian activity against Muslim fundamentalists, following increased terrorist activity by the latter. Egypt employs about 14,000 policemen and security personnel, arrests 400 suspects.

December 16-17 Israel deports 414 Hamas and Palestinian Islamic Jihad activists to Lebanon. Israel's supreme court approves the legality of the measure. Lebanon is unwilling to accept the deportees, and they are stranded between the lines. Arab League condemns the deportation. Palestinians threaten to suspend peace talks.

December 17 Eighth round of Arab-Israel bilateral peace talks ends in Washington.

December 19 UN Security Council condemns Israeli deportation of Hamas and Islamic Jihad activists.

December 27-29 Iraqi aircraft violate the no-fly zone in southern Iraq several times. US aircraft shoot down an Iraqi MiG. US transfers two additional squadrons of fighter aircraft and the aircraft carrier USS Kitty Hawk to the region.

1993

January 4-23 Iraq moves SAMs into the no-fly zone in southern Iraq. This leads to an attack on January 13 by US warplanes, with participation of a few British and French aircraft, bombing SAM sites in southern Iraq. On January 17, an Iraqi combat aircraft violates northern no-fly zone and is shot down by US aircraft. That same night 40 US cruise missiles hit an Iraqi military-industrial site at Zaafraniya, near Baghdad, that is allegedly connected with the Iraqi nuclear effort. On January 18 coalition warplanes bomb targets in the northern and southern no-fly zones of Iraq, killing 21 Iraqis. Russian Foreign Ministry calls on UN Security Council for a policy of self restraint. On January 19 Iraq announces a "goodwill ceasefire" on the eve of the inauguration of the new US president.

January 26 UN Secretary General Boutros Boutros Ghali calls on the UN Security Council to take "whatever measures are necessary" to enforce UN Security Council Resolution 799 calling on Israel to repatriate the 396 remaining Palestinians deported by Israel in December 1992.

January 28 Israel's High Court upholds the expulsion of 396 Palestinians in December.

February 1 Israel and the US reach a compromise agreement regarding the future of the deportees. Israel will permit the return of 100 of the 396 Hamas and Islamic Jihad Palestinian deportees in South Lebanon, and will allow all of them to return after one year rather than two. US administration promises Israel to block any attempt by the UN Security Council to impose sanctions against Israel for violation of UN Security Council Resolution 799.

February 18-24 US Secretary of State Warren Christopher visits the Middle East, meets President Mubarak of Egypt, President Asad of Syria, President Herawi of Lebanon, King Fahd of Saudi Arabia, King Hussein of Jordan, Prime Minister Rabin of Israel, and Palestinian leaders. Christopher seeks to assure that the peace talks proceed as scheduled in April in Washington.

February 26 An explosion in the World Trade Center in New York causes the death of six persons, wounding of several hundreds, and heavy material losses. Suspects arrested are Muslim activists from Arab countries residing in the US.

February 28 Israel test fires the Arrow ATBM for the fifth time. Missile is reportedly successful in intercepting another Arrow missile simulating an incoming SSM.

March 12 Israeli Prime Minister Yitzhak Rabin visits US, confers with US President Clinton, cuts short his visit due to an escalation in terrorist activity in Israel and the Territories.

March 30 Two Israeli policemen shot to death by Palestinians near Hadera, bringing to 15 the number of Israelis stabbed or shot to death by Palestinians from the Territories during March. Israeli government imposes a complete closure of the Territories; no laborers are allowed to work in Israel.

April 27-May 13 Ninth round of Israel-Arab peace talks held in Washington. Israeli-Palestinian attempt to draft an agreed statement of principles fails, despite active US involvement.

May Government crisis in Israel. Shas party demands the removal of Education and Culture Minister Shulamit Aloni of Meretz Party.

May 13 Ezer Weizman sworn in as seventh president of Israel.

ABREVIATIONS

AA	anti-aircraft
AAG	anti-aircraft gun
AAM	air-to-air missile
AEW	airborne early warning
AFB	air force base
AFV	armored fighting vehicle
AGM	air-to-ground missile
AP	anti-personnel
APC	armored personnel carrier
AR	assault rifle
ARV	armored reconnaissance vehicle
AS	anti-submarine warfare
AT	anti-tank
ATGM	anti-tank guided missile
ATRL	anti-tank rocket launcher
AWACS	airborne warning and control system
batt.	battalion
bil.	billion
bty.	battery
CAS	close air support
CBU	cluster bomb unit
CLGP	cannon-launched guided projectile
CW	chemical warfare
div.	division
DWT	dead weight tons
ECM	electronic countermeasures
ECCM	electronic counter-countermeasures
EW	electronic warfare
FAE	fuel air explosive bomb
FLIR	forward-looking infrared
ft.	feet
GCC	Gulf Cooperation Council
GDP	gross domestic product
GHQ	general headquarters
GPMG	general purpose machine gun

GRT	gross registered tons
h.	hour
HMG	heavy machine gun
HQ	headquarters
IAF	Israel Air Force
IAI	Israel Aircraft Industries
IDF	Israel Defense Forces
kg.	kilogram
km	kilometer
laser	light amplification by stimulated emission of radiation
LCM	landing craft, mechanized
LCT	landing craft, tank
LCU	landing craft, utility
LMG	light machine gun
LSM	landing ship, mechanized
LST	landing ship, tank
LT	light tank
m.	meter
MBT	main battle tank
MFPB	missile fast patrol boat
MG	machine gun
mil.	million
MLRS	multiple launch rocket system
mm	millimeter
MMG	medium machine gun
MRL	multiple-rocket launcher
MTB	motor torpedo boat
Naval SSM	sea-to-sea missile
NCO	non-commissioned officer
PGM	precision-guided munition
PLA	Palestine Liberation Army
PLO	Palestine Liberation Organization
port.	portable
reg.	regular
res.	reserve
RPV	remotely piloted vehicle; see also UAV
SAR	semi-automatic rifle
SAM	surface-to-air missile
SDV	swimmer delivery vehicle
SLAR	sideways-looking airborne radar

SMG	submachine gun
SP	self-propelled
sq.	square
SSM	surface-to-surface missile
Sys.	system
STOL	short take-off/landing
TALD	tactical air-launched decoy
TEL	transporter-erector-launcher (for SSMs or SAMs)
TOE	table of organization and equipment
UAV	unmanned aerial vehicle; RPV is remotely piloted, UAV is either remotely piloted or flies according to pre-planned computerized program
unconf.	unconfirmed

MAPS

Map no. 1

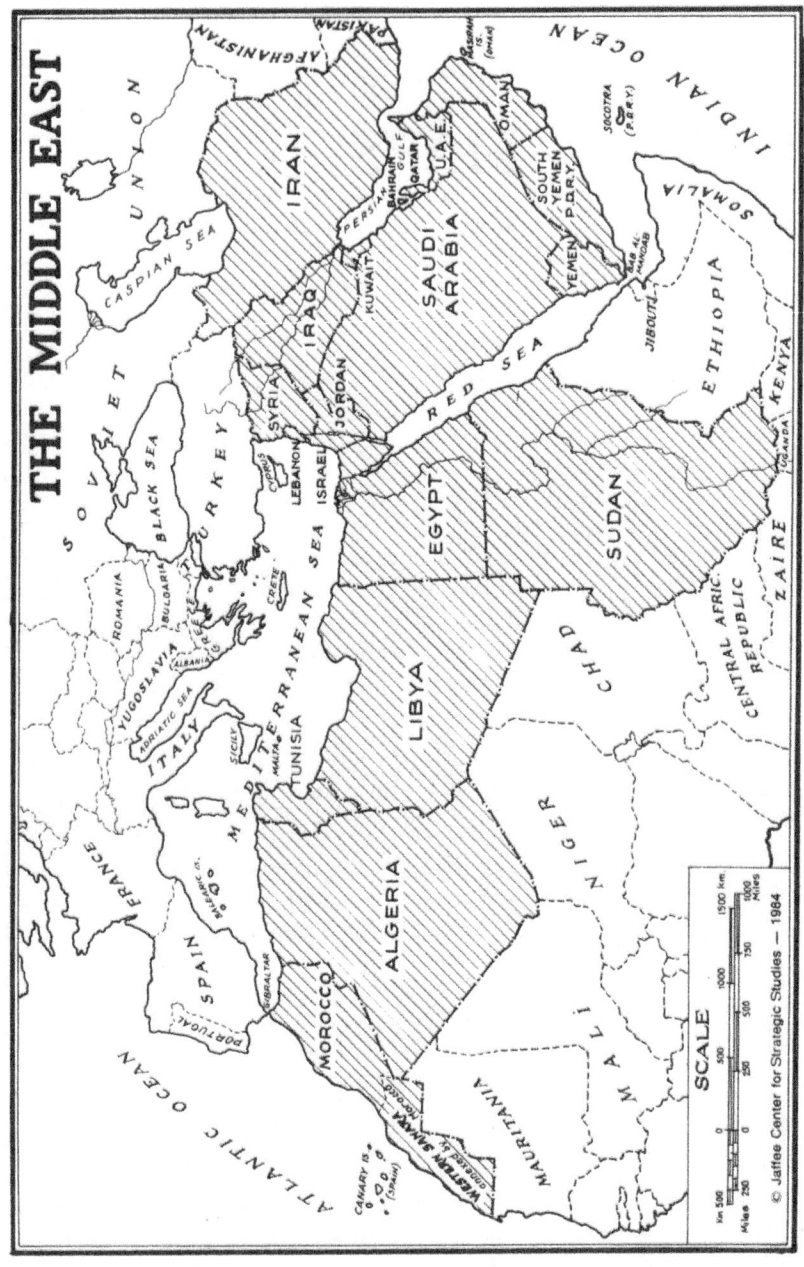

Map no. 2

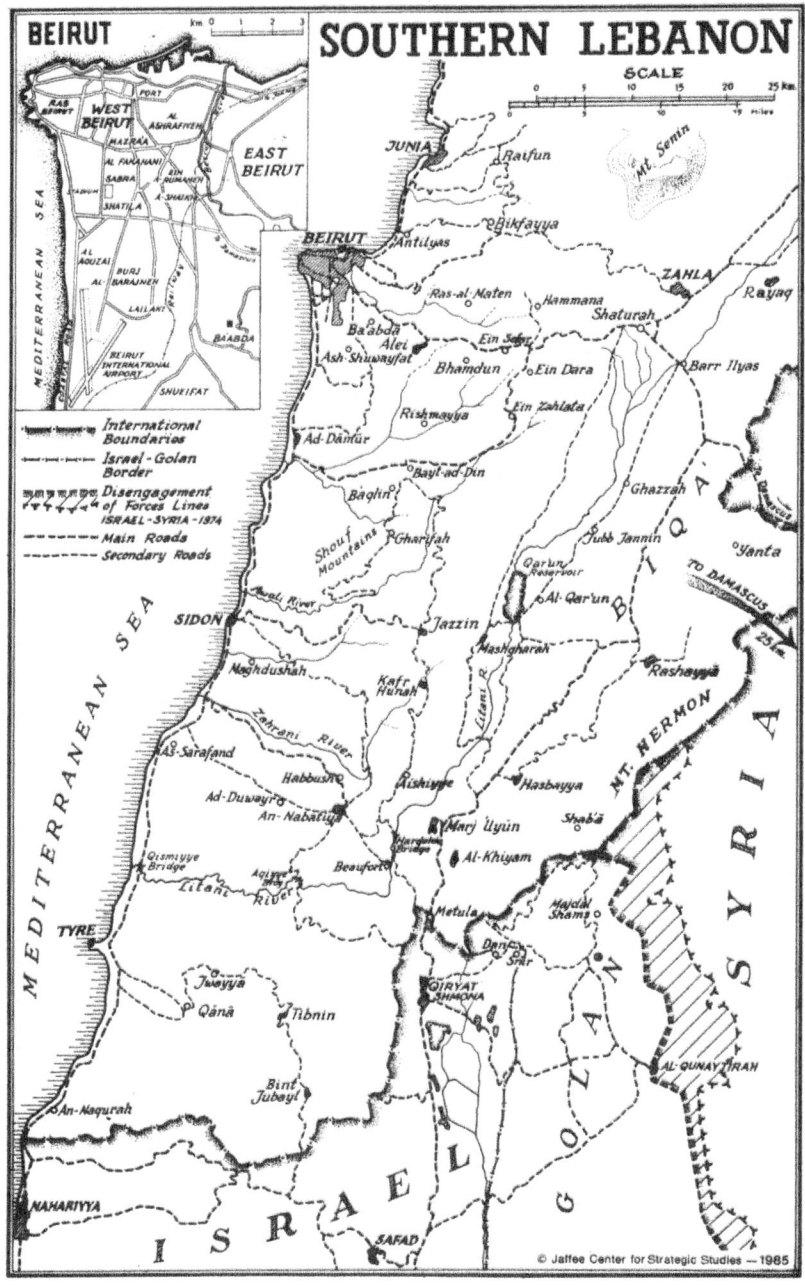

BEIRUT

WEST BEIRUT · EAST BEIRUT · PORT · RAS BEIRUT · AL ASHRAFIYEH · HAZRAA · AL FAKAHANI · SABRA · EIN RUMANEH · A-SHAIAH · SHATILA · AL OUZAI · BURJ AL BARAJNEH · LAILANE · BAABDA · BEIRUT INTERNATIONAL AIRPORT · SNUEIFAT · MEDITERRANEAN SEA

SOUTHERN LEBANON

SCALE

International Boundaries
Israel - Golan Border
Disengagement of Forces Lines ISRAEL - SYRIA - 1974
Main Roads
Secondary Roads

JUNIA · Raifun · Mt. Senin · Antilyas · Bikfayya · ZAHLA · Rayaq · Ras-al-Maten · Hammana · Shaturah · Barr Ilyas · Ba'abda · Alei · Ein Sofr · Ash-Shuwayfat · Bhamdun · Ein Dara · Rishmayya · Ein Zahlata · Ad-Damur · Bayt-ad-Din · Ghazzah · Baqlin · B I Q A · Shouf Mountains · Gharifah · Jubb Jannin · Yanta · Qar'un Reservoir · TO DAMASCUS · Litani River · Al-Qar'un · SIDON · Jazzin · Maghdushah · Nashgharah · Rashayya · Kafr Huhah · MT. HERMON · Zahrani River · As-Sarafand · Habbush · Aishiyye · Hasbayya · Ad-Duwayr · An-Nabatiya · Shab'a · Qismiyye Bridge · Marj 'Uyun · Hardula Bridge · Al-Khiyam · Litani River · Aqiyya Bridge · Beaufort · TYRE · Majdal Shams · Metula · Danny Sror · Juwayya · QIRYAT SHMONA · Qana · Tibnin · G O L A N · S Y R I A · Bint Jubayl · Al-QUNAYTIRAH · An-Naqurah · NAHARIYYA · I S R A E L · SAFAD

© Jaffee Center for Strategic Studies — 1985

Map no. 3

Map no. 4

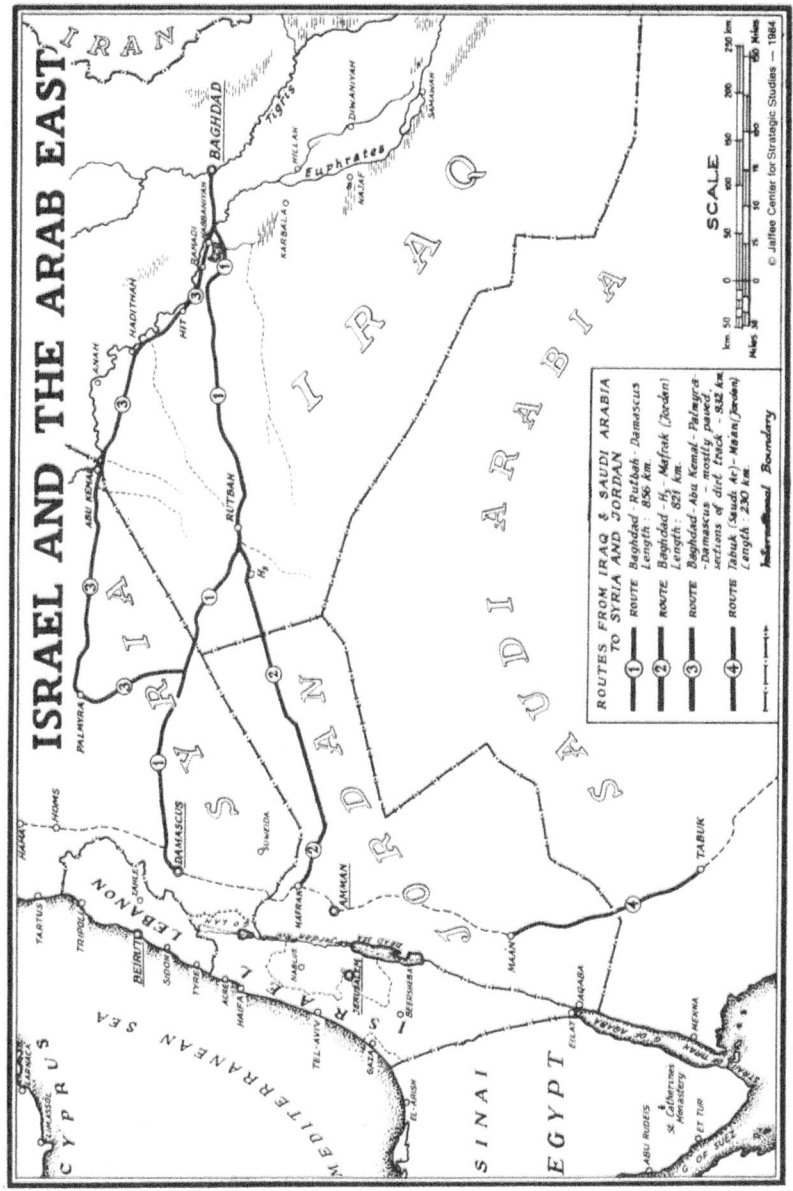

Map no. 5

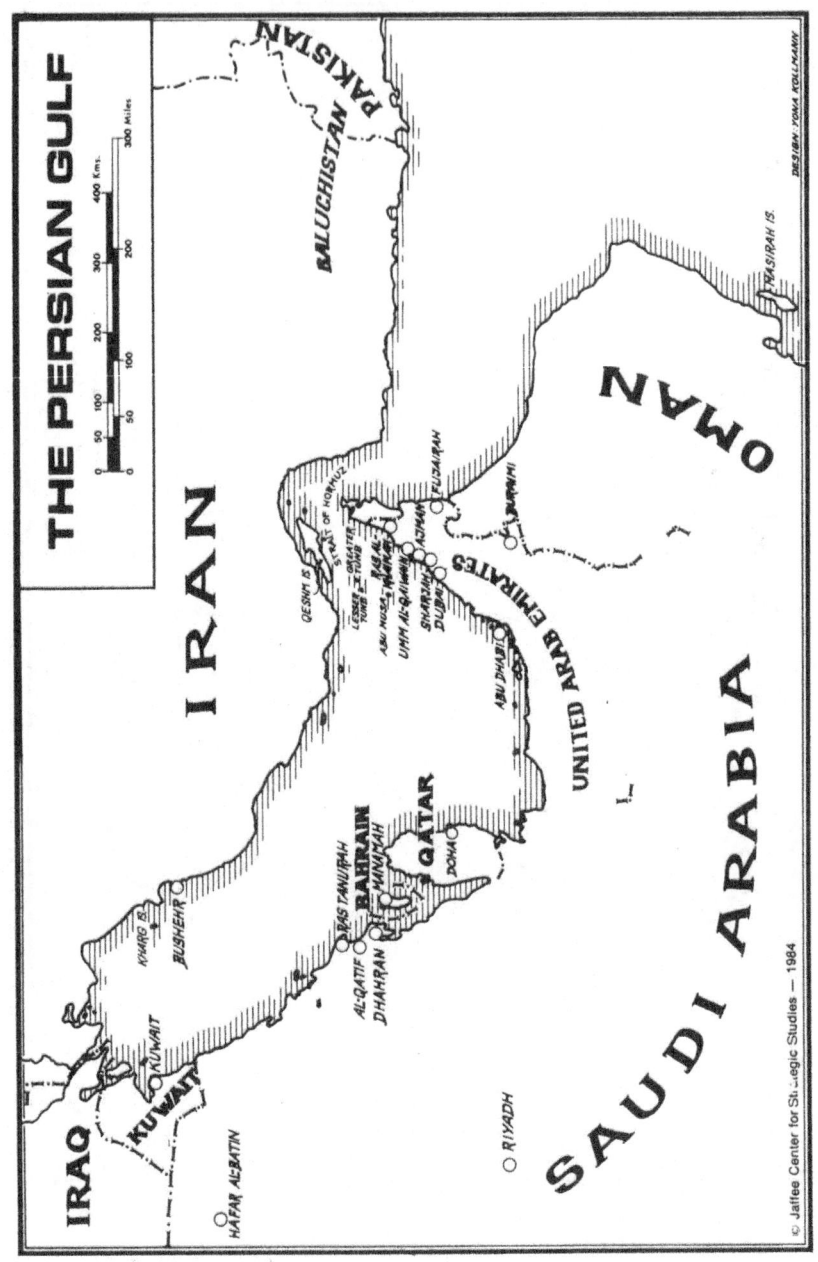

Map no. 6

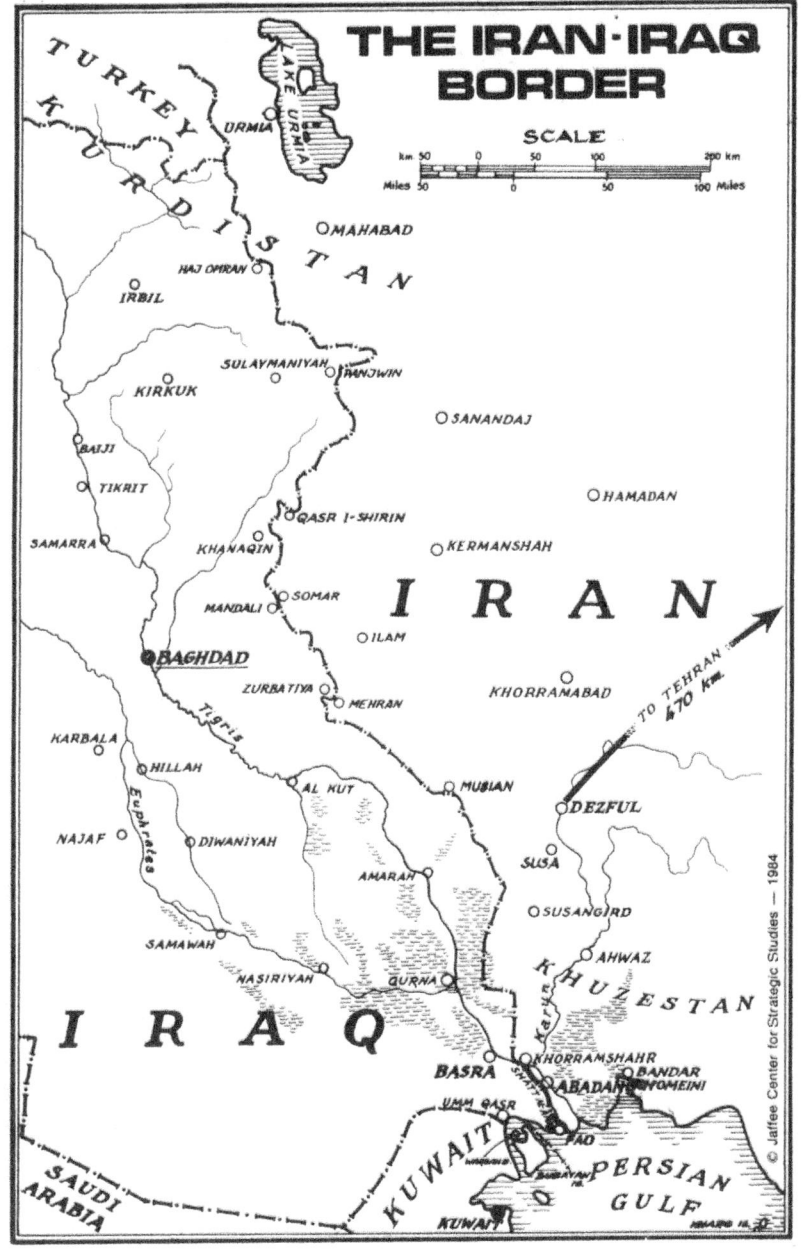

Map no. 7

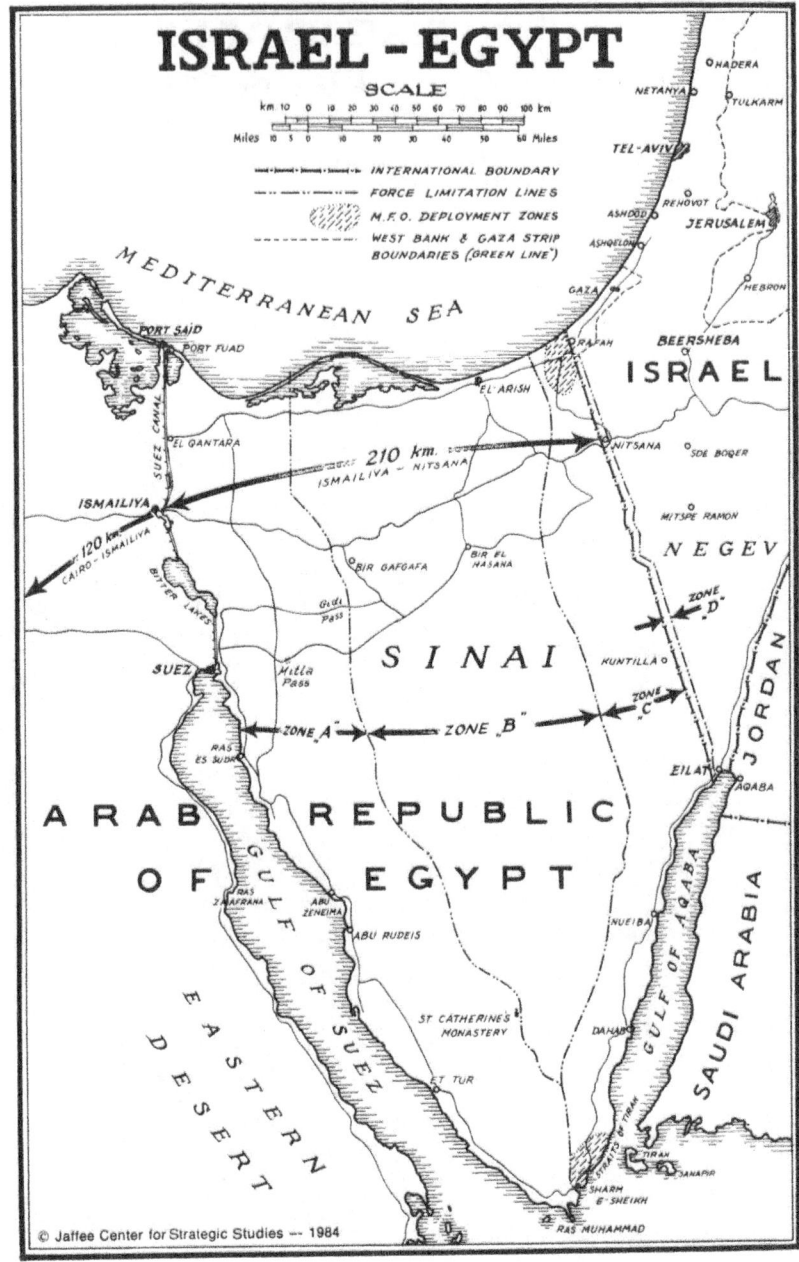

Map no. 8

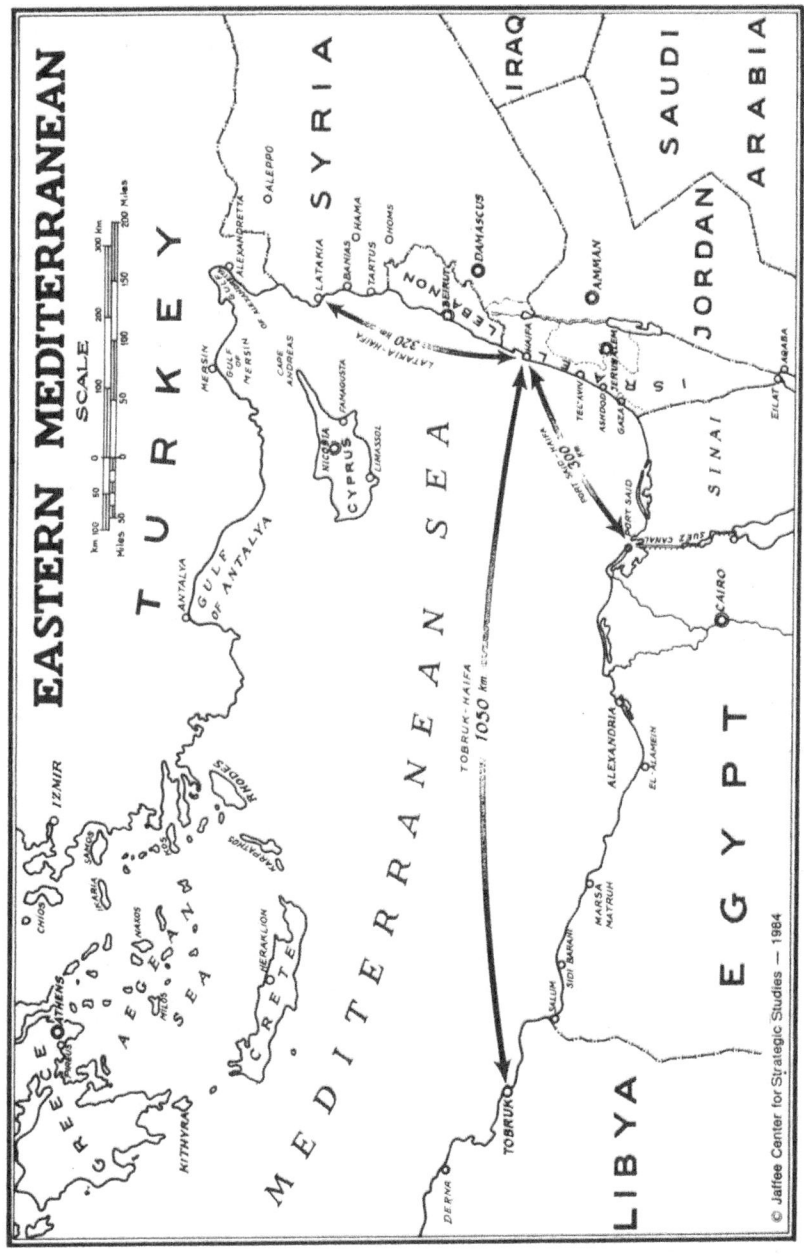

Map no. 9

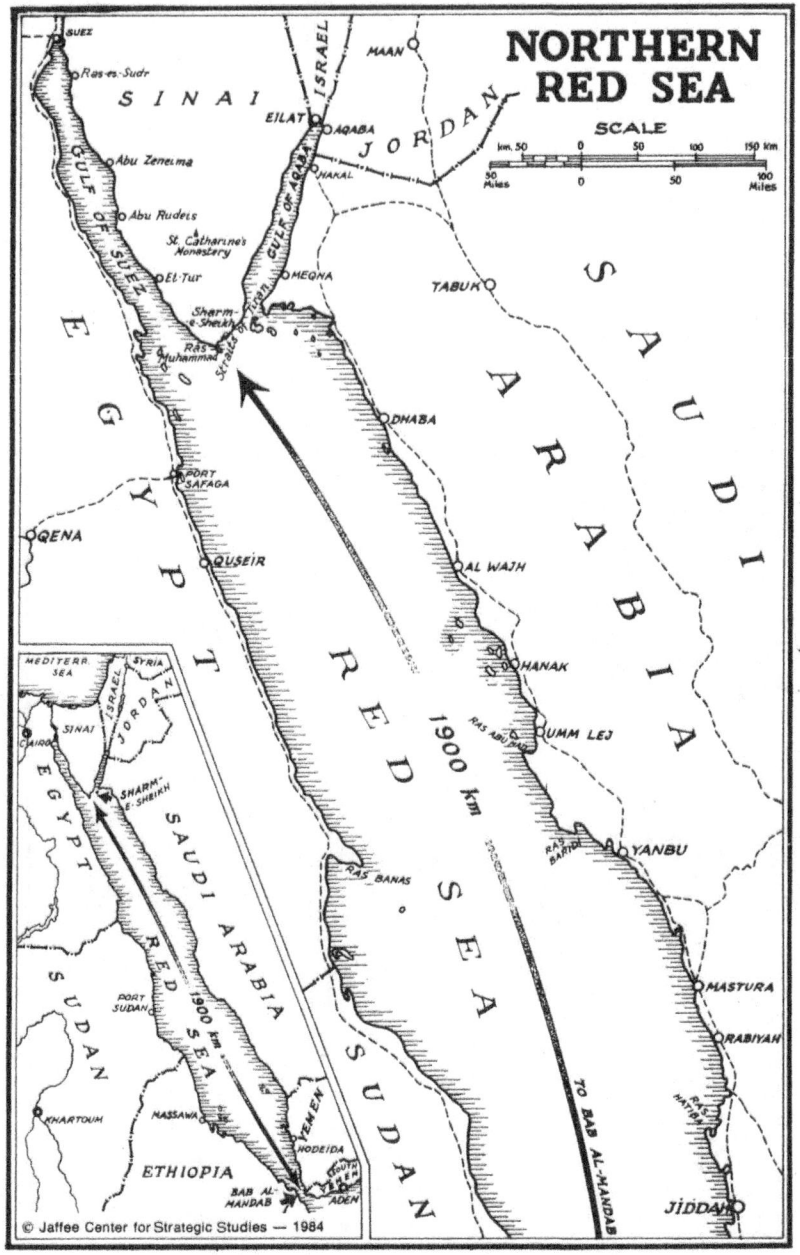

Map no. 10

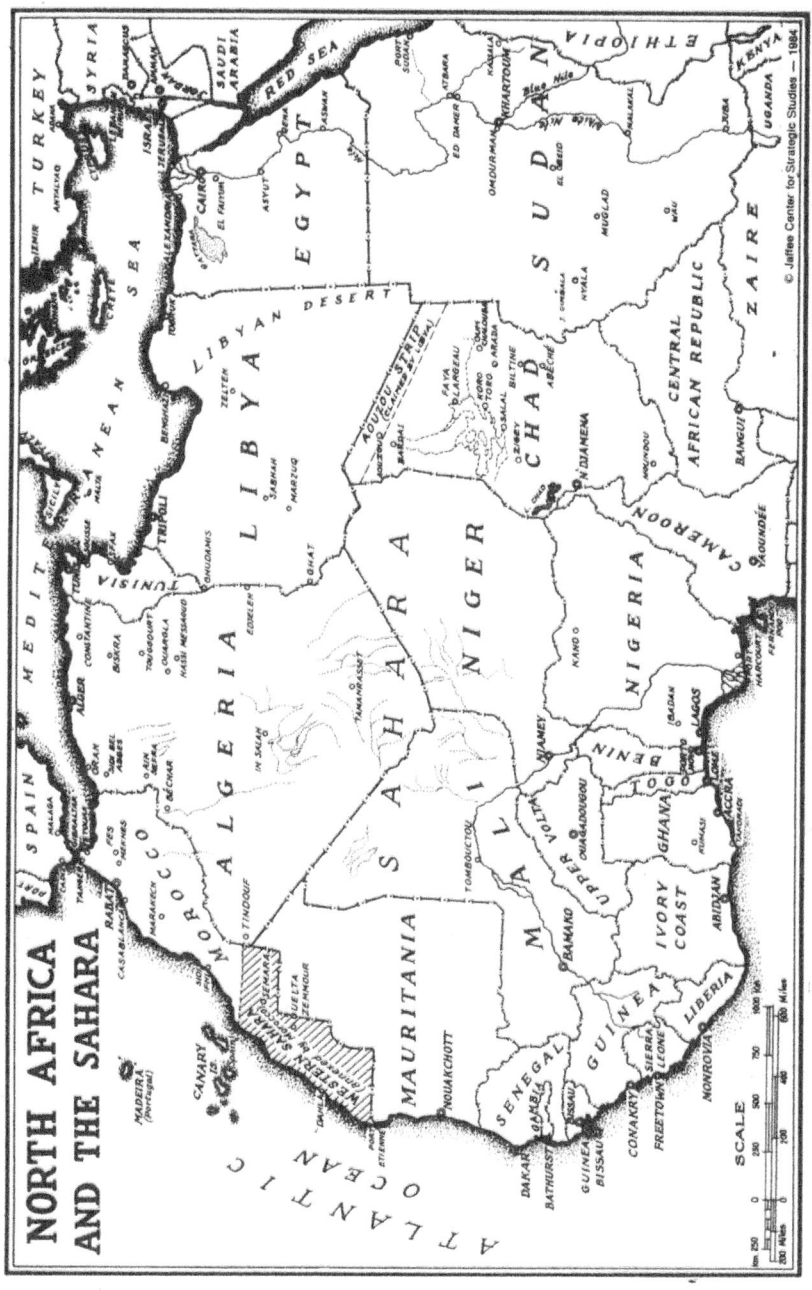